Programming
Distributed Applications
with **COM+** and

Microsoft® **COM+**

Microsoft®
Visual Basic® 6.0
Second Edition

Ted Pattison
Foreword by Don Box

PUBLISHED BY
Microsoft Press
A Division of Microsoft Corporation
One Microsoft Way
Redmond, Washington 98052-6399

Library of Congress Cataloging-in-Publication Data
Pattison, Ted, 1962-
      Programming Distributed Applications with COM+ and Microsoft Visual Basic / Ted
Pattison.--2nd ed.
            p.   cm.
      Includes index.
      ISBN 0-7356-1010-X
      1. Electronic data processing--Distributed processing. 2. Application software--
Development. 3. COM (Computer architecture) 4. Microsoft Visual BASIC.
I. Title.
QA76.9.D5 P38 2000
004'.36--dc21   00-020234

Printed and bound in the United States of America.

1 2 3 4 5 6 7 8 9   QMQM   5 4 3 2 1 0

Distributed in Canada by Penguin Books Canada Limited.

A CIP catalogue record for this book is available from the British Library.

Microsoft Press books are available through booksellers and distributors worldwide. For further information about international editions, contact your local Microsoft Corporation office or contact Microsoft Press International directly at fax (425) 936-7329. Visit our Web site at mspress.microsoft.com. Send comments to *mspinput@microsoft.com*.

Acquisitions Editor: Ben Ryan
Project Editor: Kathleen Atkins
Manuscript Editor: Ina Chang
Technical Editor: Steve Perry

To my beautiful wife, Amy, and our lovely daughter, Sophie.
I appreciate the sacrifices you make for my writing.
Our love and happiness is what makes everything in life worthwhile.

Special thanks to my parents, who have always given me every opportunity
to be both happy and successful.

TED PATTISON

Ted Pattison is an instructor and researcher at DevelopMentor (*www.develop.com*) in Los Angeles, California. He teaches professional developers how to build multitier applications using COM, MTS, and COM+ applications. He co-manages DevelopMentor's Visual Basic curriculum and has written several courses, including *Guerrilla VB* and *Essential COM(+) for VB Programmers*.

Ted is a contributing editor of *MSDN* magazine and has his own column titled *Basic Instincts* dedicated to building enterprise and Internet-style applications using Visual Basic. He has published articles in *Microsoft Systems Journal, MIND,* and *Visual Basic Programmer's Journal*. He's also a regular speaker at conferences such as VBITs, WinDev, and Tech Ed.

Ted provides consulting services through his own firm, Subliminal Systems (*http://SubliminalSystems.com*). He has worked with companies such as Hughes Aircraft, Dell Computer, Nabisco, ADP, IPS-Sendero, and PeachTree Software conducting architecture reviews and transferring technology to bring each company's programming talent up to speed for multitier development based on Windows 2000 and Windows NT technology. For more information, you can send mail to Ted at *TedP@SubliminalSystems.com*.

Contents

Contents

Contents

Contents

Foreword

A guy walks into a bar and sees two well-dressed women in their mid-fifties talking to one another just within earshot. He hears one of the women saying, "What's your IQ? Mine is 155!" The other woman replies, "Really, mine is 149! How did you interpret the impact of Nelson's micro-economic theory on the development of post–Soviet Union Eastern Europe?" At this point, two men in athletic wear enter the bar in midconversation, catching the ear of our observer. The first man says, "I just had my IQ tested. I am a solid 115!" to which the second replies, "Excellent! My IQ was 108 last time I was tested. Say, who do you like for this Sunday's Giants/Dodgers game?" Not being a sports fanatic, the attention of our eavesdropper turns to two men in their late twenties sitting in a corner booth. He overhears the first man confess, "My IQ test results just came in. I only scored 63." Trying to console his friend, the second man replies, "Don't feel bad, my IQ is only 59. By the way, which is better: C++ or Visual Basic?"

VB is dead. Finally.

OK, so VB the tool is still alive. But VB as a derogatory label, a culture, an all-encompassing worldview, is dead as a doornail.

For me, the beginning of the end was the first edition of the book you are now reading. Prior to that point, VB was considered an absolute toy amongst most of my colleagues. Worse, VB users were considered to be the people not competent enough to get jobs in documentation, testing, or marketing. VB was often viewed as society's "safety net" that provided "workfare" for those who could not make it on their own as software developers.

And then came Ted's first book.

When developers asked me about good MTS programming books, I constantly found myself recommending Ted's book. At first, I apologized for the VB-related content in the book. "Just pencil in the semicolons if you need them," I would exclaim. However, I eventually grew tired of playing the role of "VB apologist" and decided to rethink my views. At that point, I came to the following realization:

We all are VB programmers in one way or another.

VB programmers are (correctly) portrayed as being blind to a set of issues many consider to be critical. If this is the litmus test for being a VB programmer, then Dim me As VBProgrammer. I care deeply about component integration, yet I am blind to T-SQL optimizations in SQL Server 7.0. My office mate just wrote a 400-page treatise on NT security, yet he couldn't tell you the difference between an unparsed general entity and an internal parameter entity if his life depended on it. In the information-overload world we live in as software developers, selective ignorance is the only way to survive.

Ted (unlike many writers, including myself) has embraced the selective ignorance chromosome that is present in all developers, not just those who have embraced the development tool that dares not speak its name. The first edition of this book demonstrated Ted's mastery of focusing the attention of the reader on the concepts that are important. Unlike the 800-page behemoths so common in this field, Ted's book was a digestible morsel of information that made the able developer more able to solve the problems at hand. This second edition brings Ted's story up to date with the current state of the practice in COM development and will be a valuable addition to the component software canon.

Don Box
Redondo Beach, California

Acknowledgments

First and foremost, I must acknowledge DevelopMentor. For any of you who are unfamiliar with this company, DevelopMentor focuses on training and education for developers building distributed systems. DevelopMentor is made up of the brightest and most enthusiastic group of computer scientists I have ever encountered—a peer group of the highest level of technical integrity. I consider myself extremely fortunate to have been part of this community for the past six years of my life. Many of the ideas, analogies, and recommendations in this book derive from a shared viewpoint and common base of knowledge that have grown out of the DevelopMentor community.

Many thanks to Mike Abercrombie, Lorrie Trussell, and everyone else who works at DevelopMentor. I am grateful for all your hard work building this rich and nourishing environment, which has given me so many opportunities. DevelopMentor has allowed me to exchange ideas with some of the industry's top researchers and to pursue my passion for cutting-edge technology.

I'd like to give a very special thanks to Don Box. I am especially indebted to Don for his guidance and advice on so many aspects of my career. His vision has been incredibly valuable in structuring the story this book tells. If it weren't for the questionable choices Don makes time after time when buying a laptop computer, I would consider him the smartest man in the software industry today.

I'd like to thank those subject experts who reviewed chapters and provided valuable feedback and constructive criticism. You have made this book considerably better and more accurate. I had lots of support from the different product groups within Microsoft. Thanks to Robert Green from the Visual Studio team for reviewing the first five chapters. Thanks to George Reilly from the IIS teams for reviewing the chapter on IIS and ASP. Thanks to Dick Dievendorff from the MSMQ team for reviewing my messaging chapter. A special thanks to Joe Long from the COM+ team for taking the time to answer countless questions I had when writing the chapters on the internals of COM+.

There were also many people at DevelopMentor who conducted valuable chapter reviews. Thanks to Bob Beauchemin and Jason Masterman for contributing their expertise in the areas of transaction processing and COM+ distributed services. Thanks to Tim Ewald for making excellent recommendations about architectural design issues and explaining how things work way down under. Thanks to Doug Tenure for giving me feedback on some of the earlier chapters on COM. Thanks to Keith Brown, Steve Rodgers, and Dan Sinclair for thoroughly reviewing my security chapter. Thanks to Aaron Skonnard for reviewing several chapters and making excellent suggestions about how to motivate and explain software development based on IIS, ASP, and XML. Thanks to my buddy Brian Randell for his research and his passionate views on the subject of component versioning. Chapter 5 is an adapted version of an article I coauthored with Brian for *Microsoft Systems Journal*. Don't tell anyone (especially Brian), but I think a few of the paragraphs in this chapter might even have been written by him.

DevelopMentor is a great place to work because it's full of legendary characters. Mike Woodring has rewritten the Island Hopper samples using nothing but assembly language. Calvin Caldwell once paused between steps in the ATL COM AppWizard to go out back (on his ranch) and deliver a baby calf. During an intensive week-long course, Dr. Joe Hummel led a cab ride of eager students into Hollywood in the early morning hours to provide a realistic simulation of what it's like to transmit packets across the Internet. And then there's this guy, Fred Wesley, who thinks so hard and so deep that none of us really understands a word he says. The joke about Fred is that he spends so much time contemplating and debating the theory of thought that he never gets around to the practice of thinking.

I also need to thank all my other peers at DevelopMentor including Niels Berglund, Henk de Koning, Jon Flanders, Martin Gudgin, Stuart Halloway, Justin Hoagland, Simon Horrell, Kevin Jones, Paul Kirby, John Lam, Brian Meso, Jose Mojica, Gus Molina, Brad E. Needham, Fritz Onion, Simon Perkins, Brent Rector, Dave Schmitt, George Shepherd, David Smallberg, Dan Weston, and Jason Whittington. All of you have contributed in one way or another to my overall understanding of computer science and software development.

Last but surely not least, I must give recognition to Chris Sells, the evil genius of DevelopMentor. Chris, more than any other individual, is responsible for my career direction. He's the one who ultimately led me down the path to writing about Visual Basic and COM. It was Chris's overly adequate explanations of casting away *const*, template specialization, and functor objects that convinced me that I would never find happiness as a C++ programmer.

I'd like to thank everyone I have worked with at Fawcette Technical Publications. Thanks to all the hardworking people who put the VBITs conferences together, including Tena Carter, Janet Nickels, Robert Scoble, Maryam Ghaemmaghami, Jennifer Brucker, and Diamond Jim Fawcette.

Thanks to Joshua Trupin and Joseph Flanigen for publishing my articles in *MSDN Magazine, Microsoft Systems Journal,* and *MIND*. I'd also like to thank the other people at these publications who helped me get my words into print, including Joanne Steinhart, Terry Dorsey, Etna Novik, Joan Levinson, and Michael Longacre.

I would like to thank Claudette Moore and Debbie McKenna at the Moore Literary Agency for their support and assistance. Thanks especially to Claire Horne for helping me create and shop the proposal for the first edition of this book.

I am especially appreciative of all the people at Microsoft Press for helping me put this book together. This includes my acquisitions editor, Ben Ryan, and a very talented editing and production team. Many thanks to Kathleen Atkins for doing an excellent job as lead editor and project manager. Thanks, too, to Sally Stickney for her contributions editing the manuscript. I was also very lucky to have Ina Chang as the manuscript editor and Steve Perry as the technical editor. I hope to work with all of them again in the future.

Finally, I would like to thank the attorneys who work for Microsoft. In retrospect, I am very grateful that you made me spell out "Visual Basic" at every possible occasion instead of allowing me to use the friendly two-letter abbreviation that we all use when referring to our beloved development tool. You have undoubtedly added at least 10 pages to this text and you have, therefore, increased the perceived value of my book to the casual observer looking through the shelves at her local bookstore.

Introduction

Any developer who wants to create multitier applications using the Microsoft Windows platform as the foundation must rely on many separate pieces of software. Some of these pieces will be supplied by Microsoft, and you or your company will write other pieces. Still other pieces can come from third-party software vendors.

The Component Object Model (COM) is the primary glue that binds all these pieces of software together. It enables programmers and companies to distribute and reuse their code efficiently. COM+, an extended version of COM, provides a valuable runtime environment for components that run in the middle tier. COM+ and a handful of other critical Windows services, such as Microsoft Internet Information Services (IIS), Active Server Pages (ASP), and Microsoft Message Queuing (MSMQ), provide the building blocks that enable programmers and companies to create large-scale multitier applications.

WHO IS THIS BOOK FOR?

I believe that a thorough knowledge of COM and COM+ is a prerequisite to building multitier applications with Windows 2000. From my perspective, there's no way you can build scalable applications without a solid understanding of the infrastructure that supports the applications. To that end, the purpose of this book is to explain the critical parts of COM+ and Windows 2000 that affect the way you design and write components for a distributed application.

This book is for intermediate and advanced Microsoft Visual Basic programmers who want to develop for COM+ and Windows 2000. The book focuses on the architecture of the Windows platform. To this extent, it can also serve as a resource for ASP and C++ developers. Some readers might be new to COM. Other readers might already have experience with COM and Microsoft Transaction Server (MTS). My goal in this edition is to accommodate both kinds of readers.

Over the past five years, I've thought long and hard about how to craft a story that includes just the right amount of detail. Some technical details are critical. Other technical details are esoteric, and absorbing them would waste your mental bandwidth.

I've tried to cover what's important and omit what's not. I wanted to cover a lot of territory while keeping the text as concise as possible. While I make a point of avoiding unnecessary complexity, I also reserve the right to dive into low-level details in places where I think it's appropriate.

Many Visual Basic programmers don't have the motivation or aptitude to learn about COM and COM+ at this level. Visual Basic can extend a modest amount of the platform's functionality to these programmers without their needing any knowledge of the underlying technology, but they won't be able to create large information systems with COM+, IIS, ASP, and MSMQ. This book is most definitely not for them.

For Readers Already Familiar with the First Edition

I've always hated buying the second edition of a technical book just to find out that it had a new cover and the same old text. One of my main goals with the second edition has been to create something that adds value for those who have read the first edition. Over 75 percent of the text for this book is newly written for the second edition.

I have restructured my coverage of the fundamentals of classic COM and placed them as early in the book as possible. Chapter 2, which covers interface-based programming, is the one chapter that's basically the same in both editions. I've condensed the fundamentals of COM that were spread across several chapters in the first edition into Chapter 3 of this edition. Chapter 4 and Chapter 5 describe using Visual Basic to create and version components. The material in these chapters has been enhanced from the first edition with new coverage of building custom type libraries with IDL and designing components for scripting clients. For programmers who are already comfortable with COM and MTS, Chapters 2 through 5 can serve as a quick review or as a reference.

Chapter 6 and Chapter 7 cover the architecture of the COM+ runtime environment. The aim is to teach you how to write configured components that take advantage of the runtime services and thread pooling offered by COM+. Chapter 8 on transactions introduces new material that compares local transactions to distributed transactions. Chapter 9 includes new and essential coverage of IIS and ASP. Chapter 10 on messaging has coverage of MSMQ similar to the first edition, but it also adds new material about the Queued Components Service and COM+ Events. Chapter 11 is a security chapter recently written from the ground up. (I hope it isn't as painful for you to read as it was for me to write.) Chapter 12 covers application design issues that affect scalability and performance.

What Experience Do You Need?

I assume that you have a background that includes object-oriented programming and creating applications that use classes. It doesn't matter whether you learned about classes using Visual Basic, C++, or Java. It's just important that you understand why you would design a class using encapsulation and that you understand the relationship between a class and an object.

It's helpful but not essential that you have some experience in computer science or a low-level language such as C. It would be impossible for me to tell you about COM without talking about things such as pointers, memory addresses, stack frames, and threads. If you don't have this background, please take the time to contemplate what's going on at a lower level. Occasionally your temples might begin to throb. But the time and effort you invest will be more than worthwhile.

Most readers of this book will have done some work in database programming. It's hard to imagine that an intermediate Visual Basic programmer could have gotten by without having worked on at least one database-oriented application. When I describe writing transactions for COM+ objects, I assume that you have a moderate comfort level with ActiveX Data Objects (ADO) and Structured Query Language (SQL). If you don't have this background, you should acquire it on your own. The ADO and SQL code presented in this book isn't overly complicated.

In the chapter on IIS and ASP, I assume you know the basics of using HTML and creating simple ASP pages. Given the background of most readers and the availability of quality reference material on ASP, I didn't see much point in covering those details.

What's Not in This Book

This book doesn't contain many step-by-step instructions. Therefore, this book won't appeal to those who just want to know what to do but don't care why. Throughout the book, I refer you to the Microsoft Developer's Network (MSDN) to get details concerning such practices as using the administrative tools for COM+ or IIS. I don't think these are areas in which most programmers need assistance. My goal is to build your understanding of the theory behind the software.

I don't tell you much about how to automate COM+ or IIS administration through scripting or custom administrative applications. While both COM+ and IIS provide rich object models for automating administrative chores, I don't spend much time on it. I cover a little bit of these topics here and there, but I expect you to learn the details through the documentation in MSDN and the Microsoft Platform SDK.

If you're looking for a book with a great big sample application that you can use as a starting point, this isn't the right book for you. Most of my code listings are short, between 5 and 10 lines. When I present a code listing, I always try to do it in as few lines as possible to focus your attention on a particular point. I omit extraneous things such as error handling. For this reason, my style doesn't lend itself to those who are looking to blindly copy-and-paste my samples into production code. When it comes to presenting code, my goal is to teach you to fish as opposed to simply giving you fish.

WHAT'S ON THE CD?

How?

The CD included with this book contains the source code for several Visual Basic applications. These applications contain working examples of the code I use throughout this book. As a Visual Basic programmer, I've always felt that my understanding was boosted by hitting the F5 key and single-stepping through an application line by line. I'd like you to have the same opportunity. The Samples.htm file will give you a synopsis of all the applications and what they do.

The Setup directory on the CD contains the files and instructions for setting up the Microsoft SQL Server database that you need to run the Market application. The Setup.htm file can walk you through the steps. Each of the other applications that have additional setup instructions will have a Setup.htm file in its directory. I hope you find these sample applications valuable.

What Software Do You Need to Run the Sample Applications?

W2K Server 1)

MSMQ 2)

Visual Studio 6 3)

If you want to run all the sample applications I have included on the CD, you must install Windows 2000 Server or Windows 2000 Advanced Server. Either version includes COM+ and IIS as part of the default installation. If you want to run the messaging example from Chapter 10, you must also install MSMQ, which isn't part of the default installation for Windows 2000.

You should also install Microsoft Visual Studio 6 including Visual Basic 6, Microsoft Visual C++, and the most recent version of MSDN. When you install Visual Studio, be sure to select the option to *Register Environment Variables* for reasons that will become clear in Chapter 5. After installing Visual Studio, make sure to install Visual

4)

SQL Server 7 5)

6)

MS Plat SDK 7)

Studio Service Pack 3 or later. To run the sample applications from the later chapters, you must also install SQL Server 7. Once you install SQL Server, it never hurts to apply the latest service packs. The final thing to install is the Microsoft Platform SDK. Use the edition from January 2000 or later. The Platform SDK provides many important tools and utilities that will be described throughout the book.

UPDATES AND OTHER INFORMATION

Download

In my work as a researcher, an instructor, and a writer, I'm continually improving and creating new Visual Basic applications that relate to COM and COM+ programming. You're free to download the most recent collection of samples from my Web site, *http://SubliminalSystems.com*. At this site, you'll also find other information relating to this book, including a listing of any bugs and inaccuracies. If you'd like to send me feedback, mail it to me at *tedp@SubliminalSystems.com*. I hope you enjoy this book.

Chapter 1

An Overview of COM+

So, one millennium's ended and another's just begun. Just how much impact did the changeover have on your life as a professional developer? Sure, when the clocks all ticked zero, there were a few hiccups here and there. A few outdated systems had to be taken to their final resting places. But our industry as a whole didn't experience the doomsday scenarios predicted in the media. This was especially true for those of us who build applications based on operating systems and development tools created within the last decade. It's pretty humorous when you look back on it all. Rumors of the death of your company's information system were obviously greatly exaggerated.

Then again, does the press really ever know what's going on in our industry? They missed the fact that it was a century bug and not really a millennium bug. The problem was rooted in the use of two-character dates instead of four-character dates. If the human race had had the same technology 100 years earlier, we would have faced all the same issues on New Year's Eve of 1899. However, "millennium bug" sounded so much more sensational and, consequently, sold more newspapers and magazines.

Remember a few years back when the press predicted that everything would be rewritten in Java, including the United States Constitution and the Magna Carta? Now the Java buzz has subsided and we see Java for what it is—a young and promising language with its share of strengths and weaknesses. It didn't take the industry by storm. It's a language that's usable in some situations but unsuitable in others.

Now everybody's talking about XML as the cure-all technology. I know that as XML matures, we'll find more and more uses for it. It will solve lots of problems that are very hard and very real. But XML will never replace technologies such as COM, Corba, and Java, as many people have suggested. It's important that we keep all these new technologies in perspective. It's not healthy to get overly excited about a technology that might solve all your problems a few years down the road when you have to ship an application in the next few months.

WHY SHOULD YOU USE COM+?

I'll assume that you are at least considering using COM+ to build distributed applications. Many companies are using COM+ and Microsoft Windows 2000 because they provide a robust development platform. This platform is made up of several core technologies that provide the basic building blocks for constructing multitier business applications. And after all, the more the underlying platform brings to the table, the less code you have to write and debug.

I probably don't need to convince you that multitier applications offer many advantages over the two-tier applications that were in vogue in the late 1980s and early 1990s. Your company has probably already decided to abandon the two-tier approach in favor of a multitier strategy. However, I'd like to take a little time at the beginning of this chapter to review the most significant problems with two-tier applications and explain how multitier applications provide solutions to many of these problems. I'll also discuss why multitier development introduces some new problems and additional complexities.

One of Microsoft's goals in developing COM+ has been to offer companies the benefits of multitier applications while hiding as much of the inherent complexity as possible. Over the last decade, Microsoft has made many advances in creating this infrastructure for distributed applications.

The first version of COM shipped in 1993. Since that time, COM has grown from a young and complicated technology to become the core of Microsoft's multitier strategy. This chapter examines COM's most important milestones. Along the way, I'll also do my best to define all the acronyms that marketing folks have generated over the years. You've probably heard of OLE, DCOM, ActiveX, and MTS. COM+ and DNA are the two most recent additions to the list. But have you ever tried to explain the difference between these terms to someone at a cocktail party? It's not easy, is it? They all mean different things to different people.

The chapter concludes with a high-level overview of the distributed services that have been integrated into the COM+ platform. Any nontrivial multitier application requires such things as transaction support, integrated security, a Web server, messaging, and delivery of event notifications. This chapter will identify where each of these COM+ services fits in. Before drilling down into the low-level details in the chapters that follow, I'll show you how all these pieces fit together. This should give you an appreciation for COM+ as a whole and show you the light at the end of the tunnel.

From Two-Tier to Multitier Systems

One of the best reasons to use COM+ is to move a company's information systems from a two-tier architecture to a multitier architecture. This transition requires the design and creation of a middle-tier layer of business objects. Business objects usually sit between client applications and database servers. COM+ serves as the platform for these types of systems.

Two-tier applications have been widely deployed in the industry, so the problems associated with them are well known. Let's review the key shortcomings of a traditional two-tier architecture, such as the one shown in Figure 1-1.

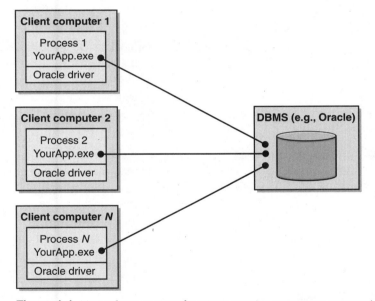

Figure 1-1 *Typical two-tier applications require a separate connection to a database server for each user, and the user's computer must have the appropriate driver for a specific database management system (DBMS).*

■ User interface code is intermingled with business logic and data access code, which makes it difficult to reuse business logic and data access code across multiple client applications. Furthermore, changes to business logic or the database often require rebuilding and redistributing client applications.

■ Each client application, complete with business logic and data access code, runs in a separate process, so you can't share resources that are process-specific, such as threads and memory. You also can't share a database connection in a two-tier application because each user requires a separate connection to the database server. The same is true for client applications that connect to a mainframe computer. This inability to effectively share resources across a set of users limits a system's overall throughput and scalability.

■ Every client computer requires one or more proprietary drivers so that it can talk to a database server or a mainframe application, which makes desktop computers more expensive to maintain and configure. The system administrator must install and maintain a set of drivers on each computer to provide access to such things as open database connectivity (ODBC) databases. If you need to swap out your back-end database—for example, if you're moving from Sybase to Oracle—the administrator must visit every single desktop. That gets expensive.

■ Client applications have a hard time accessing data from multiple data sources. In a corporate environment, it's not uncommon for critical business data to be spread across many different systems, as shown in Figure 1-2. Things get pretty tricky when an application needs to run business transactions using data that's spread across multiple computers. Things get exceptionally difficult when the data is also stored in a variety of formats.

■ Client applications are often required to run on the same local area network (LAN) as the database server or mainframe application, which makes it impossible to build distributed applications that span geographic locations. Many companies have employees all over the planet, and many of them need to create applications for customers and suppliers that could never be integrated into such a controlled environment as a corporate LAN.

■ Users are restricted to specific platforms. For example, a two-tier system often requires everybody to run the same operating system, such as a 32-bit version of Windows. In a world where any computer can potentially be connected with any other, this limitation is becoming more and more unacceptable.

■ Two-tier systems cease to be operational when computers become disconnected, such as when the database server is taken off line for maintenance or laptop users disconnect from the network while they're working in airplanes or at customer sites. A system's availability is severely limited if it experiences downtime whenever various computers can't directly connect to one another.

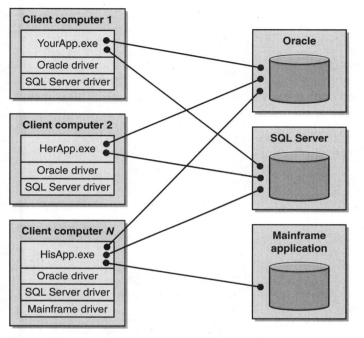

Figure 1-2 *A two-tier strategy doesn't work well when a company has multiple client applications or multiple database servers.*

Splitting out the presentation tier

The problems of a two-tier architecture can be solved as many other problems in computer science are solved—by adding a layer of indirection. You can decouple client applications from business logic and data access code by introducing a set of *business objects,* as shown in Figure 1-3. The client application containing the user interface code is often referred to as the *presentation tier.* Unless I indicate otherwise, the term *client application* in this book means a presentation-tier application that contains the elements and code for the user interface.

Business objects allow you to centralize your logic and reuse it across several client applications. In networks based on Windows 2000 and Windows NT, these business objects can be deployed using COM as the foundation. COM can also provide the basis for remote communication between client applications and middle-tier objects.

One of COM's biggest selling points is that it allows middle-tier programmers to update the code in their business objects without requiring recompilation or redistribution of client applications. It's pretty straightforward and painless to change your business logic or data access code after your components have already been put into production because client applications are shielded from your business objects' implementation details.

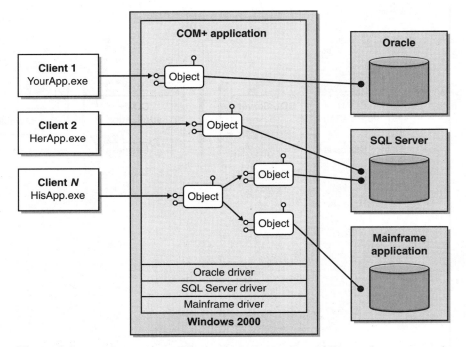

Figure 1-3 *Introducing a set of business objects in the middle tier eliminates costly dependencies between client applications and database servers.*

An application's data can change storage formats and new database servers can be brought on line without undue pain and frustration. You can often make the necessary modifications to a single Microsoft Visual Basic dynamic-link library (DLL). It's easy to recompile a DLL and replace it on a production server in the middle tier. The client applications remain in production unaltered.

In a typical multitier application like the one shown in Figure 1-3, a set of middle-tier objects runs on behalf of many users. However, all these objects often run inside a single process on a Windows 2000 server. This makes it possible to share process-specific resources such as threads, memory, and database connections across multiple users. Also, the computers running client applications don't require database drivers, as they do in the two-tier model.

Logical tiers vs. physical deployment

One of the first questions that arises in multitier development is where each of the tiers should be deployed. Figure 1-4 shows two possible scenarios. The number of tiers doesn't necessarily indicate how many computers are involved. In a small deployment, the business code and the database server might run on the same computer. In a larger system, the data can be kept on one or more dedicated computers while the business objects run on a separate host.

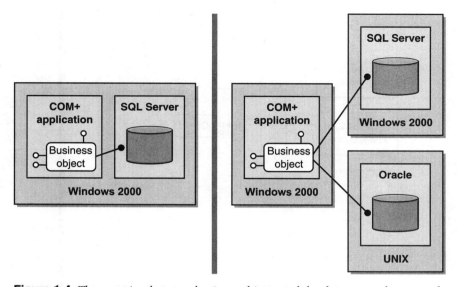

Figure 1-4 *The mapping between business objects and the data access layer can be simple at first and then become more complex without affecting client applications.*

Some physical deployment schemes are easier to set up and less expensive. Others offer higher levels of scalability, reliability, and fault tolerance. When people speak of multitier systems, they're speaking of several distinct *logical tiers*. The physical deployment can vary and can easily be changed after a system is put into production. One of COM's greatest strengths is that it allows you to make changes to the physical deployment without modifying or recompiling any application code.

Some people use the terms *three-tier* or N-*tier* instead of *multitier*. For the most part, these terms all mean the same thing—that a system has three or more tiers. Figure 1-5 shows a more complex set of physical layers. In the multitier model, the business and data access tiers can be arbitrarily complex. The best thing about this model is that client applications know only about a visible layer of business objects. All the additional complexity behind the business objects doesn't concern them. The primary design goal in a multitier system, therefore, is to hide as much of this complexity as possible from the client applications that make up the presentation layer.

Another powerful feature of COM is that it allows client applications to create and use objects from across the network. Behind the scenes, COM uses a protocol called Remote Procedure Call (RPC) to execute method calls across process and host boundaries. RPC is the first of several important protocols that you should understand before you design a distributed application with COM+.

If you have a set of users that all run COM-aware operating systems such as Windows 2000, Windows NT, and Windows 98, you can create multitier applications

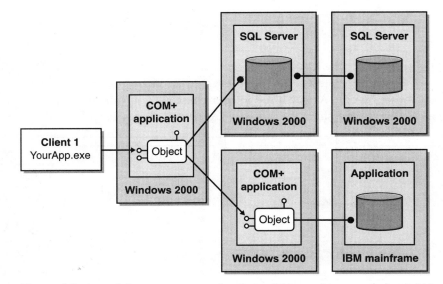

Figure 1-5 *One of the greatest strengths of a multitier architecture is that it hides the complexity of a company's evolving IT infrastructure from client applications.*

like the one shown in Figure 1-5. The computers running the client applications rely on COM to establish connections with business objects across the LAN. Once a client application creates business objects from across the network, it can use them to run transactions and retrieve information.

Although this approach works well for some applications, it's inadequate for others. This style of development usually requires that every user run a 32-bit version of Windows. It also works much more reliably when all your client applications and business objects are running inside the same LAN. You might, however, want to reach users who haven't logged on to the local network or who are running other operating systems, such as Macintosh, OS/2, or UNIX. You can reach a much larger audience by using a Web-based development strategy.

Web-based applications

The popularity of the Internet and Web-based applications has spurred the industry's adoption of multitier architectures. In a Web-based system, client applications run inside a browser. Browsers submit requests to Web servers using a lightweight protocol called Hypertext Transfer Protocol (HTTP). The presentation tier in a Web-based application is constructed with Hypertext Markup Language (HTML).

The way things work in a typical Web application is actually pretty simple. A client submits a request to the Web server, and the Web server responds by processing the request and sending an HTML-based page back to the user. The great thing about working with HTTP and HTML is that every major platform supports them. Your applications can potentially reach any user on the Internet.

Note that the Web server is the client's entry point into the middle tier, as shown in Figure 1-6. When a client submits an HTTP request, the middle-tier application must load and run business objects in order to realize the benefits of multitier development. While the code and HTML pages that make up the presentation tier live on the server, you can still separate the user interface elements, the business logic, and the data access code. As you'll see in later chapters, you can create a single set of business objects and share them across LAN-based clients as well as Web-based clients.

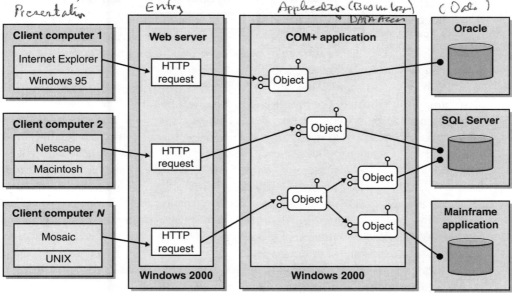

Figure 1-6 *Web-based development makes it possible to reach clients over the Internet who run a wide range of browsers and operating systems.*

If you design a Web-based application correctly, you can realize all the benefits of multitier development that I've described so far. You can share process-specific resources such as threads, memory, and database connections across a large group of users. You can respond to a single HTTP request by retrieving data and running transactions against multiple data sources. Moreover, Web-based development significantly reduces or eliminates client-side configuration issues.

When you design a Web-based application, you must decide which browsers and platforms you plan to support. If your primary goal is to reach the broadest possible audience, you should opt for a pure HTML solution. If you want to build a more sophisticated user interface, you generally have to restrict users to one specific browser or a set of modern browsers.

For instance, features such as Dynamic HTML (DHTML) and client-side JavaScript are supported by recent versions of Microsoft Internet Explorer and Netscape Navigator. If you use these features, however, users with older browsers will have trouble using your application. Typically, you must decide whether it's more important to support a wider population of users or to create an application with a more polished user interface. It's a tough decision that you should make early in the design phase.

The need for messaging

You should address one final issue during the initial design phase of a multitier application. Many of the protocols used in distributed applications, such as RPC and HTTP, are synchronous. This means that the application running on the client's computer must wait patiently during each request while the server computer performs the requested task. Also, if the server has a large backlog of requests, a client might be forced to wait for an unacceptable period of time.

Also note that applications built using synchronous protocols depend on every computer involved in the processing of a request being on line at the same time. The server must be on line for the client to make requests, and clients must be on line and issuing requests to make use of the available processing cycles that the server has to offer. If the server goes off line, clients can't issue requests. When the clients are off line, the server sits around with nothing to do. In essence, everybody has to be on line at the same time for the system as a whole to be operational.

Frequently, multiple applications need to communicate in an asynchronous and disconnected manner. *Messaging* is a mechanism for establishing asynchronous communication between two or more applications. Client applications send asynchronous messages to queues across the network. Each message typically represents a client request or some type of notification. Server applications monitor these queues and process messages either as they arrive or at a later time. Messages and queues simply provide a layer of indirection between the applications that are making requests and the applications that are processing requests.

An application built on top of a messaging protocol can continue to operate when various computers are off line. However, creating a robust messaging infrastructure that can route each message to its destination queue with the required delivery guarantees is not a trivial undertaking. A messaging infrastructure must provide an extensive set of subsystems to transparently store messages when computers are off line and then forward them to their destination later when a connection can be established.

Most companies aren't willing to invest the time and money it takes to write and debug the code for a custom messaging infrastructure. Fortunately, several messaging products that offer the benefits of asynchronous and connectionless communication are commercially available, such as the IBM MQSeries family and Microsoft Message Queuing Services (MSMQ). This eliminates the need to hand-roll a custom messaging infrastructure.

THE EVOLUTION OF MICROSOFT'S MULTITIER PLATFORM

As I mentioned earlier, Windows 2000 and COM+ offer a platform for building multitier applications. But many of the core technologies that make up this platform have been around for a long time. It's important that you understand how the various pieces of the platform have evolved over the years.

As far back as the early 1990s, influential individuals at Microsoft realized that a disproportionate amount of money was being spent on infrastructure in the development of large multitier systems. They realized that companies wanted to spend more time writing custom business logic and less time writing complex code to address issues such as sharing middle-tier resources and monitoring distributed transactions. Microsoft's entire multitier strategy is based on the assumption that companies would rather have someone else create the generic yet critical pieces of a framework for distributed applications.

As Microsoft's multitier strategy has evolved, its attempts to give it a name and a consistent identity have created some confusion. The marketing folks seem to dream up entirely new names and acronyms every year or two for technologies that have already been around for a while. For example, Microsoft's latest name for its platform is the Windows Distributed interNet Applications Architecture (Windows DNA). From a marketing perspective, Microsoft needs new fresh names to compete with similar technologies such as Corba and Enterprise JavaBeans. From your perspective as a developer, these name changes don't mean much. Try not to let them confuse you. No one's reinventing the wheel here—they're simply starting to call it a Circular Locomotion Device (CLD).

Every topic discussed in this book fits under the vast umbrella of Windows DNA. I won't even attempt to cover all the DNA-related technologies, such as DHTML and client-side scripting. The term *DNA* encompasses everything that Microsoft has ever done to help companies build multitier applications. Many programmers avoid the term altogether because they don't want to be confused with someone from the marketing department or with a nontechnical manager. If you really want to talk shop in development circles, you have to understand all the important technologies that make up the platform.

The Foundation: COM

Microsoft's multitier strategy is founded on a core technology known as the Component Object Model (COM). While COM offers many benefits, it is a complex technology that involves several challenging concepts and tons of low-level details. Some of these concepts and many of these details are critical to your understanding of how to properly build middle-tier components for a COM+ application. Many other details associated with COM are no longer relevant or are important only to programmers who are building presentation-tier applications. You need not concern yourself with such COM-related topics as object linking and embedding (OLE), ActiveX controls, and connection points (such as Visual Basic events), so I have omitted them from this book. This book focuses exclusively on the details of COM that are important for programmers who are building nonvisual components for the middle tier.

The term *COM* means many different things to many different people. On the one hand, it's a specification for writing reusable software that runs in component-based systems. On the other hand, it's a sophisticated infrastructure that allows clients and objects to communicate across process and computer boundaries. Many developers who are already COM-savvy see it as a new programming style and a set of disciplines that are required in order to work in a Microsoft-centric environment.

The COM programming model is based on the distribution of class code in binary components. This means that software (components) that adheres to COM can be reused without any dependencies on source code. Developers can ship their work as binary files without revealing their proprietary algorithms. The reuse of code in a binary form also eliminates many compile-time problems that occur when applications are assembled using a development style based on source code reuse.

Before component-based technologies such as COM were available, large applications were built by sending hundreds or even thousands of source files to a compiler in a single batch job to build one executable file. This development style, with its reliance on *monolithic applications,* requires huge executables and long build times. Also, to take advantage of a modification to a single line of source code, the entire application must be rebuilt. This makes it increasingly difficult to coordinate the programming teams working together on a large application. Maintaining and enhancing a monolithic application is awkward at best.

Component-based development solves many of the problems associated with monolithic applications. It allows development teams to ship binary files rather than source code. Binary components can be updated independently and replaced in the field, which makes it much easier to maintain and extend an application after it's been put into production. Most people agree that using COM or some other component-based technology is an absolute requirement in the development of a large information system.

COM is based on object-oriented programming (OOP). This means that COM is about clients communicating with objects. COM exploits the OOP paradigm to achieve higher levels of reuse and maintainability than is possible with other models of binary reuse. COM clients and COM classes typically live in separate binary files. COM defines an infrastructure that enables clients to create and bind to objects at runtime.

A platform based on object-oriented component reuse must provide a dynamic class-loading mechanism. This is one way in which Java and COM are alike. A client creates objects at runtime by naming a specific class that's been compiled into a separate binary component. A system-supplied agent tracks down the class code, loads it, and creates the object on behalf of the client.

Binary reuse makes it far easier to incorporate small changes to an application. For example, a minor bug fix or a performance modification can be made to a DLL. The DLL can then be recompiled and replaced in the field without adversely affecting any of the client applications that use it. Systems based on source code reuse must typically recompile every line of code in the entire application, which makes maintaining and extending software cumbersome and expensive.

The principles of binary reuse allow you to construct COM-based applications using language-independent components. When several teams are building components for a single system, each team can choose its programming language independently. Today's list of COM-enabled languages includes C++, Visual Basic, Java, Delphi, and even COBOL. Each team can select a language that matches its programming expertise and gives it the best mix of flexibility, performance, and productivity.

For example, if one team requires low-level systems code, it can use C++ for its flexibility. Another team that's writing and extending business logic and data access code for the same application can use Visual Basic for its high levels of productivity. The ability to mix and match languages makes it easier for companies to make the best use of their existing pools of programming talent.

Interface-based programming

Microsoft engineers made many important architectural decisions as they designed COM. But one of the most profound decisions was to require that COM have a formalized separation of interface from implementation. This means that COM is founded on the idea of *interface-based programming*.

The concept of interface-based programming wasn't a clever new idea from Microsoft engineers. This programming style had already been adopted by academic computer scientists and by organizations that needed to build large, extensible applications. Interface-based programming was pioneered in languages such as C++ and Smalltalk, which have no formal support for the concept of a distinct, stand-alone interface. Today languages and tools such as Java and Visual Basic have built-in support for this style of programming. So while Microsoft doesn't get credit for the idea, it should definitely get credit for seeing the elegance of interface-based programming and using it as the cornerstone of COM.

An interface, like a class, is a distinct data type. It defines a set of public methods without including any implementation. In another sense, an interface defines a very specific protocol for the communication that occurs between a client and an object. The act of decoupling the interface from the class or classes that implement it gives class authors the freedom to do many things that would otherwise be impossible. A developer writing a client application against an interface definition avoids dependencies on class definitions. Chapter 2 introduces core concepts of interface-based programming. While it might be one of the more challenging chapters of this book, its concepts are important to your understanding of how and why COM works the way it does.

Distributed COM

From the beginning, COM was designed to transcend process boundaries. The earlier releases of COM made this possible only when the client process and the server process were running on a single computer. With the release of Microsoft Windows NT 4, support was added to COM that allowed this interprocess communication to extend across computer boundaries. Microsoft created a new wire protocol for COM that made it possible to deploy distributed applications in a LAN environment. This was a significant milestone in Microsoft's strategy for enterprise computing.

At first, Microsoft struggled to come up with a marketing term to signify that COM could finally be used to create objects from across the network. The name Distributed COM (DCOM) won out over Network OLE when Windows NT 4 was first shipped in August 1995. Today neither term is in style among developers. *Distributed COM* is currently the proper term for talking about COM's wire protocol, although many developers think that COM itself is a distributed technology and that putting *Distributed* in front of *COM* is redundant.

As I mentioned earlier, COM's support for distributed applications is based on an interprocess mechanism named Remote Procedure Call (RPC). RPC is an industry standard that has matured on many platforms. Microsoft enhanced RPC with object-oriented extensions to accommodate COM, and the resulting implementation on the Windows platform is known as Object RPC (ORPC).

COM and RPC have a symbiotic relationship. COM offers RPC an object-oriented feel, and RPC offers COM the ability to serve up objects from across the network. In Chapter 3, we'll look at how COM leverages RPC to transparently call methods on remote computers by sending request and response packets between clients and objects and how clients still invoke methods as usual, as if the objects were nearby. It's remarkable how COM's architects were able to hide so many of the details required by RPC from both middle-tier programmers and client-side programmers.

From COM to MTS

The release of Microsoft Transaction Server (MTS) was a significant milestone in the evolution of the platform. MTS is a piece of software created for Windows NT Server. MTS allows business objects running on Windows NT Server to run and control distributed transactions from the middle tier. However, MTS is much more than a transaction monitor; it provided a brand-new runtime environment for COM objects running in the middle tier. MTS added lots of critical infrastructure support that wasn't included with COM. In particular, it added new support for distributed transactions, integrated security, thread pooling, and improved configuration and administration.

The name MTS has caused confusion because the software wasn't created just for companies that want to run distributed transactions. MTS provided a vehicle for Microsoft to ship the next generation of its distributed application framework. Middle-tier objects targeted for Windows NT Server should be run in the MTS environment whether or not they're involved in transactions. People get confused when they learn that MTS can be used to deploy objects that are nontransactional. To eliminate this confusion in Windows 2000, Microsoft has changed the name of the middle-tier runtime environment from MTS to COM+. The transaction support that was created for MTS is also included in COM+. If you already know how to program transactions using MTS, you don't need to learn much more to write transactional components for COM+. Things work almost exactly the same way. (Programming transactions with COM+ is covered in Chapter 8.)

In addition to supporting distributed transactions, MTS extended COM's security model. MTS security is based on the notion of _roles_. A role is an abstraction that represents a security profile for one or more users in an MTS application. At design time, a developer can set up security checks using roles in either a declarative or a programmatic fashion. At deployment time, an administrator maps a set of roles to user accounts and group accounts inside a Windows NT domain. The role-based security model of MTS provides more flexibility and more granularity than the original security model provided by COM.

Another significant feature that MTS added to the platform was a scheme to manage concurrency by conducting thread pooling behind the scenes. MTS introduced an abstraction called an _activity_, which represents a logical thread of execution in an MTS application. MTS programmers should write their applications to provide one activity per client application. The MTS runtime automatically binds logical activities to physical threads. Once the number of clients reaches a predefined threshold, the MTS runtime begins sharing individual threads across multiple clients.

Multitier applications that use a thread-pooling scheme scale better than those that use a single-threaded model or a thread-per-client model. A single-threaded model removes any chance of concurrency because it can't execute methods for two or more clients at the same time. A thread-per-client model results in unacceptable resource usage in larger applications because of the ongoing need to create and tear down physical threads. The goal of a thread-pooling scheme such as the one built into MTS is to create an optimized balance between higher levels of concurrency and more efficient resource usage. In this respect, MTS takes on a pretty tough task and neatly tucks it under the covers.

One other significant feature of MTS was improved support for computer configuration and network management. COM made it tricky and expensive to deploy and administer larger COM-based applications in a network environment. The MTS administration tools made it much easier to configure and manage the server computers that run middle-tier objects. Unlike COM, MTS makes it possible to manage many server computers from a single desktop. MTS also provides the tools to generate client-side and server-side setup programs.

Attribute-based programming and interception

declarative
attribute-based

vs

APIs

MTS introduced a significant concept to the platform's programming model: attribute-based programming. Services provided by the platform are exposed through declarative attributes. Attribute settings are determined by programmers at design time and can be reconfigured by administrators after an application has been put into production. Attribute-based programming is very different from the way that most operating systems have exposed system services in the past.

Traditionally, operating systems have exposed services through a set of functions in a call-level application programming interface (API). In this model, an application leverages system services by making explicit calls to the API. This means that you must compile explicit system-level calls into your application. If you want to change the way you use a system service after an application is already in production, you must modify your code and recompile the application. A programming model based on declarative attributes is much more flexible.

Let's look at an example to give you a clearer picture of how declarative attributes work. A component in an MTS application has an attribute that tells the MTS runtime environment whether it supports transactions. If a programmer marks a component to require a transaction, objects instantiated from the component are created inside the context of a logical MTS transaction. When a client calls one of these transactional objects, the MTS runtime automatically makes a call to start a physical transaction. It also makes the appropriate call to either commit or roll back the transaction. The point is that programmers never make explicit calls to start, commit, or abort a transaction. All the necessary calls are made behind the scenes by the MTS runtime.

Why is the attribute-based programming model better than the older procedural model, which requires explicit API calls? First, the new model requires less code. You indicate your preferences at design time by setting attributes, and the underlying runtime environment makes sure your needs are met. A second, less obvious reason is that administrators can easily reconfigure the way that an application uses a system service after it's been put into production. There's no need to modify any code or recompile your application.

interception

The attribute-based programming model of MTS relies on a mechanism known as *interception*. When a client creates an object from a component that's been configured in an MTS application, the underlying runtime inserts an interception layer, as shown in Figure 1-7. This interception layer represents a hook that allows the MTS runtime to perform system-supplied preprocessing and postprocessing on method calls. The system steals away control right before and right after an object executes the code behind each method.

Figure 1-7 *An attribute-based programming model relies on interception to leverage system services.*

The COM vs. MTS problem

One of the biggest dilemmas for programmers who are building multitier applications targeted for Windows NT Server is deciding when to use COM versus MTS. Many companies have chosen MTS because it offers many valuable built-in services that COM doesn't offer. Other companies have chosen COM because they don't understand the added value of the MTS runtime environment.

COM ships with Windows NT Server, while MTS does not. To use MTS ⟨with Windows NT⟩ you must install an extra piece of software, the Windows NT Option Pack. This means that MTS isn't really part of COM. COM has its own programming model and runtime layer; MTS has a different programming model and separate runtime layer.

You should see that MTS is simply a layer that has been built on top of COM. COM was never modified to accommodate MTS. So what does this mean? The two runtime layers aren't as tightly integrated as they could be. This results in a platform that contains a certain degree of inefficiency, ambiguity, and confusion. Things are tricky for MTS programmers because they need to know how both programming models work. Moreover, many valid COM programming techniques don't work correctly when used in an MTS application.

From COM and MTS to COM+

As the platform architects began planning changes and enhancements for Windows 2000, one thing was obvious: COM and MTS had to be unified into a single runtime layer and a single programming model. This wasn't a trivial undertaking, but it was well worth the effort.

With the release of Windows 2000, all the best ideas of COM and MTS have been integrated into a new runtime named COM+. Unlike MTS, this new runtime layer isn't optional. COM+ is part of the default installation of Windows 2000. But the good news is that the COM-versus-MTS dilemma doesn't exist on Windows 2000. Moreover, writing components for COM+ is easier than for MTS because many of the annoying idiosyncrasies associated with MTS have gone away.

Like COM, COM+ is based on binary components and interface-based programming. Method calls are remoted across process and computer boundaries through the use of a transparent RPC layer. And just like COM components, COM+ components can be upgraded and extended in production without adversely affecting the client applications that use them.

Like MTS, COM+ supports distributed transactions and role-based security. It provides a built-in thread-pooling scheme that's as transparent as the one for MTS. The COM+ programming model also uses interception to expose platform services to developers through declarative attributes. However, COM+ takes attribute-based programming much further than MTS. In addition to transaction services and integrated security, COM+ exposes services such as custom object construction, synchronization, and object pooling. Other new COM+ features, such as Queued Components and COM+ Events, are also exposed through configurable attributes.

Configured vs. nonconfigured components

If you want your components to take advantage of COM+ services, you must install them in a COM+ application. When a component is installed in a COM+ application, it's given a profile in a system catalog called the COM+ registration database (RegDB). This catalog holds configured attribute settings for components as well as for COM+ applications. A component that has been installed in a COM+ application is known as a *configured* component, primarily because it has associated COM+ attribute settings.

You'll also encounter an older type of component that doesn't have associated COM+ attributes: the *nonconfigured* component. Nonconfigured components aren't installed in COM+ applications. Instead, they are registered in a manner consistent with earlier versions of COM. Nonconfigured components can't take advantage of COM+ services, but they can run in environments other than MTS and COM+.

If you're authoring component code for a COM+ application, you'll generally produce configured components. This approach allows you to take advantage of various platform services. When you're writing your code, you're also likely to encounter nonconfigured components. For instance, the ActiveX Data Objects (ADO) library is made up of nonconfigured components. ADO objects can run in a COM+ application, but unlike configured components, they can also run in applications based on earlier versions of COM.

UNDERSTANDING COM+ SERVICES

In addition to providing a runtime environment, COM+ and Windows 2000 also include several built-in services that are important to programmers who are building multitier applications. Some multitier applications might need to leverage only one or two of these services. Others might need to use all of them. You should have a general understanding of how all these pieces fit together so that you can make informed decisions during the initial design phase. The following sections present a brief overview of the platform's most significant services for distributed applications.

Internet Information Services

IIS

Internet Information Services (IIS) is Microsoft's Web server. This product was origi-nally created for Windows NT Server. The most recent version is IIS 5, which ships with Windows 2000. Like other Web server products, IIS handles incoming HTTP requests sent by client applications. Earlier versions of IIS were primarily used to serve up static Web pages. Today many Web-based applications leverage IIS to run cus-tomized processing behind every incoming request.

IIS exposes a proprietary API called the Internet Server API (ISAPI) for devel-opers who want to create Web applications with customized server-side logic. Pro-grammers who program against ISAPI directly create software modules known as *ISAPI extensions* and *ISAPI filters*. While writing ISAPI-based software provides the highest levels of performance and flexibility, this approach also has a few significant costs—it requires development in C or C++ instead of Visual Basic and typically forces programmers to deal with low-level infrastructure details such as writing a thread-pooling manager.

ISAPI extensions filters

Many companies don't want to program directly against ISAPI because they don't have the expertise or aren't willing to invest the necessary time and money. IIS pro-vides an alternative to ISAPI with a framework known as Active Server Pages (ASP). The ASP framework is itself an ISAPI extension that allows programmers to write server-side logic using scripting languages and Visual Basic, among other options.

You should note that Web applications built using ISAPI or ASP can provide pure HTML solutions if that's what you want. You make all the decisions about what brows-ers your application will support. You can create a pure HTML solution that supports a larger, Internet-style user base, or you can exploit the strengths of one browser, such as Internet Explorer, in an intranet-style environment.

Many companies have built fairly sophisticated sites using nothing but ASP. It's pretty easy to write server-side business logic and data access code using scripting languages such as Microsoft Visual Basic, Scripting Edition (VBScript), and JavaScript and a development tool such as Microsoft Visual InterDev. However, companies have also discovered that it's hard to reuse, maintain, and extend logic that's spread across many pages. This becomes more apparent as a site grows larger. A better approach is to encapsulate business logic and data access code in compiled components.

Visual InterDev

The integration between ASP and COM+ makes it easy to create and run cus-tom business objects from an ASP page. This means that you can distribute most of your server logic using components rather than scripts embedded in ASP pages. Using components makes it easier to reuse, maintain, and extend your code. Such components can be created with Visual Basic, which offers much better testing and debugging facilities than any ASP-based development tool. Many companies have found that using ASP with Visual Basic offers the best balance between productivity, maintainability, and performance.

Microsoft Message Queuing Services

MSMQ

MSMQ is another important part of the platform. MSMQ is a middleware service that facilitates messaging between various processes in a multitier application. As mentioned earlier, messaging is important because it offers asynchronous and connectionless communication, which neither RPC nor HTTP can provide.

MSMQ is a messaging product based on the asynchronous delivery of messages to named queues. At a high level, messages model procedure calls between a client and a server except that either party can do its work in the absence of the other. The biggest conceptual difference is that a message moves only in one direction, whereas a COM method call involves both an RPC request sent to the object and an RPC response returned to the client.

With MSMQ, a client application can send request messages even when the server application is off line. It also means that the server can respond to request messages after all client applications have gone off line. In environments in which client applications and servers can become disconnected for any number of reasons, this capability allows the distributed application as a whole to stay up and running.

When would you need to use MSMQ? Let's look at a typical example. In a sales-order application, clients can submit sales orders to an order request queue even if the server application isn't running. Later the server application can open the queue and begin processing the order requests. MSMQ also makes it possible for the server application to return a response message to the sender as if it were the response to a method call. It simply takes a little more work when messaging is involved.

MSMQ is also useful to companies with users of laptop computers, who are constantly disconnecting from and reconnecting to the network. With MSMQ, you simply create client applications that send messages to a queue on the network. If a laptop computer is off line, MSMQ automatically stores messages in a temporary local queue. When the laptop reconnects to the network, MSMQ detects that the network is available and automatically forwards the cached messages to the appropriate destination queue. As you can see, the essential aspects of a store-and-forward mechanism are neatly tucked into the underlying platform.

exactly-once delivery

Messaging products such as MSMQ can also provide better delivery guarantees than products based on RPC or HTTP. An MSMQ message can be sent inside the scope of a transaction to provide *exactly-once* delivery semantics. This means that MSMQ takes many extra precautions to ensure that your messages eventually reach their destination. It also provides extra infrastructure support to transmit failure notifications back to the sender when messages time out or can't be routed to their destination. You are guaranteed that MSMQ will deliver the message to its destination or inform you that the message couldn't be delivered. MSMQ eliminates many of the lost-message issues that affect applications based on RPC and HTTP.

Queued Components

MSMQ debuted on Windows NT Server in November 1997 with the release of the Windows NT Option Pack. Since then, Visual Basic programmers have been able to leverage MSMQ to reap the benefits of asynchronous, connectionless communication. However, MSMQ programming requires extra code to create, prepare, and send messages from client applications. It also requires you to write a server-side listener application. Compared with communicating with COM method calls, communicating with MSMQ requires noticeably more work to issue a request and get back a response.

COM+ provides a service named Queued Components that allows you to take advantage of MSMQ without having to explicitly program against the MSMQ API. The Queued Components service is simply a productivity layer built on top of MSMQ. You author queued components in almost exactly the same way that you do standard COM+ components, with one or two limitations. For example, you can't design methods with output parameters or return values.

Once you create and install a queued component in a COM+ application, you must configure an attribute indicating that the interface you're providing is supposed to be queued. You must also configure the COM+ application to be queued and to be a listener. When you do this, the Queued Components service automatically creates a special queue for the application. It also sets up a system-provided listening service to handle incoming messages as they arrive.

Once the queued component is properly configured on the server, you can write client applications that use it. A client application doesn't directly instantiate an object from a queued component. Instead, it creates a special client-side proxy object called a *recorder,* which looks and feels like the actual object as far as the client is concerned. The client then begins invoking method calls as usual. The Queued Components service provides an infrastructure for recording these method calls in an MSMQ message and transporting this data over the network to the computer where the queued component has been installed. The server-side piece of the Queued Components service receives the message, creates an instance of the queued component, and replays the method calls.

As you can see, the primary design goal of Queued Components is to provide the convenience of COM method calls together with the benefits of asynchronous, connectionless communication. In essence, queued components use MSMQ as an underlying transport protocol instead of RPC. Queued components can thus get around many of the limitations of a connection-oriented, synchronous protocol.

You don't need to use the Queued Components service to take advantage of MSMQ. You can always program against MSMQ directly. The Queued Components service is a productivity-oriented framework that hides many of the tedious details of MSMQ programming. And like any other framework, it provides greater productivity at the expense of flexibility.

Quite a few things that you can do with MSMQ aren't supported by Queued Components. You should use the Queued Components service only if it supports the features you need and will save you many hours of MSMQ programming. One of its most valuable features is a server-side listener service. Creating a multithreaded listener service using only Visual Basic is next to impossible, so if you want a server-side listener application that can process many messages per second and you don't want to resort to developing with C++, Queued Components is just what you need.

COM+ Events Service

[handwritten margin note: EVENTS]

Some multitier applications require that certain users or applications receive notifications of interesting events—such as the hiring of a new employee, a change in a stock price, or a drop in inventory level that requires restocking. COM+ Events is a service for sending and delivering event notifications between applications.

[handwritten margin note: publishers / subscribers]

In the COM+ Events model, applications that send out event notifications are called *publishers*. Applications that receive event notifications are called *subscribers*. COM+ events are often called *loosely coupled events* (LCEs) because publishers and subscribers don't have any knowledge of one another. Instead, a set of events is defined inside the scope of an *event class,* and this event class is installed in a COM+ application. Publishers and subscribers know about event classes, but they never know about each other.

The decoupling of publishers from subscribers offers quite a few benefits. You don't have to worry about who's listening when you create a publisher application, so there's less code to write. And after the publisher application has been put into production, you don't have to modify it when you want to add or remove subscribers. Furthermore, you don't have to modify subscribers when you want to add or remove the publishers associated with an event class.

Here's a brief overview of how this event model works. You author an event class that implements one or more interfaces. Each interface defines a group of methods, which represents a set of events. You write subscriber components to implement these interfaces and respond to events when they're fired. Finally, you write a publisher application to create objects from the event class and call various methods when it wants to fire events. The event service takes care of processing the method and delivering the events to every subscriber.

There are two types of subscriptions: *persistent subscriptions* and *transient subscriptions*. When an event is delivered to a persistent subscription, the COM+ event service creates a new object from a configured subscriber component and invokes the method associated with the event. The event service wakes up the subscriber application if it's not already running. You should note that for a persistent subscription, an object is created and destroyed each time an event is fired.

The second type of subscription is a transient subscription. Once an application is running, the application can register itself with a specific event class to listen to events as they're fired. In this case, the event service doesn't create and destroy an object for each event. The main difference between the two subscription types is that a transient subscriber must programmatically create a new subscription and register a callback when it wants to listen for events.

Creating a transient subscriber requires more code than creating a persistent subscriber. Creating a persistent subscriber is easier because you can use the COM+ administration tools. Also, if the server holding the event class is rebooted, persistent subscribers continue to work without any problems. All transient subscribers, however, must create and register a new subscription.

A scalable event notification architecture requires asynchronous communication. If the publisher must wait for every subscriber to process its event notification, the system might prove to be inadequate. Also, some applications might require event notifications to be sent in a connectionless manner consistent with MSMQ. COM+ Events has been tightly integrated with Queued Components to provide the benefits of asynchronous, connectionless communication. Both publishers and subscribers can be configured to use Queued Components instead of RPC. For many applications, COM+ events are valuable only when used with the Queued Component service.

BUILDING DISTRIBUTED APPLICATIONS WITH VISUAL BASIC

If you use COM+ and its services to build distributed applications for Windows 2000, you'll find yourself in environment like the one shown in Figure 1-8. As you can see, there's a lot to learn.

Of all the COM-enabled development tools on the market, Visual Basic offers the highest levels of productivity. Visual Basic 3 and Visual Basic 4 both offered modest advancements in the product's COM-awareness, but Visual Basic 5 really made this development tool a viable option for building components for COM-based systems. Visual Basic 6 added even more support for COM and MTS development.

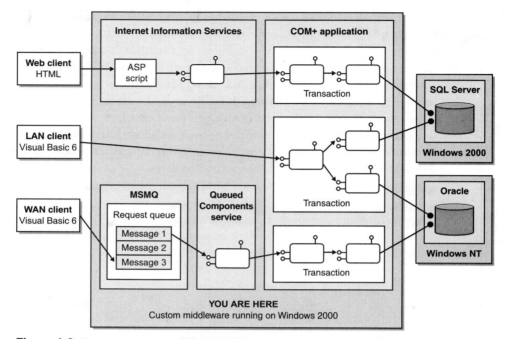

Figure 1-8 *You can create middle-tier components using COM+ and Visual Basic.*

Take a moment to consider the following questions. What is your perception of Visual Basic? Does it provide a viable option for writing the code for a large-scale application? Why are you reading this book? Respond to the following questions by choosing Visual Basic, C++, or Structured Query Language (SQL):

- Which language is the easiest for writing business logic?

- Which language offers the lowest cost of code maintenance?

- Which language offers the fastest means to enhance an existing application?

- Which is the best language for people without a classic computer science background?

Many designers and project leads would automatically answer "Visual Basic" for all these questions. But Visual Basic is in no way a cure-all language. In some cases, C++ or some other language would be a better choice for a specific component. For example, many COM interfaces, such as those exposed by OLE DB, can be readily accessed only through C++, which means that some components should be written in C++. However, companies have many opportunities to use Visual Basic in a distributed application. One of the greatest opportunities is for writing business logic and data access code for distributed objects in the middle tier of a large information system.

In the days of two-tier systems, Visual Basic was an incredibly popular tool for building the user interface. Companies used Visual Basic to build forms-based applications that ran on the desktop. Visual Basic programmers spent a good deal of their time designing forms and writing the code to deal with user interaction. Things sure have changed. More and more companies have switched to building browser-based applications for the presentation tier using HTML-based development tools such as Visual InterDev. In some ways, Visual Basic programmers have been looking for a new home.

The bright new future for Visual Basic programmers is in building nonvisual components for the middle tier. Companies that thought COM programming required C++ are changing their tune. An increasing number of shops are trying to write as much middle-tier code with Visual Basic as possible. And what's more, Visual Basic programmers have lots of support from the folks who are building the platform. The architects and implementers who have put COM+ together see Visual Basic programmers as their biggest customer.

SUMMARY

This chapter has provided a high-level overview of the things you need to know to build large-scale information systems with COM+ and Windows 2000. Many companies demand multitier applications to reach their employees, vendors, and customers. But anyone who's involved in multitier development will tell you that building a distributed application is an incredibly challenging undertaking.

The designers of COM+ have tried their best to hide the complexities of building distributed applications. What's more, Visual Basic goes a long way toward hiding many of the complexities of COM and COM+. But however "hidden" some of the intricacies of the infrastructure are, you still can't get by without a solid understanding of the core technologies and the platform's interrelated subsystems. The more you know about the underlying infrastructure the better. The philosophy you should adopt is that you will be partnering with COM+ and Windows 2000. They will do some of the work, and so will you. The secret is to let them do what they do best—provide low-level infrastructure. With this infrastructure solidly behind you, you'll be able to spend more time doing what you need to do—writing the business logic and data access code that is specific to your application.

Chapter 2

Understanding Interface-Based Programming

Getting a grasp of interface-based programming is really tough. To gain an appreciation for this style of programming, you must leave behind old habits and intuitions about writing code and look back at the evolution of object-oriented programming (OOP) and computer science over the past decade—a Darwinian saga of how the interface has made modern software designs more fit for survival. For software to survive in the ever-changing jungle of the production environment, it must have three distinct characteristics: *reusability, maintainability,* and *extensibility*. This chapter provides a general overview of interface-based programming and examines these characteristics.

COM is founded on the idea of interface-based programming, a style of programming in which the interface is separate from implementation. (COM has no meaning without the concept of the interface. Interfaces, on the other hand, exist outside the world of COM.) Interface-based programming was pioneered in languages such as C++ and Smalltalk by software engineers who discovered that using distinct interfaces could make their software, especially large applications, easier to maintain and extend. (The creators of Java saw the elegance of interface-based programming and consequently built support for it directly into their language.)

Interfaces solve many problems associated with code reuse in OOP. This chapter investigates some of these problems. In particular, when you program in a style consistent with classic OOP, a client can build inflexible dependencies on a class definition. These dependencies can make it difficult to maintain or extend the class without breaking the client. It becomes tedious or impossible to improve the code for an object over time. Certain problems are also associated with a popular OOP language feature known as *implementation inheritance*. This powerful but often misused feature is vulnerable to similar dependency problems, which compromise an application's maintainability and extensibility. This chapter describes the strengths and limitations of implementation inheritance (even though this type of inheritance is not supported by Visual Basic) in order to address some of the problems that interface-based programming was created to solve.

Visual Basic 5.0 was the first version of the product to include support for defining and implementing user-defined interfaces. This chapter shows you how to program in terms of interfaces in a Visual Basic application. After covering the basics of using interfaces, I'll demonstrate how to achieve *polymorphism* and how to use *runtime type inspection*.

As you'll see in the next chapter, COM clients must communicate with objects through interfaces. You should always keep in mind, however, that Visual Basic doesn't require you to program explicitly in terms of user-defined interfaces. At times, you actually can't create components that implement user-defined interfaces. You have to work in terms of classes with public methods. This is typically the case when you're creating servers for scripting clients.

Programming with user-defined interfaces provides benefits at the cost of additional complexity. The goal of this chapter is to prove to you that the benefits can be greater than the costs.

THE FUNDAMENTALS OF OBJECT-ORIENTED PROGRAMMING

Your first stop on the road to interface awareness must be an examination of the problems that interface-based programming was meant to solve. Many of these problems have to do with the relationship between a class and the clients that use it. Think about the following questions: What is the relationship between a client and a class definition? What must a client know about a class in order to benefit from using it? What dependencies are created in the client when a programmer writes code using a class's methods and properties?

In an object-oriented paradigm, a client typically instantiates an object from a class. The client usually creates the object by using the *New* operator followed by the class name. After creating the object, the client uses it by accessing an exposed set

New operator

of properties and methods through a variable that is a *class-based reference*. Here's a simple example that uses a variable based on a class type to access an object's public members:

— a class-based reference using the New operator

```
Dim Dog As CDog
Set Dog = New CDog
' Access a property.
Dog.Name = "Snoopy"
' Invoke a method.
Dog.Bark
```

In this example, a class-based reference makes it possible to instantiate and communicate with a dog object. The communication between the client and the object takes place through a set of publicly accessible properties and methods that are known as an object's *public interface*. The class author must use the public interface to expose the object's functionality to the client. This is what makes an object useful. Note that the method names and property names from the public interface are hard coded into the client. Future versions of the class must continue to supply these members in order to honor the dependencies built into the client.

One benefit of using classes is that they allow you to reuse code. Once a class has been written, you can use it in many different places in an application. Classes thus let you reduce or eliminate redundant code in an application. They also facilitate code maintenance. You can modify or remove any properties or methods that aren't publicly visible. You can also change public method implementations as long as the calling syntax of the methods isn't altered. When the implementation of a method in a class is improved, any client that uses the class will seamlessly benefit from the changes.

When you modify an existing class definition, you shouldn't change the calling syntax for accessing any public method or property because of the risk of breaking the dependencies that client code has built on the original class definition. As long as you hold the public interface constant, you can make any modifications to improve your class without breaking any client code.

To rephrase the key point of the last paragraph: Once you publish a property or a method signature in a class's public interface, you can't change or remove it. This means that you must properly design the public interface at the beginning of a project and use discipline as the class evolves. If you do this, you can improve and extend object code without having to rewrite any client code. You can maintain a class by fixing bugs and improving method implementations.

The rules for maintaining existing members of the public interface are cut-and-dried, but what flexibility do you have when you add new functionality to a class? What can you do to safely extend an object in later versions? It's easy and safe to add new public methods and properties to a class as long as you can make one big assumption: that the class and the clients are compiled at the same time. Old client code will continue to run as before, even though it can't take advantage of the object's new functionality. New client code written after the class has been modified, however, can take advantage of any members added to the public interface. This means you can improve an object safely over time in the production environment.

What about a situation in which a class definition is compiled separately from the client code that uses it? This creates a potential versioning problem. Let's look at an example to illustrate the problem. Let's say you compile a class into one executable and compile some client code that uses it into another. After you put both of these executables into production, you decide to add a new method to the second version of the class. After that, you create a second version of the client that uses this new method. What will happen if you put the newly compiled client into production before the newly compiled class? The newer version of the client will attempt to execute a method that the older version of the class doesn't support.

This example should lead you to the following conclusion: When you're writing classes for a component-based system, adding methods to later versions of a class can be as bad as removing or changing methods. The public interface of a class must be held constant in order to provide compatibility in every situation.

Changing the Public Interface of a Class

Problems arise in class design when you change the signature of a public method in a way that breaks an existing client. This commonly happens when you discover that the initial class design was inadequate. For instance, imagine a method that provides the behavior for a dog rolling over. The following *RollOver* method is defined with a 16-bit Integer parameter to allow the client to request a specific number of rolls in each invocation.

```
' Method defined in CDog class.
Public Sub RollOver(ByRef Rolls As Integer)
    ' Implementation code goes here.
End Sub

' Client hardcodes calling syntax.
Dim Dog As CDog, Rolls As Integer
Set Dog = New CDog
Rolls = 20000
Dog.RollOver Rolls
```

What if the requirements for a dog object weren't properly anticipated in the initial design? For instance, what if the required number of rolls exceeds the highest possible value for an Integer (about 32,000)? Perhaps your competitor has just released a dog component that supports rolling over 100,000 times. While you might be able to rewrite your implementation of *RollOver* to match or surpass your competitor's software, the bigger problem is with your method's signature. In order for your dog object to roll 100,000 times, you must change the parameter type to Long (long integer). This creates quite a design problem. The newer clients want to pass a 32-bit Long. But older clients such as the ones just shown have a dependency on the 16-bit Integer.

You have only two options. One is to modify the method signature and then rewrite all the client code that calls the method. The other is to leave things as they are and deal with the limitations of the original design. As you can see, poor class design results in either broken clients or nonextensible objects.

The intuitive solution to this problem is to make sure that the design of the class's public interface is full-featured and finalized before you write client code against it. But this isn't always possible, even for the most experienced class designer. If a class models a real-world entity that never changes, an experienced designer can create a robust, long-lasting design. In many cases, however, it's impossible to predict how external changes will affect the requirements for an object's public interface. A designer who is creating classes for an application that's expected to run for years in a rapidly changing business environment can't possibly predict what is needed. If the business model is constantly changing, your classes must change with it. Therein lies the need for extensible objects.

The use of *class-based references* results in a layer of dependencies between clients and classes. These dependencies create tight coupling between various pieces of software. As the author of a class, you want the freedom to modify and extend the functionality you expose in later versions. When you're authoring classes with public methods, however, it's easy to paint yourself into a corner. When you're months or years into a large project, you're faced with a no-win decision. Should you change the public interface defined by your class and force all clients to modify their code and recompile? Or should you freeze the functionality of your objects?

A Quick Primer on Implementation Inheritance

Many of the features of OOP are meant to give programmers higher levels of code reuse. Languages such as C++, Smalltalk, and Java offer a popular feature known as *implementation inheritance,* which offers one of many possible ways to achieve code reuse in an object-oriented paradigm. Some people argue that a language must offer implementation inheritance to be considered a real object-oriented language. This has led to a heated debate in both the software industry and the academic community—a debate that this book won't address. Instead, we'll focus on the benefits and problems associated with this powerful feature.

In implementation inheritance, one class is defined to reuse the code of another class. The class that's reused is called the *superclass*. The class that benefits from the reuse is the *subclass*. Visual Basic doesn't currently support implementation inheritance (but I'm sure you've heard all the rumors), so I'll use a Java example to illustrate what implementation inheritance looks like. Examine the following Java class *CDog*:

```
// Superclass
class CDog
{
    // Dog state
    public String Name;

    // Dog behavior
    public void Bark()
        {/* method implementation */}
    public void RollOver(int Rolls)
        {/* method implementation */}
}
```

The class *CDog* contains a property and two methods. Assume that each method has been defined with a valuable implementation. You can reuse the state and the behavior of the class by using implementation inheritance. *CDog* will be used as a superclass. A subclass that extends *CDog* will inherit both the class properties and the method implementations. The following Java code shows the syntax required to achieve implementation inheritance:

```
// Subclass                    ┌────────── inherits
class CBeagle extends CDog
{
    // Beagle state
    // Name property is inherited.
    // A color property is added.
    Public String Color;

    // Beagle behavior
    // Implementation of RollOver() is inherited.
    // Implementation of Bark() is overridden.
    public void Bark()
        {/* CBeagle-specific implementation */}
    // CBeagle extends CDog by adding a new method.
    public void FetchSlippers()
        {/* CBeagle-specific implementation */}
}
```

When *CBeagle* (the subclass) extends *CDog* (the superclass), it inherits all of the existing properties and method implementations. This means that *CBeagle* can reuse all of the state and behavior defined in *CDog*. You can then extend *CDog* by overriding existing methods such as *Bark* and adding methods such as *FetchSlippers* in *CBeagle*. You can also add new properties to the subclass definition.

You should use implementation inheritance only when a logical "is a" relationship exists between the subclass and the superclass. In this example, you can say, "A beagle is a dog." Figure 2-1 graphically depicts a relationship in which one class derives from another. As long as the "is a" requirement is met, implementation inheritance is useful for achieving code reuse. Implementation inheritance can be especially valuable when an application contains many classes that must exhibit a common behavior. The commonality of several classes can be hoisted to a superclass. For example, once the *CDog* class has been written, it can be extended by *CBeagle*, *CTerrier*, *CBoxer*, and any other class that "is a" dog. Code written to define state and behavior in the *CDog* class can be reused in many other classes.

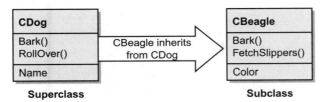

Figure 2-1 *Implementation inheritance allows one class to reuse the state and the behavior of another.*

Figure 2-2 is a graphic representation of what is known as an *inheritance hierarchy*. The hierarchy shows the relationships among the various classes in the application. This hierarchy is simple; you can create others that are far more complex. Imagine a hierarchy in which *CScottie* extends *CTerrier*, which extends *CDog*, which extends *CMammal*, which extends *CAnimal*. As you can imagine, inheritance hierarchies can become large and complex. Hierarchies containing five or more levels aren't uncommon in production code.

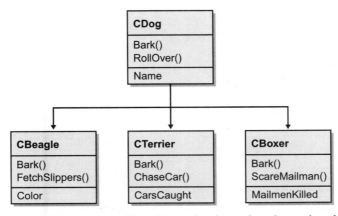

Figure 2-2 *An inheritance hierarchy shows the relationships between the superclasses and the subclasses in an application.*

When implementation inheritance is used correctly, it can be a powerful mechanism for code maintenance. When you improve the implementation of a method in a superclass, all of the classes down the inheritance hierarchy automatically benefit from the changes. A bug fix to the *CAnimal* class can potentially improve hundreds of other classes. As the inheritance hierarchy becomes larger and more complex, modifications to classes at the top can have a significant impact on many classes below. This implies that a single modification can affect the behavior of many distinct object types.

What is polymorphism?

So far, this chapter has explained how implementation inheritance offers the implicit reuse of method implementations, which results in greater maintainability through the elimination of duplicate code. Another powerful OOP feature provided by implementation inheritance is known as *polymorphism*. This is arguably the most important concept in object-oriented programming. Polymorphism allows a client to treat different objects in the same way, even if they were created from different classes and exhibit different behaviors.

You can use implementation inheritance to achieve polymorphism in languages such as C++ and Java. For instance, you can use a superclass reference to connect to and invoke methods on subclass instances. Figure 2-3 shows how a client can use a *CDog* reference to communicate with three different types of objects. Each subclass that derives from *CDog* is type-compatible with a *CDog* reference. Therefore, a client can use a *CDog* reference when communicating with objects of type *CBeagle*, *CTerrier*, or *CBoxer*.

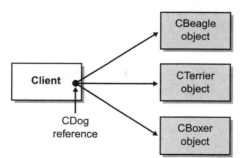

Figure 2-3 *You can achieve polymorphism by using a superclass reference to communicate with subclass instances. A client can use a* CDog *reference to communicate with any* CDog-*compatible object.*

A client can be sure that any class that extends the *CDog* class provides an implementation of the *Bark* method. The client doesn't care if the subclass uses the definition of *Bark* that was supplied by *CDog* or if the subclass has overridden this method with its own implementation. The client simply invokes the method using the calling syntax defined in the *CDog* class. But if each subclass supplies its own implementation of *Bark*, each object type can respond in its own unique way to the same request. Examine the following Java code:

```
// Method accepts any CDog-compatible object.
Public void MakeDogBark(CDog Dog)
{
    // Different objects can respond differently.
    Dog.Bark()
}
```

If this method is invoked using a *CBeagle* object, it might have very different results than if it's invoked using a *CTerrier* object. The client code knows which method to call, but it has no idea how the *Bark* method will be carried out. The calling syntax is well defined at compile time, but the actual method implementation isn't determined until runtime. Polymorphism is based on the idea of *dynamic binding* as opposed to static binding. Dynamic binding provides a degree of controlled uncertainty that makes polymorphism very powerful.

Many developers have discovered the value of creating applications with *plug-compatible* objects. Even if thousands of lines of client code have been written to *CDog*'s public interface, you can easily replace a *CBeagle* object with a *CTerrier* object or a *CBoxer* object. Such a change has little or no impact on client code because client code has dependencies on the *CDog* class but not on any of the classes that extend it.

Problems with implementation inheritance

So far, this chapter has explored the two biggest benefits of implementation inheritance: the implicit reuse of method implementations and polymorphism. It has not yet covered some of the potential problems with implementation inheritance. Unfortunately, implementation inheritance makes an application more susceptible to the kinds of dependency problems associated with class-based references because of the tight coupling between a subclass and its superclass.

With the proper use of encapsulation, you can hide implementation details from clients. This allows you to freely change the implementation details of the class without breaking client code. The problem with implementation inheritance is that it breaks the encapsulation of nonpublic members.

Languages that offer implementation inheritance provide a *protected* level of visibility in addition to public and private levels. Properties and methods that are marked as protected are hidden from a client but are accessible from subclasses. Subclasses can see implementation details that have been hidden from the client. As you hardcode the names of protected properties and methods of a superclass into a subclass, another layer of inflexible dependencies is created.

Implementation inheritance is an example of a development style known as *white-box reuse*. Applications that are built on white-box reuse often experience a tight coupling between the classes in the inheritance hierarchy. Once a subclass uses a protected property or method, you can't change the superclass's signature or remove it without breaking dependencies built into subclasses. This leads to fragility in applications with large inheritance hierarchies. Changing the classes at the top of the hierarchy often requires modifications to many subclasses. In some applications, changing a method signature or a property type at the top of the hierarchy can result in breaking tens or hundreds of classes down the inheritance chain. On the other hand, freezing the public and protected interfaces of key superclasses usually results in a system that can't evolve.

You must carefully consider whether to give a property or a method protected visibility. Proper design using implementation inheritance requires a high level of expertise and discipline to prevent what is known as the *fragile superclass scenario*. You should know whether a class will be extended by subclasses. If you expect a class to be extended, it's as important to hide implementation details from subclasses as it is to hide them from clients.

This isn't to suggest that implementation inheritance isn't useful. It's powerful in appropriate development scenarios. It's best used in smaller, controlled situations. Creating a large inheritance hierarchy that can evolve along with the requirements of an application is beyond the reach of all but the most experienced object-oriented designers.

When C++ and Smalltalk were first introduced, the OOP evangelists oversold implementation inheritance as a cure-all technique to achieve code reuse. As a result, this feature has been abused by designers who haven't understood the coupling problems that accompany white-box reuse. Over the past decade, the casual use of implementation inheritance has crippled the evolution of many large applications. Experienced developers who knew that implementation inheritance was most appropriate in small doses looked for more flexible ways to achieve reuse on a large scale. In particular, they looked for ways to achieve reuse without compromising extensibility in larger systems. This fueled the birth of interface-based programming and a development style known as *object composition*.

SEPARATING THE INTERFACE FROM THE IMPLEMENTATION

Interface-based programming offers another way to achieve reuse without the tendency toward tight coupling. Interface-based programming is based on *black-box reuse,* in which encapsulation is never compromised. Clients know only about the names and the calling syntax for an available set of requests. Clients never know about the implementation details behind the objects they're using.

Black-box reuse is achieved through a formal separation of interface and implementation. This means that the interface becomes a first-class citizen. An interface is an independent data type that is defined on its own. This is an evolution of classic OOP, in which a public interface is defined within the scope of a class definition.

At this point, you're probably thinking that this is all pretty vague. You're asking yourself, "What exactly is an interface?" Unfortunately, it's hard to provide a concise definition that conveys the key concepts of an entirely new way to write software. An interface can be described in many ways. You can get up to speed pretty quickly on the syntax for defining, implementing, and using interfaces. But the ramifications of interfaces for software design are much harder for the average programmer to embrace. Learning how to design with interfaces usually takes months or years.

At its most basic level, *an interface is a set of public method signatures*. It defines the calling syntax for a set of logically related client requests. While an interface defines method signatures, however, it can't include any implementation or data properties. By providing a layer of indirection, an interface decouples a class from the clients that use it. This means that an interface must be implemented by one or more classes in order to be useful. Once an interface has been implemented by a class, a client can create an object from the class and communicate with it through an interface reference.

You can use an interface to create an object reference but not the object itself. This makes sense because an object requires data properties and method implementations that cannot be supplied by an interface. Because it isn't a creatable entity, *an interface is an abstract data type*. Objects can be instantiated only from creatable classes known as *concrete data types*.

From a design standpoint, *an interface is a contract*. A class that implements an interface guarantees that the objects it serves up will support a certain type of behavior. More specifically, a class must supply an implementation for each method defined by the interface. When communicating with an object through an interface reference, a client can be sure that the object will supply a reasonable response to each method defined in the interface.

More than one class can implement the same interface. An interface defines the exact calling syntax and the loose semantics for each method. The loose semantics give each class author some freedom in determining the appropriate object behavior for each method. For instance, if the *IDog* interface defines a method named *Bark*, different class authors can supply different responses to the same request as long as each somehow reinforces the concept of a dog barking. The *CBeagle* class can implement *Bark* in a way that's different from either *CTerrier* or *CBoxer*. This means that *interfaces provide the opportunity for polymorphism*. Interfaces are like implementation inheritance in that they let you build applications composed of plug-compatible objects. But interfaces provide plug compatibility without the risk of the tight coupling that can occur with implementation inheritance and white-box reuse.

The Two Faces of Inheritance

Inheritance is an objected-oriented concept based on the "is a" relationship between entities. So far, I've used the term *implementation inheritance* instead of the more generic term *inheritance* because extending a superclass with a subclass is only one way to leverage an "is a" relationship. When a class implements an interface, it also takes advantage of an "is a" relationship. For instance, if a class *CBeagle* implements the interface *IDog*, it is correct to say that a beagle "is a" dog. You can use a *CBeagle* object in any situation in which an *IDog*-compatible object is required.

Interface-based programming is founded on a second form of inheritance known as *interface inheritance*. In general, inheritance doesn't require the reuse of method implementations. Instead, the only true requirement for inheritance is that a subclass instance be compatible with the base type that's being extended. The base type that's extended can be a class or a user-defined interface. In either situation, you can use a base-type reference to communicate with objects of many different types. This allows both forms of inheritance to achieve polymorphism.

Both implementation inheritance and interface inheritance offer polymorphism, but they differ greatly when it comes to their use of encapsulation. Implementation inheritance is based on white-box reuse. It allows a subclass to know intimate details of the superclass it extends. This allows a subclass to experience implicit reuse of a superclass's method implementation and data properties. Implementation inheritance is far more powerful than interface inheritance in terms of reusing state and behavior. But this reuse comes at a cost. The loss of encapsulation in white-box reuse limits the scalability of applications based on implementation inheritance.

As the term *black-box reuse* suggests, interface inheritance enforces the concepts of encapsulation. Strict adherence to the encapsulation of implementation details within classes allows for more scalable application designs. Interface-based programming solves many problems associated with white-box reuse. But to appreciate this style of programming, you must accept the idea that the benefits are greater than the costs. This is a struggle for many programmers.

When a class implements an interface, it takes on the obligation to provide a set of method implementations. Subclass authors must write additional code whenever they decide to implement an interface. When you compare this with implementation inheritance, it seems like much more work. When you inherit from a class, most of your work is already done, but when you inherit from an interface, your work has just begun. At first glance, implementation inheritance looks and smells like a cheeseburger, while interface inheritance looks like a bowl of steamed broccoli. You have to get beyond the desire to have the cheeseburger to reach a higher level of interface awareness. The key advantage of interface inheritance over implementation inheritance is that interface inheritance isn't vulnerable to the tight coupling that compromises the extensibility of an application.

Using Interfaces with Visual Basic

Visual Basic 5.0 was the first version of the product to support user-defined interfaces. You can achieve the benefits of interface-based programming with a Visual Basic project by following three required steps:

1. Define an interface.

2. Implement the interface in one or more creatable classes.

3. Use an interface reference in a client to communicate with objects.

As you can see, the basic steps for adding interfaces to your applications are pretty easy. Using interfaces also lets you add polymorphism to your application designs. We'll look at a simple example of the Visual Basic syntax required to complete these steps.

You can create user-defined interfaces in Visual Basic by using standard class modules. It would be better if the Visual Basic integrated development environment (IDE) provided a separate editor for defining interfaces, but unfortunately an editor dedicated to creating interfaces isn't currently available. You use the class module editor to create interface definitions as well as classes.

To define a new interface, you simply add a new class module to an existing project. Then you give it an appropriate name. If you're creating an interface to express the behavior of a dog, a suitable name might be *IDog* or *itfDog*. These are the two most common naming conventions among Visual Basic developers. If you're working in a Visual Basic project that's either an ActiveX DLL or an ActiveX EXE, you should also set the class module's *Instancing* property to *PublicNotCreatable*. This setting makes sense because the interface will represent an abstract data type. In a Standard EXE project, class modules don't have an adjustable *Instancing* property.

You define your interface by creating the calling syntax for a set of public methods. Don't include an implementation for any of the methods in your interface. You need only define the signatures, nothing more. In essence, you define *how* the client calls these methods, not *what* will happen. Here's an example of the *IDog* interface defined in a Visual Basic class module:

```
' Interface IDog
' Expresses behavior of a dog object

Public Property Get Name() As String
End Property

Public Property Let Name(ByVal Value As String)
End Property

Public Sub Bark()
End Sub
```

(continued)

```
Public Sub RollOver(ByRef Rolls As Integer)
End Sub
```

One of the first things you notice when declaring an interface in Visual Basic is the presence of *End Sub*, *End Function*, or *End Property* after each method signature. This makes no sense. The keyword *End* usually signifies the end of a method implementation. This is a confusing idiosyncrasy of the Visual Basic IDE and an unfortunate side effect of using the Visual Basic class module for defining both classes and interfaces. Perhaps a future version of Visual Basic will provide a module type dedicated to defining interfaces that won't require *End Sub*, *End Function*, or *End Property*, but for now you just have to grin and bear it.

Another important point is that this interface can use logical properties in addition to methods. This is reasonable when you consider that a logical property is actually a set of methods, not a data property. The client can use the logical property *Name* defined in the interface above just like a regular data property, but it must be implemented in terms of a *Property Let/Property Get* method pair.

Stop and think about this: Why can't an interface contain data members? Because an interface, unlike a class, is never used to create objects. Objects are created from a class that encapsulates the implementation details. The data layout of an object is among the most important details to encapsulate within a class definition. If an interface were to contain actual data members, the client would build dependencies on them. You know by this point that dependencies are bad.

Even though interfaces can't contain data properties, Visual Basic still lets you define a property in an interface, like this:

```
Public Name As String
```

But when you define a property in an interface, Visual Basic transparently defines it as a logical property. This is simply a convenience that Visual Basic provides when you create user-defined interfaces. The *Name* property defined in the preceding line of code still requires *Property Let* and *Property Get* in any class that implements the interface. Also note that implementing an interface has no effect on the data layout for a class definition. Any class that implements this interface should include a private data property for the physical storage of the dog's name.

After you create the interface definition, the next step is to create a concrete class that implements it. You add a second class module to your project and give it an appropriate name. For instance, you can create a concrete class *CBeagle* that implements the *IDog* interface. You must use the keyword *Implements* at the top of a class module. This is what the statement looks like:

```
Implements IDog
```

Once a class module contains this line, every method and logical property in the interface must have an associated implementation in the class module. This requirement is checked by Visual Basic's compiler. You can't compile your code without supplying every implementation. For instance, implementing the *Bark* method in the *IDog* interface requires this definition:

```
Private Sub IDog_Bark()
    ' Implementation code goes here.
End Sub
```

Visual Basic's mapping of interfaces requires each method implementation to use the name of the interface followed by an underscore and the method name. Visual Basic uses this proprietary syntax to create an entry point into an object when a particular interface is used. The Visual Basic compiler requires you to supply a similar implementation for each method and logical property in the interface. This guarantees that objects created from the class will provide an entry point for each interface member.

Fortunately, the Visual Basic IDE makes it easy to create the procedure skeletons for the method implementations if you use the keyword *Implements* at the top of the class module. The class module's editor window has a wizard bar that includes two drop-down combo boxes. If you select the name of the interface in the left combo box, you can quickly generate the skeletons for the method implementations by selecting the method names in the right combo box. An example of using the wizard bar is shown in Figure 2-4. Here's a partial implementation of the *CBeagle* class that implements the *IDog* interface:

```
Implements IDog
Private Name As String

Private Property Let IDog_Name(ByVal Value As String)
    Name = Value
End Property

Private Property Get IDog_Name() As String
    IDog_Name = Name
End Property

Private Sub IDog_Bark()
    ' Implementation code goes here.
End Sub

Private Sub IDog_RollOver(ByRef Rolls As Integer)
    ' Implementation code goes here.
End Sub
```

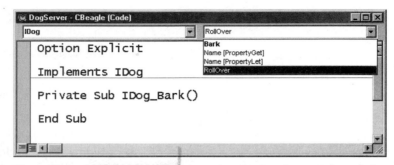

Figure 2-4 *The wizard bar makes it easy to create the procedure skeletons for implementing a user-defined interface.*

The wizard bar generates method signatures that are marked as private. This means that these method implementations aren't available to clients that use a *CBeagle* reference. They're available only to clients that use an *IDog* reference. The code above also demonstrates how the *CBeagle* class can implement the logical *Name* property by defining a private data property and implementing the *Property Let* and *Property Get* methods.

Now that you've created an interface and a class that implements it, you can use the interface to communicate with an object. For instance, a client can communicate with a *CBeagle* object through an *IDog* reference. You can use the *IDog* reference to invoke any method that the interface exposes. Here's a simple example.

```
Dim Dog As IDog ' IDog is abstract.
Set Dog = New CBeagle ' CBeagle is concrete.
' Access object through interface reference.
Dog.Name = "Spot"
Dog.Bark
Dog.RollOver 12
```

Once the client is connected to the object through the interface reference, it can invoke methods and access logical properties. The Visual Basic IDE provides the same IntelliSense features, type checking, and debugging that are available when you use class-based references. Note that you shouldn't use an interface after the *New* operator. An interface isn't a creatable type. You must use a concrete class such as *CBeagle* to create an object when you use the *New* operator.

Why Design with User-Defined Interfaces?

When Visual Basic programmers see what's required to utilize user-defined interfaces in an application for the first time, they often wonder, "Why would I ever want to do that?" or "Why should I care?" Programming with class-based references seems far more natural compared with the additional complexity required with user-defined interfaces. The previous example would have been far easier if the client code had been written against a *CBeagle* class instead of the *IDog* interface. User-defined interfaces seem like extra work without any tangible benefits.

There are several significant reasons why a Visual Basic programmer building a distributed application should care about interfaces. The first reason is that interfaces are the foundation of COM. In COM, clients can't use class-based references. Instead, they must access COM objects through interface references. As you'll see in the next chapter, Visual Basic does a pretty good job of hiding the complexities of this requirement. When you use a class-based reference, Visual Basic generates a default COM-style interface for the class behind the scenes. This means that you can work in Visual Basic without ever having to deal with user-defined interfaces explicitly. If you embrace interface-based programming, however, you'll become a much stronger COM programmer.

Another reason you should care about interfaces is that they can offer power and flexibility in software designs. Using user-defined interfaces in Visual Basic becomes valuable when you don't have a one-to-one mapping between a class and a public interface. Two scenarios are common. In one scenario, you create an interface and implement it in multiple classes. In the other scenario, you implement multiple interfaces in a single class. Both techniques offer advantages over application designs in which clients are restricted to using references based on concrete classes. While interface-based designs often require more complexity, the sky is the limit when it comes to what you can do with them.

Consider a case in which many classes implement the same interface. For example, assume that the classes *CBeagle*, *CTerrier*, and *CBoxer* all implement the interface *IDog*. An application can maintain a collection of *IDog*-compatible objects using the following code:

```
Dim Dog1 As IDog, Dog2 As IDog, Dog3 As IDog
' Create and initialize dogs.
Set Dog1 = New CBeagle
Dog1.Name = "Mo"
Set Dog2 = New CTerrier
Dog2.Name = "Larry"
Set Dog3 = New CBoxer
Dog3.Name = "Curly"
' Add dogs to a collection.
Dim Dogs As New Collection
Dogs.Add Dog1
Dogs.Add Dog2
Dogs.Add Dog3
```

The application can achieve polymorphic behavior by treating all of the *IDog*-compatible objects in the same manner. The following code iterates through the collection and invokes the *Bark* method on each object:

```
Dim Dog As IDog
For Each Dog In Dogs
    Dog.Bark
Next Dog
```

As the application evolves, this collection can be modified to hold any mix of *IDog*-compatible objects, including objects created from *CBeagle*, *CTerrier*, *CBoxer*, and any other future class that's written to implement the *IDog* interface. The *For Each* loop in the previous example is written in terms of the *IDog* interface and has no dependencies on any concrete class. You don't have to modify any of the code inside the loop when you introduce new concrete class types into the application.

Another powerful design technique is to have a single class implement multiple interfaces. If you do this, you'll have objects that support multiple interfaces and therefore multiple behaviors. When used together with runtime type inspection, this strategy becomes very powerful. Assume that the sample application adds another interface, *IWonderDog*, with the following method:

```
Sub FetchSlippers()
```

Let's say you have two classes, *CBeagle* and *CTerrier*, that both implement *IDog*. Assume that the *CBeagle* class implements *IWonderDog* but that the *CTerrier* class doesn't. A client can inspect objects created from these classes at runtime and ask them whether they support a specific interface. If an object supports the interface, the client can call upon its functionality. If an object doesn't support the interface, the client can degrade gracefully. The following code uses the Visual Basic *TypeOf* keyword to test for *IWonderDog* support.

```
Dim Dog1 As IDog, Dog2 As IDog

Set Dog1 = New CBeagle
Set Dog2 = New CTerrier

If TypeOf Dog1 Is IWonderDog Then
    Dim WonderDog1 As IWonderDog
    Set WonderDog1 = Dog1
    WonderDog1.FetchSlippers
End If

If TypeOf Dog2 Is IWonderDog Then
    Dim WonderDog2 As IWonderDog
    Set WonderDog2 = Dog2
    WonderDog2.FetchSlippers
End If
```

When the client queries the *CBeagle* object, it finds that object is *IWonderDog*-compatible. In other words, the object supports the *IWonderDog* interface. The client can then create an *IWonderDog* reference and assign the *CBeagle* object to it by casting the *IDog* reference with the *Set* statement. Once the client has an *IWonderDog* reference, it can successfully call *FetchSlippers*. Note that two references refer to the same object. When you're dealing with classes that implement multiple interfaces, code in the client becomes more complex because it takes several references to a single object to get at all the functionality.

When the *CTerrier* object is queried for *IWonderDog* compatibility, the client discovers that the interface isn't supported, which allows the client to degrade gracefully. Client code can iterate through a collection of *IDog*-compatible objects and safely call *FetchSlippers* on each object that supports the *IWonderDog* interface, like this:

```
Dim Dog As IDog, WonderDog As IWonderDog
For Each Dog In Dogs
    If TypeOf Dog Is IWonderDog Then
        Set WonderDog = Dog
        WonderDog.FetchSlippers
    End If
Next Dog
```

As you can imagine, this ability to determine the functionality of an object at runtime is very useful when you improve an application. If a later version of the *CBoxer* class implements the *IWonderDog* interface, the *For Each* loop shown above can take advantage of that without being rewritten. Client code can anticipate supported functionality in future versions of the object.

Extending a Class Definition

The example above shows how to use an object that supports more than one interface. You can also employ user-defined interfaces to safely extend the behavior of an object when an existing set of method signatures has become too limiting. For instance, the *IDog* interface defines the *RollOver* method as follows:

```
Public Sub RollOver(ByRef Rolls As Integer)
End Sub
```

If you need to extend the functionality of dog objects in the application so that clients can pass larger integer values, you can create a second interface named *IDog2*. Assume that the *IDog2* interface defines the same members as *IDog* with the exception of the *RollOver* method, which is defined like this:

```
Public Sub RollOver(ByRef Rolls As Long)
End Sub
```

A new client can test to see whether an *IDog* object supports the new behavior. If the new behavior isn't supported, the client can simply fall back on the older behavior. Here's an example of how this works:

```
Sub ExerciseDog(ByVal Dog As IDog)
    If TypeOf Dog Is IDog2 Then
        ' Use new behavior if supported.
        Dim Dog2 As IDog2, lRolls As Long
        Set Dog2 = Dog
        lRolls = 50000
        Dog2.RollOver lRolls
    Else
        ' Use older behavior if necessary.
        Dim iRolls As Integer
        iRolls = 20000
        Dog.RollOver iRolls
    End If
End Sub
```

The key observation to make about this versioning scheme is that you can introduce new clients and new classes into an application without breaking older clients and older classes. A new class can accommodate older clients by continuing to support the interfaces from earlier versions. New clients deal with older classes by using the older interface when required. In a world without interfaces, extending classes often requires modifying all the clients. Modifying clients often requires modifying classes. The versioning scheme made possible by interface-based programming allows you to make changes to an application with little or no impact on code that's already in production.

Using Interfaces in Your Application Designs

This chapter has presented a simple application to demonstrate the core concepts of interface-based programming. How can you apply these principles in a real-world application? If you're designing a large application that uses customer data from many different DBMSs, you often find that it's necessary to write separate code for each one. You can create a user-defined interface *ICustomerDataManager* and start writing lots of client code in business logic components against the interface instead of a concrete *CCustomerDataManager* class. This will make it much easier to port your application across several DBMSs. If you create several classes that implement the *ICustomerDataManager* interface (perhaps one class for accessing an Oracle DBMS and another for SQL Server), you can achieve the plug-and-play benefits of polymorphism. Different types of objects exhibit different behavior, but they're all controlled through the same interface.

From a versioning standpoint, this design lets you improve the behavior of various classes by introducing new interfaces into the application. Interfaces such as *ICustomerDataManager2*, *ICustomerDataManager3*, and *ICustomerDataManager4* let you safely extend the behavior of your objects over time. The best part about this approach is that you can revise clients and classes independently. Class authors have much more freedom to modify and extend the functionality behind their objects without breaking existing clients. Older clients and objects can use earlier interfaces, while newer clients and objects can communicate through newer interfaces. All of this is made possible through the runtime type inspection of interface support.

Interfaces and COM

The industry has adopted interface-based programming because of the limitations of other common techniques, such as the use of class-based references and implementation inheritance. User-defined interfaces bring a new level of complexity to both application design and programming, but their value is easy to measure in large applications. (In fact, this is one of the only areas in which Microsoft and Sun agree.) In a Darwinian sense, interface-based programming makes software more fit for survival. Interfaces remove the dependencies that couple various pieces of software. And this act of decoupling makes your code easier to reuse, maintain, and extend.

The next chapter presents the fundamentals of COM. As you'll see, COM is based on the following core concepts of interface-based programming:

- **COM requires a formal separation of interface and implementation** That is, it requires that clients communicate with objects exclusively through interface references. This ensures that clients never build undesirable dependencies on components (classes), which in turn allows component authors to revise their class code without worrying about breaking client code.

- **COM clients query objects for runtime type information** A client can always ask an object whether it supports a specific interface. If the requested interface isn't supported, the client can discover this and degrade gracefully. This lets programmers revise components and client applications independently. Older components and older clients can work in harmony with newer components and newer clients. Herein lies the key to versioning in COM.

SUMMARY

This chapter showed the use of interfaces in a single application. The entire application was written in a single language, and all the source code was sent to a compiler at the same time. COM, on the other hand, must work across binary component boundaries. Moreover, clients and components can be written in different languages and can run in different processes on different computers. COM must solve many problems at the physical level to achieve the benefits of interface-based programming in a distributed environment.

Chapter 3

The Fundamentals of COM

This chapter describes the essential concepts and details of the Component Object Model (COM). It examines Microsoft's original motivation for creating COM and lays out the original design goals. As you'll see, COM connects clients to objects using the principles of interface-based programming. At the physical level, many details must be addressed when code for an application is distributed in separate binary files and client-object interaction takes place across process and host boundaries.

This chapter explains how COM's architects were able to integrate many languages, including Microsoft Visual Basic, into COM. You'll see how the Visual Basic compiler works with a special type of file called a type library. Type libraries make it possible for languages such as Visual Basic to access COM objects. You'll see how and why the Visual Basic compiler builds a type library into every ActiveX DLL and ActiveX EXE. This chapter also explains how scripting clients such as VBScript and JavaScript can access COM objects by using a mechanism known as automation.

In COM, the code written for clients and the code for components are often compiled into separate binary files. Components never expose their implementation details to clients, but clients still need to create objects. But how can a client application create an object if the object's server doesn't expose a visible concrete class definition? COM provides a class-loading mechanism that clients can call upon to create and activate objects without ever knowing about a component's implementation details. This chapter explains the services and design requirements that make object activation possible.

Finally, this chapter examines how clients communicate with objects that live in different processes and on different machines. COM's remoting layer solves a very difficult problem: How do you remote a method call across thread, process, and host boundaries? The architecture of classic COM not only solves this problem, it does so in a way that is completely transparent to the majority of application programmers.

THE BIRTH OF COM

The seeds of COM were planted in 1988, when several teams at Microsoft began to build object-oriented infrastructures that provided reuse based on components. When a group of engineers from various teams were assembled with the Microsoft Office team to help out on the OLE2 project, they decided that they needed to draft a few high-level requirements for the new architecture they would be building.

These engineers came up with four high-level requirements for their new component architecture. First, the architecture had to be based on *binary reuse* because maintaining and enhancing code in large, monolithic applications causes too many problems. Systems based on binary components are much easier to assemble, maintain, and extend.

Second, the architecture had to be based on an *object-oriented paradigm*. Most of the binary reuse in Microsoft Windows had been based on traditional DLLs, which don't commonly include object-oriented extensions. This type of binary reuse can't benefit from the encapsulation that can be achieved with a class-based design.

Third, the architecture had to be *language-independent*. It would be far more powerful if each component author could select a language independently of other component authors. Every programming language requires programmers to make trade-offs in productivity, flexibility, and performance. The ability to choose a language on a component-by-component basis offers many advantages over having to use a single language for an entire application.

Finally, the architecture had to address *interprocess communication*. It was essential to compose systems of clients and objects that ran on different machines so that the architecture could be a foundation for distributed technologies. The engineers also knew that if they could hide the details of interprocess communication from the majority of programmers, their architecture would foster much higher productivity.

The efforts of these engineers debuted in production code with Microsoft's second major release of Object Linking and Embedding (OLE), a technology that allows users to link documents produced in one application with documents produced in another application. OLE requires interprocess communication among applications. The original version of OLE was based on an interprocess mechanism called Dynamic Data Exchange (DDE). This initial release was plagued with resource and performance problems, which resulted in limited acceptance within the industry. Microsoft knew that OLE's features were valuable conceptually but that making this technology usable in a production environment would mean optimizing the underlying infrastructure. In essence, OLE needed a whole new plumbing system to be viable.

OLE2 shipped with the first generation of COM in 1993. OLE and COM are distinct entities: OLE is a technology for linking and embedding documents, while COM is an architecture for building component-based systems. Unfortunately, these two technologies have a history of being confused as one and the same. As fate would have it, COM has become far more important than OLE, the technology it was created to assist.

Creating Binary Components with C++

The COM architects designed a way to compose applications based on components built into separate binary files. However, this was no easy undertaking. They had to make some tough decisions along the way. One of the most significant decisions was that client code could not be written using class-based references. The coupling that would occur would be far too damaging. It was obvious that this new object model would have to be based on a formal separation of interface from implementation.

Long before any Visual Basic or Java programmer used keywords such as *Implements* and *interface*, the C++ community was building applications using the principles of interface-based programming. Although the C++ language has no direct support for this style of programming, you can create abstract data types (interfaces) using advanced features of the language. A C++ class can define a set of method signatures without implementation. This is what is known as an *abstract base class*. In just a bit, you'll see what one of these looks like, but first let's examine why these C++ developers needed abstract base classes in the first place.

C++ has a very serious shortcoming when it comes to building component-based applications: It doesn't support encapsulation at the binary level. This can be traced back to the fact that the language was designed to build monolithic applications. When a C++ class author marks a data member as private, it's off-limits to client code, as you'd expect. However, this encapsulation is enforced only in the syntax of the language. Any client that calls *New* on a class must have knowledge of the object's data layout. The client is responsible for allocating the memory in which the object will run. This means that the client must have knowledge of each data member for a class regardless of whether it's marked public, protected, or private.

These layout dependencies aren't a problem in a monolithic application because the client always recompiles against the latest version of the class. But in component-based development, this is a huge problem. The layout of a class within a DLL can't change without breaking all the clients that use it. The following C++ code shows a client and two versions of a class in a DLL.

```
// In SERVER.DLL - Version 1
// Each object will require 8 bytes of memory.
class CDog {
public:
    void Bark(){ /* implementation */ }
    void RollOver(int Rolls){ /* implementation */ }
private:
    double Weight;
};

// In CLIENT.EXE
// Compiled against Version 1 of DLL
// Client allocates 8 bytes for object.
CDog* pDog = new CDog;

// In SERVER.DLL - Version 2
// Each object will require 16 bytes of memory.
// Replacing older DLL will break client.
class CDog {
public:
    void Bark(){ /* implementation */ }
    void RollOver(int Rolls){ /* implementation */ }
private:
    double Weight;
    double Age;
};
```

When the first version of the DLL is replaced in the field by the second version, a big problem arises. The client application continues to create objects that are 8 bytes in size, but each object thinks that it's 16 bytes. This is a recipe for disaster. For example, let's say you've rewritten the implementation of *Bark* in version 2 to access the *Age* property to determine the intensity of the dog's bark. The newer version of the object will try to access memory that it doesn't own, and the application will likely fail in strange and mysterious ways. The only way to deal with this is to rebuild all client applications whenever the object's data layout changes. This eliminates one of the biggest benefits of component-based development: the ability to modify one binary file without touching any of the others.

How can you replace the DLL without breaking any of the client applications that use it? The object's data layout must be hidden from the client. The client must also be relieved of the responsibility of calling the C++ *New* operator across a binary firewall. Some other agent outside the client application must take on the responsibility of creating the object.

It all boils down to this: the C++ language is broken. Its creators never intended it to be used for building component-based applications. Fortunately, C++ programmers are the smartest programmers in the industry. (Just ask any of them—they'll be happy to verify this fact.) They discovered that abstract base classes make it possible to separate interface from implementation. Abstract base classes allow C++ programmers to build client applications without any layout dependencies on the concrete classes they're using. This, in turn, makes it possible for class authors to freely change their layout details from version to version.

Abstract base classes as interfaces

In C++, an abstract base class is used to define method signatures that don't include any implementation. Here's an example of what an abstract base class looks like in C++:

```
class IDog {
    virtual void Bark() = 0;
    virtual void RollOver(int Rolls) = 0;
};
```

A C++ member function (a method) that's marked with *=0* is a pure virtual function. This means that it doesn't include an implementation. It also means that the class that defines it isn't a creatable type. Therefore, the only way to use an abstract base class is through inheritance, like this:

```
class CBeagle : public IDog {
    virtual void Bark()
        {/* Implementation */}
    virtual void RollOver(int Rolls)
        {/* Implementation */}
};
```

C++ programmers who use abstract base classes and a little extra discipline can achieve the reusability, maintainability, and extensibility benefits that we covered in Chapter 2. The extra discipline is required to avoid any definition of data storage or method implementation inside an abstract base class. As a result, an abstract base class can formalize the separation of interface from implementation. A C++ client application can communicate with a *CBeagle* object through an *IDog* reference, which allows the client application to avoid building any layout dependencies on the *CBeagle* class.

You should see that a C++ abstract base class is being used as a logical interface. Even though C++ has no formal support for interface-based programming, advanced techniques in C++ allow you to reap the most significant benefits of interfaces. In fact, C++ programmers pioneered the concept of interface-based programming by using abstract base classes in large component-based applications. This technique has been used in numerous projects and is well described in *Large-Scale C++ Software Design* by John S. Lakos (Addison-Wesley, 1996). The principles of interface-based programming as implemented in C++ have had a profound effect on the development of COM.

Ada (?)

The vTable as a Standard In-Memory Representation

The creators of COM concluded that if they used abstract base classes, they could achieve object-oriented binary reuse. DLLs could hold concrete class definitions. Client applications could use objects created from these DLLs as long as they communicated through abstract base classes. DLLs could be revised and replaced in the field without adversely affecting existing client applications. Arriving at this series of conclusions was a big milestone for the Microsoft engineers. They had devised a way to achieve binary reuse in an object-oriented paradigm using C++. They had achieved their first two design goals.

Interface-based programming is founded on the concept of polymorphism. As you remember from the previous chapter, polymorphism is a controlled form of uncertainty whereby the client knows what method to call but doesn't know or care how a particular object might implement it. Any language that supports polymorphism must provide a way to dynamically bind a client to any one of many possible implementations. As long as the client has been programmed against a well-known interface, an application can plug in any type-compatible object at runtime.

Different languages and compilers approach the requirement of *dynamic binding* in different ways. Because of its low-level nature, C++ happens to have one of the fastest binding techniques available. Dynamic binding in C++ is based on a highly efficient dispatching architecture that relies on the use of *virtual functions*.

The C++ compiler and linker make dynamic binding possible by generating an array of function pointers called a *vTable*. (The *v* stands for *virtual*.) This array of function pointers represents a set of entry points into an object. Each method defined in an abstract base class gets an associated pointer in the vTable. As long as the client knows the calling syntax of a particular method and acquires the appropriate function pointer, it can access the object without any knowledge of the concrete class from which it was created.

At this point, the COM architects made another significant decision. They decided to use C++-style vTables as the standard in-memory representation for all client-object communication. All COM objects must expose their method implementations through vTables. All clients must bind to vTables and invoke methods through the use of these function pointers. This is what's known as *direct vTable binding*.

Figure 3-1 shows what a vTable looks like. It's basically the same in both C++ and in COM. A vTable is a standard in-memory representation that both an object and a client agree on. On the right side of the figure is a logical view of a COM client accessing a COM object. Each lollipop represents an interface that the COM object supports. Note that an object can support multiple interfaces. An object must expose a separate vTable for each interface it implements.

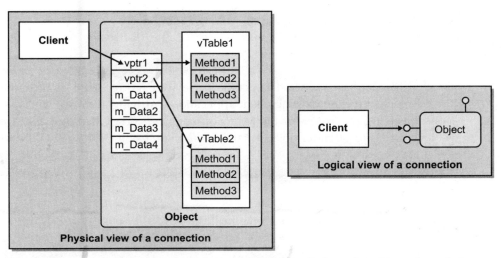

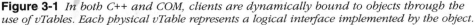

Figure 3-1 *In both C++ and COM, clients are dynamically bound to objects through the use of vTables. Each physical vTable represents a logical interface implemented by the object.*

Sometime after the completion of the OLE2 project, several of the engineers who designed the COM architecture drafted a specification for what they had done. This document, known as the *COM Specification,* defines the rules for COM programming. It also defines much of the important terminology.

COM objects are instantiated from COM-compliant classes known as *coclasses.* A coclass is a concrete implementation of one or more interfaces. You should note that the terms *coclass* and *component* can be used interchangeably. A component is a creatable data type from which a client creates objects. In practice, you'll create a *MultiUse* class for each component you want to produce.

Coclasses are compiled into and deployed in binary files called *servers.* In addition to containing the implementation code for one or more coclasses, a server must also support COM's infrastructure for object activation. As you'll see, a server does this by exposing well-known entry points.

Some people use the term *component* to mean a physical file, such as an ActiveX DLL, but I define a component as a creatable class compiled into a server. The ActiveX DLL is the server, not the component. To illustrate the potential confusion, answer the following question: If you compile two *MultiUse* classes into one ActiveX DLL, do you have one component or two? I'd say you have two. Others would say you have one. You should realize that there's no consistency with this issue. In this book, the terms *component, coclass,* and *concrete class* all mean the same thing. It's what you use to create an object. This usage is consistent with the programming models of MTS and COM+.

TYPE LIBRARIES AND LANGUAGE INDEPENDENCE

In COM, clients and objects communicate through vTable binding. This implies that clients and objects must be savvy in their use of function pointers. Luckily, the compiler helps C++ programmers by doing most of the work behind the scenes. vTables are automatically created and populated by the C++ compiler on the object side. The C++ compiler can also generate the required client-side binding code that invokes methods through the vTable function pointers. All client-side programmers have to do is compile their work against a header file that contains the definition of the abstract base class.

But what about programmers who use Visual Basic, Java, and scripting languages? Many developer tools and languages such as these have no built-in support for dealing with function pointers. To create or use COM objects, a development tool or language must follow the COM Specification, which states that vTable binding must be used to conduct all client-object communication. Many higher-level tools and languages need assistance to be able to participate in COM programming.

Visual Basic provides this assistance by adding support to its compiler and adding a Visual Basic–to–COM mapping layer in its runtime. After all, the COM Specification defines the rules clearly. The Visual Basic team knew exactly what it would take to make objects vTable-compliant. On the client side, the Visual Basic compiler automatically creates the vTable binding code required to access a COM object. Fortunately, when a language or tool such as Visual Basic uses a mapping layer, it can hide many of the underlying details from its programmers. This is why Visual Basic is so much easier to use than C++ for COM programming.

The Visual Basic compiler can't make sense of a C++ header file. Therefore, it can't use an abstract base class at compile time to build the client-side binding code. Instead, Visual Basic uses interface definitions that are published inside a special type of file called a *type library*. The type library tells the Visual Basic compiler what the vTable for each interface looks like.

A type library is a binary repository that contains type information about such things as interfaces and coclasses. It's essentially a catalog that defines a collection of COM data types. Inside a type library, each interface is defined as a set of methods; each coclass is defined as a set of one or more implemented interfaces. When you compile an ActiveX DLL or an ActiveX EXE, Visual Basic automatically creates a type library for you and bundles it into the server's executable image. This type library contains definitions for the coclasses provided by the server and a definition for each interface defined in the server's project.

When compiling a client application, Visual Basic needs to see the server's type library in order to build the client-side binding code. As long as Visual Basic's compiler can read the interface definitions from a type library, it can build the code

required for direct vTable binding. You can import a type library into a Visual Basic *Prcled*
project by opening the References dialog box from the Project menu. This dialog box
presents a list of all the type libraries registered on your development workstation.

So how do you build a type library? It turns out that different programmers build
them in different ways. With Visual Basic, it couldn't be easier. You simply compile
your server project, and Visual Basic transparently creates the type library behind the
scenes by examining your source code. However, many programmers build type
libraries using a special language called *Interface Definition Language (IDL)*.

Working with IDL

While type libraries define interfaces and coclasses in a binary format, IDL does the
same thing in a readable text-based format. C++ developers who need to create type
libraries start by using IDL. Once a developer has defined interface and coclass definitions with IDL, the resulting IDL source file can be fed to the Microsoft IDL (MIDL)
compiler. The MIDL compiler is capable of emitting many different things including
a type library.

If Visual Basic can build type libraries automatically, why can't a C++ compiler
do the same? When the COM team began formalizing the COM Specification, it became obvious that C++ and C couldn't be used to define COM interfaces. C and C++
weren't designed to define functions that can be called across process boundaries,
so they allow parameter definitions that are extremely vague. For instance, if a C++
method defines a parameter as a pointer, what does the pointer actually point to? What
data must actually move between the client process and the object process? A mere
pointer can't define what needs to be moved between the two processes. IDL solves
this problem by using syntax that describes method parameters without ambiguity.

IDL looks a lot like C, but it adds a few object-oriented extensions. It also allows the specification of attributes for entities such as type libraries, coclasses, interfaces, methods, and parameters. Here's a watered-down example of what IDL
looks like:

```
library DogServerLib {
    interface IDog {
        HRESULT Bark();
        HRESULT RollOver([in] int Rolls);
    };
    interface IwonderDog {
        HRESULT FetchSlippers();
    };
    coclass CBeagle {
        interface IDog;
        interface IWonderDog;
    };
};
```

This example shows how type libraries, interfaces, and coclasses are defined in IDL. Note that each method definition has a return value of type HRESULT. COM requires that methods return HRESULT to establish a standardized infrastructure for error reporting. This infrastructure is particularly valuable in a distributed environment in which remote objects can crash or become unreachable for any number of reasons. Chapter 4 discusses error propagation and error handling in more detail. We'll revisit the topic of how HRESULTs are used in that chapter.

When C++ programmers want to create components and interfaces, they must first create an IDL source file containing the appropriate definitions and feed it to the MIDL compiler. Visual Basic programmers, on the other hand, don't go through this process because the Visual Basic IDE creates type libraries directly from Visual Basic code. As you can see, Visual Basic programmers never have to work with IDL.

You can live a productive life as a Visual Basic programmer without ever seeing or understanding IDL. However, if you learn the basics of IDL, you'll be a better COM programmer. This is especially true if you're concerned with what's really going on behind the scenes or with interoperability among components written in other languages such as C++. With an understanding of IDL, you can see exactly what Visual Basic is doing under the covers to provide support for COM.

A COM utility named *OLEVIEW.EXE* can help you reverse-engineer a type library into readable text-based IDL code. Figure 3-2 shows how you can use this utility to examine the coclasses and interfaces built into your ActiveX DLLs and ActiveX EXEs. Be sure to set OLEVIEW.EXE to expert mode (the Expert Mode command is on the View menu) when you attempt to read a type library. If you don't do this, you won't see the type libraries in the left-side tree view control of OLEVIEW.EXE.

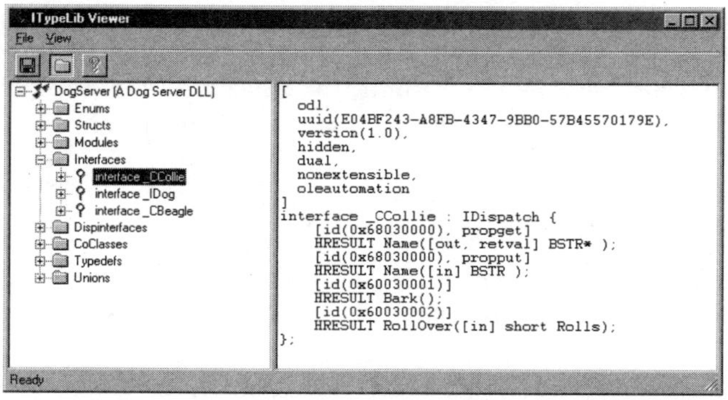

Figure 3-2 *OLEVIEW.EXE lets you examine and modify many aspects of your COM servers. This example shows how OLEVIEW.EXE lets you reverse-engineer a type library.*

How Visual Basic Maps to COM

COM requires that every object implement at least one interface. Visual Basic makes things easy for you by creating a default interface in each creatable class. All of the public methods and properties from a class are placed in a *default interface*. For instance, assume that you have (in an ActiveX DLL) a class *CCollie* with the following public interface:

```
Public Name As String

Public Sub Bark()
    ' implementation
End Sub
```

Visual Basic creates a hidden interface named *_CCollie* from the public properties and methods of the class module. The fact that this interface is marked *hidden* in the type library means that other Visual Basic programmers can't see it in the Object Browser or through Microsoft IntelliSense. (Visual Basic also hides any type name that begins with an underscore.) Visual Basic then creates a coclass named *CCollie* that implements *_CCollie* as the *default interface*. The basic IDL looks like this:

```
[hidden]
interface _CCollie {
    [propget] HRESULT Name([out, retval] BSTR* Name);
    [propput] HRESULT Name([in] BSTR Name);
    HRESULT Bark();
};

coclass CCollie {
    [default] interface _CCollie;
};
```

This transparent one-to-one mapping allows Visual Basic classes to be COM-compliant without any assistance from the programmer. Naive Visual Basic programmers have no idea what's really going on. Any Visual Basic client can contain the following code to use this class:

```
Dim Dog As CCollie
Set Dog = New CCollie
Dog.Name = "Lassie"
Dog.Bark
```

In the code above, the variable declared with the type *CCollie* is transparently cast to a *_CCollie* reference. This makes sense because a client must communicate with an object through an interface reference. This also makes COM programming easy in Visual Basic. As long as there is a one-to-one mapping between your classes and the interfaces that you want to export, you don't have to create user-defined interfaces. However, if you don't employ user-defined interfaces, you can't really tap into the power of interface-based designs.

Chapter 2 showed how to implement user-defined interfaces in a Visual Basic application. When you define an interface in Visual Basic 5 with a *PublicNotCreatable* class and implement it in a class, the resulting IDL code looks something like this:

```
interface IDog {
    HRESULT Name([out, retval] BSTR* Name);
    HRESULT Name([in] BSTR Name);
    HRESULT Bark();
};

interface _CBeagle {
};

coclass CBeagle {
    [default] interface _CBeagle;
    interface IDog;
};
```

Notice that *IDog* is defined as an implemented interface in the *CBeagle* class, yet it's not marked as the default interface. Even when your class contains no public members, Visual Basic automatically creates a default interface of the same name preceded by an underscore. You can't change this to make another interface the default. In the next chapter, you'll see that sometimes you must put functionality in the default interface, which means that you must add public members in your class. This is always the case when you create Visual Basic components for scripting clients.

Visual Basic 6 works differently than Visual Basic 5. When you mark a class module as *PublicNotCreatable*, Visual Basic 6 creates a coclass and a default interface. For instance, when you create the interface *IDog* with a property and a method in a class module marked as *PublicNotCreatable*, the resulting IDL looks like this:

```
[hidden]
interface _IDog : IDispatch {
    HRESULT Name([out, retval] BSTR* Name);
    HRESULT Name([in] BSTR Name);
    HRESULT Bark();
};

[noncreatable]
coclass IDog {
    [default] interface _IDog;
};
```

This means that in Visual Basic 6 you can't create a COM interface without an associated coclass inside your server's type library as you could in Visual Basic 5. *PublicNotCreatable* class modules always produce an interface and a *noncreatable* coclass. The *noncreatable* attribute means that the class can't be instantiated from a COM client. However, any code that lives inside the same server project can create objects from a *PublicNotCreatable* class. In Visual Basic 6, you should think of these as "public-not-externally-creatable" classes.

It turns out that the differences between Visual Basic 5 and Visual Basic 6 are hidden inside the type library. The code you write in Visual Basic 6 is the same as the code you write in Visual Basic 5. In the example above, *IDog* is a coclass and *_IDog* is a hidden interface. Whenever you use the type *IDog* with the *Implements* keyword or use it to create object references, Visual Basic silently casts it to *_IDog*.

Note that your classes can also implement interfaces that are defined in type libraries referenced in your project. To implement them, you must import the type library using the References dialog box (accessed from the Project menu). These type libraries can be built with either Visual Basic or by using IDL and the MIDL compiler. Once your project can see the interface definition, you can use the *Implements* keyword in a class module. In large projects whose designs depend on user-defined interfaces, it might make sense to distribute the interface definitions in a type library that's independent of any servers that implement them. In Chapter 5, we'll look at how to build and distribute type libraries using IDL and the MIDL compiler. More important, we'll look at some reasons why you might or might not want to do this.

Globally Unique Identifiers (GUIDs)

COM offers a scheme for identifying data types such as interfaces and coclasses that is much better than relying on their human-readable names such as *IDog* and *CBeagle*. COM uses something called a *globally unique identifier (GUID)*. A GUID is a 128-bit integer. Approximately 3.4×10^{38} values are possible for a 128-bit integer, so it's safe to assume that an unlimited supply of these identifiers is available for use in COM. Most compilers and databases don't support 128-bit integers, so GUIDs are usually stored in other formats.

C++ programmers use a structure (equivalent to a user-defined type in Visual Basic) that represents a 128-bit value with a set of smaller integer values. A GUID can also be expressed in 32-character hexadecimal form, which makes it somewhat readable. This is known as the *Registry format* because that's how GUIDs are stored in the Windows Registry. Here's an example of what a GUID looks like in the Registry:

{C46C1BE0-3C52-11D0-9200-848C1D000000}

COM supplies a system-level function named *CoCreateGUID*, which is used to generate new GUIDs. The function relies on an algorithm that uses information such as the unique identifier from the computer's network card and the system clock to create a GUID that is guaranteed to be unique across time and space. Programmers creating interface or coclass definitions in IDL can use a utility named GUIDGEN.EXE to generate GUIDs. This allows them to copy and paste GUIDs into IDL source files as well as C++ source code. Visual Basic programmers never have to worry about this because the Visual Basic IDE generates GUIDs behind the scenes when they're needed.

GUIDs are used in many places in COM, but you should start by examining their use with interfaces and coclasses. Each COM interface has an associated GUID called an *interface ID (IID)*. Each coclass has an associated GUID called a *class ID (CLSID)*. When you examine IDL, you'll notice that each interface and coclass has a *uuid* attribute (where *uuid* stands for *universally unique identifier*). Don't let the *uuid* attribute confuse you. A uuid is the same thing as a GUID. Here's an example of an IID and a CLSID in IDL:

```
[ uuid(3B46B8A8-CA17-11D1-920B-709024000000) ]
interface _IDog {
    // methods
};

[ uuid(3B46B8AB-CA17-11D1-920B-709024000000) ]
coclass CBeagle {
    // interfaces
};
```

When you build an ActiveX DLL or an ActiveX EXE, all required CLSIDs and IIDs are transparently generated and compiled into the server's type library. The GUID then becomes the physical name for an interface or a coclass. When a client application is compiled against the type library, these GUIDs are also compiled into the client's binary image. This enables the client application to ask for a specific coclass and interface whenever it needs to create and bind to an object at runtime.

Visual Basic does a pretty good job of hiding GUIDs from programmers. When you reference a type library in a Visual Basic project, you simply use the friendly names of interfaces and coclasses in your code. Visual Basic reads the required GUIDs out of the type library at compile time and builds them into the EXE or DLL when you choose the Make command from the File menu.

When you create a COM server, Visual Basic also hides the GUIDs from you. It automatically generates GUIDs for your interfaces and coclasses on the fly whenever you build a server using the Make command. This is convenient, but sometimes it would be nice if Visual Basic offered a little more flexibility. It doesn't allow you to take a specific GUID and associate it with an interface or a coclass. For instance, you might have a cool designer GUID like this:

```
"{DEADBEEF-BADD-BADD-BADD-2BE2DEF4BEDD}"
```

Unfortunately, the Visual Basic IDE won't let you assign this GUID to one of the coclasses in your Visual Basic server. Visual Basic also requires that you build your server projects with an appropriate compatibility mode setting. If you don't, your GUIDs will change from build to build. Chapter 5 covers compatibility in greater depth.

LOADING COMPONENT CODE DYNAMICALLY

What do you know about COM so far? You know that a client must communicate with an object through an interface and that a client binds to an object at runtime and invokes methods through direct vTable binding. You also know that Visual Basic clients learn about components and interfaces by examining type libraries at compile time. These rules are the foundation on which COM is built.

But think about the following questions: How does a client create and bind to an object if it only knows two GUIDs, the IID and the CLSID? How does a client obtain the first interface reference to an object? COM provides an infrastructure that helps the client. However, the client must know how to call into the system to ask for assistance.

COM exposes a library of system-level functions that are collectively known as the *COM library*. This library is exposed through a set of DLLs that are installed on any COM-enabled operating system. The COM library is part of Windows 2000, Windows NT 4, Windows 98, and Windows 95. (But the runtime files in future versions of COM+ will probably be decoupled from the operating system.)

Client applications written in C++ typically interact with the COM library through calls to OLE32.DLL. Visual Basic programmers are shielded from this DLL by their runtime layer. Figure 3-3 shows the differences in the layers between a COM application written in C++ and one written in Visual Basic.

Client applications must call upon the services provided by the COM library to create and connect to objects. The sequence of object creation must be carefully orchestrated because a client must bind to an interface, not to a class. This leads to a catch-22: How can a client create an object when it can never see the definition of the creatable class? The following sections describe exactly how COM makes this possible.

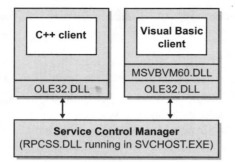

Figure 3-3 *C++ programmers talk to the COM library directly. Visual Basic programmers are shielded from this library by the Visual Basic runtime layer.*

Object Activation

A client application can discover the CLSID of a coclass as well as which IIDs it supports at compile time through inspection of a type library. However, COM requires that no other dependencies be built between clients and components. As long as a client knows which CSLID and IID to use, it can create and bind to an object. Once the binding has taken place, the client can invoke methods on the object by accessing the vTable associated with the IID. The act of creating and binding to an object is called *activation*. When a client wants to activate an object, it must make a call to the COM library and pass a CLSID and an IID.

Activation support must be built into COM's infrastructure because clients must always be shielded from the definitions of concrete classes. This is a fundamental principle of interface-based programming. After all, if a client could see the definition behind a component, it could generate a dependency on the object's data layout at compile time. Instead, COM puts the responsibility of allocating memory and creating the object on the server. The infrastructure support supplied by COM simply plays the role of middleman. It takes an activation request from the client and forwards it to the server. The server is the one calling *New* on the class when the object is instantiated.

The COM service that helps clients with activation is known as the *Service Control Manager (SCM)*. It's affectionately called "the scum" by COM programmers who are in the know. During in-process activation, a session of the SCM is loaded into the client process from OLE32.DLL. To assist with out-of-process activation in Windows 2000, a session of the SCM is loaded from RPCSS.DLL into an instance of SVCHOST.EXE, as shown in Figure 3-3. Note that in Windows NT, the SCM is a service that runs as RPCSS.EXE.

A client application always interacts with the SCM through OLE32.DLL. C++ programmers activate objects by directly calling a function named *CoCreateInstance* (or a related function named *CoCreateInstanceEx*). Visual Basic programmers can activate objects by using the *New* operator or the *CreateObject* function. When a client application calls *New* or *CreateObject* on a component that resides in a COM server, Visual Basic has enough information to determine the associated CLSID and call *CoCreateInstance* on its behalf.

For example, when a client application makes a call to the *New* operator on a component in an ActiveX DLL, the Visual Basic compiler embeds the component's CLSID in the client's executable image. At runtime, the call to *New* is translated by the Visual Basic runtime into a call to *CoCreateInstance*.

When the Visual Basic runtime passes the CLSID to *CoCreateInstance*, the SCM uses configuration information in the Windows Registry to locate the server's binary image. This is typically a DLL or an EXE. This means that a COM server requires an associated set of Registry entries, including a physical path to its location. Each COM server is responsible for adding its configuration information to the Registry when asked.

CLSIDs and the Windows Registry

The SCM is entirely dependent on information stored in the Registry. Every loadable component associated with an in-process server or an out-of-process server must have a Registry entry that associates it with a physical path to a server's binary image.

The Registry key HKEY_CLASSES_ROOT\CLSID lists the components available to client applications on the machine. Each CLSID key contains one or more subkeys that hold configuration data about the associated component, as shown in Figure 3-4. Components in an in-process server such as an ActiveX DLL require an InprocServer32 subkey, while components in an out-of-process server such as an ActiveX EXE require a LocalServer32 subkey. These keys hold the physical path to the server file; the SCM uses them to find and load the servers during object activation.

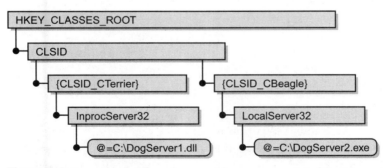

Figure 3-4 *Every creatable coclass must have an associated Registry entry to map the CLSID to the server's location. The SCM uses this mapping information to find and load a server during an activation request.*

There are other important Registry entries in addition to those for the CLSID. The Registry key HKEY_CLASSES_ROOT\TypeLib tracks the physical location of every registered type library on the local machine. By the way, when you bring up the

References dialog box, Visual Basic examines this key to fill in the list of available references.

As you'll see later in this chapter, each IID plays an important role in binding an object to a client that's running in another process. Every interface that is remotable must have associated configuration data in the Registry key HKEY_CLASSES_ ROOT\Interface. This configuration data makes it possible to make connections that span process and machine boundaries. You'll see more specifics about this later in the chapter.

All modern COM servers are self-registering. That means that a server, when asked politely, should write all of its required information into the local computer's Registry. In the early days of COM, C++ programmers had to write registration code by hand against the Win32 API. Fortunately, Visual Basic automatically generates self-registration code when you build a server. A Visual Basic server is capable of registering all the information about its CLSIDs, IIDs, and type library.

Registering a server

In-process servers such as ActiveX DLLs are passive and can't register or unregister themselves without a little help. You can register and unregister them using the Win32 SDK utility REGSVR32.EXE. You can run this utility from the command line by passing the path to the DLL with the appropriate switch, like this:

```
REGSVR32.EXE DOGSERVER.DLL
REGSVR32.EXE /u DOGSERVER.DLL
```

REGSVR32.EXE doesn't actually register the server. It simply loads the server and calls a well-known function exposed by the DLL. The DLL responds to this call by writing its required configuration information to the Registry.

Out-of-process servers such as ActiveX EXEs register themselves each time they're launched. If you double-click the icon for an ActiveX EXE, the server launches and registers itself. Once the server process is running, it realizes that it has no client and unloads. The polite way to register and unregister an EXE-based server is to use a standard command-line switch, as follows:

```
DOGSERVER.EXE /RegServer
DOGSERVER.EXE /UnregServer
```

When you build a server using the Make command, the Visual Basic IDE automatically registers it on your development workstation by using one of the two methods just described. When you build an ActiveX DLL, Visual Basic builds in the self-registration code and then registers the server using REGSVR32.EXE. This makes it easy to build and test a client application after you build the server. Keep in mind that it's one thing to configure a server on a development workstation and another to register it on a production machine. Both are equally important for your server to run correctly.

The SCM in Action

So, you have an ActiveX DLL with a *MultiUse* class named *CBeagle*. The DLL has been installed and registered on the local machine. A client application calls *New* on this class to activate an object. The Visual Basic runtime translates the call to *New* into a call to *CoCreateInstance* and passes both a CLSID and an IID to the SCM.

The SCM starts by looking up the CLSID in the Registry and finding the path to the associated DLL file. The SCM loads the DLL into the client's process. The SCM then calls into the DLL through a well-known entry point and forwards the activation request by passing both the CLSID and the IID.

The server responds by creating a new instance of the requested class. It then passes an interface reference (based on the requested interface) back to the SCM. The SCM simply forwards this interface reference back to the client. Once the client gets this interface reference, it has been successfully bound to the object. In other words, the client has taken hold of one of the object's vTables. The client can now begin making method calls on the object.

As you can see, the SCM is really just a matchmaker. Once it binds a client to an object, it's no longer needed. The client and the object can have a long and fruitful relationship. However, for this architecture to work properly, the SCM must have a predefined way of interacting with the server. Every COM server must therefore provide support for object activation by exposing a well-known entry point through which the SCM can make activation requests.

Servers must expose class factories

The rules for activation support inside a COM server are defined in the COM Specification. COM uses a common software technique known as the *factory pattern,* in which the code that actually calls *New* on the class is contained in the same binary file as the class itself. This eliminates the need for the client or the SCM to know about the class definition behind the object being created. The key advantage to this technique is that it allows class authors to revise their code without worrying about client dependencies such as the need to know an object's data layout.

When the SCM interacts with a server to activate an object, it must acquire a reference to a special type of object called a *class factory*. A class factory object is an agent that creates instances of the class associated with a specific CLSID upon request. A COM server must provide a class factory object for each supported CLSID. When the SCM receives an activation request, it must acquire a reference to the appropriate class factory object. It does this in different ways, depending on whether the server code is in an in-process DLL or an out-of-process EXE. Figure 3-5 shows how a single class factory object can be used to create many instances of a particular coclass.

Every COM server, including those built with Visual Basic, must provide class factories for the SCM. When you compile an ActiveX DLL or an ActiveX EXE, Visual

Basic transparently builds in class factory support for each public creatable class. Visual Basic creates class factories in a reasonable and boilerplate fashion. You can't influence how it does this. You can't even see the class factories. You have to take it on faith that they're there. Visual Basic also automatically builds the required entry points for the SCM so that it can get at your class factories.

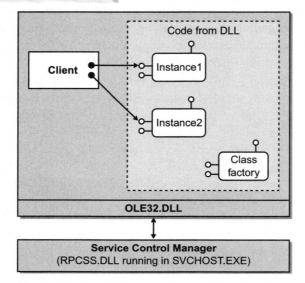

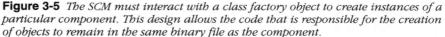

Figure 3-5 *The SCM must interact with a class factory object to create instances of a particular component. This design allows the code that is responsible for the creation of objects to remain in the same binary file as the component.*

ProgIDs and the *CreateObject* Function

A ProgID is simply a text-based alias for a specific CLSID. A ProgID consists of two parts. The first part is the name of the server project that holds the component. The second part is the friendly class name of the component itself. An example of a ProgID is *DogServer.CBeagle*. ProgIDs are especially important for scripting clients. When a scripting client wants to activate an object of a specific type, it usually must know the ProgID ahead of time.

The self-registration code in a Visual Basic server adds Registry entries to map a ProgID to each supported CLSID to support activation for applications such as scripting clients. For instance, there will be a Registry key HKEY_CLASSES_ROOT\DogServer.CBeagle that holds a named value to map it to a CLSID.

You might also see that some ProgIDs have a number on the end in the form of DogServer.CBeagle.1 and DogServer.CBeagle.2. One of this kind is known as a version-dependent ProgID. One without a trailing number is a version-independent ProgID. Office applications and COM servers made with C++ frameworks such as the

Active Template Library (ATL) often use version-dependent ProgIDs. However, Visual Basic doesn't support version-dependent ProgIDs. The ProgIDs created by Visual Basic don't get a number on the end. They're always version-independent.

When you call the *CreateObject* function from a Visual Basic application, you must pass the *ProgID* for a specific component. However, a client application can't directly activate an object with a ProgID through the SCM. Instead, the client must call a system-level function in the COM library to resolve a ProgID into a CLSID. This is true of the Visual Basic runtime as well as scripting interpreters.

Once a client application has translated a ProgID into a CLSID, it can then call *CoCreateInstance*. Of course, this is all done behind the scenes. You should see that a call to *CreateObject* is usually just like a call to the *New* operator. It's just that the implementation of the *CreateObject* function requires one extra call to the COM library before it can call *CoCreateInstance*.

You should be aware of one more difference when you're deciding whether to create objects with the *New* operator or the *CreateObject* function. When you call *CreateObject*, the Visual Basic runtime will always attempt to activate the object through the SCM with a call to *CoCreateInstance*. This is not always the case when you use the *New* operator. If one class instantiates an object from another class in the same project using the *New* operator, the Visual Basic runtime creates and binds the object without any help from the SCM. For example, if you have two *MultiUse* classes in an ActiveX DLL project and one class creates an instance of the other using the *New* operator, the SCM doesn't get involved. While this might appear to be a valuable optimization, it can be problematic for components that are configured in either COM+ or MTS. Chapter 6 will introduce configured components and provide a motivation for letting the SCM handle all activation requests. As you'll see, at times you'll want to avoid using the *New* operator.

UNDERSTANDING *IUNKNOWN* AND *IDISPATCH*

The best thing about a COM object is that it acts in a predictable way. After it's activated, it waits patiently to service your method requests. It knows when you've finished using it, and it politely excuses itself from the application by destroying itself and releasing all its resources back to the system. It can answer intelligently when you ask it what interfaces it supports. What's more, a COM object lets you navigate among all of its interfaces so that you can get at all of the functionality it offers.

The next part of this chapter explains how COM objects provide this base level of functionality through an interface named *IUnknown*. Although this interface is completely hidden from Visual Basic programmers, you should understand its purpose and functionality. We'll also look at a standard interface named *IDispatch*, and you'll see how objects provide access to scripting clients through the use of a COM mechanism called *automation*.

The *IUnknown* Interface

COM has one interface from which all other interfaces derive: *IUnknown*. Every interface must derive directly from *IUnknown* or from an interface that has *IUnknown* at the root of its inheritance chain. *IUnknown* is the only interface in COM that doesn't derive from another interface; it's always at the top of every COM interface hierarchy. This means that the three methods defined in *IUnknown* (*QueryInterface*, *AddRef*, and *Release*) are always at the top of any COM-compliant vTable, as shown in Figure 3-6. Any connection to an object is made through an *IUnknown*-compatible reference.

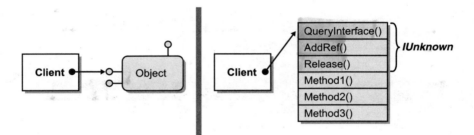

Figure 3-6 *The three methods of the* IUnknown *interface always appear at the top of a COM-compliant vTable. Any connection to an object guarantees a client the ability to call these methods.*

IUnknown expresses the base behavior of a COM object as opposed to a domain-specific behavior that you experience through a user-defined interface. *IUnknown* allows every COM object to manage its own lifetime. It also allows a client to query an object to see whether it supports a given interface and to dynamically cast the object to any of the supported interfaces.

Note that Visual Basic programmers are never directly exposed to *IUnknown*. On the server side, Visual Basic transparently builds in an implementation of *IUnknown* behind every component. On the client side, Visual Basic's mapping layer hides all of the code that deals with *IUnknown*. While you can declare variables of type *IUnknown*, you can't invoke *IUnknown*'s methods because they're marked as restricted in the type library STDOLE2.TLB.

In COM, an object is expected to manage its own lifetime. However, an object needs help to make an informed decision about whether to terminate itself or continue running. The client of an object is responsible for calling *AddRef* whenever it duplicates an interface reference and for calling *Release* whenever it drops an existing connection. If all clients live up to their responsibilities, an object can provide a simple implementation of these two methods to properly manage its lifetime. The object maintains a count of connected references and releases itself from memory whenever this count drops to 0.

Visual Basic and lifetime management

When you work in Visual Basic, you don't have to worry much about lifetime management. You really need to remember only two rules: Hold the object reference when you want to keep the object alive, and release the reference when you no longer care about the object. Visual Basic handles all calls to *IUnknown* for you. Take a look at the following example:

```
Sub CreateAndUseDog()
    Dim Dog As IDog
    Set Dog = New CBeagle ' AddRef is called.
    Dim Dog2 As IDog
    Set Dog2 = Dog ' AddRef is called.
    Set Dog2 = Nothing ' Release is called.
    ' Release is called on Dog when reference goes out of scope.
End Sub
```

This code results in several calls to *AddRef* and *Release*. When an object is activated, it experiences an *AddRef* call. When you create a second reference to the object, the Visual Basic runtime automatically calls *AddRef*. If you explicitly set an interface reference to *Nothing*, the Visual Basic runtime automatically calls *Release* for you. If you don't explicitly set a reference to *Nothing*, Visual Basic detects when an active reference is going out of scope and calls *Release* on the object just before dropping the connection.

On the object side, Visual Basic automatically implements *AddRef* and *Release* to conduct standard reference counting. A Visual Basic object keeps running as long as active clients remain connected. When the client holding the last connection calls *Release*, the Visual Basic object terminates itself. Once again, there's nothing you can do in Visual Basic to influence how an object manages its lifetime, but it's important to understand how your objects will behave.

Although the fact that Visual Basic calls *AddRef* and *Release* behind the scenes might make you think that you don't need to set local object references to *Nothing*, many problems have been associated with failing to do so. For example, countless programmers have created memory leaks and other various problems when they've forgotten to set object references to *Nothing* before the variables that hold them go out of scope. Early versions of Data Access Objects (DAO) and ActiveX Data Objects (ADO) were among the tools that created frustrating problems. Consequently, many Visual Basic programmers are in the habit of always setting object references to *Nothing* when they're done using an object.

One of the trickier aspects of lifetime management involves *circular references,* such as when object A holds a reference to object B and object B holds a reference to object A. Even after all interested clients have dropped their connections, the objects remain in memory because of the outstanding references they hold on each other.

If your design involves circular references, you must be sure that objects go away when they're no longer needed. One common way to prevent circular references from keeping objects alive forever is to create an explicit method in one of the objects that breaks a connection, causing the composite to break down.

The *QueryInterface* Method

The first and arguably most profound method of *IUnknown* is *QueryInterface,* which allows clients to navigate among the various interfaces supported by an object. This act of dynamically navigating between different interfaces is known as *type casting*. A client can also use *QueryInterface* simply to test whether an object supports a particular interface. The capabilities provided by *QueryInterface* are essential to COM. Without *QueryInterface*, COM couldn't achieve polymorphism or offer runtime type inspection, which are required in an interface-based programming paradigm.

A COM object must implement at least one interface, but it can implement as many as it likes. Objects that implement multiple interfaces must allow clients to navigate among them by calling *QueryInterface*. A client passes a desired IID when it calls *QueryInterface*, and the object responds by returning a reference to the interface. If the client asks for an interface that's not supported, the call to *QueryInterface* fails. If the call fails, the client can determine that the requested functionality isn't available and thus degrade gracefully.

The Visual Basic runtime layer silently calls *QueryInterface* when you assign an object to a variable of a specific reference type. Take a look at the following example:

```
Dim Dog As IDog
Set Dog = New CBeagle
' To get at another interface
Dim WonderDog As IWonderDog
Set WonderDog = Dog ' QueryInterface is called.
WonderDog.FetchSlippers
```

If you've already acquired an *IDog* reference to an object and you want to retrieve an *IWonderDog* reference, you can simply use the *Set* statement to cast one interface reference to another. A trappable "Type mismatch" error will occur if the interface is not supported. If the cast is successful, you can use the new interface reference to invoke methods on the object.

Some Visual Basic programmers prefer to blindly cast interface references, as shown in the previous example. If you try to cast to an interface that isn't supported, the Visual Basic runtime layer deals with an unsuccessful call to *QueryInterface* by raising a trappable runtime error in your code. If there's a chance that the cast will fail, you must be prepared to trap and deal with this error. If you'd rather avoid dealing with runtime errors, you can query an object for interface support by using Visual Basic's *TypeOf* syntax, like this:

```
Dim Dog As IDog
Set Dog = New CBeagle
' Test for support before using interface.
If TypeOf Dog Is IWonderDog Then ' Call QueryInterface.
    Dim WonderDog As IWonderDog
    Set WonderDog = Dog ' Call to QueryInterface
    WonderDog.FetchSlippers
Else
    ' Degrade gracefully if interface isn't supported.
End If
```

A Visual Basic object automatically implements *QueryInterface*. When you implement one or more user-defined interfaces in a class, Visual Basic provides an implementation of *QueryInterface* that allows clients to move among interface references. As in the case of *AddRef* and *Release*, the Visual Basic implementation of *QueryInterface* is fairly straightforward, but you can never see it. You have to take it on faith that it works perfectly.

Client-side activation revisited

[handwritten: Service Control Manager]

Earlier, I described how object activation works with a client, the SCM, and an in-process server. However, I couldn't go into the exact details of what occurs inside the Visual Basic runtime because I hadn't yet described the *QueryInterface* method. Now that you know how and why a client would call *QueryInterface*, you can appreciate what Visual Basic does during object activation. Examine the following code:

```
Dim Spot As CDog
Set Spot = New CDog
```

[handwritten: Interface ID]

When the Visual Basic runtime calls *CoCreateInstance*, it passes the CLSID for the component *CDog* and also passes the IID for *IUnknown*. Once it has activated the object with an *IUnknown* reference, it calls *QueryInterface* to obtain a second reference by passing the IID for the default interface _*CDog*. The client is then bound to the desired interface and things can proceed as you'd expect. However, what if you have a component with a user-defined interface and you write client-side code that looks like this?

```
Dim Fido As IDog
Set Fido = New CBeagle
```

It turns out that the Visual Basic runtime conducts a sequence of calls that isn't so intuitive. First it calls *CoCreateInstance*, passing the CLSID for *CBeagle* and the IID for *IUnknown* to activate the object. Next it calls *QueryInterface* to obtain a second reference by passing the IID for the default interface _CBeagle_. The Visual Basic runtime performs this step regardless of whether the client uses the interface. Finally, the Visual Basic runtime calls *QueryInterface* one more time to obtain the desired interface by passing the IID for *IDog*. The main point here is that using the *New* operator on a class name results in the Visual Basic runtime calling *QueryInterface* to obtain a reference to the default interface. It doesn't matter whether the client is using it.

This last point might seem a bit esoteric. However, you can run into frustrating problems when you're trying to version components and you can't understand why things aren't working correctly. We'll revisit this point in Chapter 5 after a thorough discussion of component versioning. As you'll see, you need to keep the IID for a component's default interface constant whenever you compile a later version of the server. This is the case even when the default interface has no methods.

The *IDispatch* Interface and Automation

In the early days, COM was accessible only to C and C++ programmers because of the low-level nature of vTable binding. IDL and type libraries then made it possible for development tools such as Visual Basic 4 to generate the required vTable binding code at compile time. However, some clients still can't make sense of a type library or the equivalent C/C++ header files. Today, scripting clients written in VBScript and JavaScript are the primary examples of such clients.

Because a scripting client can't read an interface definition from a type library, it can't generate the required client-side binding code to access the vTables associated with a COM object. However, these clients still have a way to invoke methods in a special type of object known as an *automation object*. An automation object is an object that implements a special interface named *IDispatch*.

Microsoft was motivated to build automation into the development culture of COM because such an extension would result in many more COM programmers. Automation gives COM greater language independence. The original version of automation (called *OLE automation*) shipped at roughly the same time as Visual Basic 3. Previous versions of Visual Basic didn't include any COM support, so automation was the first means by which a Visual Basic programmer could create client-side code to access a COM object.

The COM team and the Visual Basic team worked together to make automation work with Visual Basic 3. Since the release of Visual Basic 4, the product has had support for programming against type libraries, so there's no longer any need to use automation from the client side. However, many languages and tools still rely on automation. For instance, most of Microsoft's Web-based technologies use languages such as VBScript and JavaScript, which can't build custom vTable bindings. Programmers in these languages rely instead on automation when they need to access a COM object. If you're creating components for scripting clients, you should gain an understanding of how automation works.

Late binding through *IDispatch*

Automation relies on an interface named *IDispatch*, which allows clients to create method bindings at runtime in a process known as *late binding*. The vTable that ~~Late binding~~ represents *IDispatch* is shown in Figure 3-7. *IDispatch* extends *IUnknown* by adding four methods. Automation clients use the two methods *GetIDsOfNames* and *Invoke* to achieve late binding. As in the case of *IUnknown*, Visual Basic programmers never deal with this interface directly. Instead, the Visual Basic mapping layer translates your code and makes the calls to *IDispatch* methods. The same is true of client-side code written in VBScript or JavaScript. The scripting interpreter makes all the necessary calls to *IDispatch* behind the scenes.

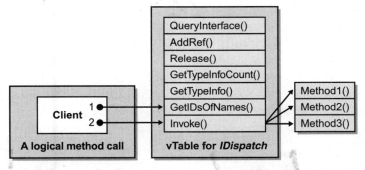

Figure 3-7 *Automation clients bind to a vTable based on the* IDispatch *interface. An automation client achieves late binding by calling* GetIDsOfNames *and then* Invoke.

Here's how automation works. After a client receives an *IDispatch* reference, it can ask an object whether it supports a particular method by calling *GetIDsOfNames*. The client must pass the name of the method as a string argument in the call. If the object doesn't support the requested method, the call to *GetIDsOfNames* fails. If the method is supported, *GetIDsOfNames* returns a logical identifier for the method called a DISPID. A DISPID is simply an integer that an object provides to identify one of its ~~DISPID~~ methods. Positive DISPIDs indicate that a method is user-defined, while negative DISPIDs are reserved for methods with special purposes.

A client armed with a valid DISPID can execute a method through automation by calling *Invoke*. In fact, *Invoke* is the only way to execute a user-defined method through the *IDispatch* interface. As you can see, *IDispatch* is a single physical interface that allows less sophisticated clients to get at any number of logical interfaces. In essence, *IDispatch* represents a standard vTable with a highly extensible invocation architecture. This arrangement allows clients such as the VBScript interpreter to access many different types of COM objects while knowing about only a single vTable layout. This effectively eliminates the need for a client to build custom binding code from information in a type library.

Whenever you compile a *MultiUse* class in an ActiveX DLL or an ActiveX EXE project, Visual Basic automatically builds in an implementation of *IDispatch* for the public methods in the default interface. This means any COM-capable scripting clients can create and use objects from a Visual Basic server. Without this support, you wouldn't be able to use Visual Basic components from scripting clients such as Active Server Pages (ASP) or the Windows Scripting Host (WSH).

While *IDispatch* is very flexible, it isn't very efficient compared to direct vTable binding. Every logical call through *IDispatch* requires two physical calls. The first call to *GetIDsOfNames* requires a string lookup in the object to return the proper DISPID to the client. The call to *Invoke* also requires quite a bit of overhead. This overhead is necessary because of the open-ended nature of this dispatching architecture.

A method can have an arbitrary number of parameters, which can come in all shapes and sizes. Automation deals with this by requiring the client to pass all parameters as an array of variants in the call to *Invoke*. The array allows the method to define any number of parameters, and the variant type allows each parameter to be self-describing. An object responds to a call to *Invoke* by resolving the DISPID and unpacking the variant arguments to their proper types. After the object processes a call to *Invoke*, it must pass any output parameters and the return value back to the client as variants.

You should note two key facts about late binding and *IDispatch*: Late binding is great for clients that can't deal with direct vTable binding, but it offers pretty slow execution times compared with direct vTable binding. When you're dealing with an in-process object, you can expect a call using direct vTable binding to be a few hundred times faster than a call through *IDispatch*.

A Visual Basic client can access an automation object through *IDispatch* by using the *Object* data type. You should note that you can't use the type *IDispatch* in your Visual Basic source code because it's marked as restricted in the type library STDOLE2.TLB. However, you're really creating an *IDispatch* reference when you define a parameter or a variable using the *Object* data type. Here's an example of using the *Object* data type to access an object through *IDispatch*:

```
Dim Dog As Object
Set Dog = CreateObject("DogServer.CBeagle")
Dog.Name = "Rex"
Dog.Bark
```

When the object is created, an *IDispatch* reference is assigned to the *Object* variable *Dog*. A logical call to a property or a method translates to a call to both *GetIDsOfNames* and *Invoke*. Visual Basic could optimize automation by caching the

DISPIDs of properties and methods, but it doesn't. Each logical call results in two round-trips between the client and the object. When you add the overhead of a call to *Invoke*, you can see that you don't want to use the *Object* data type if you don't have to.

Another important thing to keep in mind when you use the *Object* data type is that you have no type safety. The Visual Basic environment assumes at compile time that any method call through *IDispatch* will succeed. This means you lose out on wonderful features of the Visual Basic IDE such as compile-time type checking and IntelliSense, yet another reason to avoid using the *Object* data type.

Dual Interfaces

So far, you've seen two types of clients—those that access custom interfaces through direct vTable binding and those that access methods through the *IDispatch* interface and late binding. Each type of client has a preferred style of interface. Clients that are capable of direct vTable binding don't want to go through *IDispatch* because it's much slower. Scripting clients can't access custom interfaces because they can't generate the required client-side binding code. However, a third style of interface is a hybrid between the other two. It's called a *dual interface*. Figure 3-8 compares all three types.

A custom interface derives directly from *IUnknown*, whereas a dual interface derives directly from *IDispatch*. The key here is that the vTable behind a dual interface contains user-defined methods in addition to the methods of *IDispatch*. Clients can access a dual interface either through direct vTable binding or through late binding. A dual interface offers the speed and efficiency of direct vTable bindings to sophisticated clients created with tools such as C++ and Visual Basic. A dual interface also provides *IDispatch*-style entry points for automation clients such as VBScript and JavaScript.

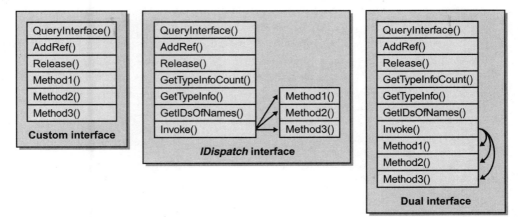

Figure 3-8 *A dual interface is a hybrid of an* IDispatch *interface and a custom interface.*

As of version 5, every interface that Visual Basic creates is defined as a dual interface. You don't have to ask Visual Basic to publish dual interfaces in the type library of your server, and there's nothing you can do to prevent this behavior. When you choose the Make command from the File menu, Visual Basic generates a full-blown implementation of the dual interface behind every component in your server. To do this properly, it must also provide a standard implementation of *IDispatch*. This means that your Visual Basic objects can cater to both custom vTable-bound clients and scripting clients.

A quick review of available binding techniques

You can experience three types of binding when you create a client with Visual Basic. *Late binding* is used whenever the *Object* data type is used, and this is true whether or not you include a type library for the object. Late binding provides the worst performance and no type checking at compile time. Use late binding only when you have no other choice. You can almost always avoid it in client-side code written in Visual Basic.

DISPID binding occurs when you have an *IDispatch*-only component that has an associated type library. In Figure 3-8, an *IDispatch*-only interface is the type in the middle as opposed to a dual interface on the right. The client can read the DISPIDs from the type library at compile time and embed them in the client executable. This eliminates the need for a call to *GetIDsOfNames*, but the client still goes through *Invoke* to execute a method. DISPID binding is faster than late binding, but it's still noticeably slower than direct vTable binding. DISPID binding also allows the Visual Basic IDE to perform compile-time type checking and to use IntelliSense.

DISPID binding occurs only if you have a type library for an *IDispatch* object that doesn't provide a dual interface. You don't find many components that meet these criteria. Older C++ components built using the Microsoft Foundation Class (MFC) framework are probably the most common example. Here's another interesting fact: When you place an ActiveX control on a form, Visual Basic uses DISPID binding instead of direct vTable binding because these controls must use the *IDispatch* interface to support dynamic properties.

You should always favor direct vTable binding because it's significantly faster than the other two binding techniques. Visual Basic clients always use direct vTable bindings as long as the following are true:

- The client project contains a reference to the component's type library.

- The reference is typed to an interface or a creatable class (the default interface).

- The object exposes vTables for custom interfaces or a dual interface—that is, the object isn't *IDispatch*-only.

Some Visual Basic programmers assume that the *CreateObject* function always results in late binding as opposed to direct vTable binding. This assumption is incorrect. It doesn't matter how you create or connect to an object. What matters is the type of the variable or parameter you use when connecting to an object. The rules remain the same. If you use the *Object* data type, you'll experience late binding. If you use the name of a class or user-defined interface, you'll experience direct vTable binding regardless of whether you use *CreateObject* or the *New* operator.

One final note here is that different programmers use the term *early binding* to mean different things. Some developers use the term to mean DISPID binding. Others use the term to mean direct vTable binding. Just remember that there isn't any consensus on the meaning of the term. The only thing that everybody agrees on is that early binding is different from late binding.

TAKING COM OUT OF PROCESS

So far, this chapter has described the interaction between a client and an object only in the scope of a single process running under a single thread of execution. When a client is bound to an in-process object, it can directly invoke methods through the use of function pointers that are stored in a vTable. The interaction is very efficient because the client code and the object code share the same thread, the same call stack, and the same set of memory addresses. Unfortunately, when the object runs in another process, none of these resources can be shared.

The function pointers stored in vTables have no meaning across process boundaries. A client can't use a remote function pointer to access an object in another process. How, then, can COM remote a method call from the client's process to the object's process? COM makes remote communication possible with a pair of helper objects called the *proxy* and the *stub*.

Figure 3-9 shows how the proxy and the stub are deployed. The proxy runs in the client's process, while the stub runs in the object's process. The proxy and the stub establish a communication channel using an interprocess communication mechanism called *Remote Procedure Call (RPC)*. RPC is a connection-oriented protocol that is based on synchronous request/response pairs. The proxy and stub use the RPC channel to pass data such as method parameters back and forth during the execution of each method. However, in order to do this, the proxy and stub must serialize this data into a form that can be transmitted across process and host boundaries. The act of serializing method-related data for transmission across the proxy/stub layer is known as *marshaling*.

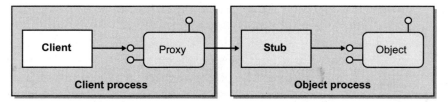

Figure 3-9 *COM's remoting architecture requires that a proxy/stub layer be intro-duced between the client and the object. The proxy and the stub establish an RPC channel between them to transmit method-related data back and forth.*

When the client invokes a method on the proxy, the proxy forwards the request to the stub. To properly transmit this request, the proxy marshals the method's in-bound parameters and then transmits them to the stub across the RPC channel. When the stub receives the request, it unmarshals the inbound parameters and performs the actual call on the object. After the object completes the method and returns con-trol back to the stub, the stub prepares a response by marshaling outbound parame-ters and a return value. The data is then transmitted back to the proxy. Finally, the proxy unmarshals the data in the response and returns control back to the client.

You should be asking yourself an important question: Who creates proxies and stubs? The answer is that they're usually created by the COM runtime. When a client calls *CoCreateInstance* to create an object in another process, the proxy and stub are created automatically by the system. By the time the client has successfully activated the object, the proxy and stub have already been created. However, the client is bound to the proxy instead of the object. And it's the stub, not the client, that gets bound to the object.

In most cases, the COM runtime simply detects the need for proxies and stubs and inserts them wherever they're needed. The idea is simple. When an interface reference is exported from the object's process, the COM runtime builds a stub. When the interface reference is imported into the client's process, the COM runtime builds a proxy. The communication channel that is established between the proxy and the stub makes it possible to remote method requests from the client to the object and back.

What about the case in which an object reference is passed across process boundaries in a COM method call? Again, the COM runtime automatically does the right thing. It knows to build a proxy/stub pair whenever the object and the client who receives the reference live in different processes. Things couldn't be any easier for you. While C++ programmers can get into sticky situations in which they're re-quired to explicitly build proxies and stubs by calling functions in the COM library, Visual Basic programmers really never have to worry. Proxies and stubs always get built for them behind the scenes.

The best part about COM's remoting architecture is that neither the client nor the object can tell that calls are being remoted. The client thinks that the proxy is the object. The object thinks that the stub is the client. This allows COM programmers to write code for both clients and objects without regard to whether objects will be activated in-process or out-of-process. This powerful feature is known as *location transparency*.

You should note that there is a proxy/stub pair for each connected interface. This means that a client and an object can have two or more proxy/stub pairs connecting them at any one time. It makes sense that the proxy/stub pair is associated with the interface because it's the interface definition that describes the methods that need to be remoted.

The key to generating the code to build proxies and stubs lies in interface definitions. As you know, COM interfaces can be defined in either IDL source files or type libraries. In fact, IDL is a language that was originally created to solve the problem of marshaling function parameters from one machine to another. This is why IDL requires you to specify parameters with attributes such as *[in]*, *[out]*, and *[in, out]*. These parameter attributes tell the proxy and stub which direction to marshal all the relevant data for a remote method call.

A type library is like an IDL source file in the sense that it can hold interface definitions. One of the main differences between the two is that a type library exists in a binary format. It's easier to parse at runtime. As it turns out, COM provides a service that can build proxies and stubs on an as-needed basis by examining interface definitions in a type library. This service is known as the *universal marshaler*. It goes by other names as well, such as the *type library marshaler* and the *automation marshaler*. However, the term *automation marshaler* can be somewhat misleading because the marshaler doesn't require that clients and objects communicate through *IDispatch*.

The Role of the Universal Marshaler

The proxy and the stub have their work cut out for them. They must work together to give both the client and the object the perception that they're running in a single process on a single thread. They create this illusion by constructing a call stack in the object's process that is identical to the one in the client's process. Any data sitting on the call stack in the client's process must be marshaled to the object's process. What's more, any pointers on the client's call stack require the proxy to marshal the data that the pointer refers to. The stub is responsible for unmarshaling all the data and setting up the call stack. This might involve unmarshaling data items that aren't stack-based and then setting up stack-based pointers that point to them.

As you can imagine, the code that accomplishes the marshaling behind a proxy/stub pair can become quite complicated. Fortunately, you can rely on the universal marshaler to build the required proxy/stub code. The universal marshaler is part of OLEAUT32.DLL. When you're dealing with interfaces that rely on the universal marshaler, the COM runtime calls upon code inside OLEAUT32.DLL whenever it determines that a proxy or a stub is needed.

You should note that C++ programmers often build their own custom proxy/ stub code instead of using the universal marshaler. They have to deal with a few more issues that aren't a concern for Visual Basic programmers. It's safe to assume that the interfaces you implement in Visual Basic components will rely on the universal marshaler to build their proxies and stubs.

The universal marshaler uses interface definitions in type libraries to build proxies and stubs. Earlier in the chapter, you saw that Visual Basic also uses interface definitions in type libraries to generate direct vTable binding code at compile time. Now, you see that type libraries have another important role at runtime: They're the key to building interprocess connections between clients and objects.

Interfaces that rely on the universal marshaler are defined in type libraries and in IDL with the *[oleautomation]* attribute. This is what differentiates interfaces that use the universal marshaler from interfaces that provide their own custom proxy/stub code. When a type library is registered, a key is placed in the Registry that tells the universal marshaler where to find it. At registration time, configuration information is also added to the Registry for each IID declared with the *[oleautomation]* attribute.

Remember that every proxy/stub pair is based on a specific IID. When the COM runtime needs to build either a proxy or a stub, it examines the Registry key HKEY_CLASSES_ROOT\Interface to locate configuration information for the interface in question. Figure 3-10 shows the Registry entries for an oleautomation IID. There is a ProxyStubClsid32 key, which tells the COM runtime where to find the code to build proxies and stubs. For oleautomation interfaces, this is the CLSID for the universal marshaler.

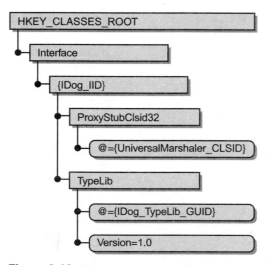

Figure 3-10 *The Registry settings for an interface marked with the* [oleautomation] *attribute tell the COM runtime to use the universal marshaler. They also tell the universal marshaler which type library holds the interface definition.*

Interface ID

Globally Unique Identifier

When the COM runtime determines that it needs to build a proxy or a stub for an oleautomation interface, it forwards the request to the universal marshaler. The universal marshaler then inspects the Registry to find the GUID for the type library associated with the IID. The universal marshaler then locates the type library using the information shown in Figure 3-11. Once the universal marshaler has the path, it can load the type library, read the interface definition, and build a proxy or a stub.

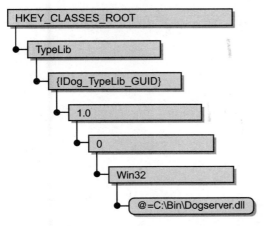

Figure 3-11 *The universal marshaler uses the TypeLib key to find the physical path to the type library. This path can point to either a stand-alone .TLB file or a COM server with an embedded type library.*

In later chapters, you'll see that the COM+ runtime builds proxies and stubs in a few other situations as well. I'll also introduce *contexts* and *apartments*. A context is a set of objects running inside an apartment. An apartment is a set of contexts running inside a process. Client and object often communicate through proxies and stubs even when they're running inside the same process. I'll explain why this is the case. For now, let's concentrate on proxies and stubs that allow method calls to flow across process and host boundaries.

context
apartment
process

It's important to see that the client and object both require a type library to successfully build a proxy/stub pair. When the client and object are running on different machines, both computers must have a local copy of the type library. Because the object always has a local version of the server, it can rely on the type library inside the server's binary image. The client computer, on the other hand, doesn't require the server. It needs only the type library. It's common practice to generate a stand-alone type library for installation on client machines when they'll be activating objects from across the network.

Observations About Out-of-Process COM

First and foremost, you should be ecstatic that *the low-level details of out-of-process communication have been abstracted away and hidden beneath the covers*. RPC is essential to COM, but the manner in which COM creates and uses an RPC connection doesn't require your attention. Imagine how much harder it would be to create a distributed application if you had to directly program against an interprocess communication layer such as RPC or sockets.

Next, you should note three important performance-related points about out-of-process COM. The first is that *out-of-process method calls take much longer than in-process calls*. Generally, you can expect an out-of-process call to take at least 1000 times as long as an in-process call with direct vTable binding. The proxy/stub layer requires thread switching and marshaling, so it adds a significant amount of overhead.

The second thing to note is that *remote method calls on Visual Basic objects are always conducted synchronously*. This is due to the synchronous nature of RPC. When the client invokes a method on a remote object, the calling thread in the client's process is blocked until the call returns. This means that the client must wait it out while the RPC request message travels to the stub, the stub executes the call, and, finally, the RPC response message makes its way back to the proxy. Although new asynchronous RPC support has been added to Windows 2000, you must program in C++ to take advantage of it. Every RPC-based COM method call you make to or from Visual Basic code is conducted synchronously.

The third key point is that *objects created with Visual Basic can be passed only by reference and never by value*. Don't be fooled into thinking that you can simply pass a Visual Basic object from one machine to another. Your methods can define parameters that are object references but not actual objects. The current version of Visual Basic lets you put the *ByVal* keyword in front of object types in parameter definitions, but these parameters are still interpreted with pass-by-reference semantics. When you have a reference to an out-of-process object, access to each method or property in the object requires an expensive round-trip.

Out-of-process objects created with Visual Basic are bound with proxies and stubs built by the universal marshaler. This technique for binding a client to an out-of-process object from the information in a type library is a form of *standard marshaling*. Many programmers who use languages other than Visual Basic also use standard marshaling because it's easy to set up.

C++ programmers can forgo standard marshaling in favor of *custom marshaling*. Those who are willing to write their own marshaling code by implementing a special interface named *IMarshal* can optimize the communication channel in ways that are impossible with standard marshaling. For instance, you can implement pass-by-value semantics with custom marshaling code. However, you should note a few important limitations with custom marshaling. First, it requires the use of C++ on the object side. Second, it's not supported for configured components in either COM+ or MTS. It can be used only with nonconfigured components.

As a Visual Basic programmer, you can't produce components that support custom marshaling. However, you might come into contact with one common nonconfigured component that does support custom marshaling. The ADO Recordset objects implement *IMarshal*. This means that you can define method parameters and return values in terms of the ADO Recordset component and all the data for the recordset (not just a reference) will flow over the network across the proxy/stub layer. Note that you must use disconnected, client-side recordsets in order for this to work. Marshaling ADO recordsets is one of several techniques for moving data around the network in an efficient manner. We'll revisit this topic in greater depth in Chapter 11.

Object activation and location transparency

In the previous edition of this book, I explained how object activation works in an out-of-process server such as an ActiveX EXE. I've decided to omit these details from this edition because they're no longer relevant to developers who are using COM+ to create distributed applications. Chapter 6 describes how out-of-process and remote activation occur in a COM+ application. What's important to note is that clients and objects can't tell whether they're running in the same process or even on the same machine.

Figure 3-12 shows three different deployment scenarios. The components you create in an ActiveX DLL can be configured to run in-process, locally, or across the network. It's all transparent to client code as well as component code. You can move back and forth between all three deployment scenarios without ever rebuilding your servers or your client applications. Changing the location of the client or a component requires minimal effort using a simple administrative tool.

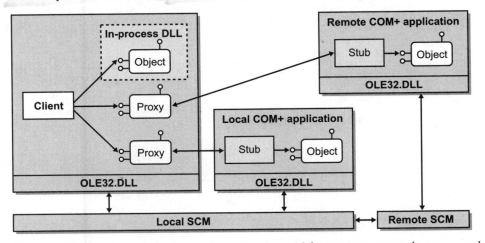

Figure 3-12 *Location transparency eliminates the need for programmers to be concerned with the details of remote activation or interprocess communication.*

The ability of programmers to write both client code and object code for an in-process relationship and have the code work automatically across process boundaries is one of the most powerful features of COM. This location transparency eliminates the need for programmers to be concerned with the grungy details of interprocess communication. It also means that components can be redeployed around the network with little or no impact on code. You can redirect a client that is programmed to activate a certain object from an in-process DLL so that it activates a remote object by making just a few minor adjustments. You don't have to rewrite a single line of code.

However, the mere fact that your component code automatically works in both in-process and out-of-process situations doesn't mean that it's efficient. Code written for in-process objects might not scale when deployed in an application that's running across the network. Quite a few coding techniques work adequately in in-process scenarios but result in unacceptable performance when the proxy/stub layer is introduced. Chapter 11 explains the importance of designing interfaces that work efficiently across the proxy/stub layer.

SUMMARY

This chapter described the essential concepts and details of COM. You must have a firm understanding of COM before you can understand how all of the new features of COM+ have been layered on top of it. For the rest of the book, I'll use the term *COM* when I refer to the aspects of the Windows platform that I've covered in this chapter. When I use the term *COM+,* I'm talking about a runtime layer and a programming model specific to Windows 2000. The distinction between COM and COM+ can be somewhat fuzzy because of the fact that COM+ is built on top of COM. When you're talking about Window 2000, the COM runtime and the COM+ runtime are one and the same.

The original version of COM meets four important design requirements: It's based on binary reuse, it's object-oriented, it's language-independent, and it provides a foundation for interprocess communication. After reading this chapter, you know that COM's original architects had to deal with countless details in order to meet these requirements.

COM is based on a formal separation of interface from implementation. At the physical level, the vTable serves as the in-memory representation for an interface. Some clients access objects through direct vTable binding, while others, such as scripting clients, require automation objects that expose functionality through the *IDispatch* interface.

Visual Basic hides COM's goriest details. On the component side, Visual Basic builds in support for programmers who don't want to deal with the extra complexities involved with user-defined interfaces. On the client side, it builds in support for direct vTable binding by inspecting interface definitions in type libraries at compile time. You should have an appreciation for why objects implement *IUnknown* and *IDispatch*. But at the same time, you should be grateful that Visual Basic takes care of all the details for you behind the scenes. *(Service Control Manager)*

The SCM is a dynamic class loader that clients use to create objects on demand. The requirements of interface-based programming don't allow servers to expose concrete classes. Instead, every server must support a somewhat complicated activation protocol. Clients make activation requests to the SCM, and the SCM forwards the request to the server. Once again, the Visual Basic compiler steps in and takes care of all these details behind the scenes. You don't have to do much in order for clients to be able to activate objects from your components.

The last part of this chapter discussed the fundamentals of COM's remoting layer. The proxy/stub layer provides the architecture for remoting method calls across processes and host boundaries while keeping clients and objects ignorant of what's really going on. These details are the responsibility of the COM runtime and the universal marshaler. The universal marshaler creates the code for remoting method calls by inspecting an interface definition from a type library. You can thus conclude that interfaces are the key to seamless distribution in COM.

Chapter 4

Building and Designing Servers

This chapter begins by explaining how to package components for distribution and describing the options you have when compiling a server. One of the first issues you must address is whether to distribute your components in an in-process DLL or an out-of-process EXE. In-process objects are faster, while out-of-process objects provide higher levels of fault tolerance and better security. You'll also see why COM+ requires you to package your components in ActiveX DLLs as opposed to ActiveX EXEs.

This chapter also delves into a variety of issues relating to server design, such as exposing components and interfaces, using enumerations and user-defined types (UDTs), and modifying procedure attributes. It also covers designing components that support scripting clients.

The chapter concludes with an explanation of error handling in COM. You'll learn how Microsoft Visual Basic maps its own internal error-handling model onto COM exceptions in a manner that is very transparent. You'll see, however, that errors are propagated from objects to clients in a language-neutral fashion. This will give you an appreciation for all the work Visual Basic does for you behind the scenes and will lead to a discussion of the best techniques for raising errors from the components in your servers.

COMPILING COMPONENTS INTO SERVERS

A COM server must expose one or more components to be useful to a client application. In this sense, you can simply define a server as a binary file that packages a set of components. As you know, each component is defined as a coclass in the server's type library. In addition to defining coclasses, a server's type library can define other COM data types such as interfaces, enumerations, and UDTs.

COM supports two server types. COM DLLs are *in-process servers* (also known as *in-proc servers*), and COM EXEs are *out-of-process servers.* You must decide whether to serve up your components through an in-process DLL or an out-of-process EXE.

The Visual Basic integrated development environment offers three Project Type settings for building COM servers. You specify this setting when you create a new project, and you can change it afterward in the Project Properties dialog box. You use an ActiveX DLL project to create an in-process server, and you use an ActiveX Control project to create a more specialized type of visual in-process server. (This book doesn't cover ActiveX Control projects.) You use an ActiveX EXE project to create an out-of-process server.

In-Process Servers

An in-process server such as an ActiveX DLL is typically the most efficient choice for packaging components. Your code gets loaded into the address space of the client application. An object from an in-process server can usually be directly bound to the client without any need for a proxy/stub layer (as described in Chapter 3). Direct binding allows the client and the object to share the same thread, the same call stack, and the same set of memory addresses. Once the object is activated, the communication between the two is as fast as it would be if the class were defined within the client application. Better performance is often the primary advantage of using an in-process server.

An in-process server also imposes a few significant limitations. There is no easy way to share data between two different client applications using the same ActiveX DLL because all variables are process-specific. An in-process server is also not as robust as an out-of-process server because it's tightly coupled to the client application process in which it's loaded. A defective object can crash the client application, and if the client application crashes on its own, the object also crashes.

An in-process server is also somewhat inflexible when it comes to security. An object activated from an in-process server usually runs under the same security context as the client application. For instance, if two users, Bob and Sally, use your ActiveX DLL, some of your objects will run under Bob's identity and others will run under Sally's identity. This isn't always a problem, but sometimes you'll want all the objects activated from a particular server to run under a dedicated user account rather than taking on the identity of the client application. When client applications activate Visual

Basic objects from in-process DLLs, you don't have the option of specifying a dedicated user account. This security issue becomes particularly important when you want to deploy middle-tier applications. We'll revisit this topic in greater depth in Chapter 11.

Out-of-Process Servers

An out-of-process server is implemented in Visual Basic as an ActiveX EXE. The executable file that Visual Basic builds when you compile an ActiveX EXE can launch and control its own Win32 process. When a client activates an object from an out-of-process server, COM's Service Control Manager (SCM) finds or loads the server process and negotiates the creation of a new object. Once the object and the client have been bound together, a proxy/stub layer exists between them. As you know, this layer adds significant overhead. Calls to objects in out-of-process servers are much slower than calls to objects loaded from in-process servers.

A *local server* runs on the same computer as the client application, while a *remote server* runs on a different computer. In terms of COM servers, it doesn't really matter whether your ActiveX EXE runs locally or on a computer across the network. An ActiveX EXE is always configured to run as a local server. Once the server has been configured to run as a local server, you can add a few configuration changes to the Registry to allow remote clients to use it as well. You don't need to do anything special to an ActiveX EXE project to differentiate between these deployment options.

Out-of-process servers are more robust than in-process servers. They're at least as robust as the operating system on which they're running. With an in-process server, either the client or the object can potentially crash the other. An out-of-process relationship has a built-in level of fault tolerance. A client can detect that an object has died by inspecting the HRESULT returned by any method. You'll see how this is done later in the chapter. The infrastructure of COM can also detect a dead client and notify the object that the connection is no longer valid. With an out-of-process server, either the client or the object can continue to live a productive life after the other has passed on.

So how do you decide between an ActiveX DLL and an ActiveX EXE? You should think about performance first. If your objects can be used exclusively by a single client application, it makes sense to package your components in an ActiveX DLL. This is the best approach when your code calculates a value such as sales tax or an interest rate. You can install your DLL on the user's desktop computer along with the client application and provide the best possible performance.

But what if you need to run your objects from across the network? One seemingly intuitive solution is to create an ActiveX EXE project because an ActiveX EXE can serve up objects to remote clients. However, another option gives you far more flexibility: serving up distributed objects with a surrogate process provided by COM+, as described in the next section.

Packaging Components for COM+

Much of Microsoft's strategy for creating distributed applications is based on the concept of *surrogate processes*. A surrogate process is a system-supplied runtime environment that acts as a host for your objects. For example, COM+ provides a container application named DLLHOST.EXE. Each COM+ server application runs in its own separate instance of DLLHOST.EXE. When you want to run your objects in this runtime environment, you can't package your components in an ActiveX EXE. Your only choice is to package them in an ActiveX DLL.

Once you compile your components into an ActiveX DLL and properly install them in a COM+ server application, clients can activate objects from across the network. Although you must package your components in an in-process server, COM+ can still provide the benefits of an out-of-process server. You have added fault tolerance, the ability to share memory, and the ability to have all objects run under a dedicated user account.

The difference between an out-of-process server that will be used by one or two client applications and an out-of-process server that will run objects for hundreds of client applications is significant. With an out-of-process server that will be accessed by a large user base, you must deal with more scalability issues, such as thread pooling, security, and database connection management. A COM+ server application provides a scalable architecture, while an ActiveX EXE does not. For this reason, I'll spend much more time in this book discussing ActiveX DLLs than ActiveX EXEs. Your time will be much better spent concentrating on how to create components for COM+ applications.

The idea of a universal runtime environment such as the one supplied by COM+ is appealing for a few reasons. First, it makes things easier for developers because it provides much of the infrastructure code that's required to scale a middle-tier application. Second, it allows Microsoft to maintain all this infrastructure in a single code base and, consequently, share it across many different languages. Finally, it allows COM objects to run and behave in a consistent manner, even if they were created with different languages and tools. Chapter 6 will introduce configured components and describe how to use all these built-in system services. The main point I want to emphasize is that you'll almost always ship your components in ActiveX DLLs.

Building a Server

Visual Basic makes some things incredibly easy. Even a four-year-old can build an ActiveX DLL or an ActiveX EXE in the Visual Basic IDE using the Make command on the File menu. This command opens a dialog box with various options and an OK button. You simply click OK to build the current project into a binary server.

Several important things happen behind the scenes when you choose the Make command. Figure 4-1 depicts what Visual Basic builds into the server. First, Visual Basic automatically publishes information in a type library and bundles it into your server's binary image. The type library is important for use by other development tools that need to create vTable bindings for your objects at compile time. The universal marshaler also uses this type library to build proxies and stubs at runtime.

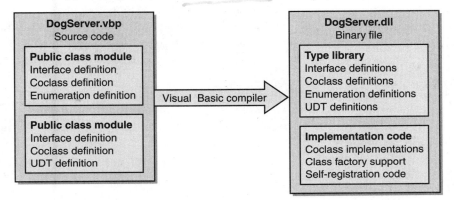

Figure 4-1 *When you build a server using the Make command on the File menu, Visual Basic does lots of work for you.*

Second, for every component Visual Basic generates an implementation of each interface that's supported as well as an implementation of both *IUnknown* and *IDispatch*. Third, Visual Basic adds class factory support for each component. Finally, Visual Basic adds the code to your server to support self-registration. The self-registration code adds entries to the Registry for each CLSID and IID. It also adds a set of entries for the type library.

After Visual Basic finishes building the server, it registers it on your development workstation. When you build an ActiveX DLL, Visual Basic uses the REGSVR32.EXE utility to register your server. When you build an ActiveX EXE, it uses the appropriate command-line parameters to register it as an out-of-process server.

Dealing with Registry madness

It's safe to say that, of all the developers in the industry today, Visual Basic programmers don't have the reputation of being the most disciplined. However, the discipline of properly registering and unregistering servers on your development workstation at the proper times is worth striving for.

How can you tell if you aren't as disciplined as you should be? Here's a good test. Bring up the References dialog box from the Project menu. If you see two or more type libraries with exactly the same description, you know that you should pay more attention to what's being written to your Registry. If you see 10 or more type libraries with the same description, you're one of the programmers who've earned the Visual Basic community an unjust reputation for lacking discipline.

As you know, Visual Basic builds in self-registration code and then registers the server when you build an ActiveX DLL. What if you create a second build of the server and overwrite the first build? The Visual Basic IDE unregisters the first build before deleting it. There's not much that you have to be concerned with. However, if you create the second build of the DLL in a different location and don't overwrite the first build, you might leave entries for the first DLL in the Registry. That's probably not what you want. To make things worse, if you delete a registered DLL without unregistering it first, you delete the only code that knows how to remove those DLL entries from the Registry.

The point is that there are two situations in which you should always unregister a DLL: when you've built a newer version in a different location and before you delete the DLL. Adhering to these two rules keeps the Registry on your development workstation young and vital. Unregistering a DLL that isn't registered doesn't hurt anything; forgetting to unregister a DLL pollutes your Registry. Most experienced COM developers know that there's only one sure-fire way to restore the Registry once it's been abused by undisciplined programmers, and as you've guessed, it starts with the following command:

```
FORMAT C:
```

Generating a stand-alone type library

As you know, the universal marshaler needs the type library for building proxies and stubs at runtime. But what if the server runs on one computer while all the client applications run on other computers? On the computer that holds the server, the universal marshaler can simply use the type library bundled into the server's image. However, the client computer also needs a copy of the type library. The universal marshaler can't build a proxy without it. You could copy the server file to each client computer, but that would be inefficient. The server file includes all the component implementations, and the client computers need only the interface definitions.

Visual Basic lets you create a stand-alone type library by selecting the Remote Server Files check box on the Component tab of the Project Properties dialog box. When you select this check box for an ActiveX DLL or an ActiveX EXE project, the Make command creates a separate type library file with the .TLB extension in addition to the type library it builds into the server. The primary motivation for selecting the Remote Server Files check box is to create a stand-alone type library for distribution to the client computers in a network environment. This type library allows the universal marshaler on a client machine to build proxies as needed.

Miscellaneous compilation options

Before getting into server design issues, I want to quickly cover a few of the options you have when compiling a server. The Project Properties dialog box has a check box for Unattended Execution that tells the Visual Basic compiler to avoid anything that involves user interaction. For example, when you select this check box, all MsgBox statements are converted into application event logs.

When you invoke a MsgBox statement from your component, you hang the current thread, which can be a terrible thing to do in a COM+ application that's running in production. So you should consider the Unattended Execution option as a safety precaution. It is recommended for production builds of your servers. However, if you like to bring up message boxes during debugging, you should compile debug builds without this option.

If you select the Unattended Execution check box, the Retained In Memory check box also becomes available. Selecting this check box prevents the hosting application from unloading the code in your DLL. The DLL stays loaded for the lifetime of the hosting process. This option is recommended for servers that will be used in middle-tier environments such as COM+ and Microsoft Internet Information Services (IIS). You want to reduce the number of times that the code from a DLL is loaded into an application. If the DLL refuses to unload, it doesn't need to be reloaded later. If you select this option, you should be able to assume that the hosting application will continue to use the code from your server throughout its lifetime. This is usually a safe assumption in a COM+ application.

SERVER DESIGN ISSUES

In the first step of the design phase, you should plan which types of clients you want to support. You should split the potential clients of your components into two categories: clients that use direct vTable binding and scripting clients that use late binding. Table 4-1 shows the types of clients produced by a few popular languages.

Table 4-1 **TYPES OF CLIENTS PRODUCED BY VARIOUS LANGUAGES**

Languages That Produce Direct vTable-bound Clients	*Languages That Produce Late-bound Clients*
Visual Basic 6	VBScript
Visual Basic 5	JavaScript
Visual Basic 4	Visual Basic 3
C++	
Delphi	

If you can assume that your component will be used by clients from only one category, your life will be easier. If your components will be accessed exclusively by clients that use direct vTable binding, you'll have more options: You'll be able to design components in terms of user-defined interfaces, enumerations, and UDTs, features you should generally avoid when you create components for scripting clients.

Clients that use direct vTable binding rely on information in your server's type library. Scripting clients never use type libraries—they rely on ProgIDs and late binding. We'll concentrate first on clients that use type libraries and address design issues for scripting clients later in the chapter.

When you design a server, you should start by thinking about what you want published in the server's type library. The information in the type library is what the outside world sees and is the means, at the most basic level, by which your components expose their functionality to their clients.

We'll start by looking at high-level attributes for a type library, and then we'll work our way down to attributes for components and methods. You'll also learn how to publish user-defined interfaces, enumerations, and UDTs in your type libraries and use them in method definitions.

Projectwide Type Library Attributes

When you create a new server project, you should immediately open the Project Properties dialog box and change the Project Name and the Project Description, as shown in Figure 4-2. These important pieces of information become high-level attributes of your type library. The Project Name creates a namespace for the components within it. Client applications that reference the type library can refer to components in your server with a fully qualified name such as *DogServer.CBeagle*. You should also note that the Project Name is always the first part of the ProgID for all components in the server project.

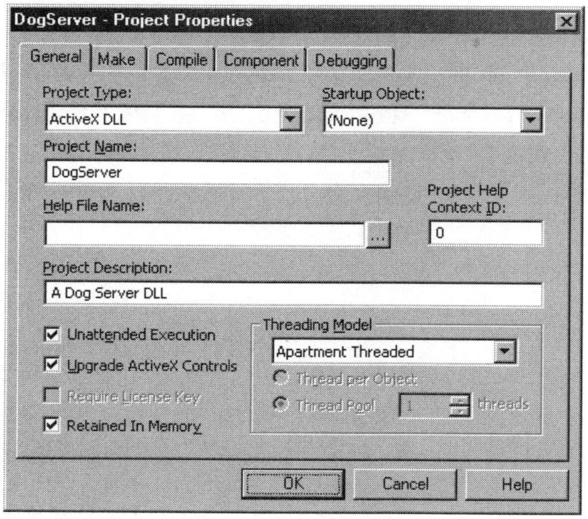

Figure 4-2 *In the Project Properties dialog box, you can assign a Project Name and a Project Description to your server. These settings become top-level attributes of the server's type library.*

The Project Description is used as the friendly description of the type library itself. Once your server has been registered on other developers' workstations, these developers will see this description when they add your server to their projects using the References dialog box. If you don't include a description, Visual Basic uses the Project Name as the description.

When you write client-side code, you should use the fully qualified name *DogServer.CBeagle* rather than the short name *CBeagle*. Most of the time, using the short name isn't a problem, but at times it can get you in trouble. For instance, using the short name creates ambiguity if the Visual Basic project for a client application has references to two different type libraries and each has a *CBeagle* component. Visual Basic simply resolves this ambiguity by selecting the *CBeagle* component from whichever type library was referenced first. As you can imagine, this approach can produce undesirable results. While the References dialog box allows you to change the priority of referenced type libraries, using the fully qualified name is a much better solution to this problem.

The Component *Instancing* Property

The *Instancing* property settings of class modules have a profound effect on what is published in your server's type library: They determine what coclasses and interfaces are seen by the outside world. The following are the available settings ranked in terms of usefulness to a COM+ programmer:

- **MultiUse**   The class module generates a creatable coclass and a dual interface. This interface is built from the public members and is marked as the default for the coclass. Visual Basic generates a CLSID and an IID for the class module. The class becomes a component that clients can use to instantiate objects through the SCM.

- **PublicNotCreatable**   The class module generates a noncreatable coclass and a dual interface. This interface is built from the public members and is marked as the default for the coclass. Visual Basic generates a CLSID and an IID for the class module. The class is not a true component because clients can't use it to instantiate objects through the SCM.

- **Private**   The class module has no effect on what is published in the type library. It has neither a CLSID nor an IID. The class can be used only by client code in the local project. The SCM is never involved when objects are instantiated for the class.

- **GlobalMultiUse**   This setting is like MultiUse, but it also allows client applications to access methods of the class as if they were global functions.

■ **SingleUse (for out-of-process servers only)**   This setting is like MultiUse, but the server guarantees that each object instantiated from the class lives in its own process. That is, there is a separate ActiveX EXE server process for each instance of this class.

■ **GlobalSingleUse**   This setting is like SingleUse, but it also allows client applications to access methods of the class as if they were global functions.

When you create ActiveX DLLs for a COM+ application, the most common setting for the *Instancing* property of a class module is *MultiUse*. In fact, you might never use another setting. *MultiUse* is also the default setting when you create a new class module. Each *MultiUse* class you compile in an ActiveX DLL can be configured as a COM+ component.

The other *Instancing* setting you might use is *PublicNotCreatable*. One reason to use a *PublicNotCreatable* class module is to create a user-defined interface. (Chapter 2 discussed how to create and implement an interface defined in a *PublicNotCreatable* class module.) A *PublicNotCreatable* class module has an associated IID to identify the interface in the type library. However, unlike with *MultiUse* classes, Visual Basic doesn't build in support for activation through the SCM. Client applications can't create objects from a *PublicNotCreatable* class.

If you're creating servers with Visual Basic that you don't intend to run as configured components in the COM+ runtime environment, there are other reasons why you might use a *PublicNotCreatable* class module. For example, *PublicNotCreatable* classes can be used to instantiate objects from client code within the same project. Note that the client code must use the *New* operator to do this. The *CreateObject* function won't work because a *PublicNotCreatable* class module doesn't get Registry entries for its CLSID, nor does it get any built-in activation support. When you use the *New* operator, the Visual Basic runtime instantiates the object without the help of the SCM.

Creating objects from *PublicNotCreatable* classes can be problematic in COM+ because the new object is not initialized in a valid context. This means that the object can't use any of the built-in services the COM+ runtime offers. For a component to benefit from these COM+ services, its objects must be activated through the SCM. We'll talk more about this topic in Chapter 6, but for now keep in mind that objects created from *PublicNotCreatable* classes can't take advantage of what COM+ has to offer.

Private classes suffer from the same shortcoming as *PublicNotCreatable* classes when used in a COM+ application. *Private* classes don't support activation through the SCM. They also can't define an interface, and they have no IID in the type library. They are invisible to all clients that look at the type library. The only reason to use a *Private* class is to create a behind-the-scenes object that doesn't use any of the built-in services COM+ provides.

SingleUse classes are of no use to COM+ programmers because they can exist only in ActiveX EXE projects. In COM+, you can use only components compiled into ActiveX DLLs. However, *SingleUse* classes do serve a purpose. For example, if you're creating a simple ActiveX EXE server that you plan to run on each user's desktop, a *SingleUse* class has some interesting uses. If you create two objects from a *SingleUse* class, each object is created in a separate server process. If you're running two instances of a client application on a user's desktop and they activate the same type of object, you can use a *SingleUse* class to give your objects an extra level of fault protection. Each client activates its object in a different process. *SingleUse* classes also provide a simple way to achieve multithreading because each process gets its own thread. Once again, you should use this technique sparingly and only with a very limited number of clients.

MultiUse and *SingleUse* both allow you to make a class "global." This simply makes the class easier for the client to use. If you have a standard *MultiUse* class that calculates a tax rate, for example, you access the object like this:

```
Dim Obj As CTaxCalculator, Tax As Currency
Set Obj = New CTaxCalculator
Tax = Obj.CalculateTax(28600)
```

When you set the instancing property of the class to *GlobalMultiUse*, the client can access the method as if it were a global function, as shown here:

```
Dim Tax As Currency
Tax = CalculateTax(28600)
```

Global classes save the client the trouble of instantiating an object before calling a method. Visual Basic provides this feature by marking the coclass with the *AppObject* attribute in the type library. On the client side, Visual Basic creates an invisible object behind the scenes when it is first needed and maps all global calls to method calls on this invisible object. Visual Basic is currently the only development tool that provides the convenience of transparently mapping global method calls on the client side. A programmer creating a client application using C++ or Java can't tell the difference between a class marked *GlobalMultiUse* and a class marked *MultiUse*. Global classes simply provide a syntactic sugar for other Visual Basic programmers.

You need to consider a few issues when you're designing with *GlobalMultiUse* classes. First, they work correctly only when the client code that uses them lives in a different project. One class can't take advantage of the global aspects of a *GlobalMultiUse* class when both classes are in the same project. Moreover, you don't have much control over when the invisible object gets created or destroyed. It is created on first use and is destroyed when the client application terminates. This can result in inefficient code when a *GlobalMultiUse* object holds expensive resources.

Often, you're much better off instantiating objects from standard *MultiUse* classes and explicitly setting references to *Nothing* when you want to release them.

Modifying Procedure Attributes

You can influence how Visual Basic sets attributes for the methods and properties of your classes and interfaces by choosing the Procedure Attributes command from the Tools menu while the code for the class module you want to modify is in the active window. Figure 4-3 shows the dialog box that appears.

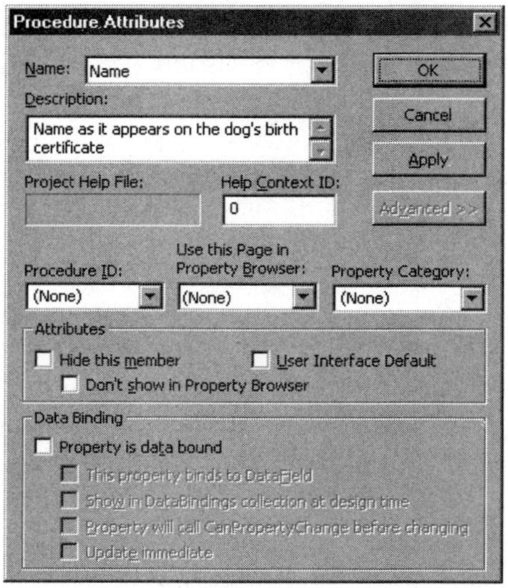

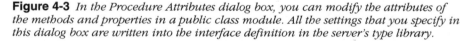

Figure 4-3 *In the Procedure Attributes dialog box, you can modify the attributes of the methods and properties in a public class module. All the settings that you specify in this dialog box are written into the interface definition in the server's type library.*

You use the Description setting to document the semantics of the method or property. Other Visual Basic programmers will see your descriptions when they examine your server's type library with the Object Browser. Providing descriptions is pretty easy to do, and it makes your server seem more polished.

You can also set the Procedure ID to a different value. For instance, if you set the Procedure ID for a property to Default (the value 0), the property will be recognized as the default property of the object. Here's what the resulting IDL looks like:

```
[
    id(00000000),
    propput,
    helpstring("Name as it appears on birth certificate")
]
HRESULT Name([in] BSTR Name);
```

Now a client can access this property both explicitly and implicitly, like this:

```
Dim Dog1 As IDog, Dog2 As IDog
Set Dog1 = New CRetriever
Set Dog2 = New CRetriever
' Name property is accessible explicitly.
Dog1.Name = "Milli"
' Name property is also accessible implicitly.
Dog2 = "Vanilli"
```

As you can see, you can set several options in the Procedure Attributes dialog box. You can also hide methods from other programmers. In short, you can make your server more polished by adding certain method attributes. Note that many of the settings are relevant only to programmers who are building ActiveX controls. Many options, such as Don't Show In Property Browser and User Interface Default, aren't useful to programmers who are creating nonvisual components for the middle tier.

Friend Methods

Marking a method as a friend in a Visual Basic *MultiUse* class creates an interesting effect. A friend method is accessible to any code in the server project, but it isn't exposed to the outside world. You could say that it's public on the inside and private on the outside. Or you could say that in a public class, private members provide modulewide access, friend members provide projectwide access, and public members are available to any client inside or outside the server. When you mark a method or a property as a friend, it isn't published in a type library. It has nothing to do with COM.

Although friend methods might seem attractive during the design phase, you're better off avoiding them. First of all, many programmers use this friend syntax without realizing that they're breaking encapsulation. Later, after removing or changing a friend method, they end up having to modify all client code that had a dependency on the method.

The second (and more significant) reason to avoid using friend methods is that they don't get published in the type library. This is problematic because the COM runtime uses the interface definitions in the type library to build proxies and stubs. The only time you can use a friend method is when you're absolutely sure you don't need a proxy or stub between the client and the object. As you'll see in Chapter 6, objects created from components configured in a COM+ application are connected to their client through a lightweight proxy. Because of this, you should definitely avoid friend methods when you create configured components.

Using Enumerations

As a COM developer, you should try to use enumerations in your designs as much as possible. Enumerations let you declare logically related sets of constants in your type library. Once these enumerations are defined in the type library, you can use them for method parameter and return value types. You can also use them to define sets of error codes. Here's what an enumeration definition looks like in a Visual Basic class module:

```
Enum FetchItemEnum
    dsSlippers
    dsNewspaper
    dsBeer
End Enum
```

Now let's put this enumeration to work by using it to define a method parameter. If you define a method like this

```
Sub Fetch(ByVal Item As FetchItemEnum)
    ' Visualize your implementation here.
End Sub
```

a client can call the method passing one of the enumeration values like this:

```
Dim Spot As CRetriever
Set Spot = New CRetriever
Spot.Fetch dsBeer
```

Enumerations make the client code more readable. Moreover, when you use an enumeration for a parameter type, the IntelliSense that's built into Visual Basic provides client-side programmers with a drop-down list of available choices. This makes your components much more convenient to program against.

You must declare enumerations in a public class module to publish them in the server's type library. When you create an ActiveX DLL project, your best choices for a public class module are those with an instancing setting of *MultiUse* or *PublicNotCreatable*. Enumerations declared in .BAS modules are private to the project and can't be used in public method definitions.

What's not very intuitive is that the enumerations you declare in a class module are scoped at the type library level, not at the class level. The class instancing property has no effect on an enumeration's scope. If you want to create a separate class module just to hold your enumerations, you should mark it as *PublicNotCreatable*. You can also simply declare enumerations in a *MultiUse* class that defines a component. Just realize that all the enumeration values in your project are part of one big namespace. Therefore, every enumeration value that you declare should be given a unique name.

C++ Programmer Prospects Still Bright

By John H. Mayer

It may not be the newest technology on the block – more recently developed object-oriented languages attract more attention these days – but there's still a lot of life left in the job market for Java C++ developers.

"A C++ background is still the hottest thing in the job market today," says Brett Kosineski, a recruiter and placement firm Hall Kinion in Burlington, [Mass.] While many companies are moving to Java, "has a good Java developer is more valuable [...]"

Part of the rap on C++ has been that it is harder to learn, use, and maintain for many developers. Much of that opinion can be attributed to the fact that, unlike many other application development environments, [...] developers to manage

[PROGRAMMERS page 14]

September

The next Visual C++ Developers Conference and Exposition will feature more than 75 sessions and workshops, say organizers. Scheduled to run September 19 through 23 at the Orlando World Center Marriott Resort and Convention Center, the conference will host sessions on a broad array of topics, including ATL windowing, COM+ Jumpstart, XML for C++ programmers, ATL templates for OLE DB, and how to create applications with ADO and Visual C++. The conference will also feature a full-day tutorial on Microsoft's

development kits; co-marketing [resources], including the right to [use] the Visual Studio logo; [dis]closure of future [...]ies.

...thriller

...tecturally charming but long-vacant old building in the blighted downtown of Newcastle, Massachusetts would be home to the Magic Box, a community-run children's museum-cum-book and toy store.

Strewn about the floor before him were piles of new lumber, some sawhorses, a table saw, a bucket of nails, one sledge and three claw hammers, a pry-bar, heaps of splintered wood and smashed Sheetrock, a paint-splattered floodlamp, an electric saw sitting atop a tangle of bright orange extension cords, and a few cartons — early shipments from orders placed at the Toy Fair a month ago. Until tonight, the bare concrete floor had been covered with depress-ing blue-grey industrial carpet — cheap to start with, and never cleaned in thirty years of use. Nick had spent the last six hours ripping it up with his bare hands and cutting it into sections with construction-grade razor blades. Strips of the carpet stuck out of two brown plastic garbage cans amid the rubble, making them look like matching Muppets with spiky blue-grey industrial hair, lin-

Here's something else to think about: When a client application uses several type libraries, each of which defines its own set of enumerations, all the combined enumerations from every server are visible to the client application in a single projectwide scope. The enumerations from two servers will conflict if they have the same name. The popular convention of using server-specific prefixes was created to prevent such conflicts. The enumerations in the preceding example were defined with the prefix *ds* to comply with this convention. However, there's still a potential conflict, which you can resolve in the client application by preceding the name of the enumeration with the project name, like this:

```
DogServer.dsBeer
```

Using UDTs

Prior to Visual Basic 6, you could define only user-defined types (UDTs) that were private to a project. With Visual Basic 6, you can define COM methods using a UDT as the type for a parameter or the return value. (The equivalent construct to a UDT in C and C++ is known as a *structure* or a *struct*.)

You face a few important restrictions when you use UDTs in COM methods. First, you must mark all UDT parameters as *ByRef* rather than *ByVal*. Second, you must use a version of the universal marshaler that's recent enough to know how to convert between a UDT and a Variant. If you don't have an updated version, the universal marshaler will fail when it attempts to create a proxy or a stub for an IID that contains UDTs. Windows 2000 and Windows 98 computers have the updated version of the universal marshaler. If you're using Windows NT Server, you must install Service Pack 4 or later. If you're using Windows 95, you'll need a recent version of the DCOM upgrade.

Like enumerations, UDTs must be declared in public class modules to be published in a server's type library. Here's a simple example of a UDT definition:

```
Type DogInfo
    Name As String
    Rank As String
    SerialNumber As String
End Type
```

Once you define the UDT, you can use it in a method signature as a parameter or return value type, like this:

```
Sub SetDogInfo(ByRef Data As DogInfo)
    ' Implementation
End Sub
```

(continued)

```
Function GetDogInfo() As DogInfo
    ' Implementation
End Function
```

Here's an example of a client calling the *SetDogInfo* method and passing a UDT as a parameter:

```
Dim Spot As CRetriever
Set Spot = New CRetriever
' Create and fill UDT instance.
Dim SpotInfo As DogInfo
SpotInfo.Name = "Spot"
SpotInfo.Rank = "Sergeant"
SpotInfo.SerialNumber = "K9"
' Pass UDT instance as a parameter.
Spot.SetDogInfo SpotInfo
```

UDTs are useful in many situations. In Chapter 11, which delves into marshaling and interface design, you'll see various techniques for moving data efficiently across the network using UDTs, arrays, property bags, and even ADO recordsets. For now, it's more important that you understand the basic COM data types that you can define in a type library. So far in this chapter, you've seen that Visual Basic publishes type information for coclasses, interfaces, enumerations, and UDTs.

Remember that some clients can make use of your server's type library and others can't. If you can assume that all your component's clients are written in Visual Basic or C++, you can use all the data types that we've discussed so far in this chapter, including enumerations and UDTs. It also means that you can design your components and applications in terms of abstract and concrete classes. If you want to make use of the design features exploited by user-defined interfaces, that's fine. However, if you'd like to avoid the extra work and complexity associated with user-defined interfaces, you can program in terms of the default (and automatic) interface behind a component. It's your choice.

DESIGNING COMPONENTS FOR SCRIPTING CLIENTS

Up to this point, we've focused on clients that use type information obtained from type libraries. These clients know how to access custom vTables and are compiled along with CLSIDs and IIDs. But scripting clients are much different. They never know or care about your type library. All they know about is your ProgIDs and the names of your methods and properties.

Designing components for scripting clients poses several limitations that make it impossible to use some of the techniques that we discussed earlier in this chapter.

You shouldn't design using UDTs because most scripting languages don't offer the syntax to access UDT members. You can define methods using enumerations because the scripting client sees an enumeration type as an integer. However, enumerations aren't nearly as handy when the client can't get their definitions out of a type library.

When you design a method that has *ByRef* parameters, you should define each of these parameters as a Variant instead of using a more precise type because most scripting hosts can't execute methods with strongly typed output parameters. For example, VBScript can deal with *ByRef* parameters only of type Variant. A VBScript client will fail with a "Type mismatch" error if it attempts to call a method with a *ByRef* parameter based on a data type such as Integer, Double, or String.

Scripting Clients and User-Defined Interfaces

Many COM programmers have worked hard to get up to speed on the concepts and practice of interface-based programming. User-defined interfaces require extra work when you design and write an application, but the benefits they provide in larger projects are easy to measure.

When you define your interfaces separately from your creatable components, you can achieve higher levels of reuse, maintainability, and extensibility. You can create polymorphic designs based on plug-compatible components. Your client applications can adapt to any version of a component by conducting runtime tests to see whether an object supports a certain interface. You can also create a robust versioning scheme that makes it possible to safely upgrade a component or client application without disturbing any of the other components or client applications already in production.

Once you grasp its key concepts, interface-based programming becomes addictive. Many Visual Basic programmers have fallen in love with user-defined interfaces and try to use them wherever possible. However, there's an unfortunate problem: Once you create a component that implements user-defined interfaces, it's difficult or impossible to use it directly from a scripting client. That's a problem if you're creating components that will be used by scripting clients such as Web sites built with Active Server Pages (ASP).

What's the problem?

The problem is rooted in the fact that scripting clients are written in typeless languages. For example, when you write VBScript in an ASP page, all your variables and parameters are defined as Variants. When you establish a connection to a COM object, you can't specify which interface you want to use. Instead, a VBScript client is always connected to a COM object through its default interface. Also, the default interface must be an *IDispatch*-style interface or a dual interface. *IDispatch* allows a scripting client to access the object through late binding.

In COM, clients navigate from one interface to another by calling *QueryInterface*. C++ clients can call *QueryInterface* directly. Visual Basic clients can call *QueryInterface* indirectly by assigning object references to variables and parameters that have the desired interface type. However, scripting clients can't call *QueryInterface* either directly or indirectly. They can't navigate to a secondary interface. In essence, they're stuck with the default interface to which they were originally connected. As you can see, scripting clients simply don't provide the required support to take advantage of components that implement more than one interface.

Another problem related to Visual Basic makes things even worse. You can't configure Visual Basic to use a user-defined interface as the default interface behind a *MultiUse* class. This is true of user-defined interfaces defined in *PublicNotCreatable* class modules as well as interfaces defined in IDL.

The only way you can define the default interface for a *MulitUse* class is by adding public methods to the class module itself. For example, let's say you've defined a dual interface named *IDog* in IDL that looks like this:

```
Interface IDog : IDispatch {
    HRESULT Bark();
    HRESULT RollOver([in, out] short* Rolls);
};
```

Once you compile your IDL into a type library, you can register the type library on your development workstation. (You'll see how to do this in the next chapter.) Once you register the type library, you can reference it in an ActiveX DLL project and implement your interface in a *MultiUse* class named *CDingo*, like this:

```
Option Explicit
Implements IDog

Private Sub IDog_Bark()
    ' Your implementation
End Sub

Private Sub IDog_RollOver(ByRef Rolls As Integer)
    ' Your implementation
End Sub
```

Even though *IDog* is the only interface you want your class to support, it's not marked as the default interface. In fact, there's nothing you can do in Visual Basic to make *IDog* the default interface. If you reverse-engineer the type library that Visual Basic builds into the DLL, you can see the following definitions, which illustrate the problem.

```
interface _CDingo : IDispatch {
    // Empty because there are no public methods in CDingo
};
```

```
coclass CDingo {
    [default] interface _CDingo;
    interface IDog;
};
```

Visual Basic always defines a dual interface from the public members of a *MultiUse* class and marks it as the default—even when the class doesn't have any public methods. Any user-defined interface that you implement using the *Implements* keyword is always a secondary, nondefault interface. This means that a scripting client can't navigate to the methods in your interface.

What are the implications of not being able to navigate to a secondary interface? It means when you create components with Visual Basic, your scripting clients can get to only the public methods in your creatable classes. It means you can't define your interfaces separately from the classes that hold your implementations. It also means that you can't really benefit from the principles of interface-based programming when you deal with scripting clients.

So, after all this hard work in the design and coding phase, you end up with a sticky problem: Clients that can call *QueryInterface* can access the user-defined interfaces behind your components, but scripting clients can't. How do you deal with this situation? Let's start by discussing what not to do.

Hacking away at the problem

The first technique we'll look at is for programmers who love a challenge. Scripting clients can't navigate to a secondary interface on their own. However, you can give them a little help. Look at the following code in a *MultiUse* class and notice the new method *GetIDog*:

```
Option Explicit
Implements IDog

Private Sub IDog_Bark()
    ' Your implementation
End Sub

Private Sub IDog_RollOver(ByRef Rolls As Integer)
    ' Your implementation
End Sub

' Entry point for a scripting client
Public Function GetIDog() As IDog
    Set GetIDog = Me
End Function
```

GetIDog is a public method in the default interface and is therefore accessible to a scripting client. This method has a return type of *IDog*, which results in an implicit call to *QueryInterface*. By calling *GetIDog*, a scripting client can navigate from the default interface to a secondary interface. Here's an example of some VBScript code that connects to *IDog* and calls the *Bark* method:

```
Dim ProgID, Ref1, Ref2
ProgID = "DogServer.CDingo"
Set Ref1 = Server.CreateObject(ProgID)
Set Ref2 = Ref1.GetIDog()
Ref2.Bark
Ref2.RollOver 3
Set Ref1 = Nothing
Set Ref2 = Nothing
```

As you can see, this technique allows a scripting client to access a user-defined interface such as *IDog*. Note that you should define *IDog* as a dual interface that derives from *IDispatch* as opposed to a custom interface that derives from *IUnknown*. A dual interface allows a scripting client to use late binding when calling methods such as *Bark* and *RollOver*.

On the surface, this approach seems to provide a nice solution. It allows you to design an application with scripting clients that benefits from the principles of interface-based programming. However, this approach has a significant problem: It doesn't work when the client and the object run in different processes. In fact, it doesn't even work when the client and object run on different threads inside the same process.

The problem with this approach is that it breaks COM's remoting layer. Every connection between a client and an object is based on a specific IID. For instance, there should be one proxy/stub pair for the default interface behind *CDingo* and another proxy/stub pair for *IDog*. However, in some situations the second required proxy/stub pair for *IDog* never gets created.

When a scripting client calls the *GetIDog* method on a remote object, things don't work correctly because COM's remoting layer attempts an optimization. It sees that there's already one *IDispatch* connection, so it doesn't attempt to create a second *IDispatch* connection. Even though each dual interface has a different IID, the typeless scripting client always asks for *IDispatch*. As a result, a call to *GetIDog* returns a redundant reference to the default interface. The scripting client doesn't navigate from one interface to another in the intended manner. When the scripting client attempts to call *Bark*, the call fails because the default interface behind *CDingo* doesn't support *Bark*.

So maybe this technique isn't so great after all. It works when the client and the object don't need a proxy/stub layer between them, but it breaks in all other cases. When will this get you in trouble? Let's say that you create a component and an ASP script client that use this technique. You install the component in a COM+ library application on the same machine as the ASP code. Things will work just fine at first, but what happens if the system administrator decides to reconfigure your component to run in a COM+ server application for reasons related to security or fault tolerance?

Your code won't work anymore because you created a dependency that broke when the component was reconfigured. This type of dependency is something you probably want to avoid.

Don't implement *IDispatch* more than once

Scripting clients know about only one interface, *IDispatch*. When you implement two dual interfaces in one component, you create an ambiguity because you implement *IDispatch* more than once. As you've seen, this ambiguity can be problematic. From a design perspective, a component should expose only one *IDispatch* implementation. COM's designers made this assumption when they designed their remoting layer.

Recall that Visual Basic components always expose the default interface as a dual interface. This is the interface that's built from the class's public methods. This means that a Visual Basic *MultiUse* class already has an *IDispatch* implementation before you implement any secondary interfaces. All secondary, user-defined interfaces you implement should derive from *IUnknown* instead of *IDispatch*. Following this rule will ensure that your components don't provide multiple implementations of *IDispatch*. (You'll learn how to define such an interface using IDL in Chapter 5.)

So, we still haven't solved the problem. If you have a component that implements user-defined interfaces, how do you access those interfaces from a scripting client? The solution is to flatten out all the user-defined interfaces into a single *IDispatch*-style interface. This interface will be a superset of all methods in all other interfaces. You implement it by using public methods in a *MultiUse* class.

Let's extend our example. Assume that you have a *MultiUse* class that implements two different user-defined interfaces, *IDog* and *IWonderDog*. Also assume that these two interfaces derive from *IUnknown* instead of *IDispatch*. Look at the *MultiUse* class definition in Listing 4-1. The public methods in the *MultiUse* class module serve as an entry point for a scripting client. Each method of each interface has a corresponding public method that can be called by a scripting client. The public method simply forwards the call to the interface method. Although adding scripting client support like this can be somewhat tedious, it does solve our problem. A scripting client can call any method that the component implements.

```
Implements IDog
Implements IWonderDog

Private Sub IDog_Bark()
    ' Your implementation
End Sub

Private Sub IDog_RollOver(ByRef Rolls As Integer)
    ' Your implementation
End Sub
```

(continued)

```
Private Sub IWonderDog_FetchSlippers()
    ' Your implementation
End Sub

' Scripting support added to default interface
Public Sub Bark()
    Call IDog_Bark ' Forward call.
End Sub

Public Sub RollOver(ByRef Rolls As Variant)
    Dim iRolls As Integer
    iRolls = Rolls
    Call IDog_RollOver(iRolls) ' Forward call.
    Rolls = iRolls
End Sub

Public Sub FetchSlippers()
    Call IWonderDog_FetchSlippers ' Forward call.
End Sub
```

Listing 4-1 *You can add public methods to a* MultiUse *class to map calls made by scripting clients to the private methods of user-defined interfaces.*

Creating wrapper components for scripting clients

While the approach just described gets the job done, at times you might need another technique that doesn't require modifying the original component—such as when you're dealing with a component that implements user-defined interfaces and you can't modify its source code. Instead of adding public methods to the original component, you can create a complementary wrapper component that provides access for scripting clients. This wrapper component is an adapter that plays the role of an "impedance matcher" between a scripting engine and a component that's not script-friendly.

A wrapper component typically creates an object from the original component and maps its public methods to methods in all the user-defined interfaces. Look at the code for the *CDingo* component defined in Listing 4-2. A scripting client can't access it because it exposes all its functionality through user-defined interfaces.

Listing 4-3 shows the code for a wrapper component *CDingoWrapper*. This wrapper component uses the *Class_Initialize* event handler to create a *CDingo* object. During its initialization, the wrapper component acquires a separate connection for each user-defined interface. The wrapper component uses these connections to forward public method calls to interface method implementations.

Once you flatten out all the user-defined interfaces into one big default interface, a scripting client can access every method. The scripting client simply instantiates an object using the wrapper component and calls methods directly. Here's an example of some VBScript code in an ASP page.

```
Dim ProgID, Dog
ProgID = "DogServer.CDingoWrapper"
Set Dog = Server.CreateObject(ProgID)
Dog.Bark
Dog.RollOver 3
Dog.FetchSlippers
Set Dog = Nothing
```

When you define and implement the methods in the wrapper component, you must forward parameters passed from the scripting client to the component you're wrapping. In many cases, you can forward the parameters without any casting or conversion. In some cases, however, you might need to cast the parameters to types that are compatible with whatever scripting clients you're using.

Note that you're responsible for modifying your wrapper component whenever anyone extends the original component to support another interface. You should also realize (and be thankful) that your versioning concerns aren't as complicated as they could be because the wrapper component supports only scripting clients. We'll get into all the details associated with component versioning in the next chapter.

```
' MultiUse class CDingo
Implements IDog
Implements IWonderDog

Private Sub IDog_Bark()
    ' Your implementation
End Sub

Private Sub IDog_RollOver(ByRef Rolls As Integer)
    ' Your implementation
End Sub

Private Sub IWonderDog_FetchSlippers()
    ' Your implementation
End Sub
```

Listing 4-2 *This class definition produces a component that scripting clients can't access directly.*

```
' MultiUse class CDingoWrapper
' CDingo wrapper component for scripting clients
Private Ref1 As IDog
Private Ref2 As IWonderDog

Private Sub Class_Initialize()
    Set Ref1 = New CDingo    ' Create object and
    Set Ref2 = Ref1          ' establish connections.
End Sub
```

(continued)

```
Public Sub Bark()
    Ref1.Bark ' Forward call.
End Sub

Public Sub RollOver(ByRef Rolls As Variant)
    Dim iRolls As Integer
    iRolls = Rolls
    Ref1.RollOver(iRolls) ' Forward call.
    Rolls = iRolls
End Sub

Public Sub FetchSlippers()
    Ref2.FetchSlippers ' Forward call.
End Sub

Private Sub Class_Terminate()
    Set Ref1 = Nothing
    Set Ref2 = Nothing
End Sub
```

Listing 4-3 *This wrapper class allows scripting clients to access the interfaces implemented by the* CDingo *class.*

Observations About Scripting Clients

So, scripting clients take something as elegant as interface-based programming and make it less than elegant. When you decide to create a component with user-defined interfaces, you should assume that the component will be accessed exclusively by clients that can call *QueryInterface*. Such a component won't support scripting clients directly.

The good news is that you can still program in terms of abstract and concrete classes when scripting client support isn't required. For instance, you can create a set of user-defined interfaces that define the manner in which your business logic components interact with the components that contain your data access code. This approach works great as long you can assume that all your business components will be created with Visual Basic or C++.

If you're creating a component that will support scripting clients, you're usually better off avoiding user-defined interfaces. Simply create your components using public methods in *MultiUse* classes. Scripting clients can call any method directly.

In an imperfect world, you can't always plan your fate so carefully. For instance, if you're creating a Web site in which an ASP client must access a vendor-provided component that implements user-defined interfaces, you have to do a little extra work. One of the best approaches is to create a wrapper component like the one shown in this chapter. Its purpose is to flatten out all the user-defined interfaces into a single interface that is accessible to scripting clients. Your scripting clients can thus get up and running using the path of least resistance.

RAISING ERRORS FROM A SERVER

There will undoubtedly be times when a client will call upon your component to perform a task but your code can't fulfill the request. This might happen if the database server has gone off line, for example, or if the caller doesn't have the proper authorization. Perhaps the client has attempted to run a transaction that violates one of your business rules. As a component author, you must anticipate these problems. In these situations, you must raise errors and propagate them from your code back to the caller.

If you're a long-time Visual Basic programmer, you're probably comfortable with Visual Basic's native support for raising and handling errors. When you want to propagate an error back to the caller, you simply use the *Raise* method of the built-in *Err* object. On the client side, you handle errors by using *On Error* statements and creating error handlers. However, COM is all about integrating code from different languages. When an error propagates across component boundaries, it must do so in a language-neutral fashion.

Let's say you created a component with Visual Basic that raises an error. When other Visual Basic programmers access your component, they'll handle your error in the same fashion as any other runtime error. However, other client-side programmers might access your component using different languages, such as C++, VBScript, and JavaScript. Fortunately, COM provides a way for these types of clients to handle your errors as well.

COM provides two language-independent mechanisms for reporting error conditions. A COM object uses both HRESULTs and COM exceptions to inform the client when a call can't be completed successfully. The HRESULT is the standard return value that ultimately tells the client whether a call was successful. COM exceptions are layered on top of HRESULTs and are used to propagate rich error information from an object back to a client in a language-neutral fashion.

Visual Basic had its own native support for raising and handling errors before the COM team created their own exception-handling model. The Visual Basic and COM team worked hard so that Visual Basic's error-handling model could be directly mapped on top of COM exceptions. The Visual Basic runtime deals with the HRESULTs and COM exceptions behind the scenes. You simply raise errors from your components and handle errors in your client code. Visual Basic does the automatic conversion for you behind the scenes. This is great news for Visual Basic programmers—you don't have to change your style of programming when you start creating components.

HRESULTs

HRESULTs indicate the success or failure of method calls in COM. They're particularly important in calls that extend across the network. COM has standardized on this return value so that the remoting infrastructure (the RPC layer) can inform the client that a problem has occurred when an object can't be reached. Therefore, if an object that's part of an active connection meets an untimely death, the client can discover this fact and respond appropriately.

In COM, every remotable method must return an HRESULT. To be remotable, a method must be callable across a proxy/stub layer. As it turns out, every method you ever create or call using Visual Basic returns an HRESULT. However, the Visual Basic team has tried its best to hide all traces of the existence of HRESULTs. If you use OLEVIEW.EXE to inspect your servers, you'll see that every method you've created is defined with an HRESULT as a return value—including Visual Basic methods that are defined as functions. For example, a method defined in Visual Basic as

```
Function GetTaxRate() As Double
```

is expressed in IDL like this:

```
HRESULT GetTaxRate([out, retval] double*);
```

Whenever a method needs a logical return value, IDL accommodates this requirement by providing the *[retval]* parameter attribute. There can be only one *[retval]* parameter in a COM method, and it must appear last in the parameter list. Visual Basic and Java are examples of languages that transparently map these special parameters so that programmers can use them as return values instead of as output parameters. Mapping makes calling a function more natural and also relieves programmers from manually inspecting HRESULTs. Visual Basic's runtime layer inspects the HRESULT, and the client receives an error in the event of a failure.

Why does COM need a standard return value? A standard method return value allows COM's infrastructure to return well-known errors back to the client in certain situations. To demonstrate the value of standard return values, let's suppose that a client is connected to a remote object that lives across the network. There's a chance that the object will die or become unreachable while the client still holds a connection—for example, if the server process crashes or if an overzealous administrator reboots the server computer. In either case, the client application will have an outstanding reference to an object that no longer exists. This situation can also occur if network problems make it impossible to route a method request between the client and the object. In all such cases, a remote method call will fail.

The underlying RPC layer is capable of informing the client that the server is unavailable. This is one of the primary reasons that the COM team chose to standardize on HRESULTs. A client can inspect an HRESULT to see whether the call was successful. If the client determines that the call was not successful, it can also examine the HRESULT to find out more specific information about the problem at hand. The HRESULT tells the client whether the error came from the object itself or from another subsystem such as the underlying RPC layer.

As it turns out, only C++ programmers deal with HRESULTs directly. Visual Basic makes things much easier. On the client side, the Visual Basic runtime always inspects HRESULTs for you behind the scenes. If a call returns without an error, it means that the Visual Basic runtime determined that the HRESULT indicated success. But if the Visual Basic runtime sees an HRESULT that indicates failure, it raises a runtime error.

Do you ever have to deal with HRESULTs as a Visual Basic programmer? Only in rare situations. The Visual Basic runtime knows about many well-known HRESULTs that are reported by the COM library as well as by other various COM-related subsystems. The Visual Basic runtime translates these HRESULTs into standard runtime errors. However, the Visual Basic runtime doesn't handle certain other situations as elegantly. If it encounters an HRESULT that it doesn't know about, it raises an error and places the raw HRESULT value in *Err.Number*.

Visual Basic 6 added support for catching most of the HRESULTs that indicate that an out-of-process object is dead or unreachable. When the Visual Basic runtime sees HRESULTs from the RPC layer that report a dead object, it raises error number 462 along with this description: "The remote server machine doesn't exist or is unavailable." This runtime error assists you in many of the cases in which you need to handle a dead or unreachable object. However, Visual Basic 5 doesn't include the same support. If you're using Visual Basic 5, you must examine a raw HRESULT to determine that an object has died. At times like these, it's helpful to know exactly what's inside an HRESULT.

An HRESULT is a 32-bit value that contains three distinct pieces of information. Figure 4-4 shows how the physical memory of an HRESULT is segmented to hold a severity level, a facility code, and an application-specific error code. The severity level stored in bit 31 indicates whether the method call was successful. If the bit is left off, the method call succeeded. If the bit is turned on, the method call failed.

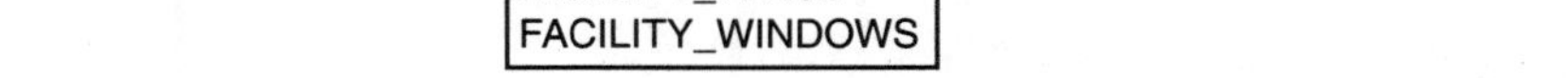

Figure 4-4 *All remotable methods in COM return HRESULTs at the physical level.*

The set of bits in the middle of an HRESULT, known as the *facility code*, tells the client where the error originated. Standard COM errors use the code FACILITY_NULL. An object, on the other hand, should use FACILITY_ITF when it wants to send an interface-specific error code to the client. Table 4-2 shows other possible values for the facility code. As you can see, errors can be generated from many different subsystems in Windows 2000.

How do you know when you're dealing with a raw HRESULT in *Err.Number*? It's actually pretty easy to tell because the value is a very large negative number. When you see a value such as −2147220992, you know it's an HRESULT indicating failure. The most significant bit of an HRESULT tells the caller whether the call was successful. If this bit is turned on, the call failed. However, Visual Basic always sees this bit as an indicator of whether the integer is positive or negative because Visual Basic always uses signed integers rather than unsigned integers.

If you experience a runtime error that passes you a raw HRESULT, you can attempt to find out what happened by inspecting both the facility code and the error code. However, to extract the facility code or the error code, you must perform a bitwise operation using the AND operator. Look at the following function:

```
Function GetFacilityCode(ByVal HRESULT As Long) As Integer
    GetFacilityCode = ((HRESULT And &HFFF0000) / 65536)
End Function
```

This function extracts the bits of the HRESULT that are specific to the facility code. It uses a bit mask to ignore all the other bits. It then divides by 65536 to calculate the actual facility code. Table 4-2 shows all the facility code values that are defined in Windows 2000.

Table 4-2 **FACILITY CODES IN WINDOWS 2000**

Facility Code	Value
FACILITY_NULL	0
FACILITY_RPC	1
FACILITY_DISPATCH	2
FACILITY_STORAGE	3
FACILITY_ITF	4
FACILITY_WIN32	7
FACILITY_WINDOWS	8
FACILITY_SECURITY	9
FACILITY_CONTROL	10
FACILITY_INTERNET	12
FACILITY_MEDIASERVER	13
FACILITY_MSMQ	14
FACILITY_SETUPAPI	15
FACILITY_SCARD	16

By examining the facility code, you can try to determine where the error occurred. Facility codes such as FACILITY_RPC, FACILITY_WIN32, and FACILITY_WINDOWS mean that the error was reported by the underlying infrastructure. These codes might also mean you have a dead or unreachable object. Unfortunately, you can't be sure that receiving one of these facility codes really means the object has died. You might receive a failure with one of these facility codes when the parameters of a method call couldn't be marshaled to or from the object. In such a case, the next call to the object might be successful.

After you determine the facility code, you should look at the error code in the lower 16 bits of the HRESULT if you really want to know what happened. Here's a function that looks at the lower 16 bits of the HRESULT and ignores everything else:

```
Function GetErrorCode(ByVal HRESULT As Long) As Integer
    GetErrorCode = (HRESULT And 65535)
End Function
```

Once you find both the facility code and the error code, you can look up the error in the header file WINERROR.H, which is part of the Win32 SDK. This file should include all system-generated HRESULTs. As you can imagine, working at this level can be very tedious for the average Visual Basic programmer. Remember that you won't have to work with HRESULTs very often—only when you receive an error generated by the system and the Visual Basic runtime doesn't know about it.

COM Exceptions

An HRESULT can convey whether a method has succeeded. It can also contain an application-specific error code. But it can't convey a text-based error message or any information about where the error actually occurred. You can use *COM exceptions* to pass a richer set of error information from an object back to its clients. Support for COM exceptions is provided by a handful of functions and interfaces in the COM library.

Before examining the inner workings of COM exceptions, you should note that all these details are hidden from Visual Basic programmers. The Visual Basic team took Visual Basic's proprietary error-handling model and cleanly mapped it on top of COM exceptions. As a result, Visual Basic programmers don't have to know a thing about COM exceptions.

Here's how COM exceptions work. Any COM object that throws exceptions must advertise this fact by supporting a standard interface named *ISupportErrorInfo*. This interface allows a client to query the object on an interface-by-interface basis to see whether the object supports exceptions for a specific IID. The object can tell the client, "Yes, I support COM exceptions for the interface you're using."

When an object wants to throw an exception, it must create an error object by calling a function in the COM library named *CreateErrorInfo*. This function creates the error object and returns an *ICreateErrorInfo* reference. The object then uses this reference to populate the newly created error object with information such as a description and an error source. Next, the object must call *SetErrorInfo* to associate the error object with the logical thread of the caller. (The term *logical thread* refers to a chain of method calls that might span several physical threads.) Finally, the object must return an HRESULT that tells the client that something has gone wrong.

An exception-savvy client can query an object to see whether it supports the *ISupportErrorInfo* interface. If it does, the client calls a method through *ISupportErrorInfo* to test for support on the interface that the client is currently using. If the object indicates that it supports exceptions on that interface, the client can be sure that an error object will be generated with contextual information about the nature of the problem whenever a failed HRESULT is returned. So, if the client inspects an HRESULT and finds that a method call was not successful, it calls *GetErrorInfo* to retrieve an *IErrorInfo* interface reference to the error object. This interface lets the client retrieve all the error information sent by the object. As you can see, COM exceptions require a lot of work on both sides. It's fortunate that Visual Basic does all this work for you behind the scenes but still lets you participate in this language-neutral error-handling scheme.

One point you should understand is that COM exceptions are pretty efficient. If an object raises a COM exception and the client is on another machine, all the error information is sent along the wire as the call returns. There's no need for a second round-trip between the client computer and the server computer to pick up extra error information. This relative ease is made possible by optimizations to COM's remoting layer. The contextual information associated with a COM exception is always marshaled across the wire with the method's response. The client can simply retrieve all this error information from a local cache.

Visual Basic errors are mapped to COM exceptions

If you have used Visual Basic's error-handling model, you know that it's much easier to use than COM's exception-handling model. It's fortunate that the two models work so well together. Visual Basic programmers continue to raise and trap errors in the same way that they have for years, and the details are transparently mapped by the runtime layer to conform to the language-independent model required by COM.

Every Visual Basic component has built-in support for *ISupportErrorInfo*. When you explicitly raise an error from a Visual Basic server with *Err.Raise*, the runtime layer automatically creates and populates a COM error object. It also makes the other necessary calls to properly throw a COM exception. All you really need to do is provide code, as shown in the following example:

```
Dim MyErrorCode As Long, Source As String, Description As String
MyErrorCode = vbObjectError + 512
Source = "DogServer.CBeagle.Bark"
Description = "The cat's got the dog's tongue."
Err.Raise MyErrorCode, Source, Description
```

When you call *Err.Raise*, you must pass a user-defined error code. Visual Basic provides the intrinsic constant *vbObjectError* as the starting point for your user-defined error code. The constant *vbObjectError* maps to a failed HRESULT with a facility code of FACILITY_ITF. However, the COM team recommends that you actually start your custom-defined error codes at *vbObjectError + 512* to avoid any conflicts with Microsoft-defined error codes.

The previous example also shows how to populate the *Source* and *Description* properties of an error object. The source should tell the client application where the problem occurred. This information is most useful during debugging. The description should give the client an indication of what went wrong in a human-readable form. It's common practice to display the description to the user, so keep that in mind. If the error condition has a remedy, it's often valuable to make that known in the description as well.

All the user-defined errors raised by your servers should have corresponding error codes. The error codes for a server should be published in the type library using enumerations. You can define a set of error codes in the following manner:

```
' Dog Server Error Codes
Enum ErrorCodesEnum
    dsDogUnavailable = vbObjectError + 512
    dsDogUnagreeable
    dsDogNotCapable
    dsDogNotFound
    dsUnexpectedError
End Enum
```

Visual Basic's mapping of COM exceptions on the client side is just as transparent as it is on the object side. When a method returns an HRESULT indicating failure, the mapping layer uses the *ISupportErrorInfo* interface to determine whether the object supports COM exceptions. If it does, the mapping layer retrieves the COM error object and uses it to populate a standard Visual Basic *Error* object. The Visual Basic runtime then raises an error back to the caller. You can use a *Select Case* statement in a client application to create a handler, like this:

```
Sub MakeDogBark(Dog As IDog)
    On Error GoTo MakeDogBark_Err
    Dog.Bark
' Exit if successful.
Exit Sub
' Enter handler on error.
MakeDogBark_Err:
    Select Case Err.Number
        Case dsDogNotCapable:
            ' Perform necessary handling in client.
            MsgBox Err.Description, vbCritical, "Error: Dog Not Capable"
```

(continued)

```
        Case Else
            ' Always provide a last-chance handler.
            MsgBox Err.Description, vbCritical, "Unexpected Error"
    End Select
End Sub
```

It is also acceptable for your components to raise errors based on HRESULTs defined by Microsoft. For example, if you conduct a runtime test in one of your methods and determine that the caller doesn't have the proper authorization to perform a task, you should raise an error. However, instead of defining your own custom error code, you should use the standard HRESULT that indicates that access has been denied. Here's an example of how to use this HRESULT in your code:

```
Const E_ACCESSDENIED = &H80070005
Err.Raise E_ACCESSDENIED, , "Access has been denied"
```

You can look at the file WINERROR.H to see what other HRESULTs Microsoft has defined. You also might have noticed that the previous code example defines the HRESULT constant using a hexadecimal format. You can also use the equivalent decimal value –2147024891. Either way is fine. It's just that WINERROR.H uses the hexadecimal format, which makes it easier to copy and paste these values into your Visual Basic source code.

Error-Raising Conventions

When you distribute COM servers, you are expected to follow the rules defined by COM as well as the rules used by Visual Basic programmers. This expectation is especially firm if you work in environments in which some components and clients are written with tools and languages other than Visual Basic. Here are some rules that you should keep in mind:

- All COM exceptions that leave your server should be explicitly raised by your code. This means that only errors explicitly generated with *Err.Raise* should leave your server. You must prevent any unhandled errors from leaving your server. Most Visual Basic programmers know that an unhandled error in a client application results in the application's termination. A Visual Basic server, on the other hand, deals with an unhandled error by passing it to the client. For instance, if a method in your server experiences a division-by-zero error that isn't handled, the runtime layer simply forwards the error to the client application.

    It's considered bad style to let exceptions leave your server that haven't been explicitly raised. The rules of COM state that any COM object that implements *ISupportErrorInfo* can pass only its own exceptions.

To follow these rules, you must catch any error generated by methods such as those in the Visual Basic runtime and the ADO library. If your server experiences an error that it can't deal with, raise an application-specific "unexpected error" exception back to the client.

■ Always include a helpful text description when you raise an exception. Try to create informational descriptions at the place where the error occurred. The procedure in which the error occurs usually has the most contextual information. It's easy to propagate this description back to the original caller from anywhere in the call chain. A description such as "Order for $2000.00 could not be accepted. The customer has a credit balance of only $1250.00" is far more valuable than "Order submission failure." The handler in the client application often displays this error message to the user. Remember that error codes are for programmers and that error descriptions are for users.

■ Always use enumerations to define custom error codes. This practice will allow other programmers to see your error codes through the type library. Visual Basic programmers using your server will be able to see these error codes with the Object Browser.

■ Always define custom error codes using *vbObjectError + 512*. The lower error codes are reserved by the COM team and have special meanings. If you use the *vbObjectError* constant and add 512, you can be sure that your codes won't be misinterpreted as system-defined error codes.

■ Try to supply documentation with your servers that describes errors to other programmers. You can convey only so much information with an enumerated value such as *dsDogNotCapable*. If possible, you should include a list of remedies and workarounds for each error condition.

■ Never display a message box in your server's error handlers. The decision to interact with the user should always be left to the client application. With an out-of-process server, an error handler that displays a message box will hang the server, and that is something you want to avoid. Although you can display a message box to the user from an in-process server, doing so is considered bad style. The client application programmer should ultimately control all interaction with the user.

Handling Errors in Scripting Clients

Your component's clients might be written in ASP scripts or as Microsoft Windows Script Host (WSH) files using languages such as VBScript and JavaScript. If you're writing components for scripting clients such as these, you can and should raise errors in the manner just described whenever a method can't complete its work. This means that scripting clients shouldn't be treated any differently than other clients. However, you should be aware that the manner in which the error-handling code is written in a scripting client is not very elegant. Let's look at an example of a client written in VBScript:

```
' VBScript in a WSH file
Const dsDogNotCapable = &H80040202
On Error Resume Next
Dim Spot
Set Spot = CreateObject("DogServer.CBeagle")
' Call method.
Spot.Bark
' Test for success or failure.
Select Case Err.Number
    Case 0
        ' Things are good. The call did not experience an error.
    Case dsDogNotCapable
        MsgBox "The dog isn't capable of barking at this moment"
    Case Else
        MsgBox "Unexpected error #" & Err.Number & ": " & Err.Description
End Select
' Be sure to clear error object.
Err.Clear
' Now call other methods and test for errors in similar fashion.
```

If your component uses enumerations to publish error codes, a scripting client usually can't use this information. One easy way to deal with this problem is to simply use constants in the scripting clients to map error codes to readable names. Also note that you are limited to the *On Error Resume Next* statement when you handle errors in VBScript. This means you must inspect *Err.Number* after each method call. If *Err.Number* is not equal to zero, a runtime error has occurred. Also note that once you handle a runtime error, you must clear the *Err* object using the *Clear* method before attempting another call.

SUMMARY

This chapter covered the basics of designing and building servers with Visual Basic. You must first decide whether to package your components in ActiveX DLLs or ActiveX EXEs. The way you package your code affects your server's performance, robustness, and security. Many distributed application designs require that your objects be deployed in an out-of-process server. However, sophisticated runtime environments such as COM+ and IIS provide a surrogate process, which means that you still distribute your code in an ActiveX DLL.

As you've seen, Visual Basic automatically builds lots of support into your servers at compile time. The Visual Basic compiler and runtime layer work hard to hide many of the details required by COM. Your job as a component author is to concentrate on how to expose functionality through interfaces defined in the type library and how to provide an implementation of those interfaces in your components.

This chapter discussed advanced techniques such as using user-defined interfaces, enumerations, and UDTs when you design your components. You also saw that many of these techniques create problems when scripting clients are involved. It's best if you can make assumptions early in the design phase about which types of clients will use your components.

This chapter also exposed you to the important issues of raising and handling errors. It's comforting that Visual Basic provides a transparent mapping on top of COM exceptions. Visual Basic objects and clients can participate in exception handling with components written in other languages. In most situations, Visual Basic hides all the gory details of HRESULTs and COM exceptions, so you can raise and handle errors in the manner that Visual Basic programmers have always used.

Chapter 5

Versioning Components

Component versioning is critical in the production environment. To harvest COM's most powerful features, you must be able to revise your servers and replace them in the field without adversely affecting any client applications. This chapter shows you the options that Microsoft Visual Basic gives you to accomplish this. For some readers, this might prove to be the most valuable topic in the book.

We'll examine the most important versioning issues a Visual Basic programmer faces when creating and maintaining components for an application. These guidelines apply whether your application is based on COM+, MTS, or earlier versions of COM. You'll learn when and how to use Visual Basic's binary compatibility scheme. I'll also point out a few important limitations of using binary compatibility and show you an alternative technique for versioning Visual Basic components. This technique involves defining interfaces with Interface Definition Language (IDL) and building custom type libraries.

My goal in this chapter is to arm you with enough knowledge to realize one of COM's biggest promises: the ability to easily maintain and extend your application code once it's been put into production.

VERSIONING IN COM

Interface ID p962

COM was founded on the notion of interface immutability. Once a COM interface (a custom vTable layout identified by an IID) has been published, its set of methods can never change. This condition means you can't modify, remove, or add method definitions in an interface that's already in production. If you violate these rules, you void the versioning warranty that comes with the COM Specification. If you adhere to the rules of interface immutability, however, you can version a component to your heart's content. If you want to change or extend a component's behavior, you simply define a new interface and implement it.

As long as your component continues to implement all previously supported interfaces, any new version of the component will work with older clients as well as newer clients. Moreover, a client can query an object at runtime to determine whether a particular IID is supported, which allows a newer client to degrade gracefully when it encounters an older version of the component. In short, COM makes it possible to put a new version of a client or a component into production without having to change other code that's already in place.

Much of Visual Basic's success is due to the fact that it hides the complexity of the underlying platform. In the spirit of making programming easier, the Visual Basic team has hidden many of the complex and grotesque details associated with COM. For instance, COM requires a formalized separation of interface from implementation, but Visual Basic doesn't require a COM programmer to work in terms of user-defined interfaces.

Let's say you're creating an ActiveX DLL named DOGSERVER.DLL for a COM+ application. When you create a *MultiUse* class named *CCollie* with a few public methods, Visual Basic creates a coclass and a default interface definition for you. The coclass is given the logical name of *CCollie* and the interface definition is named *_CCollie*. When you build the DLL, Visual Basic compiles the coclass and interface definitions into a type library, which it bundles into the server's executable image. You, as the component author, don't have to define a separate interface.

Programming from the client side in Visual Basic is just as easy. When a client application creates an object reference of type *CCollie*, Visual Basic knows to silently cast this reference to the default interface *_CCollie*. Visual Basic clients and objects communicate using valid COM interfaces, but Visual Basic programmers don't have to work in terms of user-defined interfaces.

Given that many Visual Basic programmers create components without explicitly creating user-defined interfaces, the Visual Basic team wanted to provide a versioning scheme for components that rely on default interfaces. One goal of this scheme is to allow component authors to add methods to later versions of a component.

Globally Unique ID,
Interface ID,
Class ID,

As you'll see, this versioning scheme is controlled through a project's *version compatibility* setting. You must understand how Visual Basic uses this setting to control how it manages GUIDs such as IIDs and CLSIDs from build to build. You should also understand Visual Basic's convoluted mechanism that allows you to add methods to later versions of the component. We'll examine these issues in a moment.

Let's start our discussion of component versioning by asking an important question: What types of clients will use your component? As I explained in Chapter 4, you can generally split client code into two categories: scripting clients that access your objects through late binding and more sophisticated clients that access your objects through direct vTable binding.

If you can assume that your component will be accessed only by clients from one of these categories, your versioning concerns are less complicated. Versioning components for direct vTable-bound clients is harder. Moreover, sometimes you'll need to support both types of clients as you version a component. In these situations, you must understand how versioning is handled behind the scenes.

Versioning a Component for Scripting Clients

It's not hard to version a component for scripting clients because a scripting client has few dependencies on the component. For example, client code in an ASP script typically includes the component's ProgID and the names of some methods and properties. However, scripting clients never have dependencies on IIDs or custom vTable layouts because scripting clients use late binding.

Creating a component in Visual Basic for scripting clients is pretty easy. You simply create a new *MultiUse* class and add a few public methods and properties. Visual Basic always creates a dual interface containing the public methods and properties, which serves as the component's default interface. This default interface can be accessed through either late binding or direct vTable binding. When a scripting client instantiates a new object from your component, the scripting client is always connected through the default interface. Once connected, the scripting client uses late binding to access public methods or properties.

I described in the preceding chapter the problems that occur when you mix scripting clients and user-defined interfaces. If you're going to create components for scripting clients, you shouldn't develop them in terms of user-defined interfaces. If you already have a Visual Basic component that implements user-defined interfaces, it's a pain to access it from scripting clients. Typically, you have to write extra code to connect a scripting client to methods that are not part of the default interface.

Once you accept the fact that scripting clients require *MultiUse* classes with public methods and properties, it's simple to create and version your components.

You add a few methods to your class and then compile and distribute your DLL. When you want to add another method or two, you simply modify the class and recompile and redistribute your DLL. It doesn't even matter what version compatibility mode you're in when you rebuild the DLL. Older scripting clients can use the old version of your DLL or the new version. Newer clients can use the newer version of the component and make use of the new methods.

The only situation you have to watch out for is when a newer scripting client comes in contact with an older version of the component. For example, if you add a method to a later version of a component and call it from a scripting client, the client will have problems when it attempts to use the earlier version of the DLL. The newer scripting client will try to bind to a method that doesn't exist, which will result in a runtime error. As long as you're prepared to deal with this scenario, things aren't very complicated.

Versioning a Component for Direct vTable-Bound Clients

Things get more complicated and far more interesting when you version Visual Basic components for clients that use direct vTable binding. You have a choice between using binary compatibility or using IDL. Binary compatibility is a good choice if you're relying on Visual Basic to define your interfaces for you behind the scenes. If you want to define your interfaces separately from your components, you should use IDL and build type libraries using the MIDL compiler.

We'll begin by looking at binary compatibility and the versioning support that's built into Visual Basic. First, you must understand how a project's version compatibility setting affects your components from build to build. If you set things up properly, you can safely upgrade and extend your components. If you configure your project with the wrong compatibility setting, your life can be downright miserable.

Before I explain how this setting works, let's review what Visual Basic does when you create an ActiveX DLL. In our example, we're creating a DLL named DOGSERVER.DLL with a *MultiUse* class named *CCollie*, which contains a few public methods. When you build the DLL, Visual Basic creates a definition for a coclass named *CCollie* and a default interface named _CCollie and publishes them in the server's type library.

Let's turn our attention to what's in the server's type library. There's a coclass named *CCollie* and a default interface named _CCollie. However, these are just logical names for these COM types. COM requires GUIDs to identify coclasses and interfaces at the physical level.

You can explicitly generate a GUID by calling a system-level function in the COM library named *CoCreateGUID* or by using a utility named GUIDGEN.EXE. COM developers who use C++ often generate GUIDs this way. To make component creation painless, the Visual Basic team decided that GUID generation and management would be a transparent feature of the development environment.

At compile time, Visual Basic transparently generates the required GUIDs and assigns them to your coclasses and interfaces where applicable. The transparent generation of GUIDs makes it easy for you to create components quickly. It's also what gets many Visual Basic developers into trouble.

The logical name of your coclass is *CCollie*, but its physical name is a CLSID that looks something like {259D5370-DD2D-11D2-8319-0080C7067BA1}. Visual Basic also generates an IID for the default interface *_CCollie*. In addition, Visual Basic marks the default interface as *[hidden]* to hide it from naïve programmers.

In addition to CLSIDs and IIDs, Visual Basic generates a GUID to identify the type library that's built into the DLL. This GUID is referred to as a LIBID. Visual Basic might generate other GUIDs for enumerations and user-defined types (UDTs) as necessary.

Let's say that you add these two public methods to the *CCollie* class:

```
Public Sub Bark()
    ' Implementation
End Sub

Public Sub RollOver(ByRef Rolls As Integer)
    ' Implementation
End Sub
```

When you add these methods to *CCollie*, you're also adding them to the default interface named *_CCollie*. Remember that while the logical name for the default interface is *_CCollie*, client applications and the COM runtime always refer to this interface by its IID.

When you build the first version of your DLL and ship it to other programmers, they'll reference the built-in type library and begin programming against the *CCollie* component. When they compile their code, their applications will have dependencies on the CLSID for *CCollie* as well as the IID for the default interface. These client applications will use direct vTable binding to access *CCollie* objects.

Everything will be fine until you decide to upgrade or extend the *CCollie* component. Before you ship a second version of your DLL, you must configure your project with the proper version compatibility setting. The version compatibility setting is controlled on a project-by-project basis on the Component tab of the Project Properties dialog box, as shown in Figure 5-1. The three settings are as follows:

- **No Compatibility** This setting causes Visual Basic to regenerate all GUIDs, including IIDs, CLSIDs, and the LIBID. A project that is compiled with this setting will have all internal type library version numbers reset to 1.0.

- **Project Compatibility** This setting causes Visual Basic to regenerate all IIDs. However, the LIBID is held constant so that other programmers don't have to rereference the type library after you rebuild your server.

- **Binary Compatibility** This setting causes all GUIDs, including IIDs, to be retained across builds in order to support previously compiled clients that use direct vTable binding. Visual Basic also runs compatibility tests to make sure method signatures haven't changed.

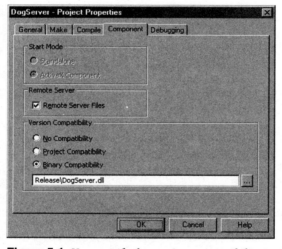

Figure 5-1 *You specify the version compatibility setting on a projectwide basis using the Component tab of the Project Properties dialog box.*

Let's spend a little time discussing each of these settings. No Compatibility means that Visual Basic regenerates all GUIDs for everything in the type library and performs no compatibility checks. This is exactly what happens when compile your component for the very first time.

Project Compatibility and Binary Compatibility require you to point the Visual Basic compiler to a previously compiled version of the server. Specifically, Visual Basic must examine the type library bundled into a previous build of your server to compare GUIDs and conduct compatibility checks on the latest version of your source code. You can use the text box below the three version compatibility radio buttons to add a path to the server file that will serve as a reference.

The Project Compatibility setting has different results depending on what version of Visual Basic you're using. In Visual Basic 5, the compiler keeps the GUID of your type library but regenerates your CLSIDs and IIDs. In Visual Basic 6, the compiler only regenerates your IIDs. The CLSIDs are retained across builds.

The change between versions was intended primarily to make it easier to deal with scripting clients that embed CLSIDs into their source code using the OBJECT tag (ActiveX controls, for example). Note that scripting clients using the OBJECT tag use late binding. This means that they have dependencies on CLSIDs but not on IIDs.

Regardless of the version of Visual Basic, when you compile under Project Compatibility mode, the compiler performs no checks to see whether your interfaces have changed. Instead, Visual Basic simply dumps all the IIDs and generates a new set. You should also note that the GUIDs associated with enumerations and UDTs are regenerated as well.

The No Compatibility and Project Compatibility settings change every IID each time you rebuild the DLL. This is problematic when you have clients that have dependencies on the IIDs that were thrown away. If another programmer compiles a client application against an earlier version of your DLL, the application will fail when it attempts to activate an object from the new version. Users will become upset and moody because they'll encounter error dialog boxes like the one shown in Figure 5-2.

Figure 5-2 *If a client application attempts to activate an object using an IID that's not supported by the component, Visual Basic raises error 430.*

What goes wrong? The client attempts to bind to an object by using the IID from a previous build. However, this IID isn't supported in later builds of the DLL. To prevent this unfortunate situation, the obvious solution is to change your project's version compatibility setting to the final choice, Binary Compatibility.

Binary Compatibility

Binary Compatibility is the only setting that allows you to rebuild a server that supports existing vTable-bound clients. The compiler retains all GUIDs across builds, including the IIDs. The Visual Basic compiler also performs compatibility checks to make sure you haven't made any illegal changes to your interfaces, enumerations, or UDTs.

Here's a simple summary of the version compatibility rules that Visual Basic uses when it's in Binary Compatibility mode: As long as you haven't modified any existing method signatures or reordered any enumeration values or UDT fields, the compiler will accept your changes and recompile your component. If Visual Basic doesn't complain when you attempt to recompile, the new version has passed the compatibility checks. The new version of the DLL will be compatible with previously compiled clients. If, however, you do something like remove a method or change a parameter's data type, the Visual Basic compiler will complain with a large dialog box similar to the one shown in Figure 5-3.

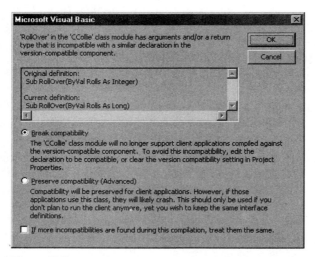

Figure 5-3 *Visual Basic presents this dialog box if you're in Binary Compatibility mode and you attempt to compile an interface that's incompatible with the previous version.*

This "incompatibility detection" dialog box offers you two choices. The Break Compatibility option does two things. First, it changes all the IIDs and resets every interface version number to 1.0. Second, it increments the version number of your server's type library by one full point. Selecting Break Compatibility is similar to rebuilding your project with a version compatibility setting of Project Compatibility.

The Preserve Compatibility (Advanced) option isn't all that useful in most cases. It allows you to retain the IID for an interface even if the calling syntax for one or more methods has changed. You should realize the implications of using this option. It can result in catastrophic failure for client applications that are compiled against earlier versions of your server.

The custom vTable-binding code that Visual Basic builds into client applications is very particular. Bad things usually happen when a client and an object disagree on how to pass a parameter when a method is invoked. Your client can easily crash with unsightly system-generated error messages like the one shown in Figure 5-4.

Figure 5-4 *This Win32 dialog box is a sign that your client application has died a cruel and sudden death.*

When you use the Break Compatibility option or the Preserve Compatibility option, you should assume that all previously compiled clients will be discarded. When you see the dialog box shown in Figure 5-3, the best thing to do is to modify your source code to make it compatible with earlier versions of the server. Once you can compile your DLL without the dialog box appearing, you know that your DLL is compatible with all existing clients.

Extending the default interface

When you work in Binary Compatibility mode, you can't alter existing method signatures. This means that you can't change the name of any method, the type of the return value, or the type of any parameter. You also can't add optional parameters to the end of a method signature. Your intuition might tell you that adding an optional parameter should be allowed because it doesn't require a change in the client's calling syntax. However, optional parameters require placing a variant on the stack at the physical level during method execution. Therefore, adding an optional parameter to an existing method makes the entire interface incompatible.

Of course, as long as you hold your method signatures constant, you can safely change any existing method implementations when you compile under Binary Compatibility mode. When you think about it, this is what COM is all about. You should always be able to change an implementation as long as you don't change the physical nature of the interface. However, Visual Basic lets you go one step further and add new methods to a *MultiUse* class.

When you add new public methods in a second version of a component, you're really adding new methods to the default interface. Visual Basic must create a new default interface that is a superset of the original default interface. The new interface is said to be *version-compatible* with the old interface. Because each interface must be represented by its own vTable, Visual Basic must use two different IIDs.

Let's revisit our example. Version 1 of the *CCollie* class defines two public methods, *Bark* and *RollOver*. The first time you build the server, Visual Basic automatically creates an interface named _CCollie (with an IID) that defines these two methods. If you add a new method named *FetchSlippers* to version 2 of *CCollie* and rebuild the server in Binary Compatibility mode, Visual Basic generates a new IID for the new default interface that contains all three methods. However, Visual Basic must also provide support in the new version to deal with clients that use the old IID. Figure 5-5 depicts both interfaces and their associated vTables.

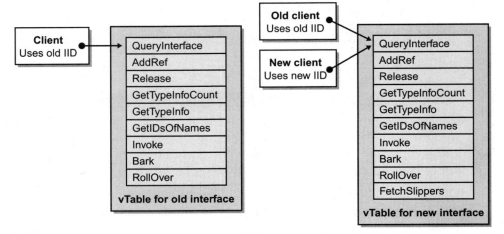

Figure 5-5 *The extensibility scheme provided by Binary Compatibility mode is based on the notion of version-compatible interfaces. The new interface is version-compatible with the old interface because its vTable represents a superset of the methods represented by the old vTable.*

Here's where things get a little weird. The compiler-generated implementation of *QueryInterface* behind the *CCollie* object hands out a reference for the new interface when a client asks for either the new interface or the old interface. Clients that were built against the original version of the DLL get bound to a vTable based on the new IID, but they know about only the first two of the three methods. Because the new interface is version-compatible with the old one, it meets the expectations of the client and things work fine.

You should note that the type library built for the version-compatible DLL contains the interface definition only for the new IID. The interface definition for the old IID is not included. However, the COM runtime might need to build proxy/stub code based on the old IID. Proxy/stub code for Visual Basic objects is generated at runtime by the universal marshaler. The universal marshaler builds proxies and stub by examining interface definitions in type libraries.

But how can the universal marshaler build a proxy or a stub for the old interface when it doesn't have access to the interface definition? It does so using *interface forwarding*. The self-registration code in a version-compatible DLL adds a key to the Registry for the old IID, as shown in Figure 5-6. This key contains forwarding information that points the universal marshaler to the newer, version-compatible IID. The universal marshaler can thus build version-compatible proxies and stubs using the interface definition associated with the new IID even when a client requests a connection based on the old IID.

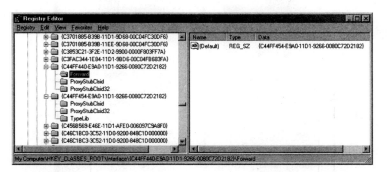

Figure 5-6 *Visual Basic and the universal marshaler use interface forwarding to make version-compatible interfaces work in the production environment.*

Visual Basic lets you build version upon version of compatible servers. For instance, version 4 can be compatible with version 3, which can be compatible with version 2, which can be compatible with the original version. A client that knows about only the original version of the interface might be forwarded across many compatible interfaces before it reaches one that's defined in a type library that exists on the host computer.

What Really Happens Behind the Scenes?   Once you compile the DLL, you can use OLEVIEW.EXE to decompile the type library to see what Visual Basic has actually done and thus see how Visual Basic manages your GUIDs across builds. Here's a watered-down version of what you see after you compile version 1:

```
[ // GUID for default interface - IID1
    uuid(C44FF440-E9A0-11D1-9266-0080C72D2182),
    version(1.0), hidden, dual, oleautomation
]
interface _CCollie : IDispatch {
    HRESULT Bark();
    HRESULT RollOver([in, out] short* Rolls);
};

[ // This GUID is the CLSID.
    uuid(EDE2823B-DE19-11D2-9A2C-0080C7067BA1),
]
coclass CCollie {
    [default] interface _CCollie;
};
```

When other programmers want to use the *CCollie* component in a client application, they must reference the server's type library using Visual Basic's References dialog box. Once they reference the type library, they can write the following code to activate and access an instance of the *CCollie* component:

```
Dim Dog As CCollie
Set Dog = New CCollie
Dog.Bark
Dog.RollOver 14
Set Dog = Nothing
```

Every COM-based connection between a client and an object must be based on a specific IID. When a Visual Basic client makes a reference to *CCollie*, the reference is automatically cast to the default interface behind the component. In this case, the connection is made using the IID of the default interface behind *CCollie*. This IID is compiled into any client application that is built against version 1 of the DLL.

After testing and debugging your code, you install DOGSERVER.DLL in a COM+ application on your production server. After you set things up properly, your users will use client applications to access the *CCollie* component from around the network. Version 1.0 of the client application and the server will be in sync. Life will be good.

Let's say that you decide to add a new method named *FetchSlippers* to *CCollie* in a second release of your DLL. When you attempt to rebuild under Binary Compatibility mode, the Visual Basic compiler detects that the default interface is compatible with the previous version but is not identical. It creates a second IID for the new version of the default interface. Here's what the IDL looks like after the second build:

```
[ // Different GUID for default interface - IID2
    uuid(C44FF454-E9A0-11D1-9266-0080C72D2182),
    version(1.1), hidden, dual, oleautomation
]
interface _CCollie : IDispatch {
    HRESULT Bark();
    HRESULT RollOver([in, out] int* Rolls);
    HRESULT FetchSlippers();
};

[ // This GUID is the CLSID.
    uuid(EDE2823B-DE19-11D2-9A2C-0080C7067BA1),
]
coclass CCollie {
    [default] interface _CCollie;
};
```

The items shown in bold are those that Visual Basic changes from the first build to the second. Visual Basic creates a version-compatible component. The interface definition for the first IID is not included in the type library. However, using OLEVIEW, you can find another new entry in the server's type library that provides a mapping back to the old IID:

```
typedef [
    uuid(C44FF440-E9A0-11D1-9266-0080C72D2182),
    version(1.0), public
]
_CCollie CCollie___v0;
```

This entry helps Visual Basic provide support for the old IID in later builds. As you've seen, Visual Basic simply maps the old IID to the new IID. Old clients can successfully bind to newer versions of the object. In addition, clients that are compiled against the newer version of the DLL will work because they bind using the new IID. The only time that version-compatible interfaces do not work is when a new client attempts to bind to an old version of the object using the new IID. We'll examine how to solve this problem in the next section. Table 5-1 summarizes what works and what doesn't.

Table 5-1 COMPATIBILITY BETWEEN VERSIONS OF CLIENT AND COMPONENT

Client Version	*Component Version*	*IID Version Used*	*Does It Work?*
Old client	Old component	Old IID	Yes
Old client	New component	Old IID	Yes
New client	New component	New IID	Yes
New client	Old component	N/A	No

What's evident is that Visual Basic's support for COM was designed to be easy and uncomplicated. However, this ease of use comes at the price of inflexibility. You can use binary compatibility to retain all GUIDs, including IIDs, across builds in order to support previously compiled clients that use direct vTable binding. Binary compatibility also supports creating version-compatible interfaces. However, as you now know, it doesn't guarantee complete compatibility.

When binary compatibility isn't enough

As you've seen, Visual Basic can publish and version your interfaces for you behind the scenes. However, if you're willing to get a little more involved, you have another option: You can define your interfaces using IDL and compile them into a custom type library. This approach offers you much greater control and lets you avoid some of the problems you might encounter when using binary compatibility.

Using IDL makes it necessary for component authors and client-side programmers to work in terms of user-defined interfaces. You can't configure a user-defined interface to be the default interface behind a *MultiUse* class. This means that you must understand the principles of interface-based programming and differentiate between concrete types and abstract types. Getting up to speed on this style of programming has its costs. However, in many cases the benefits of defining interfaces in IDL outweigh these costs. This is especially true for large projects in which the shortcomings of binary compatibility are most evident.

What are the most significant problems associated with programming exclusively against your component's default interface and relying on Visual Basic's binary compatibility scheme? First, you lose a degree of control over managing the definitions of your interfaces, enumerations, and UDTs. Second, you lose the ability to exploit polymorphism and create plug-compatible components. Finally, your clients can't adapt to use older versions of your servers. Let's look at each of these problems in a little more detail.

You lose control over defining and managing what goes into your type library because Visual Basic does everything for you behind the scenes. All you can really do is adjust the version compatibility setting on a projectwide basis. However, if you work directly with IDL to define your interfaces separately from your servers and components, you can decide when to change, retain, and publish your IIDs on an interface-by-interface basis.

If you're relying on the default interface behind each of your *MultiUse* classes, you can't create plug-compatible components because there's a limiting one-to-one relationship between your components and interfaces. If you want to design an application based on a polymorphic design with plug-compatible components, you must work in terms of user-defined interfaces. (Actually, you can also achieve polymorphism with late binding, but let's assume that you want to stick with clients that use direct vTable binding.) Once you create a user-defined interface, you can implement it in several components.

When you rely on binary compatibility, you also lose one of the major benefits of interface-based programming. A new client can't adapt to use an older version of the component. This means you're forced to replace each and every server in production whenever you want to deploy a new version of a client application that uses it.

Let's provide a little more background so you really understand this last point. As you know, Visual Basic (in Binary Compatibility mode) creates a new IID each time you add one or more methods to a new version of a component. The component supports the old IID as well as the new IID. However, only the interface definition for the new IID is published in the new build of the type library. If an old client requests a connection based on the old IID, the vTable layout is generated from the new IID. This works because the vTable behind the new IID is a superset of the vTable behind the old IID. The newer vTable is version-compatible with the older one.

You've already seen how Visual Basic deals with version-compatible interfaces at the physical level. Now let's look at things at a higher level to get a sense of what can go wrong. When you compiled the first version of *CCollie* with two public methods,

Visual Basic published a default interface named *_CCollie* with a specific IID. Let's call this *IID1*. When you add another method, *FetchSlippers*, and rebuild the server with binary compatibility, Visual Basic creates a second IID for the new interface definition with all three methods. Let's call this *IID2*. When a Visual Basic client application references the DLL containing the latest version of the component, it knows about only *IID2*. It can't test for *IID2* and then degrade gracefully to use *IID1* when it encounters a DLL containing the original version of the component. This can create serious problems. The client knows about only the IID for the default interface, but the IID for the default interface might change with every new build of the DLL.

Is this really a problem? What if you roll out version 1 of the DLL along with a client application? Say that the DLL was installed in a COM+ application. Now say that you're going to roll out an upgrade that contains both a new version of the DLL and a new version of the client. During the upgrade process, clients get upgraded, but due to an unexpected delay, the DLL on the server doesn't get upgraded. When users attempt to activate an object, they receive that obnoxious error 430, "Class does not support Automation or does not support expected interface." One thing should be clear: You should use version-compatible interfaces only if you can guarantee that new clients will always be rolled out with the most recent version of the DLL.

If you want your new clients to be able to adapt to older versions of your components, you must work in terms of user-defined interfaces. For instance, suppose you define an interface named *IDog* and implement it in the original version of the *CCollie* component. In the second version, you want to add another method. You define a second interface named *IDog2* that includes all the methods from *IDog* plus a new method. If you implement *IDog2* in addition to *IDog* in the second version of the component, you can write client code like this:

```
Dim Ref1 As IDog
Set Ref1 = New CCollie
' Test to see if component supports IDog2.
If TypeOf Ref1 Is IDog2 Then
    ' Cast to new IID.
    Dim Ref2 As IDog2
    Set Ref2 = Ref1
    ' Access object through Ref2 (new IID).
Else
    ' Degrade gracefully.
    ' Access object through Ref1 (old IID).
End If
```

This is an example of client code that's far more adaptable than the scheme used by binary compatibility. For business systems that are large and constantly changing, working in terms of user-defined interfaces offers many advantages (as described in Chapter 2).

CREATING USER-DEFINED INTERFACES

Before going any further, I want to reiterate one key point: When you use user-defined interfaces, you must make the major assumption that all clients will use direct vTable binding to access the objects created from your component.

As I mentioned in the preceding chapter, user-defined interfaces don't mix well with scripting clients. You should provide access to scripting clients through public methods in *MultiUse* classes. For the rest of this chapter, let's assume that all our client code will be written in Visual Basic or some other tool that's capable of direct vTable binding and navigating between the various interfaces supported by an object.

You have two choices when it comes to creating user-defined interfaces: You can define your interfaces with Visual Basic using *PublicNotCreatable* class modules or you can define your interfaces using IDL. Let's start with the easier approach—using Visual Basic.

Visual Basic makes it pretty simple to create user-defined interfaces. You saw the nuts and bolts of how to do this in Chapter 2. However, you must still decide whether to define your interfaces in the same server project as your components. Your other option is to generate a stand-alone type library with interface definitions that is separate from your servers.

In a smaller project, it might not make sense to publish interface definitions in a separate type library, especially if the project involves only one small team or a lone developer. It's easier to define the interfaces in the same server project as your components. If your project doesn't benefit from maintaining interfaces and components independently, the administrative overhead of building separate files is likely to be more trouble than it's worth.

For larger projects, it usually makes sense to publish user-defined interfaces in a separate type library. This approach makes it easier to use the same interface definition across multiple servers. For instance, what if you want to create two ActiveX DLLs, each of which contains a component that implements the same interface? When a designer publishes an interface in a separate type library, two independent DLL authors can easily reference this library and implement the interface. This allows several COM servers to serve up objects that are type-compatible with one another. This is valuable when a system is designed around the idea of plug-compatible components.

Creating a stand-alone type library of interface definitions with Visual Basic is fairly easy but a bit awkward. You simply create an ActiveX DLL project and define your interfaces in class modules marked as *PublicNotCreatable*. On the Component tab of the Project Properties dialog box, you must select the Remote Server Files check box to ensure that a stand-alone type library file (with a .TLB extension) is created when you build the DLL. You can throw away the DLL and distribute the .TLB file to other programmers.

An awkward thing about using the Visual Basic IDE is that you must include at least one creatable class in any ActiveX DLL project. The Visual Basic IDE assumes that you want to create servers only; you have to trick it into building an "interface-only" type library. You must create one dummy class module with the instancing setting of *MultiUse*. It's a little confusing because anyone who uses your type library must ignore this dummy class, but this is the only way you can build a .TLB file using the Visual Basic IDE.

Defining Interfaces with IDL

Although it's possible to create user-defined interfaces inside a Visual Basic project using *PublicNotCreatable* class modules, you'll have much more control if you work with IDL directly. Once you create your interface definitions in an IDL source file, you can build a custom type library using the MIDL compiler.

IDL has a somewhat confusing history. The language was originally designed to define RPC-style interfaces. An RPC-style interface definition in IDL can be fed to a compiler to generate code that will remote function calls across the network. Microsoft extended IDL for COM-based interfaces by adding attributes and some object-oriented features. The MIDL compiler is capable of generating remoting code for COM-style interfaces.

A few years back, COM programmers used two different languages for describing components and interfaces: IDL and Object Definition Language (ODL). They used IDL to create the remoting code and used ODL to build type libraries. They used an older utility named MKTYPLIB.EXE to compile an ODL file into a type library.

With the release of Windows NT 4, Microsoft's original versions of IDL and ODL were merged into the current version of IDL. You use the MIDL compiler to create both the type libraries and remoting code. Using IDL and the latest release of MIDL to build type libraries is preferable to using ODL and MKTYPLIB. Also note that you should use the very latest version of MIDL available in the Platform SDK. Earlier versions of MIDL don't support some of the later features of IDL. (The examples from this chapter are based on MIDL 5.03.0280.)

Now it's time to learn how to build a Visual Basic–friendly type library with IDL. First, you must decide what types of definitions you want publish in your type library. You can add interfaces, enumerations, and UDTs to your IDL source file. However, coclasses defined in IDL pose a problem. Although you can define a coclass in IDL and compile it into a custom type library, you can't use the coclass definition from within a Visual Basic project. The only coclass definitions that Visual Basic uses are the ones that it automatically builds into the type libraries associated with servers. This means you can't write IDL to influence how Visual Basic defines a coclass.

You should use one IDL source file for each type library you want to build. You can create and modify this IDL source file with a simple text editor such as Notepad. If you edit your IDL files in the Visual C++ development environment, the source code will be color-coded. This can be a real convenience when you're learning a new language.

If you want to build a type library named DOGLIBRARY.TLB, you should start by creating an IDL source file named DOGLIBRARY.IDL. Here's the starting skeleton for this IDL source file:

```
// DOGLIBRARY.IDL
[
    uuid(46373B81-4106-11d3-AB39-2406D0000000),
    helpstring("The Dog App Type Lib"),
    version(1.0)
]
library DogLibrary {
    importlib("STDOLE2.TLB");
    // Enum and UDT definitions go here.
    // Interface definitions go here.
};
```

This template includes the boilerplate code for defining the attributes of a type library. You expand this template by adding other definitions to the *library* block. You should notice that the *library* block requires a *uuid* attribute (a GUID). A utility that ships with Visual Studio named GUIDGEN.EXE makes it easy to generate new GUIDs and copy them to the Clipboard. You can then simply paste the GUIDs into your IDL source file. Be sure to use the Registry format when you copy your GUIDs. You'll have to trim off the *{* and *}* characters that GUIDGEN adds.

This library block you've just seen also includes two other optional attributes. The *[helpstring]* attribute serves as a description for the type library. This is the description that Visual Basic programmers see when they view the type library through the References dialog box. You can also include a *[version]* attribute.

The library template code shown above imports another type library named STDOLE2.TLB. You must import STDOLE2.TLB because it defines standard COM interfaces such as *IUnknown* and *IDispatch*. In addition, it marks *IUnknown* as *[hidden]* and *IDispatch* as *[restricted]*. It also marks all the methods from both these interfaces as *[restricted]*. The Visual Basic compiler and runtime rely on these methods being restricted, so it's critical that you import STDOLE2.TLB into every Visual Basic–friendly type library you build. You might be required to import other type libraries as well if the definitions in your IDL source file rely on external types such as ADO recordsets.

Now let's define an interface using IDL. Here's a good starting point for a Visual Basic–friendly interface definition:

```
[
    uuid(A0E89184-40BE-11d3-AB39-2406D0000000),
    oleautomation,
    object
]
interface IDog : IUnknown {
    // Method signatures
};
```

The interface includes three important attributes. The *[uuid]* attribute is required. It becomes the IID for the interface. You can generate the IID using the GUIDGEN utility just as you would any other GUID. Also notice that the interface is defined with the *[oleautomation]* attribute. This attribute restricts the data types used in the interface to those that are compatible with Visual Basic. It also tells the COM runtime to use the universal marshaler when building proxy/stub code. Finally, the *[object]* attribute informs the MIDL compiler that this is a COM-style interface as opposed to an RPC-style interface. Recent versions of the MIDL compiler don't require you to use the *[object]* attribute when you define an interface inside the body of a type library.

The next thing you should notice is that this interface derives from *IUnknown*. Visual Basic–compatible interfaces must derive directly from *IUnknown* or *IDispatch*. An interface that derives from another custom interface is incompatible with Visual Basic. For example, what happens if you derive a user-defined interface named *IDog2* from another user-defined interface named *IDog*? Look at the following two interface definitions:

```
// Can be implemented in VB class
interface IDog : IUnknown {
    HRESULT Bark();
    HRESULT RollOver([in, out] long* Rolls);
};

// Can't be implemented in VB class
interface IDog2 : IDog {
    HRESULT FetchSlippers();
};
```

You can't implement this version of *IDog2* in a Visual Basic class because it derives from *IDog*. Visual Basic supports only a single level of interface inheritance. If you want to implement *IDog2* in a Visual Basic class, it must derive from *IUnknown* or *IDispatch*.

Despite Visual Basic's lack of support for multiple levels of interface inheritance, you'll often want to create one interface that's a superset of another. For example, what should you do if you want to extend the functionality of an interface? Here's the IDL that provides a workaround for this problem:

```
interface IDog2 : IUnknown {
    HRESULT Bark();
    HRESULT RollOver([in, out] long* Rolls);
    HRESULT FetchSlippers();
};
```

You must duplicate the method definitions in both versions of the interface. This isn't an elegant solution in terms of object-oriented beauty, but it gets the job done. Once you define *IDog* and *IDog2* in this manner, you can implement both of them in version 2 of the *CCollie* component, like this:

```
Implements IDog
Implements IDog2
```

Unfortunately, each interface requires a separate set of entry points in the class module for the duplicate methods. For example, both interfaces define a method named *Bark*. However, in most cases you'll want both entry points for *Bark* to forward to a single method implementation. This makes for a somewhat tedious chore. You have to modify your class so it looks something like this:

```
Public Sub IDog_Bark()
    ' Implementation code
End Sub

Public Sub IDog2_Bark()
    ' Forward call
    Call IDog_Bark
End Sub
```

You should also notice that *IDog* and *IDog2* derive from *IUnknown* instead of *IDispatch*. The reason for this is simple. The only time you need to derive from *IDispatch* is when you want to create a dual interface to support scripting clients. However, scripting clients are always connected to objects through the default interface. Moreover, scripting clients can't navigate from one interface to another. A scripting client can't access a method in a user-defined interface. This means that the interfaces defined in IDL are consumed exclusively by clients that use direct vTable binding. Deriving from *IUnknown* is all that you need, and it requires less overhead than deriving from *IDispatch*.

Defining Method Signatures in IDL

Now let's see how to define the actual methods in an interface. You must learn how to define the type and direction for each parameter. Let's say you want an interface with a set of methods that looks like this:

```
Sub Test1(ByVal i As Long)
Sub Test2(ByRef i As Long)
Function Test3() As Long
```

The required IDL looks like this:

```
HRESULT Test1([in] long i);
HRESULT Test2([in, out] long* i);
HRESULT Test3([out, retval] long*);
```

For those of you who aren't familiar with C, the * character is used to define a parameter passed with a pointer. You must use this pointer syntax any time you want to pass output parameters from the object back to the client. You should define *ByRef* parameters using pointer syntax and the *[in, out]* attribute. Function return values should be defined using pointer syntax and the *[out, retval]* attribute and should be defined as the rightmost parameter.

IDL provides equivalents to all the usual VBA types, including String, Date, and Variant. Table 5-2 shows Visual Basic–to–IDL data type mappings.

Table 5-2 VISUAL BASIC–TO–IDL DATA TYPE MAPPINGS

Visual Basic Data Type	*IDL Data Type*	
Integer	short	
Long	long	
Byte	unsigned char	
Single	float	
Double	double	
Boolean	VARIANT_BOOL	
String	BSTR	
Variant	VARIANT	
Currency	CURRENCY	
Date	Date	
Array	SAFEARRAY	
Object	*IDispatch	

All Visual Basic arrays map into IDL as SAFEARRAYs. A SAFEARRAY is a data structure with a lot of associated metadata. An array can be passed as a *ByRef* parameter or as a function return value. Note that the universal marshaler can move the contents of a SAFEARRAY across the network in a single round trip. Here are two Visual Basic methods, one that receives an array and one that returns an array:

```
Sub Test4(ByRef x() As Long)
Function Test5() As Long()
```

Here's how to express the equivalent methods in IDL:

```
HRESULT Test4([in, out] SAFEARRAY(long)* x);
HRESULT Test5([out, retval] SAFEARRAY(long)* );
```

What do you do when you want to pass an object? Well, you should first realize that you'll be passing an object reference as opposed to an actual object. At the physical level, you'll really be passing a pointer to the vTable associated with an interface such as *IDog*. This means that object references are always passed in terms of pointers. A *ByVal* parameter allows the pointer to pass from the client to the object, as is shown in the following IDL code:

```
HRESULT Test6([in] IDog* Dog);
```

A *ByRef* parameter or a function return value based on an object reference must be passed as a pointer to a pointer. This means that you need two * characters. Look at the following method definitions:

```
HRESULT Test7([in, out] IDog** Dog);
HRESULT Test8([out, retval] IDog**);
```

The code you write in Visual Basic to implement these methods will look something like this:

```
Sub Test6(ByVal Dog As IDog)
Sub Test7(ByRef Dog As IDog)
Function Test8() As IDog
```

You can learn more about how to write method definitions in IDL by reading the online MIDL documentation that ships with Microsoft Developer Network (MSDN). However, there's a handy shortcut that will move you along the IDL learning curve much faster. You start by defining a few method signatures in a Visual Basic class module. You compile your code into an ActiveX DLL and use OLEVIEW to decompile the type library that gets built into the DLL. You can copy method signatures from OLEVIEW's Type Library Viewer and paste them directly into an IDL interface definition.

Once you paste method definitions into your IDL source file, you should trim off the *[id]* attributes because they're required only when your clients connect through *IDispatch*. You might also consider adding a *[helpstring]* attribute to each method definition to document its semantics for other programmers.

You should be aware that some syntax generated by decompiling the type library from a Visual Basic server doesn't always work because Visual Basic creates its type libraries using some older ODL-style data types. OLEVIEW occasionally produces syntax based on ODL instead of IDL as well. When you decompile a type library, some of this ODL syntax will not compile properly with the MIDL compiler. It doesn't happen very often, but it's frustrating when it does. The two most common problems you will encounter are the *single* data type and UDT definitions.

The *single* data type is defined by ODL but not by IDL. If you copy and paste code produced by OLEVIEW, you must replace the *single* data type with its IDL equivalent, *float*. As far as defining UDTs, we'll get to that in just a little bit. For now, make a mental note that you can't simply copy and paste UDT definitions from decompiled code into your own IDL source files.

Once you become more fluent in IDL, you can create or modify the signatures by hand. But be sure to follow these rules:

■   All methods must return HRESULTs.

■   Mark *ByVal* parameters as *[in]* and *ByRef* parameters as *[in, out]*.

■   You can't define parameters marked as *[in]* using pointers.

■   A parameter marked as *[out]* must also be marked as *[retval]* and must be the rightmost parameter.

■   Methods names can't start with an underscore (_).

■   Don't use parameters that are typed as unsigned integers.

Using Enumerations and UDTs

Now that you know how to define an interface in a type library, it's time to add an enumeration and a UDT definition as well. Note that you must define a type before you use it in an IDL file. For instance, let's say you want to define a UDT and a method in an interface that uses the UDT as a parameter. If you define the interface before the UDT, the IDL file will not compile. If you define all your enumerations and UDTs before your interfaces, you can avoid this problem. Alternatively, you can use the forward-declaration syntax that's available in IDL.

Let's add an enumeration to your type library. An enumeration defines a set of integer-based constants. As you know, enumerations are useful for defining parameter and return value types. Many programmers also use enumerations to define sets of error codes. Here's an example of an enumeration definition in IDL:

```
typedef
[uuid(CC316146-9B37-4EF6-9E6D-2A68ACDCA908)]
enum {
    // 0x80040200 = vbObjectError + 512
    dsDogUnavailable = 0x80040200,
    dsDogUnagreeable = 0x80040201,
    dsDogNotCapable = 0x80040202,
    dsDogNotFound = 0x80040203,
    dsUnexpectedError = 0x80040204,
} DogErrorCodes;
```

Note that the enumeration is defined using the *typedef* keyword. This example shows how to define a set of error codes that can be raised by the *CCollie* component. The starting number for this enumeration is *vbObjectError + 512*, the conventional starting point for your user-defined error codes (as explained in Chapter 4).

Now let's turn our attention to defining UDTs. You should define UDTs in IDL using the *struct* keyword. However, before you start using UDTs in your method signatures, you should consider two significant points. First, everyone must use Visual Basic 6 or later. All previous versions of Visual Basic lack support for UDTs in COM method calls. Second, your code must run on computers that are running a recent version of the universal marshaler, as explained in Chapter 4.

Working with UDTs in IDL can be a little confusing at first. You should start by acquiring the latest version of the MIDL compiler to avoid incompatible-syntax problems. The technique I'm about to show you doesn't work with many earlier versions of MIDL.

You have to use the *struct* keyword, but you should avoid the *typedef* keyword. While you can use a *typedef* to define a UDT in IDL, it causes a few sticky problems for the MIDL compiler. Here's how you should define a UDT in IDL:

```
// UDT defined inside type library DogLibrary
[uuid(173CF18E-99DA-11D2-AB73-E8BE3D000000)]
struct DogData {
    BSTR Name;
    BSTR Rank;
    BSTR SerialNumber;
};
```

Each UDT definition needs it own identifying GUID. Now let's use the UDT in a method signature. Here's where a little extra attention is required. Look at the following method definitions:

```
// Method signature that uses the UDT
HRESULT Test9([in, out] struct DogData* Data);
HRESULT Test10([out, retval] struct DogData*);
```

UDT instances must be passed by reference instead of by value. This means that you must define UDT parameters using *[in, out]* or *[out, retval]*. Also, you must define UDT parameters as pointers by using the * character. Also notice that the keyword *struct* must be used inside the method definition—that is, the parameter type in these methods is *struct DogData** as opposed to *DogData**.

Once you define the UDT in the type library, it will look something like this in the class that implements it:

```
Private Sub IDog3_Test9(Data As DogData)
Private Function IDog3_Test10() As DogData
```

Compiling Your Type Library

Once you finish writing your IDL code, it's time to build a type library by sending the IDL source file to the MIDL compiler. If you don't already have the MIDL compiler on your development machine, you must acquire it. As I've mentioned, you should acquire the MIDL compiler by installing the latest version of the Platform SDK. Note that it's very important to select the Register Environment Variables option during the SDK installation so the MIDL compiler will be in the system path.

It's pretty simple to build a type library by running the MIDL compiler from the command line. Here's an example of what you type at the command prompt:

```
MIDL /win32 DogLibrary.idl
```

Another convenient trick is to create and run a batch file that looks like this:

```
MIDL /win32 DogLibrary.idl
Pause
```

If there's a problem compiling the IDL source file, the MIDL compiler reports the error in the console window. If the MIDL compiler runs without any errors, it generates a type library named *DogLibrary.tlb*.

The MIDL compiler has quite a few command-line parameters. However, many of them don't concern you. Most are intended for developers who are generating files other than type libraries. If you want to review the complete list of available MIDL command-line parameters, run the following command from the command prompt:

```
MIDL /?
```

Distributing and Configuring Your Type Library

Once you build your type library, you must register it on any system that will use it. This includes production machines as well as development machines.

The type library is required on production machines because the universal marshaler uses it to create proxies and stubs. After a type library is registered, there are Registry entries that map each *[oleautomation]* IID to a LIBID and map the LIBID to a path and filename for the type library. The universal marshaler uses this information to locate the interface definition at runtime. The universal marshaler needs the interface definition in order to build proxy/stub code.

You must register the type library on development machines so tools such as Visual Basic can provide wizard support and Microsoft IntelliSense. Once a type library is registered, you can locate its description in the References dialog box. Note that the Visual Basic compiler needs the type library to build vTable-binding code into client applications.

A type library can be more difficult to register than an ActiveX DLL. You can't register a type library with REGSVR32.EXE because the type library contains no self-registration code. Instead, you must register a type library by calling a function in the COM library named *RegisterTypeLib*. (Actually, you have to call another function named *LoadTypeLib* first.) When you call *RegisterTypeLib*, it adds all the Registry entries for the type library. It also adds Registry entries for each interface defined in the type library with the *[oleautomation]* attribute.

It's much easier to call *RegisterTypeLib* in C++ than it is in Visual Basic because this function has parameters based on pointer data types. Fortunately, there are several utilities you can use that will call *RegisterTypeLib* for you.

The utility named REGTLIB.EXE ships with Visual Studio. You can run this utility from the command line by passing the name and path of your type library. You can also use this utility to unregister a type library.

A second way to register a type library is by using the Browse option in the References dialog box from within the Visual Basic development environment. Simply select Browse and find the type library. When you add the type library to your project, Visual Basic calls *RegisterTypeLib*. Note that the Visual Basic IDE doesn't provide a way to unregister a type library.

The last way to register a type library is by adding it to a COM+ application or an MTS package. It's a bit tricky because you must add a DLL server at the same time that you add the type library. When you add the type library, it is automatically registered on the local machine. What's more, the client-side setup programs created by COM+ and MTS automatically install and register the type library on the client machines. (Installing components and type libraries into COM+ applications is covered in greater depth in the next chapter.)

One More Sticky Point

Let's say you've defined your interfaces in IDL and compiled them into a type library. Then you create a server with one component that looks like this:

```
Option Explicit
Implements IDog

Private Sub IDog_Bark()
    ' Your implementation
End Sub

Private Sub IDog_RollOver()
    ' Your implementation
End Sub
```

Once you define all your interfaces in a custom type library, your server's type library defines only coclasses. Logically, you conclude that the server's type library isn't being used to define any interfaces. It seems as if all the important IIDs that clients are programming against live in the custom type library and not in your server's type library.

So here's a critical question: When you compile later versions of the server, should you care about the version compatibility mode? Well, obviously you shouldn't recompile using No Compatibility because the CLSID will change. But does it matter whether you use Binary Compatibility versus Project Compatibility?

The intuitive answer to this question is "no." In theory, it shouldn't matter because both compatibility modes keep the CLSID constant across builds (as long as you're using Visual Basic 6, that is). If you compile in Project Compatibility mode, the IIDs in the server's type library will change, but you assume that this isn't important because you don't care about the IIDs in the server's type library.

This assumption will get you in trouble. As you know, it's more important how things work in practice than in theory. In practice, you must often recompile in Binary Compatibility mode even when your component contains no public methods. Things will go wrong if you use Project Compatibility.

Here's why. In Chapter 3, I mentioned an esoteric point about what the Visual Basic runtime does on the client-side during object activation when the client has called *New*. The Visual Basic runtime calls *CoCreateInstance* using *IUnknown*, and then it calls *QueryInterface* to obtain a reference to the default IID behind the component. This is true whether the client is using the default interface or a user-defined interface. In other words, a Visual Basic client has a dependency on the IID for the default interface behind your component even when the client doesn't explicitly program against the default interface. If the default IID changes across builds, older clients will fail when they attempt to activate objects from the new version of the server.

Don't spend too much time wondering why Visual Basic works this way. It doesn't matter whether this makes sense to you. It's just the way things are. What you should take away from this is that binary compatibility is always required when you have Visual Basic clients that use direct vTable binding and the *New* operator. (This isn't a problem when clients are creating objects with the *CreateObject* function.) You must rebuild your servers using Binary Compatibility mode even when your components are serving up functionality exclusively through interfaces defined in a custom type library. But then again, you're a COM+ programmer. Yours is not to reason why.

SUMMARY

Versioning components is an essential aspect of developing and maintaining a dynamic system. COM was designed from the ground up to support component versioning. And certainly, Visual Basic adds its own special twist to COM's versioning story. You have to keep on top of many details, and you have many responsibilities. The most important thing to do is to ask the right questions at the start of any project.

Do you want to support scripting clients? Do you want to support clients that use direct vTable binding? Should you rely on Visual Basic to define and version your interfaces for you behind the scenes? Would it be beneficial to maintain your interface definitions in IDL?

Developers will answer these questions in different ways. However, as long as you have the knowledge to answer these questions correctly, you can draw up a versioning scheme that will be effective for the project at hand. And, most important, Visual Basic error 430 will be a distant memory instead of a daily cause of pain and frustration.

Chapter 6

Working with Configured Components

Chapter 1 presented a high-level overview of the fundamental principles of the COM+ programming model. In Chapter 3, we looked more closely at how COM's programming model relies on interfaces, dynamic class loading, and the transparent creation of RPC-based connections between clients and objects. This chapter focuses on a crucial aspect of the programming model that wasn't part of COM in the early days— the principle that *platform services are exposed through declarative attributes*. The primary goal of this chapter is to demonstrate how this principle affects the way you write code and deploy your components.

Declarative attributes first debuted in MTS, where they provide support for distributed transactions and integrated security. COM+ builds on this idea by exposing additional services through declarative attributes. For readers who are transitioning from MTS to COM+, I've included a few sidebars to illustrate the most significant differences between the two platforms. For those of you who are starting fresh with Microsoft Windows 2000, you don't have to worry about how the details of MTS differ from those of COM+. COM+ has been reengineered to be simpler and less confusing.

In this chapter, we'll examine how COM+ tracks and makes use of attribute settings for components and applications. We'll also look at how COM+ allows you to activate objects from configured components in out-of-process and remote deployment scenarios. I'll cover the fundamentals of creating COM+ components with Visual Basic as well as configuring them to run in a COM+ application.

It's important that you understand how the COM+ runtime uses contexts and interception. The interception scheme allows COM+ to provide the services requested through declarative attributes. In addition to setting attributes, you must also write some code against the COM+ Services Type Library. I'll take some time to show you the most common interfaces and system-supplied objects you'll use when you interact with the COM+ runtime.

At the end of the chapter, we'll take a brief look at how to test and debug configured components created with Visual Basic. You'll see that debugging configured components inside the Visual Basic debugger is relatively easy but that you face one or two limitations. You'll also learn a few other debugging techniques that are more tedious and complicated but provide a better simulation of what really happens when your code runs in production.

THE BASICS OF CONFIGURED COMPONENTS

Exposing system services through configurable attributes is very different from exposing system services through a set of functions in a traditional API. In the older API-based model, you must write code to tell the system what services you want and how you want to use them. When you want to modify the manner in which an application uses a system service, you must modify code and recompile and redistribute the application. Moreover, Visual Basic programmers are often at a disadvantage because their language makes it impossible or impractical to call upon several system services exposed by the C-based Win32 API. The new way in which COM+ and declarative attributes expose system services is more flexible and makes your work easier.

Working with declarative attributes offers two primary benefits. First, you don't have to write as much code. You indicate your requirements by configuring attributes at design time and letting COM+ do the work for you at runtime. The second benefit is that you can configure attributes after an application has been put into production. You don't have to modify any code or recompile your application when you want to change the way you use a system service. This is really convenient when you make hardware changes to your application's physical deployment and you need to change a database connection string or tune a middle-tier application to take advantage of a more powerful computer.

COM+ Applications

In COM+, every configured component needs a home. The programming model defines an abstraction known as a *COM+ application*. Each COM+ application defines a set of configurable attributes that tells the system such things as where to activate objects and how to set up security. Every component that carries declarative attributes must belong to exactly one COM+ application. You can think of a COM+ application as a set of one or more configured components set up to run on a specific computer. In addition to its own attributes, a configured component also inherits a set of attributes from its hosting application. As you'll see later, COM+ also tracks configured attributes for interfaces and methods.

MOVING FROM MTS

What's in a Name?

MTS uses the term *package* in the same way that COM+ uses the term *application*.

In Chapter 3, I talked about the confusion surrounding the term *component*. Some people use the term to refer to a concrete class, while others use it to refer to a physical server file such as an ActiveX DLL. Still others go as far as to use *component* interchangeably with *object*. Because the term *component* has several possible meanings, you often must read between the lines to interpret how it's being used. In this book, I use the term to refer to a concrete class identified by a specific CLSID. More specifically, in terms of COM+ development using Visual Basic, a component is a *MultiUse* class compiled into an ActiveX DLL. This view is consistent with COM+ because each COM+ application contains a *Components* collection, which holds a set of concrete classes. However, you still have to stay on your toes. The COM+ documentation in MSDN often uses the term *component* to describe a physical server file as opposed to a concrete class. So much for consistency.

The COM+ registration database (RegDB)

When you create a new COM+ application, the system creates a new profile for it in a system catalog called the *COM+ registration database (RegDB)*. This catalog holds attribute settings for applications, components, interfaces, and methods. The details of storing and accessing data in RegDB are abstracted away behind a system-supplied component called the *Catalog Manager*, as shown in Figure 6-1. The Catalog Manager generates a new GUID (known as an Application ID or AppID) to identify each application.

There are two common ways to create and administer a COM+ application. You can do it manually by using a built-in utility called the Component Services administrative tool. You can also do it programmatically by writing administrative scripts or full-blown Visual Basic applications against a set of system-supplied components known as the Component Services Administration (COMAdmin) Library. Both administrative techniques leverage the Catalog Manager to do their work.

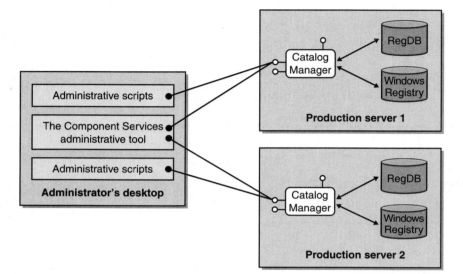

Figure 6-1 *The COM+ Catalog Manager handles reading and writing configuration information to RegDB and the Windows Registry.*

A component is considered a *configured component* once it's been added to a COM+ application. As you saw in Chapter 3, earlier versions of COM relied on Registry keys to hold configuration information about type libraries, CLSIDs, ProgIDs, and IIDs. COM+ relies on these same Registry keys in addition to other attribute settings stored in RegDB. For various reasons, the COM+ team decided to avoid changing the traditional way that COM configuration information is stored. They also decided that keeping duplicate settings in RegDB was a bad idea. This means that configured components have configuration information both inside and outside RegDB.

MOVING FROM MTS

Configured Components and MTS

The term *configured component* wasn't really formalized until the emergence of COM+. However, you should think of a component that's installed in an MTS package as a configured component. It's really the same thing. MTS components are like COM+ components in that they have declarative attributes.

The concept of a standard catalog manager is very valuable. Component registration is easier and more foolproof because administrators and developers are never responsible for writing to or reading from the Registry or RegDB. You don't have to be concerned about how registration data is physically stored in RegDB. Moreover, the Catalog Manager is a COM+ component that supports remote activation. An administrator can easily create a COM+ application and configure components on remote machines using scripts or the Component Services administrative tool. This means that COM+ provides a built-in scheme for network management.

This is important because an administrator can configure many production servers from a single desktop computer. It's also fairly easy to move a component from one computer to another when an application requires changes to its physical deployment. This is often the case when a company adds additional computers to an application to achieve higher levels of throughput, fault tolerance, or security. In the early days of COM, configuring servers was much tougher because it typically required visiting each computer involved.

Configured vs. nonconfigured components

In addition to configured components, you'll also encounter an older type of component that doesn't have COM+ attributes—the *nonconfigured component*. Nonconfigured components are not installed in COM+ applications. Instead, they're registered in a manner consistent with earlier versions of COM. For example, you should register an in-process DLL containing nonconfigured components by using REGSVR32.EXE. Note that nonconfigured components can't take advantage of COM+ services. They can, however, run in environments other than MTS and COM+.

If you're authoring component code for an application based on COM+, you'll generally produce configured components. This approach allows you to take advantage of various platform services. When you write your code, you're also likely to encounter nonconfigured components. For instance, ADO is a library made up of nonconfigured components. ADO objects can run in an application based on COM+, but they can also run in applications based on earlier versions of COM.

You should note that Visual Basic knows almost nothing about COM+ administration. When you build an ActiveX DLL, the Visual Basic IDE builds in traditional self-registration code and calls REGSVR32.EXE. In other words, after you build an ActiveX DLL on a Windows 2000 computer, your *MultiUse* classes are set up as nonconfigured components. You must explicitly add your classes to a COM+ application to turn them into configured components.

Creating and Deploying Configured Components

One of the main reasons that so many companies use Visual Basic to write middleware is that it's easy to create components for a COM+ application. All you need to do is create a simple ActiveX DLL with one or more *MultiUse* classes. You add a few public methods, implement them, and build the DLL. It's that easy.

Before we get started, I'd like to throw out a few recommendations for creating configured components:

■ Be careful when using the *New* operator.

■ Don't change the DLL's threading model to single-threaded.

■ Don't use public variables in .BAS modules.

■ Don't hold database connections open across method calls.

Now you know what not to do, but it'll take a little longer for me to tell you why. I'll attempt to explain the reasoning behind these recommendations over the next few chapters.

The easiest way to create a new COM+ application and add the components from a DLL is to use the Component Services administrative tool, which is shown in Figure 6-2. If you're not familiar with this tool, look at the platform SDK documentation in MSDN and search for *Creating and Configuring COM+ Applications*. This section walks you through the steps of COM+ administration. It can also get you started writing administrative scripts and applications with the COMAdmin Library.

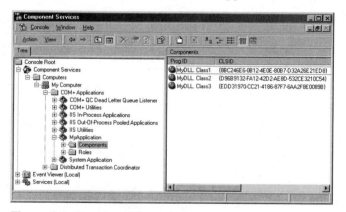

Figure 6-2 *You should learn how to create COM+ applications and configure components with the Component Services administrative tool.*

Also note that the *COM+ Administration Reference* in the platform SDK documentation briefly explains each configurable attribute. The topic titled *Applications Collection* lists each application attribute. The topic titled *Components Collection* lists each component attribute. I recommend that you take some time to become familiar with these resources.

When you create a new COM+ application with the Component Services administrative tool, a wizard asks you to set the application's *identity* property. In a production application, this property should be assigned a special user account dedicated to running middle-tier objects. However, while you're writing and testing your components, the default setting of Interactive User is the easiest and most common choice.

When you add a component to a COM+ application, it gets a new set of attributes. Each attribute is given a default value at creation time. You should review the component attributes list in MSDN to see what all the default values are. In certain cases, they won't be what you're looking for and you'll have to do a little extra work to set things up properly.

You can't predefine any of these configurable attributes (with the exception of transaction support) from within the Visual Basic IDE. You must add your components to a COM+ application and then configure them at deployment time. You can make these adjustments programmatically or by hand using the Component Services administrative tool. Future versions of Microsoft development tools and COM+ are likely to allow you to configure component attributes at design time, but they aren't quite that elegant yet.

In addition to properly configuring your component and application attributes, you must also write code that interacts with the COM+ runtime. To do this, you must reference the COM+ Services Type Library in your ActiveX DLL projects, as shown in Figure 6-3. This type library is crammed full of definitions for the components, interfaces, UDTs, and enumerations that are defined by COM+.

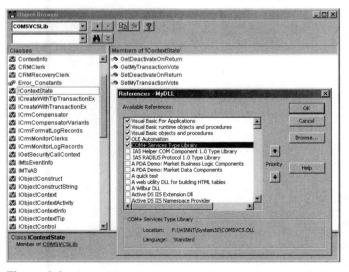

Figure 6-3 *The COM+ Services Type Library contains several interface and enumeration definitions that you'll use when you interact with the COM+ runtime.*

In most cases, the DLLs you create for the middle tier will contain configured components because configured components can take advantage of COM+ services. However, configured components also carry a dependency on the COM+ runtime. When a component is written against the COM+ Services Type Library and relies on configured attributes, it can't be run in other environments.

In some less common scenarios, you might want to create components that don't have a dependency on the COM+ runtime. This might be the case, for example, if you have a component that calculates sales tax or validates user input and you want to use the component on desktop computers running Windows 95 in addition to using it in a COM+ application. If you avoid dependencies on COM+ attributes and the COM+ Services Type Library, you can run your classes as either configured components or nonconfigured components. Just realize that nonconfigured components can't take advantage of most COM+ services.

You might be wondering: Is it me, or is all this computer theory getting a bit fuzzy? Let's look at an example of creating a component that makes use of a few configurable attribute settings. This example will show you how to put all this theory to work.

Using an object constructor string

Each configured component has a configurable object constructor string. You can use the constructor string for any purpose, but in this example I'll use it to hold an OLE-DB database connection string. The two important configurable attributes in this example are *ConstructionEnabled* and *ConstructorString*. Note that you can configure these two attributes in the Component Services administrative tool on the Activation tab of the component's Properties dialog box.

When the SCM creates an object from a configured component that has been assigned a declarative constructor string, the COM+ runtime calls into the object and provides an opportunity to load the string value from RegDB.

Let's walk through the details of how the COM+ runtime interacts with the new object. During object creation, the SCM looks to see whether the component's *ConstructionEnabled* attribute is turned on. If it is, the SCM performs a *QueryInterface* on the new object to obtain a reference to an interface named *IObjectConstruct*. As long as your component implements this interface, the COM+ runtime calls the *Construct* method and passes a reference to a constructor object. Examine the following code:

```
Implements COMSVCSLib.IObjectConstruct
Private MyConnectionString As String
```

```
Private Sub IObjectConstruct_Construct(ByVal pCtorObj As Object)
    Dim cs As IObjectConstructString
    Set cs = pCtorObj
    MyConnectionString = cs.ConstructString
End Sub
```

As you can see, this custom implementation of the *Construct* method loads the object constructor string into a module-level variable named *MyConnectionString*. Note that the reference passed by the *pCtorObj* parameter is cast to the *IObjectConstructString* interface. This interface exposes a single property, *ConstructString*, which makes it possible to obtain the configured value from RegDB and store it in a module-level variable. After the object has been created, the constructor string is available to any other method implementation in the class.

The most valuable aspect of using a constructor string is that the actual string value doesn't get compiled into the DLL. The administrator can easily reconfigure the connection string using the Component Services administrative tool. If the database's connection information changes, you don't have to modify any code. This example demonstrates how COM+ lets you do more work declaratively, which lessens the need for programming and recompiling. This example also shows you how to implement an interface that's defined in the COM+ Services Type Library.

Library Applications vs. Server Applications

Chapter 3 discussed how the SCM activates objects from an in-process server such as an ActiveX DLL. However, earlier versions of the SCM are unaware of the extended attributes made available by COM+. The COM+ team rewrote the SCM for Windows 2000 to examine the activation setting behind a configured component's application. This activation setting tells the SCM where and how to activate objects.

Every COM+ application must be configured as either a *library application* or a *server application*. The distinction between these two activation settings is quite simple. Take a look at Figure 6-4. Objects created from library application components are activated and run in the process of their creator. Objects created from server application components are activated in their own surrogate process. Furthermore, clients can activate objects from local server applications as well as from remote server applications running across the network. The ability to deploy a component in any one of these deployment scenarios without modifications or recompilation is known as *location transparency*.

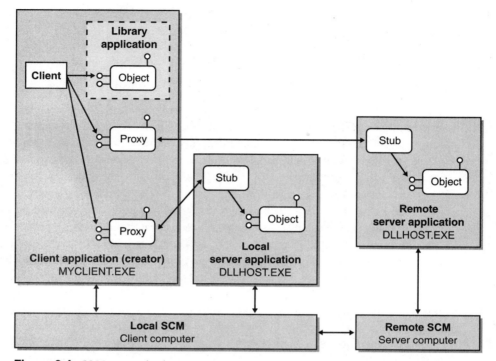

Figure 6-4 *COM+ provides location transparency. Components can be reconfigured to run in-process, locally, or across the network without requiring changes to code or recompilation.*

Out-of-Process Activation

Each server application runs in a separate instance of the surrogate container application DLLHOST.EXE. When a client creates an object from a component in a server application, the SCM locates the appropriate instance of DLLHOST.EXE. If the server application process isn't already running, the SCM launches it before creating the object. This scheme allows COM+ to start applications on an on-demand basis.

MOVING FROM MTS

The Name of the Container Application Has Changed

In MTS, the surrogate container application is MTX.EXE instead of DLLHOST.EXE.

MOVING FROM MTS

You Don't Need the Refresh Components Command Anymore

In both COM and COM+, the CLSID key for a component in an ActiveX DLL must have an *InProcServer32* subkey pointing to the server's path. When you build a Visual Basic ActiveX DLL, the compiler automatically builds in self-registration code. Once the DLL has been built, it is registered with the utility REGSVR32.EXE.

The SCM uses information in the CLSID key when it needs to create an object. However, the SCM in Windows NT 4 doesn't know how to properly create an MTS object using configured attributes. MTS requires CLSIDs to be configured differently from the way COM and COM+ do. The MTS team had to devise a way to steal activation requests from the SCM.

When you add a component to an MTS package, the Catalog Manager changes entries under the CLSID key to redirect activation requests to the MTS runtime. A component in an MTS library package requires an *InProcServer32* key pointing to MTXEX.DLL. A component in an MTS server package requires a *LocalServer32* key pointing to the container application MTX.EXE.

This gets pretty confusing. With Windows NT 4, you can register a CLSID in three different ways: the original COM way and two MTS ways. To make matters worse, the self-registration code built into a Visual Basic DLL knows only the COM way to register a CLSID. If you call REGSVR32.EXE on a Visual Basic DLL after it's been installed in an MTS package, the CLSID entries get messed up.

Many programmers have gotten into trouble when building and testing DLLs on an MTS machine because Visual Basic always calls REGSVR32.EXE at the successful completion of every build. There's nothing you can do to suppress this behavior in the Visual Basic IDE. Things don't work correctly when you try to test an MTS component that's been reconfigured as a standard COM component.

To solve the problem, MTS offers a Refresh Components command. When you run this command on an MTS package, the MTS Catalog Manager simply looks through the Registry and makes sure that each CLSID is configured in the proper MTS way instead of the COM way. There's also a Visual Basic add-on that automatically calls upon the MTS Catalog Manager to refresh MTS components whenever the associated ActiveX DLL server is rebuilt.

(continued)

> In COM+, the CLSIDs from an ActiveX DLL are always registered in a manner consistent with the original version of COM. There's always an *InProcServer32* key that holds the path to your DLL. This is true for both configured and nonconfigured components. Configured components differ from nonconfigured components only in that they have additional information about their attributes and activation requirements in RegDB. The good news in COM+ is that you don't have to worry about using the Refresh Components command, as you did in MTS.

Once the SCM locates the process of the target server application, it forwards the request for the new object. However, as you'll remember from Chapter 3, the code that actually creates objects lives in the class factories in your DLLs. When a server application is launched, the COM+ runtime loads all its associated DLLs in order to register each class factory. Once the class factory for the requested CLSID has been loaded, the server application can successfully create the object.

The server application uses a class factory to create the object, and it returns an object reference to the SCM. The reference is then forwarded to the client. After a successful out-of-process activation, the client is really holding on to a proxy that wraps an RPC-based connection to the object.

By default, the process for a server application remains loaded in memory for three minutes after the last object has been released. However, you can configure this time interval on the Advanced tab of a server application's Properties dialog box in the Component Services administrative tool. (You can also configure a server application to run indefinitely or to shut down immediately after the last object has been released.)

In addition to letting you control when a process is shut down, COM+ also supports prelaunching a server application. Prelaunching an application provides an optimization because the first client doesn't have to wait while the server process is launched. As with most other administrative chores, you can prelaunch a server application manually or programmatically.

Remote Activation

Activating an object in a remote server application is more complex than in-process or local activation because it requires the participation and coordination of the SCM on two different computers. When the client-side SCM determines that a client wants to activate an object from a component that lives at a different network address, it forwards the activation request to the SCM on the server computer. The server-side SCM is responsible for creating the requested object and returning a reference.

When the server-side SCM receives an activation request from a client across the network, it performs a standard out-of-process activation from the server application that holds the requested CLSID. After all, from the perspective of the server computer, the activation is performed locally. Once the object has been created, a reference is passed from the server application to the server-side SCM, then to the client-side SCM, and finally back to the client. As with a local out-of-process activation, the client is connected to the object across a proxy/stub pair.

Note that client computers don't have to be running Windows 2000. They require only a version of Windows that has Distributed COM (DCOM). Computers running Windows NT 4 and Windows 98 are already DCOM-compliant. If you want to run client applications on computers running Windows 95, you must install the required DCOM software by downloading the appropriate installation files from Microsoft's Web site (*www.microsoft.com/com/resources/downloads.asp*).

As you learned in Chapter 3, software created with Visual Basic relies on the universal marshaler to build proxies and stubs. The universal marshaler must create a proxy on the client computer by inspecting the appropriate interface definition in a type library. This means that a copy of the type library must be copied to and registered on every client computer. A client computer must also have information about IIDs, CLSIDs, and ProgIDs.

You can configure any client-side computer running a DCOM-enabled version of Windows to redirect activation to a remote computer on a CLSID-by-CLSID basis. The SCM redirects an activation request when it determines that a CLSID has an associated AppID with a valid network address.

You'll probably never be required to add these client-side Registry entries by hand, but here's how you'd do it. First, add an *AppID* key with a *RemoteServerName* named value, as shown in Figure 6-5. Second, set the *RemoteServerName* value to an IP address, a Domain Name System (DNS) address, or a NETBIOS name. Finally, add an *AppID* named value to the Registry key for each CLSID to associate it with the remote server name. When everything is set up correctly, the client-side SCM redirects every activation request for any of the CLSIDs to the remote server computer. That is how things worked with DCOM prior to Windows 2000. Windows 2000 stores the AppID in the same way (in the Registry), but it stores CLSID and ProgID information in RegDB instead of in the Registry.

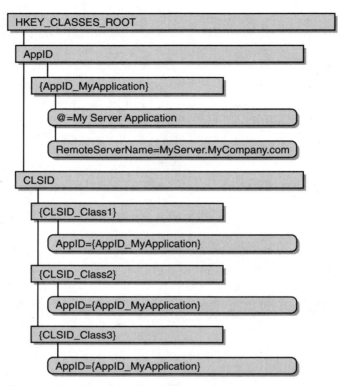

Figure 6-5 *A CLSID configured for remote activation must have an AppID with a valid* RemoteServerName *value. The CLSID should not have an* InProcServer *subkey or a* LocalServer32 *subkey.*

If you configure a CLSID for remote activation using an *AppID*, it's important that the CLSID key not have an *InProcServer32* or a *LocalServer32* subkey. The client-side SCM redirects activation to a remote computer only if both the *InProcServer32* and *LocalServer32* values are absent. Some programmers and users have gotten in trouble by registering the DLL on the client machine and unknowingly adding the *InProcServer32* subkey. In this case, the SCM performs a local in-process activation instead of calling across the network to create the object.

You should keep one more thing in mind about remote activation. You don't have to rely on the *RemoteServerName* value for selecting a target server. Instead, you can select the address of a remote computer programmatically using Visual Basic's *CreateObject* function. Visual Basic 6 added a second optional parameter to *CreateObject* that accepts the name of a remote server. This parameter always overrides the *RemoteServerName* value in the Registry. As in the case of the *RemoteServerName* value, the parameter can be an IP address, a DNS address, or a NETBIOS name.

Application Proxies

A few paragraphs back, I said that you'll probably never have to add client-side configuration information by hand because COM+ allows you to create a client-side setup program that automatically copies type libraries and writes all the required configuration information. This client-side setup program is known as an *application proxy*.

You can build an application proxy by running the Export command from the Component Services administrative tool. When you choose the Export command to create an application proxy, COM+ generates an .MSI file (a Windows Installer file). Note that the setup program runs differently on Windows 2000 computers than it does on computers running other DCOM-enabled version of Windows. On Windows 2000 computers, it writes entries for the CLSID and ProgID to RegDB and it writes type library and IID entries to the Registry. RegDB doesn't exist on earlier versions of Windows, so the setup program adds all entries to the Registry.

You'll notice a new application in the COM+ Applications folder in the Component Services administrative tool after an application proxy has been installed on a Windows 2000 computer. Every Windows 2000 computer has an Applications collection that contains application proxies in addition to server applications and library applications. The difference is that an application proxy holds the CLSIDs for a set of components that live on another machine.

You should note several more important issues concerning application proxies. First, you can explicitly set the remote server name that gets built into the application proxy. If you don't explicitly set this value, COM+ simply uses the computer on which the application proxy is built. If you want the application proxy to point to a different computer, you should change the remote server name using the Component Services administrative tool before building the application proxy. You can adjust the remote server name value on the Options tab of the My Computer Properties dialog box.

A second issue is that your client computers might require an updated version of the Windows Installer in order to install an application proxy. Windows NT, Windows 98, and Windows 95 all require updated versions. If you receive an error while installing an application proxy, you can find the required update in the Platform SDK for Windows 2000. Once you install the most recent version of the Windows Installer, the application proxy should be installed without any problems.

The third issue is that you should be sure that all the relevant type libraries have been added to the server application before the application proxy is built. Be sure to add components to a server application using the Install command rather than the Import command. The Install command adds the type libraries embedded in your ActiveX DLLs, while the Import command doesn't. If you've built any custom type libraries using IDL and the MIDL compiler, you should also add them to the server application before building the application proxy. This can be a bit tricky the first time you do it because the Component Services administrative tool only allows you to install a .TLB file in a server application at the same time that you install components from a DLL.

The fourth and final issue has to do with a bug that prevents you from building application proxies in certain situations. The client computers need type libraries but they don't need the DLLs that hold your configured components. When you select the Remote Server Files option in an ActiveX DLL project, the Visual Basic IDE builds a stand-alone .TLB file in addition to the type library that it builds into the DLL. You can add a stand-alone TLB file to a server application when you add the components from the DLL. The motivation for doing this is to prevent the application proxy from copying the entire DLL to each client computer.

However, there's a problem. If you add the .TLB file to a server application in addition to the DLL, COM+ can't build the application proxy because of an incompatibility between COM+ and Visual Basic–generated type libraries. This bug can be frustrating because things work correctly under MTS but they don't under COM+. I have no information about when this bug will be addressed.

What are the implications of this bug? If you rely on application proxies to set up client-side computers, you must copy all your DLLs to the client computers. This can present a security hole if your DLL contains sensitive passwords. A user could bypass your security scheme by installing the DLL in a local server application and executing a method.

One workaround is to move all your passwords out of your compiled DLLs and into declarative constructor strings. A second workaround is to avoid using COM+ application proxies when you configure client computers. Instead, you can copy type libraries and write all the required configuration information to client computers using another technique. Visual Basic provides an alternative technique for setting up client computers using .VBR files and the CLIREG32.EXE utility.

Distributed Garbage Collection

What happens if a client application crashes while holding an outstanding reference to an object in a remote server application? The object must have a way to determine that its client application has expired. You saw in Chapter 4 that a client can discover when an object has died by inspecting HRESULTs. However, an object needs a little more assistance to determine whether the client has passed away.

COM provides an infrastructure for distributed garbage collection that allows the server-side computer to determine when a client with an outstanding object reference has died. When the server-side computer discovers that a client has died, it informs the object by calling *Release*. This means that a remote object is automatically released from memory if its client crashes. The need for garbage collection is extremely important in distributed applications that are meant to stay running for long periods of time.

COM's mechanism for distributed garbage collection is based on the client machine pinging the server machine with a notification that says, "I'm still alive." The client pings the server every two minutes. If the server doesn't hear from the client for six minutes (three missed pings), the server informs the object that the client has died.

The ping algorithm has been optimized to avoid excessive network traffic. Pings aren't sent for individual interface references or for individual objects. Instead, the client computer transmits a single machinewide ping to the server with information about every connection between the two machines. Note that each ping doesn't transmit all the information about every outstanding interface reference. Instead, it transmits the information about what has changed since the last ping. This "delta" algorithm significantly reduces what needs to be transmitted across the network.

Partitioning a Distributed Application

You should notice that each server application is associated with exactly one process per computer. Objects created from components in the same server application run in the same process and can therefore share process-specific resources. Objects created from different server applications run in separate processes and can't share process-specific resources.

So, how do you decide between using server applications and library applications? And if you decide to use server applications, how many should you create? Should you add five components to the same server application or add each component to its own server application? You can choose from several approaches, each of which comes with trade-offs in performance, fault tolerance, and security.

The main advantage to using a library application is that it provides better performance because it eliminates or decreases the need for cross-process calls. However, library applications do not support remote activation. The client application must be running on the local computer in order to activate an object from a library application.

Each server application adds another process and therefore another level of fault tolerance. You can think of each server application as its own fault-isolation domain. An object that crashes can take down all the objects in the same server application. However, a crash in one process doesn't necessarily affect objects running in other processes.

To provide an additional level of fault tolerance, each COM+ process has a *failfast policy*. If the COM+ runtime detects that something unusually bad has happened when it's running a method implementation, it assumes that the entire process has become corrupt. This triggers COM+ to terminate the entire process. The failfast policy is also triggered whenever a component raises a Win32 error or a C++

exception. However, you can't trigger the failfast policy by raising a Visual Basic error with *Err.Raise*. Visual Basic errors (which, as you know, are really COM exceptions) propagate to the caller without any problem. Note that COM+ writes an error message to the Windows event log whenever it terminates a process with the failfast policy.

While you can add all your components to a single server application, you also have the option of spreading out your components across several server applications. The trade-off is that calls across process boundaries take significantly longer than in-process calls. If you decide to use multiple server applications spread out across multiple computers, it's possible to distribute the processing load across more processors. The obvious trade-off to this approach is that calls across computer boundaries are even more expensive than local cross-process calls.

So, when would you want to use a library application? Two scenarios are common. In the first scenario, you have a utility component that you want to share between two or more server applications. If you add the utility component to a library application, an object running in any server application can create an in-process object from the utility component. You can thus share a component across several server applications while eliminating expensive cross-process calls.

In the second scenario, you use a library application to create objects in a hosting application other than DLLHOST.EXE. For example, let's say you're deploying a component for use in a Web application and the client is an ASP page running in the IIS Web server process INETINFO.EXE. If you configure the component in a library application, your objects will be created in the Web server process instead of in an instance of DLLHOST.EXE, as shown in Figure 6-6. You'll experience better performance because you eliminated the need for cross-process calls. However, fault tolerance won't be as good as it could be. Your component can potentially crash the entire Web server process.

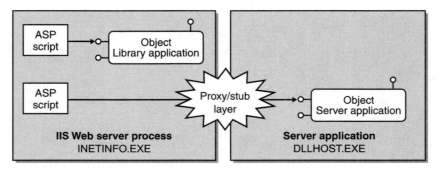

Figure 6-6 *In a Web application based on ASP pages, library applications generally offer better performance because they eliminate the need for cross-process calls. Server applications provide better fault tolerance as well as the ability to run components on a separate computer.*

UNDERSTANDING CONTEXTS

This section is critical to your understanding of how configured components work. Attribute-based programming relies on a mechanism known as *interception*. When a client creates an object from a component that's been configured in a COM+ application, the underlying runtime inserts an interception layer between them. This layer represents a hook that allows the COM+ runtime to perform system-supplied preprocessing and post-processing on a per-method-call basis. The system steals away control right before and right after an object executes its method implementation.

The COM+ interception layer is set up based on the notion of *contexts*. A context can be loosely defined as a set of objects running in a process. In actuality, processes are subdivided into apartments and apartments are subdivided into contexts. (Apartments are discussed in the next chapter.) The COM+ runtime performs interception whenever a call crosses over a context boundary.

Every object created in a COM+ application is created within the scope of a specific context, as shown in Figure 6-7. COM+ doesn't intercept calls when a caller and an object live in the same context. However, COM+ does intercept calls that go across contexts. The term *context switch* refers to system-supplied code that's run automatically whenever a call crosses over a context boundary.

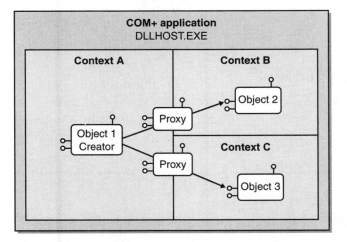

Figure 6-7 *The COM+ runtime sets up an interception scheme based on the notion of contexts. A system-provided proxy performs a context switch whenever a call crosses over a context boundary.*

Thread-Switching Proxies vs. Lightweight Proxies

When one object creates another object in a separate process, by definition the two objects live in different contexts. Therefore, the COM+ runtime builds the appropriate interception code into the proxy/stub layer. Note that this Windows 2000 version of a proxy/stub layer is more sophisticated than the one I described at the end of Chapter 3. Now the proxy/stub pair has two responsibilities. First, it must remote a method call across process and host boundaries by performing a thread switch and marshaling parameters. Second, it must perform the required context switch. This represents a big change from versions of Windows before Windows 2000, in which the proxy/stub layer didn't know anything about contexts or interception.

Windows 2000 introduces a new type of proxy to deal with the situation in which the caller and the object run in different contexts but run in the same process on the same thread. As you can see in Figure 6-6 (shown earlier), there is no need for a proxy/stub pair, only a simple *lightweight proxy*. This proxy performs a context switch but doesn't need to perform a thread switch. As in the case of the thread-switching proxy, the COM+ runtime builds a lightweight proxy by inspecting an interface definition in a type library at runtime.

MOVING FROM MTS

Context Wrappers Have Gone Away

The interception layer in MTS is set up through an invisible system-supplied object called a *context wrapper*. Like context-aware proxies in COM+, the MTS context wrapper conducts preprocessing and post-processing on each method call. However, in MTS a single context wrapper is created when a client activates a new object. This means that there's only one context wrapper per MTS object. In COM+, an object can have many associated context-aware proxies. The new interception scheme in Windows 2000 is more flexible because the COM+ runtime continues to create context-aware proxies for an object on an as-needed basis.

When Are Contexts Created?

Contexts are typically created by the SCM when a client activates a new object by calling the COM library function *CoCreateInstance*. As you know from earlier chapters, the Visual Basic runtime calls *CoCreateInstance* when a client application creates an object using the *CreateObject* function or the *New* operator. (There's a gotcha with the *New* operator that I'll discuss in a moment.) However, you should note that the SCM doesn't always create a new context when you create an object. Sometimes it does and sometimes it doesn't.

Let's cover the basic rules. Every object activated in a COM+ application is created within a valid context. The SCM has three different ways to handle an activation request:

■ Create the new object in the context of its creator.

■ Create the new object in a newly created context.

■ Create the new object in the default context of a different apartment.

It turns out that the first two approaches are much more common than the third, so let's look at them first. At activation time, the SCM must decide whether a new object needs its own set of contextual information to describe its COM+ attributes. When COM+ creates a context, it creates a private object known as the object context, which it uses to store context-specific information for all objects that belong to that context. If a new object needs its own contextual information, COM+ creates a new context for it. If a new object doesn't need its own contextual information, COM+ adds it to the context of its creator.

In most cases, an object created from a nonconfigured component is created in the context of its creator, while an object created from a configured component gets its own new context. Figure 6-8 shows what happens when a COM+ object creates an ADO object such as a connection or a recordset. Like any other object created from a nonconfigured component, an ADO object doesn't need its own context because it doesn't have any declarative attributes.

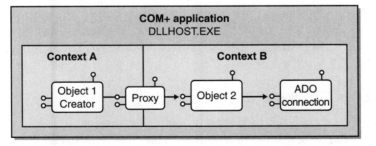

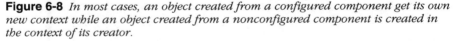

Figure 6-8 *In most cases, an object created from a configured component get its own new context while an object created from a nonconfigured component is created in the context of its creator.*

In almost every situation, an object created from a configured component needs its own context because the COM+ runtime needs to know about quite a few things in order to run the interception code correctly and provide reliable system services. The object context holds valuable information such as an object's association with a specific activity and a specific transaction.

MOVING FROM MTS

Calls to *CreateInstance* Are No Longer Needed

One of the most significant programming changes you'll experience as you move from MTS to COM+ is that you don't need to call the *CreateInstance* method of the *ObjectContext* interface anymore. In MTS, you must call *CreateInstance* to send an object activation request to the MTS runtime instead of to the SCM.

In COM+, the SCM is context-aware. This means that in contrast to the SCM in Windows NT 4, the SCM built into Windows 2000 knows how to activate an object in an appropriate context. Calls to *CreateObject* are always handled correctly. Calls to *CreateInstance* are still supported, but only for backward compatibility. A call to *CreateInstance* does the same things as a call to *CreateObject*.

Of the three ways that the SCM can handle an activation request, the last is by far the least common. The SCM creates a new object in the default context of a different apartment only when the creator and the object being created have incompatible threading models and thus can't run on the same thread. An example of this is when an apartment-threaded object creates an object from a nonconfigured component that's free-threaded. The new object can't run in the context of its creator because it's the wrong apartment type. (A context must live in one specific apartment.) However, COM+ doesn't need to create a new context for the object because it doesn't carry any COM+ attributes. In such situations, the COM+ runtime creates the new object in the *default context* of another apartment. If you're using only apartment-threaded components such as the ones created with Visual Basic, you don't have to worry about this third scenario.

Watch Out for the *New* Operator

You have to be careful not to get into trouble when you write code in one configured component that calls *New* on another configured component. When you use the *New* operator, you must consider two scenarios. In the first scenario, the creator component and the component used to create the new object live in separate DLLs. In this case, a call to *New* is sent down to the SCM just like a call to *CreateObject*. This allows the SCM to create the new object in the proper fashion. In the second scenario, the creator component and the component from which the new object is being created are compiled into the same DLL. The problem here is fairly subtle, but it can lead to lots of frustration when you're trying to determine why your code isn't working correctly.

When a Visual Basic object calls *New* on a class name that's compiled into the same DLL, the Visual Basic runtime creates and binds the object on its own without involving the SCM. The new object isn't properly created by the SCM and the COM+ runtime doesn't even know it exists. COM+ doesn't have the opportunity to set up the interception scheme correctly. The bottom line is that if you call *New* at the wrong time, your code can exhibit strange and mysterious behavior.

As it turns out, sometimes you can use the *New* operator in a method of a COM+ component. You can always use *New* to create objects from components that are external to the creator's DLL. For example, you can use *New* whenever you create a new ADO object.

Contexts and Object References

The COM+ rules concerning object references are fairly straightforward. A client is directly bound to an object when they both live in the same context. A client must communicate with an object through a system-provided proxy if it lives in a different context. So, when and how are these proxies created? The answer is refreshing: The COM+ runtime creates proxies transparently whenever they're needed.

As a COM+ programmer, you'll commonly do two things that result in the transparent creation of a context-aware proxy: You'll activate new objects from a configured component with the *CreateObject* function, and you'll pass object references in standard method calls using parameters and return values.

When you create an object from a configured component, the COM+ runtime will more than likely create a new context. However, the COM+ runtime doesn't return a direct reference back to the creator. COM+ determines that the object and creator live in different contexts, so it creates a context-aware proxy and returns that to the creator instead. This means that all calls from the creator to the object go through the proxy. The proxy performs the required context switch at runtime whenever control passes back and forth between these two contexts.

As you've seen, COM+ automatically creates a proxy when an object is created in a different context from its creator. The second common case in which COM+ creates a proxy is when an object reference is passed across context boundaries in a standard method call. Because the COM+ runtime intercepts calls as they travel across context boundaries, it can also determine when the recipient of an object reference needs a new proxy.

Let me present an example to illustrate how things work. Look at Figure 6-9. Assume that *Object1* creates *Object2* by calling the *CreateObject* function. *Object1* is in *Context A* while *Object2* is in *Context B*. Now assume that *Object1* calls the following method on *Object2*:

```
Function CreateObject3() As Class3
    Dim obj As Class3
    Set obj = CreateObject("MyDll.Class3")
    Set CreateObject3 = obj
End Function
```

When *Object2* creates *Object3*, it's passed a reference to a proxy that knows how to perform a context switch between *Context B* and *Context C*. You should note that *Object1* can't use this proxy because it lives in *Context A*. *Object1* needs a different proxy that can perform the proper context switch between *Context A* and *Context C*. However, things work out fine. When the call to *CreateObject3* returns from *Context B* back to *Context A*, the COM+ runtime automatically builds a new proxy for *Object3* that can be used in *Context A*.

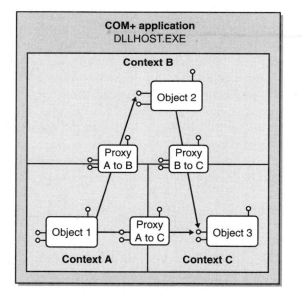

Figure 6-9 *Object references are always context-relative. You can think of a context-aware proxy as an adapter between two specific contexts.*

This example demonstrates an important point about the COM+ programming model: *All object references are context-relative.* If you follow the rules, things are pretty easy. When you need to share an object reference between two or more objects, you should design methods to pass references between them. However, you still have to watch out. You can get into trouble if you try to share object references using other techniques. For instance, it's a bad idea to place an object reference in a public variable in a .BAS module.

Let's revisit our example. What happens if *Object2* creates *Object3* and stores the returned reference in a .BAS module variable? You should see that the reference can be legally used only by code running in *Context B*.

If *Object1* accesses the .BAS module variable and acquires the reference, things don't work correctly. *Object1* needs a proxy that knows how to perform the context switch between *Context A* and *Context C*. However, the reference held by the .BAS module variable points to a proxy that was built to perform the context switch between *Context B* and *Context C*. You should see that this style of programming breaks the interception scheme set up by COM+. Likewise, it's a bad idea to store object references with other shared memory mechanisms using the Shared Property Manager. (You'll see how to use the Shared Property Manager in the next chapter; for now, just remember that you'll use it to store raw data as opposed to object references.)

MOVING FROM MTS

Calls to *SafeRef* Are No Longer Needed

In MTS, any object with an associated context wrapper must always call *SafeRef* when passing some other entity a reference to itself. A call to *SafeRef* passes a reference to the context wrapper as opposed to a raw reference to the object itself. If you don't call *SafeRef* at the appropriate times, you can defeat the MTS interception scheme.

The way that COM+ sets up the interception scheme is more transparent and more adaptable. There's no need to call *SafeRef*. As long as you follow the rules outlined in this chapter, the COM+ runtime builds context-aware proxies whenever they're needed.

THE COM+ PROGRAMMING MODEL

When you create configured components, you should reference the COM+ Services Type Library in your ActiveX DLL project. This type library defines many of the interfaces that you'll use when you interact with the COM+ runtime. Table 6-1 lists the context-related interfaces that Visual Basic programmers use most commonly.

The COM+ programming model differentiates between two types of context: *object context* and *call context*. Object context is created when the SCM creates a new context, and it doesn't generally change across method calls. A call context contains call-specific information and flows across contexts as control is passed from one method to the next.

Table 6-1 CORE COM+ INTERFACES USED BY VISUAL BASIC PROGRAMMERS

Interface	Type	Uses	Available in MTS?
ObjectContext	Object context and call context	Transaction control; Programmatic security; Obtaining references to ASP objects such as *Request*, *Response*, and *Application*	Yes
ContextInfo	Object context	Obtaining contextual information about the current context, activity, and transaction	No
IContextState	Object context	Transaction control	No
SecurityCallContext	Call context	Programmatic security	No

Programming Against the Object Context

Each context gets an object context, which is a system-provided COM object that holds context-related information. (See Figure 6-10.) The object context also exposes methods that allow you to interact with the COM+ runtime. Some of these methods allow your objects to query the COM+ runtime for information, and others allow you to tell the COM+ runtime to do things for you.

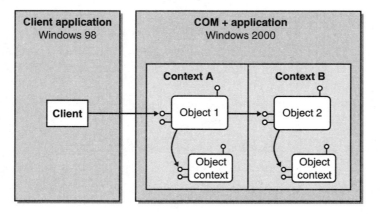

Figure 6-10 *An object can retrieve a reference to its object context by calling* GetObjectContext.

Let's look at a quick example. I'll cover writing COM+ transactions in depth in a later chapter; for now, I'll show a simple example of an object that has finished its work and wants to commit the current transaction. Examine the following code:

```
Dim oc As COMSVCSLib.ObjectContext
Set oc = GetObjectContext
oc.SetComplete
```

A call to *GetObjectContext* allows an object to retrieve a reference to its object context. In this example, the object uses its object context to tell the COM+ runtime that it has completed its work and is voting for the transaction to be committed. Note that you don't have to create an explicit *ObjectContext* reference. Here's a shorthand version of the previous code that does the same thing:

```
GetObjectContext.SetComplete
```

A call to *GetObjectContext* is performed very quickly (because the COM+ runtime stores a reference to the object context in a quickly accessible place known as *thread local storage*). In general, you won't optimize your code by attempting to minimize the number of calls to *GetObjectContext*. For example, it doesn't really speed things up when you call *GetObjectContext* and store the returned reference in a module-level variable. This approach makes your component code more complex without providing any noticeable performance improvements.

Note that an object should never access an object context from a foreign context. In Figure 6-10, for example, *Object2* should never acquire a reference to the object context for *Context A*. This means that you should never pass a reference to an object context in a method. The only context an object should ever use is the one that it acquires with a call to *GetObjectContext*.

The MTS programming model also includes the *ObjectContext* interface. In both MTS and COM+, the *ObjectContext* interface deals with object context as well as call context. When the architects redesigned things for COM+, they decided to add a few new interfaces that were specific to either object context or call context.

The *ContextInfo* interface is specific to the object context. This interface allows you to retrieve contextual information (primarily the identifying GUIDs) for the current context, activity, and transaction. You can get a reference to a system-provided object that implements the *ContextInfo* interface through the ObjectContext interface. Here's an example of using the *ContextInfo* interface to retrieve the GUID that identifies the current context:

```
Dim ci As COMSVCSLib.ContextInfo
Dim MyContextID As String
Set ci = GetObjectContext.ContextInfo
MyContextID = ci.GetContextId
```

As you can see, the object that implements *ContextInfo* is contained in the object context. This means that there are two separate objects. In COM-speak, you can say that there are two separate identities.

In addition to exposing a subobject that implements *ContextInfo*, the object context in COM+ also implements interfaces other than *ObjectContext*. Some of these other interfaces are accessible only through C++, but one that is accessible through Visual Basic is *IContextState*.

The *IContextState* interface, like *ContextInfo*, is specific to the object context. You use this interface to gain control over your transactions. You might notice that this interface exposes some functionality that's duplicated in the *ObjectContext* interface. I'll wait until Chapter 8 to get into the details. For now, I'll just show a quick example of acquiring and using an *IContextState* reference:

```
Dim cs As COMSVCSLib.IContextState
Set cs = GetObjectContext
cs.SetMyTransactionVote TxCommit
```

You acquire the reference by calling *GetObjectContext* and casting the return value to the type *IContextState*. Moreover, once you call *GetObjectContext*, you can cast back and forth between the *ObjectContext* interface and the *IContextState* interface. You can do this because they represent two interfaces implemented by a single COM identity.

```
Dim oc As ObjectContext, cs As IContextState
Set oc = GetObjectContext
Set cs = oc
```

In this example, the second line acquires an *ObjectContext* connection to the object context. The next line results in a call to *QueryInterface* to obtain a second reference to the same object. When you understand why this style of casting works the way it does, you'll be glad that you've invested so much time and energy into learning about interface-based programming.

Understanding Call Context

While the object context resides in a single place, the call context travels along with the flow of a chain of method calls. Let's look at an example to get a better understanding of the important concepts. Let's say you've created a form-based client application that's running on a Windows 98 computer. Assume that this client application creates an object in a COM+ server application on a Windows 2000 server and that this object creates a few more objects (some of which are on another Windows 2000 server), as shown in Figure 6-11. When the client application makes a method call that flows across these objects, a logical call chain extends across three different computers. However, as control passes across context, process, and computer boundaries, lots of contextual information flows along with it.

This passing of contextual information along with method calls is made possible through the notion of *causality*, which was part of COM before MTS and COM+. A causality can be defined as a chain of Object RPC (ORPC) method calls. When the client on the Windows 98 computer invokes a method, the COM runtime creates a new causality and generates a GUID (known as a *causality ID*) to identify it before making the initial outbound call. As the call is transmitted across the wire, you already know that the method's parameter values are sent along with it. However, you should see that the causality ID and other security-related information are automatically propagated as well. The causality remains alive while the flow of control moves from *Object1* to *Object2* to *Object3* and then all the way back to the client. It seems as if one big call stack extends across the network.

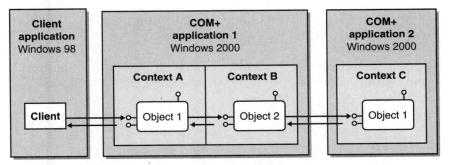

Figure 6-11 *As a chain of method calls flows across a set of objects, it represents a causality that carries related information known as the call context. In this scenario, a new causality is created each time the client calls a method.*

The primary reason for caring about call context relates to security. One interface deals specifically with the call context: *SecurityCallContext*. This interface allows an object to determine whether COM+ security has been turned on and who the caller is. Here's an example of using this interface:

```
Dim scc As COMSVCSLib.SecurityCallContext
Dim IsMyAppSecure As Boolean
Set scc = GetSecurityCallContext
IsMyAppSecure = scc.IsSecurityEnabled()
```

You might notice that a few methods are available in both the *SecurityCallContext* interface and the *ObjectContext* interface. This is due to the fact that MTS was designed to provide one-stop shopping through the *ObjectContext* interface. You can use either interface, but the *SecurityCallContext* interface includes functionality that isn't available in the *ObjectContext* interface. For this reason, I recommend being consistent and using the *SecurityCallContext* interface for all your programmatic security.

TESTING AND DEBUGGING COM+ COMPONENTS

Once you compile a component into an ActiveX DLL, you can easily install it into a COM+ server application using the Component Services administrative tool. One easy way to test your component code is to create a simple form-based application with Visual Basic that will serve as a test harness for your COM+ objects. You can create this test harness by creating a new Standard EXE project and including the reference to your ActiveX DLL. When you run this test client, any objects created from a configured component are loaded by the COM+ runtime into a private instance of DLLHOST.EXE.

You can run the test client from a compiled EXE or in the Visual Basic IDE. In either case, you should be able to look at the COM+ Services administrative tool and verify that your objects are being created inside your server application.

You typically end up constantly rebuilding your DLLs as you modify and test your code in the COM+ runtime environment. By default, however, a server application is configured to stay loaded in memory for three minutes after all of its objects have been released. If you try to rebuild the DLL while the server application is still loaded, you'll receive a "Permission denied" error. You can get around this problem by right-clicking on the server application in the Component Services administrative tool and choosing the Shut Down command. Configuring the server application to shut down immediately when all objects have been released is also a good idea during development.

You must also close the test client project before you can rebuild the DLL because the test client project holds a reference to the type library bundled into the DLL. Once you close the client project that references the DLL and make sure that the server application isn't running, you should be able to rebuild the DLL without any problems.

Of course, some programmers have found that they can take the "Permission denied" rebuilding problem a step further. If you manage to load the DLL into the Web server process, INETINFO.EXE, you must shut down INETINFO.EXE before you can rebuild the DLL. When you build components for a Web application, don't test them while they're registered as nonconfigured components or are configured to run in a library application. If you configured your component in a server application, your DLL won't be loaded into INETINFO.EXE and rebuilding during testing shouldn't be a problem.

Running Configured Components in the Visual Basic Debugger

The debugger in Visual Basic 6 includes support for debugging components in a simulated version of the COM+ runtime environment. This support was originally added for MTS development, but it works in a similar fashion on both platforms. As you'll see, this debugging strategy is definitely the fastest and easiest one to use. However, this technique has a few shortcomings in simulating the actual COM+ runtime environment, so I'll also show you a few other techniques.

The Visual Basic debugger simulates the COM+ runtime environment by creating objects from components in library applications. This allows Visual Basic to load and run objects in its debugger (VB6.EXE). If your components have already been added to a library application, everything is already set up as it should be. If your components have been added to a COM+ server application, starting the Visual Basic debugger changes it into a library application. If your components haven't been added to a COM+ application, the Visual Basic IDE creates a hidden library application for them on the fly.

All three cases work in the same way. When you run an ActiveX DLL project that's been configured properly, the COM+ runtime is loaded into the process of the Visual Basic debugger along with your component code. The important thing is that you can configure an application and all of its components using the Component Services administrative tool before you start debugging. You definitely want all of your attributes set correctly before you start testing and debugging your code. This means that you should always add and configure your components in a COM+ application before you start debugging.

Here's how to set things up. In Visual Basic 6, each *MultiUse* class module in an ActiveX DLL project has an *MTSTransactionMode* property setting. If you set this property to a value other than *NotAnMTSObject*, you can debug your COM+ components in the Visual Basic IDE. For example, you can set the *MTSTransactionMode* property to *NoTransactions* for your class modules and Visual Basic will run your objects under the control of the COM+ runtime.

The Visual Basic team could have made things less confusing by providing two class-level properties instead of one. For example, if a *MultiUse* class had a *COM+Debugging* property that could be set to *True* or *False* in addition to the setting for the transaction mode, it would be easier to understand what's going on. However, you should note that the *MTSTransactionMode* property controls both debugging and transaction support. It's confusing because these two things aren't really related.

Earlier in the chapter, I mentioned that it is incorrect to call *New* on a class that's compiled into the same DLL. Now I'd like to point out that the *New* operator causes even more frustrating problems when you're trying to debug configured components inside the Visual Basic IDE. Inside the Visual Basic debugger, the rules for when to avoid the *New* operator are even more strict. You must avoid the *New* operator when the client and the class being used to create the new object are inside the same project group. In other words, a call to *New* and the class you're calling *New* on can't be running inside the same session of the Visual Basic debugger. Let me provide a little background to illustrate why this is such a problem.

Let's say you have a client application project and an ActiveX DLL project in the same project group. Your motivation for adding them to the same project group is to debug both projects in a single session of the Visual Basic IDE. When the client application calls *New* on a class in the DLL project that you're trying to debug as a configured component, the Visual Basic debugger creates the new object without the assistance of the SCM. The result is that the new object doesn't get created by the COM+ runtime in a valid context.

This situation has unfortunate side effects that are pretty easy to recognize. All of your calls to *GetObjectContext* and *GetSecurityCallContext* will return a null reference, which typically results in a series of run-time errors. If you repeatedly see Error 91 ("Object variable or With block variable not set"), the cause is likely that your code is trying to invoke methods using these null references.

What it comes down to is that you can't run your test client project and an ActiveX DLL in the same project group if the client application is using the *New* operator. It's just as bad if you try to debug two ActiveX DLL projects in the same project group if code in one DLL is using the *New* operator to create objects from a class in the other DLL. If you want to be sure that the SCM properly creates your objects in a valid context, you must use the *CreateObject* function instead of the *New* operator.

As you've seen throughout the chapter, there are many reasons to prefer the *CreateObject* function over the *New* operator in COM+ development. Here's yet another. Many COM+ programmers use *CreateObject* exclusively so they don't have to worry about problems caused by the *New* operator.

Now that I've talked about what you should avoid doing, let me summarize a list of steps you should follow to make debugging configured components work smoothly:

1. Launch a session of the Visual Basic IDE, and open an ActiveX DLL project or a project group of ActiveX DLL projects that contain your configured components. Make sure to use *CreateObject* when activating objects across DLL projects.

2. Be sure that each project is set up for binary compatibility. This means that you must build each DLL at least once before you debug it.

3. Change the *MTSTransactionMode* property for each *MultiUse* class to something other than *NotAnMTSObject*. If you're not creating transactional components, use a setting of *NoTransactions*.

4. Be sure that you've installed your components into a COM+ application and configured all your attributes appropriately. If your components aren't configured in a COM+ application, all attributes are given default settings.

5. If you've added your components to a server application, be sure that the server application process isn't running when you start the Visual Basic debugger. If the server application is running, use the application's Shut Down command in the Component Services administrative tool.

6. Set the breakpoints you want, and start the Visual Basic debugger by choosing the Start With Full Compile command from the Run menu.

7. Run the client application. You can run the client from its compiled executable, from another session of the Visual Basic IDE or from the same session of the Visual Basic IDE that's running the DLL projects. If you decide to run the client application inside the same session of the Visual Basic IDE as your DLLs, make sure your client uses *CreateObject* instead of the *New* operator.

It's common to switch back and forth between running your component code in DLLHOST.EXE and the Visual Basic debugger. Just be sure that the client application releases all of its objects and you shut down the server application or the Visual Basic debugger before switching over to the other. This ensures that the activation setting of your application is switched back and forth between a server application and a library application without any hiccups.

You face a few important limitations with the Visual Basic debugger. First, your code doesn't run in an instance of DLLHOST.EXE. Your code runs in VB6.EXE. Second, the Visual Basic debugger is limited to a single thread. There's no way to simulate concurrency. Third, if you haven't configured your components in a COM+ application, your application and component attributes are assigned default values during debugging.

Other Useful Debugging Techniques

At times you might want to debug your code in DLLHOST.EXE instead of the Visual Basic debugger. The only way to debug your code in an actual instance of DLLHOST.EXE is to run your Visual Basic components in the Visual C++ debugger. The primary reason for doing this is to test how your code works in situations in which objects running on separate threads try to access the same resource concurrently. In MTS, you have to use the Visual C++ debugger to test security-related code. Fortunately, this isn't necessary with COM+.

To run compiled Visual Basic components in the Visual C++ debugger, you must build your ActiveX DLL with symbolic debug information. You access this option on the Compile tab of the Project Properties dialog box. This adds extra information to your compiled DLL that associates instructions with lines from your Visual Basic source code. Next, you must load the DLL and your Visual Basic class modules into the Visual

C++ IDE. (See the item in MSDN titled *Debugging Compiled Visual Basic Components* for details on how to get everything up and running.)

You should keep two other quick-and-dirty debugging techniques up your sleeve. You can generate simple debug messages by using the *MsgBox* statement or writing to the Windows event log. Let's start by generating debug messages with your old friend the *MsgBox* statement.

You might regard the use of *MsgBox* as a trick for novice programmers, but it's a quick-and-dirty way to see the values of your variables and see how your code is branching at runtime. When you need to quickly debug a configured component running in DLLHOST.EXE, this can be the fastest way to get the job done.

To use the *MsgBox* statement, you must do two things. First, you must be sure that your server application is running under the identity of the interactive user so that your objects can access your local computer's display console. Second, you must be sure that the Unattended Execution option isn't selected when you rebuild your server. If you follow these two rules, you can use a message box to send a debug message, as shown here:

```
Dim Msg As String
Msg = "Your debug message here"
MsgBox Msg, vbMsgBoxSetForeground, "Poor Man's Debugger"
```

The painful thing about this style of debugging is that you have to remove these statements before you distribute your code. If you don't, one of these calls can hang a thread in your application. You might consider using a conditional compilation argument so that you can easily switch between builds that generate debug messages and those that don't.

The other useful technique is sending debug messages to the Windows event log. Visual Basic provides a built-in *App* object that exposes the *LogEvent* method. You can easily append a message to the Windows event log with the following code:

```
Dim Msg As String
Msg = "Your debug message here"
App.LogEvent Msg, vbLogEventTypeInformation
```

When you test your components, you can use the Windows Event Viewer to examine your debug messages. You might find, by the way, that logging Windows events is useful for more than just debugging. You can use events to audit recurring errors in the production environment. You should consider logging all unexpected errors that your components raise. Note that the second parameter of the *LogEvent* method can take a value of *vbLogEventTypeInformation*, *vbLogEventTypeWarning*, or *vbLogEventTypeError*.

SUMMARY

So what has this chapter taught you? You should understand now that the COM+ programming model is all about declarative attributes and context. You must look for opportunities to do more declaratively and less programmatically. The secret is to let the COM+ runtime do as much work as possible. You should also look for ways to keep the things that change out of your compiled code so you don't have to recompile and redistribute your DLLs as often.

Knowing how COM+ administration works is important. Even after you create a COM+ application and add your components, you still have to explicitly configure several attributes. Some of you will learn to write administrative scripts, and some of you will rely on the Component Services administrative tool. Either approach can get the job done. Over the next few chapters, I'll discuss many more application and component attributes in greater detail. At this point, it's important that you simply understand when and how to configure them.

In this chapter, you saw how COM+ tracks attribute values and contextual information in a running application. An understanding of this architecture is critical to mastering how COM+ works internally. Every context has its own object context that stores contextual information. You also saw how to programmatically interact with the object context, and you saw how call context flows along as control is passed from method to method.

I ended this chapter by describing various resources for testing and debugging configured components. This information and the other ideas presented in this chapter should pave the way for the chapters ahead. I think you'll agree that attribute-based programming changes the world in which you live. Your components are definitely not in Kansas anymore.

Chapter 7

Sharing Resources in a COM+ Application

A typical COM+ application can run on many different hardware configurations. That's the beauty of COM and location transparency. But while you have many options, you can use only one physical deployment configuration at a time. Maybe you're running your application on a server computer with a single 166 MHz processor. Maybe you're running it on a computer with four 400 MHz processors. Maybe you're lucky enough to have a server farm with lots of processors spread out across many computers. Whatever your configuration, you should always write applications to make the most of the hardware that's currently available. This is the secret to writing an application that's scalable.

What is scalability? Apart from being a much-abused marketing term, scalability is an application's ability to serve a growing number of users without experiencing a drop-off in response times and overall system throughput. If your application provides one-second response times when it has 20 users, it's considered scalable if it can offer the same response times when it has 10,000 users. If your application can't handle all of these users when running on a server with a single 166 MHz processor, you can't determine whether it's scalable or not. If your application can't offer one-second response times no matter how much you spend on hardware, it's definitely not scalable.

There are two sides to scaling an application: acquiring more powerful hardware and writing your code to take advantage of whatever hardware it's running on. To write scalable components and applications, you must know how the COM+ runtime works. This chapter explains how to work with the COM+ runtime to handle as many concurrent users as possible.

Let's break down the parts of a distributed application. A distributed application is a set of one or more processes running on one or more computers. If objects are the atoms of your application, processes are the molecules. You partition your application into processes by configuring your components in various server applications and library applications. In some deployment scenarios, you might want more processes. In other scenarios, you might want fewer processes. In this chapter, I'll focus on the factors that allow each individual process to serve the largest possible set of clients.

A multitier application can offer greater scalability than a two-tier application because it can share process-specific resources across a set of clients. The COM+ runtime makes it possible to share threads, memory, database connections, and poolable objects. The main theme of this chapter is that code running on behalf of a single client should never be selfish. It should acquire its resources as late as possible and release them as soon as possible. Applications that share resources efficiently scale better than those that don't.

This chapter focuses on process-specific scalability issues. In later chapters, we'll examine designs that allow a distributed application to be spread across multiple computers. As you'll see, you should avoid certain programming techniques if you want to run your application in a server farm. For now, we'll limit our discussion to a single process running on a single computer.

SHARING THREADS

Threading is an important issue for any middle-tier application that will experience moderate to heavy traffic. High-traffic periods typically occur when online users are issuing many client requests per second. A scalable process must be able to handle each request with an acceptable level of responsiveness. A process isn't considered scalable if its responsiveness and overall throughput decrease in a linear fashion as the number of requests per second increases.

A process that's based on a single thread can't scale because it can't execute more than one method at a time. In other words, it doesn't allow for concurrency. During heavy-traffic periods, incoming requests are simply queued up and run serially. Furthermore, a single-threaded model is incredibly limiting when a process is running on a computer with multiple processors. The process simply can't take advantage of what the hardware has to offer.

A process that spawns a new thread for each client also has problems with respect to scalability. Physical threads must be created and torn down as clients come and go. Moreover, as the number of clients (and threads) increases, the operating system must spend a larger percentage of its time switching threads in and out of its processors. As this administrative overhead increases, the process's overall throughput decreases.

Years of experience led the industry to an important conclusion: To attain the highest levels of scalability, a middle-tier process must provide some type of thread-pooling scheme. The goal of such a scheme is to create an optimized balance between higher levels of concurrency and more efficient resource usage. However, writing the code to manage a pool of threads and efficiently dispatch them across a set of clients isn't a trivial undertaking.

Fortunately, COM+ provides a built-in scheme for thread pooling, and it does so in a way that's transparent to you, the programmer. You never have to think about the details of how the COM+ thread pool manager works when you write Visual Basic components. In essence, you write your components from a single-threaded perspective and let the COM+ runtime spread out your objects across a set of threads at runtime.

While the COM+ threading scheme is largely transparent, you must keep in mind several important threading concepts when you design Visual Basic components. For that reason, I'll take a little time to cover the fundamental threading concepts of the Microsoft Windows operating system and of COM. This will, in turn, lead to a discussion of the COM+ thread-pooling scheme, which is based on an abstraction called an *activity*. My goal is to give you the information you need to take advantage of the activity-based concurrency model and avoid programming techniques that diminish the scalability of your applications and the correctness of your code.

A Win32 Threading Primer

The Win32 programming model is based on two high-level abstractions called *processes* and *threads*. A process is a running instance of an application that owns an address space of virtual memory as well as various other resources. A thread is a schedulable entity that's owned by one and only one process. The operating system recognizes each thread in every process and is responsible for scheduling threads for time in the system's processors, as shown in Figure 7-1.

Every thread gets its own call stack. The scheduler allocates processing cycles by giving each thread a time slice. When the time slice is over, the running thread is preempted and another thread is given a turn. A preempted thread can keep enough information on its call stack to remember what it was doing and how far it got before being switched out of the processor. When it gets another time slice, it can pick up where it left off. The combination of threads and the scheduler is powerful because it allows a single-processor computer to appear to be doing more than one thing at a time.

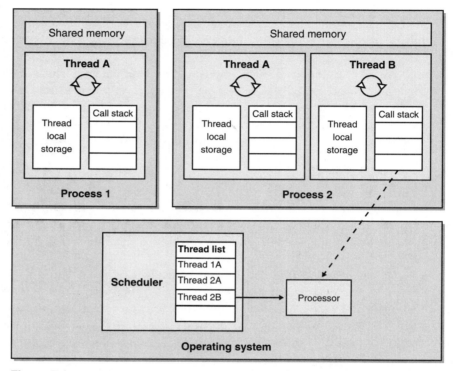

Figure 7-1 *Every Win32 process owns one or more threads. Each thread has an associated call stack and can store data in a private area known as thread-local storage (TLS).*

Each process begins its life with a *primary thread*. This system-created thread serves as the entry point into the application. In a typical Windows-based application with a user interface, the primary thread is used to create the application's main window and to set up a message pump to monitor incoming messages sent by the operating system. For example, if a user clicks on a main window, the system sends a WM_MOUSEDOWN message to a message queue associated with the window. The primary thread pulls this message off the queue and responds to it. A thread that sets up a pump to monitor the incoming messages in this manner is called a *user interface thread*.

Often when a user interface is written in C or C++, someone must set up the pump by writing a loop to monitor the message queue associated with the window.

Fortunately, Visual Basic programmers have always been shielded from having to deal with a message pump directly. The Visual Basic runtime sets up a message pump in the background. Creating a Visual Basic application with a user interface is simple because the Visual Basic runtime translates these Windows messages into Visual Basic events.

Once an application is up and running, the Win32 API lets you spawn additional threads using a Win32 API function named *CreateThread*. C and C++ programmers typically create secondary threads to carry out lower-priority background tasks. In most cases, the secondary thread doesn't monitor a message queue and therefore doesn't require as much overhead. This type of thread is often referred to as a *worker thread*. The obvious benefit of the second thread is that a background task can be run without blocking the responsiveness of the user interface.

Concurrency and synchronization

If you write multithreaded applications by calling *CreateThread*, you must exercise extreme caution. When two threads run concurrently in a single process, you can encounter problems that don't exist in a single-threaded process. In particular, shared memory that's accessed by multiple threads is vulnerable to inconsistency and corruption because of a phenomenon known as *concurrency*. In a preemptive multithreading environment such as Windows 2000, the scheduler switches threads out of the processor arbitrarily. There's no way to guarantee that a thread has completed its work. When another thread is switched into the processor, it might see shared memory left in an invalid state by some other thread that was preempted in the middle of a series of changes.

For example, imagine that the variables x and y represent the position of a point. The initial position of the point is (10,10), and thread A begins to change the position of the point to (20,20). If thread A is preempted after changing the x position but before changing the y position, the logical point is left in an invalid state—the position (20,10). The only valid positions for the point are (10,10) and (20,20), but thread B might see the point as (20,10). As you can tell, concurrency makes an application vulnerable to data inconsistency.

Multithreading also makes an application vulnerable to data corruption. Take a look at another example with a particularly unhappy ending. When thread A inserts a new entry into a linked list, it must modify a set of pointers to accomplish the task. If thread A is preempted in the middle of the operation, thread B can easily get hold of an invalid pointer when it tries to scan the list. When thread B tries to use the invalid pointer, the entire process will probably crash.

Multithreading makes it difficult to write code that is correct and robust. A Win32 programmer who wants to create a multithreaded application must lock and synchronize any shared memory that's vulnerable to inconsistency or corruption. The Win32

API exposes a set of synchronization primitives for this purpose. Critical sections, mutexes, semaphores, and events are all examples of Win32 synchronization objects. These objects are tricky to work with, but they let experienced programmers write safe, robust code that can benefit from multithreading.

The problems associated with concurrency arise only when two or more threads access the same data items in shared memory. You can avoid these problems by using local variables on the call stack instead of using shared memory. These local variables are private to a particular thread. The Win32 API also allows a thread to store persistent data in a private memory area known as *thread-local storage (TLS)*. Using TLS solves many concurrency problems because you don't have to worry about synchronization.

Although TLS solves concurrency problems, it creates a few problems of its own. Data stored in TLS can be accessed only by the owning thread. Objects that store data in TLS generate a dependency on the thread that created them. Visual Basic objects are heavy users of TLS, so every Visual Basic object has a dependency on the thread that created it. A Visual Basic object can never be accessed by any other thread. This condition is known as *thread affinity*. As you'll see later, thread affinity becomes a limiting factor in environments that use thread pooling.

COM's Threading Models

Many programmers—especially those who write business logic in languages such as Visual Basic—don't think about concurrency and synchronization. They assume that their code will run in an environment under a single thread of control or else they don't think about threading at all. They never worry about synchronizing their data during method calls. They're generally much more productive than programmers who spend time on issues relating to concurrency.

As you can see, you can write code in two very different ways. You can write a component with synchronization code that's thread-savvy or you can write a component from the single-threaded perspective. The creators of COM looked for a way to integrate the two types of components in a single application. More specifically, they looked for a way to integrate components that didn't include their own synchronization code in a multithreaded process. Their solution was to offer system-provided synchronization to any object that needs it.

COM can provide automatic synchronization through an abstraction known as an *apartment*. Apartments allow components without custom synchronization code to safely run in multithreaded processes. Moreover, apartments allow objects that exhibit thread affinity, such as those created with Visual Basic, to run safely in multithreaded processes.

In COM, every object must be created in a specific apartment and every apartment must exist in a specific process. You can view an apartment as a set of objects with compatible synchronization requirements. However, that's not the entire story. Every COM-aware thread is associated with exactly one apartment, so you can define an apartment as a set of objects and threads in a process.

You should note that apartments have been around longer than MTS or COM+. This means that apartments were part of the programming model before the introduction of contexts. With the release of Windows 2000, you can define an apartment as a set of contexts running in a process. That means that processes can be partitioned into apartments and that apartments can be partitioned into contexts.

Before Windows 2000, there were only two types of apartments: the *multithreaded apartment* (*MTA*) and the *single-threaded apartment* (*STA*). The MTA provides an environment for components with custom synchronization code. An STA is a safer environment for running objects that were written without concern for locking and synchronization. STAs were designed to eliminate the need for programmer-assisted synchronization.

Over the last few years, two different sets of terminology have been used to describe these two threading models. The Win32 SDK documentation uses the terms *multithreaded apartment* and *single-threaded apartment,* while other authors and development tools use the terms *free-threaded* and *apartment-threaded.* A free-threaded component is written to run in the MTA, and an apartment-threaded component is written to run in an STA. When you hear the term *apartment,* you can generally infer that this means an STA.

So, how does an STA prohibit concurrency? As its name implies, an STA is based on a single thread of execution. This thread is the only one that's allowed to directly touch any of the objects in the STA. This restriction is all that's needed to prohibit concurrency and provide a safe environment for objects that exhibit thread affinity. However, an STA must be capable of processing method calls originating from other apartments. To meet this requirement, the STA gets some assistance from the underlying RPC layer and a Windows message queue.

When the COM runtime creates an STA, it also creates an invisible window. Note that the STA doesn't really need the window; it just needs the message queue associated with the window. This queue allows the STA to set up a standard message pump, as shown in Figure 7-2. The RPC layer responds to method calls targeted for the STA by posting a standard Windows message to this queue using the Win32 *PostMessage* function. The thread in the STA runs a message pump just like the primary thread in an application with a user interface does. This allows the STA to respond to method requests by processing these messages on a first-in, first-out basis.

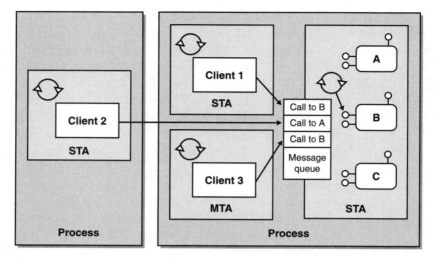

Figure 7-2 *Every STA includes a user interface thread, a Windows message queue, and a message pump. This architecture allows STAs to serialize incoming calls and run objects that exhibit thread affinity.*

When the STA is busy processing a call, other incoming requests are queued up and must wait their turn. The STA's thread eventually works its way to the bottom of the queue and goes into idle mode when the queue is empty. While this invocation architecture requires a good deal of overhead, the STA eliminates the need for programmers to be concerned about concurrency and synchronization.

When the Visual Basic team originally added multithreaded COM support to their product, they had a tough decision to make. They had to decide whether their programmers should be exposed to synchronization issues. They decided that requiring programmer-assisted synchronization was unacceptable in a tool intended to provide the highest levels of productivity. They decided that all Visual Basic objects would be required to run according to the STA model. They also made the assumption that it was acceptable to use TLS in the code that's automatically built into every Visual Basic component. This is why Visual Basic objects exhibit thread affinity.

You must use another language, such as C++, to create free-threaded components. A C++ programmer writing a free-threaded component must typically deal with concurrency by writing custom synchronization code using Win32 locking primitives. This style of programming becomes increasingly complex and grungy, but it yields components that are potentially faster and more responsive.

Windows 2000 introduced a third threading model called the *thread-neutral apartment (TNA)*. Unfortunately, Visual Basic programmers can't take advantage of this new model because of the issues relating to thread affinity. But this new model is definitely of interest to C++ programmers, especially those who have previously built components for the MTA.

Before Windows 2000, the rules of COM required a thread switch in almost all situations for calls that cross over an apartment boundary. While these rules help to guarantee the synchronization scheme built into the STA model, they are unnecessarily taxing for objects running in the MTA. In particular, a call from a client in an STA to an object in the MTA can require an expensive and unnecessary thread switch. An object running under the TNA model, however, can be directly accessed by any thread in a process. For this reason, the TNA is the preferred threading model for Windows 2000. Of course, you can use this model only if your tools and language are capable of creating objects that don't exhibit thread affinity.

Visual Basic components and the *ThreadingModel* attribute

As you know, each component has an associated CLSID key in the Windows Registry. The SCM uses the information in this key during object activation. The Registry key *CLSID\InprocServer32* can be marked with a *ThreadingModel* attribute to indicate which apartment types are compatible with the component. A Visual Basic component has either a *ThreadingModel* attribute of *Apartment* or no threading model attribute at all, as shown in Figure 7-3. A few other settings are possible for the *ThreadingModel* attribute, but they're not pertinent to developing with Visual Basic.

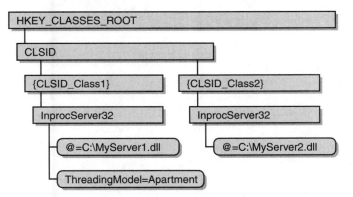

Figure 7-3 *You can specify an apartment type for a component by providing a* ThreadingModel *attribute in the* CLSID\InprocServer32 *key. Components without this attribute are considered single-threaded.*

You can explicitly assign the *ThreadingModel* attribute to the components in an ActiveX DLL project by adjusting the Threading Model setting on the General tab of the Project Properties dialog box. Two settings are possible. The default setting of Apartment Threaded ensures that each component is marked with a *ThreadingModel* attribute of *Apartment*. This setting indicates that a new object must be loaded into an STA. However, the new object can be loaded into any STA. As long as the object's creator is running in an STA, the object is created in the same apartment, which means that the two can communicate without a thread switch.

If you specify the other Threading Model setting, Single Threaded, each component is configured without a *ThreadingModel* attribute. When the SCM creates an object from a component that doesn't have a *ThreadingModel* attribute, it does so in the safest possible manner. Because the SCM can't make any assumptions about the component, it creates every object on the same thread. More specifically, it creates every object in the first STA created in the hosting process. The first STA created is known as the *main STA*. A component that lacks a *ThreadingModel* attribute is often called *single-threaded* or *main-threaded*.

Single-threaded DLLs are problematic because they cause unnecessary thread switches. If a creator is running in any STA other than the main STA, a thread-switching proxy/stub layer must be inserted between the creator and the object. Single-threaded DLLs are especially undesirable in environments such as COM+ and IIS. Apartment-threaded DLLs are almost always preferable because they allow a client in any STA to bind to an object in that same STA, which avoids the overhead of a thread-switching proxy/stub layer.

NEVER CALL *CREATETHREAD* FROM VISUAL BASIC

A Win32 thread can't participate in COM programming without making an explicit COM library call to either *CoInitialize* or *CoInitializeEx*. These functions associate a thread with an apartment. It's illegal and usually fatal for a thread to participate in any COM-related activities before calling one of these functions. Fortunately, the COM+ runtime makes this call for you when it creates a thread. If you're creating a Standard EXE or an ActiveX EXE, the Visual Basic runtime makes all of the required calls to *CoInitialize* behind the scenes.

Working directly with Win32 threads and COM apartments is difficult and, for all practical purposes, beyond the capabilities of the Visual Basic programming language. However, when Visual Basic 5 first shipped, many unfortunate programmers tried to directly call the *CreateThread* function in the Win32 API by using Visual Basic's new *AddressOf* operator. The programmers found that they could successfully call *CreateThread* but that their applications often died strange and mysterious deaths.

The problem with calling *CreateThread* is that it creates a new Win32 thread that knows nothing about COM or apartments. It's therefore illegal to use this thread to invoke a method on a COM object. This creates quite a problem because all Visual Basic objects, including forms and controls, are also COM objects. Such an object can be directly accessed only by the thread running in the object's apartment. When the newly created thread tries to change a value in a text box, the application crashes. This is a pretty good reason to never use *CreateThread* directly from Visual Basic code.

A determined Visual Basic programmer with knowledge of COM's threading models might try to take things to the next level. You can associate a thread with an STA by calling a function such as *CoInitialize* directly. However, once you associate the thread with an apartment, the complexity increases. For instance, you're typically required to write code for marshaling interface references (which are really interface pointers at this level) from one apartment to another. If you pass the interface references in a COM method call, the proxy and the stub are created automatically. However, if you pass them using another technique, the requirements increase dramatically. You must make two complicated calls to the COM library—a call to *CoMarshalInterface* to create a stub in the object's apartment and a call to *CoUnmarshalInterface* to create a proxy in the caller's apartment. What's more, you also have to know enough about COM to decide when these calls are necessary. Add in the complexities related to the rules of COM+ and contexts, and you should come to an important conclusion: Never call *CreateThread* from Visual Basic. If you really need to spawn your own threads, you should be using C++ and you should know a great deal about the underlying plumbing of COM.

I must admit that this entire sidebar is just an opinion. Some of the icons of the Visual Basic world, such as Matt Curland, advocate spawning threads directly from Visual Basic code in the manner I just described. Matt can tell you about the details of this undertaking in a book he's written titled *Advanced Visual Basic 6: Power Techniques for Everyday Programs* (published by Addison Wesley).

If you feel comfortable with all the COM details I covered in Chapter 3 and you're looking for more in-depth coverage, Matt's book can take you to the next level. Matt has worked on the Visual Basic team for quite a few years and he has intimate knowledge of how the Visual Basic runtime interacts with the COM library. He describes many techniques that involve calling into the COM library directly from Visual Basic code.

The activity-based concurrency model

Apartments were the primary mechanism for system-provided synchronization in earlier versions of COM. In the COM+ programming model, system-provided synchronization is the responsibility of a new abstraction called an *activity*. An activity can be defined as a set of contexts whose objects are protected from concurrent access. Creating one or more objects in an activity relieves you from having to write custom synchronization code. For this reason, you can say that *an activity is a synchronization domain*. Or you can say that *an activity represents a logical thread*.

An activity does the same job as an STA with respect to serializing method calls. However, an activity accomplishes its mission more efficiently. It doesn't need to pin each object to a specific thread. Instead, the COM+ runtime prohibits concurrency in an activity through an internal locking scheme.

The COM+ runtime tracks activities on a per-process basis using an internal data structure. Each activity has an identifying GUID and an exclusive lock. Any thread must acquire this lock before entering an activity and accessing any of its objects. Once a thread has the lock, all other threads will block when they attempt to enter the activity. Once a thread has entered an activity, it must release the lock on its way out. This allows the next thread to enter. As you can see, this locking scheme prevents concurrency much as an STA does. However, it does so without restricting access to a single thread or requiring an invisible window along with its associated message queue. In essence, it provides automatic synchronization without all the baggage associated with an STA.

Apartments are still part of the COM+ programming model, but their role has been scaled back. Now they're used primarily to manage objects that exhibit thread affinity. An activity doesn't restrict access to a single thread. Only an STA can guarantee that an object with affinity to one specific thread is never touched by another thread. As a consequence, every Visual Basic object running in a COM+ application must live in an STA. A Visual Basic object should also live in an activity as well (although it's not a requirement).

The *Synchronization* attribute

The association between a context and an activity is established when the context is created. As you know, the COM+ runtime creates a new context when it creates an object that needs its own contextual information. Each configured component has a *Synchronization* attribute that tells the COM+ runtime whether a new context should be associated with an activity. If the COM+ runtime creates a new context that needs an activity, the *Synchronization* attribute also indicates whether the context should inherit the creator's activity or get a new activity of its own. Table 7-1 describes how COM+ matches up new objects and contexts to activities.

In practice, you don't need to think too much about the differences between the synchronization settings when you create components with Visual Basic. You should use the default setting Required. I'll explain why in a moment. C++ programmers, on the other hand, can create components without thread affinity that don't need to run in an STA. This offers many more options with respect to how the *Synchronization* attribute is set. Therefore, C++ programmers typically choose a synchronization setting based on whether they want automatic synchronization. (The issues involved in designing COM+ components with C++ are a topic for another book.)

Table 7-1 How COM+ Matches New Objects and Contexts to Activities

Synchronization Attribute	Method Used for Matching
Not Supported	The object is created in a context that has no activity.
Supported	If the creator is running in an activity, the object is created in a context that shares that activity. If the creator isn't running in an activity, the object is created in a context that has no activity.
Required	If the creator is running in an activity, the object is created in a context that shares that activity. If the creator isn't running in an activity, the object is created in a context with a new activity.
Requires New	The object is created in a context with a new activity.
Disabled	The SCM ignores the synchronization property when deciding whether the object requires its own context. The object will be in an activity only if it's placed in the creator's context and that context has an activity.

MOVING FROM MTS

All MTS Objects Run in an Activity

Activities were first introduced with MTS. In MTS, every object must run in an activity. You can think of every MTS component as having a synchronization setting of Required. MTS also requires every object to run in an STA. This is pretty much the way things are for Visual Basic objects in COM+. However, unlike COM+, MTS makes it impossible to take advantage of C++ components with more sophisticated threading capabilities.

Apartment-threaded objects and activities

Figure 7-4 shows the layout of Visual Basic objects in a typical server application process with multiple clients. The basic premise behind the COM+ concurrency model is that each client should get its own activity. You should generally avoid designs in which a single client requires more than one activity. You should always avoid designs in which two clients map to the same activity.

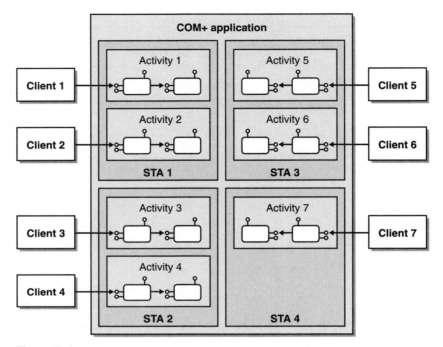

Figure 7-4 *Each client should be associated with exactly one activity. The COM+ runtime binds logical activities to physical STA threads when apartment-threaded objects are involved.*

When would a client be associated with multiple activities? It can happen if a client running outside the COM+ runtime creates two separate objects. Note that the client isn't running in an activity. If the client creates two objects from components that require synchronization, the COM+ runtime creates a separate activity for each object. A better approach is to have the client create the first object and then have this object create the second object. The second object is created in the same activity as the first object as long as its component has a synchronization attribute of Required.

Why is it important for both objects to share the same activity? It has to do with consuming fewer resources and avoiding unnecessary thread switches. With respect to resource utilization, it should be obvious why you want to limit each client to a single thread. A client doesn't need more than one. It's also much faster for one object to call another without a thread switch.

If object A will be calling object B, you should make sure they're both in the same STA. The COM+ runtime guarantees that if two apartment-threaded objects are running in the same activity and in the same process, they will also run in the same

STA. This is the main reason that you should always use the Required synchronization setting.

Now you know that it's bad for one client to own more than one activity. As it turns out, it's even worse for two or more clients to map to one activity. The COM+ architects made the assumption that *each activity is associated with exactly one client*. When a client calls into an activity, it should wait for the call to return before issuing another call. This model wasn't designed to accommodate situations in which two or more clients make calls into the same activity independently. It's equally bad if a single client application tries to make calls into the same activity using two separate threads. The main rule to keep in mind is that you should never make a call into an activity before the previous call returns.

An object that is shared across multiple clients is often called a *singleton*. Developers typically design with singletons in order to share data across multiple clients. While the use of singleton objects might be acceptable in some single-user scenarios, you should definitely avoid it in COM+ applications. Every client should get its own private objects. If multiple clients require access to the same data, you should store this data in shared memory or in a database. You can then devise a design in which each client creates a private object that accesses this shared data.

You should note that COM+ doesn't restrict an activity to a single process. Figure 7-5 shows an example of an activity that spans processes. If object A is running in an activity in server application 1 and it creates object B in server application 2, the new object and its context inherit the activity of the creator. This model, of course, assumes that the component used to create object B requires synchronization.

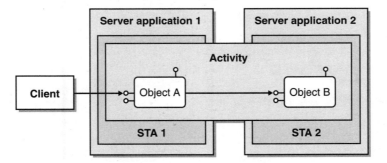

Figure 7-5 *An activity can span process and computer boundaries.*

As you can see, COM+ flows contextual information about the activity from object A to object B during activation. In Chapter 8, you'll see that objects must be in the same activity in order to be in the same COM+ transaction. But it's possible for two objects to participate in the same transaction even when they're running on different computers. They just need to be in the same activity.

You should be aware of one limitation of activities. The COM+ runtime doesn't guarantee activitywide synchronization across processes. The locking scheme used by COM+ works only within the scope of a single process. It would be too expensive for COM+ to check locks in other processes before allowing a thread to enter an activity. In Figure 7-5, what would happen if one client were to call into object A at the same time that another client calls into object B? COM+ wouldn't be able to prevent two calls from executing in an activity at the same time. However, this limitation should never cause a problem because your designs should never allow for this situation to occur. As long as you never allow two separate clients to map to the same activity, the single-process locking scheme shouldn't be an issue.

The STA thread pool

Each COM+ server application maintains two separate thread pools. One thread pool services STA objects, and the other one services all the other objects. As a Visual Basic programmer, you should obviously be more concerned with the STA thread pool. The COM+ runtime sets up the STA thread pool based on the following rules:

- The initial pool size is 7 plus the number of processors.

- The maximum pool size is 10 times the number of processors.

- The thread pool size increases based on the number of queued requests.

- During times with less traffic, the thread pool size decreases based on system-supplied code triggered by idle timers.

MOVING FROM MTS

Thread Pool Size in MTS

In MTS 2, each server package process maintains a single pool of STA threads. This pool has an initial size of 1 and a maximum size of 100. The pool size increases based on the number of activities. Unlike the situation in COM+, the MTS thread pool never decreases in size.

After looking at these rules, many developers ask this question: How can my application scale if it's limited to 10 threads? Your intuition might tell you that increasing the number of threads will always make things better. However, this simply isn't the case. You can scale only so far when your application is running on a computer with a single processor. Naively increasing the number of threads to 50 or 100 or 1000 will hurt the overall throughput of your application.

The thread-pooling scheme that's built into COM+ is self-tuning with respect to the number of available processors on the host computer. The best way to accommodate a growing user base is to upgrade your hardware. Acquiring a new server computer that has more processors or faster processors or both is the best place to start. Obviously, you should also make sure the computer has more than enough physical memory to serve the expected number of users.

Here's another question that everyone always asks: How many users can a COM+ application handle? The answer is, of course, that it depends. With the right hardware in place, an application can handle several hundred users. Later in this book, I'll talk about using HTTP as opposed to COM and RPC for client-to-server communication. As you'll see, HTTP has many scaling advantages over RPC, which is especially important when an application has thousands or tens of thousands of users. For this reason, many distributed applications use COM and RPC for server-to-server communication and rely on HTTP for client-to-server communication.

Activities and STA threads

You should observe that your application has a finite number of STA threads to work with. At first, COM+ assigns each activity to its own thread. However, when the number of activities exceeds the number of STAs, COM+ must map multiple activities to the same STA. It's important to note that a client is pinned to an STA thread when an activity is created. In an application with many users, each STA has its own set of clients.

Remember that STAs are physical threads, while activities are logical threads. When two activities share the same STA, the COM+ runtime manages the multiplexing of STAs in and out of activities. The multiplexing provided by COM+ is pretty sophisticated.

Let's look at an example to see how things work. Take a look at Figure 7-6. Assume that client 1 calls a method on object A. A split-second later, client 2 attempts to call a method on object B. Object B is in a different activity than object A, but they share the same STA.

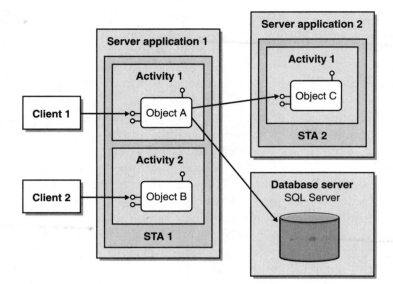

Figure 7-6 *An activity releases control of its STA thread when it returns or when it makes an outbound call.*

While the STA thread is busy executing the method call for client 1, the call from client 2 is blocked. You should see that this blocking isn't enforced by activity-based locks. The blocking is due to the single-threaded nature of the STA. But what happens if object 1 makes an outbound call to another process while executing its method? Perhaps object 1 makes a COM call to another object in a different server application or an OLE-DB call to a database server. Will the call from client 2 block while object 1 is waiting for this outbound call to return? Fortunately, the answer is no. The multiplexing scheme is smart enough to free up the STA thread. Once the call from object 1 leaves the STA, another activity can take control of the thread.

These locking semantics are fairly complex. The call to object B can start executing after the call to object A but still finish before it. This behavior helps to improve concurrency, but it relaxes the rules of synchronization. When objects in an STA make outbound calls, the STA doesn't guarantee that calls will be serialized. However, calls are serialized from the perspective of each activity.

I want to show one other example of how the relaxed rules of synchronization might catch a programmer off guard. Let's say a programmer creates an object from a Visual Basic component that doesn't support synchronization. The object is created in an STA, but it doesn't have an associated activity. Now assume that two different clients hold references to this object. (I know you'd never share an object across two clients, but imagine that you have a friend who does this.)

Assume that client 1 makes a method call on the object. When this method starts to execute, it changes a module-level variable to 5 and then makes an outbound call. Now let's say client 2 calls a method that executes while the object is waiting for this outbound call to return. If the method called by client 2 changes the module-level variable to 6, client 1 sees inconsistent data.

When the outbound call was issued, the variable value was 5. When the outbound call returned, the value was 6. The call from client 1 wasn't run in a serialized fashion. If the object had been created in an activity, however, there wouldn't be any problems. The call from client 2 would block until the call from client 1 returned. This example provides another good reason to stick with the default synchronization setting of Required for all Visual Basic components. It also shows how sharing objects across clients can get you in trouble.

SHARING MEMORY

In the initial design phase of a distributed application, you must decide how to share data across a set of clients. Using shared memory in a COM+ application is typically the fastest way to accomplish this goal. It's faster than accessing a database because the data is close at hand. Moreover, you don't have to go through a database engine to read or write a data item. However, the use of shared memory in a COM+ application requires attention to synchronization. Different objects running on different threads will all access the same information.

Apartments and Standard Module Variables

Many veteran Visual Basic programmers get confused the first time they run their code in a multithreaded environment such as a COM+ application because public variables defined in standard (.BAS) modules aren't really global variables. These public variables are scoped at the STA level rather than at the process level. This changes things for programmers who are used to defining global, applicationwide variables in earlier versions of Visual Basic. The rules change when you start programming for the middle tier.

When your component runs in a multithreaded process, two objects see the same public standard-module data only when they're in the same STA. Objects in separate STAs see different instances of these public variables, as shown in Figure 7-7. This creates random behavior in a COM+ application because of the arbitrary way in which objects are matched with STA threads.

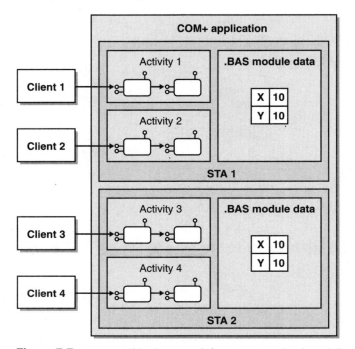

Figure 7-7 *Any variable that you define in a standard module in an ActiveX DLL project is held in TLS. This means that objects running in different STAs can't share data.*

When the Visual Basic team added support for the STA threading model, they had to decide how to handle the public variables defined in standard modules. If they decided to store this data in shared memory, someone would have to be responsible for synchronizing access to it. As in the case of the COM support they built into Visual Basic components, the team felt that it was unacceptable to require any type of programmer-assisted synchronization. Therefore, they opted to store the data defined in a standard module in TLS.

When the Visual Basic runtime encounters a new STA, it creates a fresh copy in TLS of each variable defined in a standard module. The Visual Basic runtime also calls *Sub Main* once in each STA. This lets you initialize the data on a per-STA basis. The important point to note is that there are several copies of each piece of data. While it can be acceptable to use constants or variables that are read-only once they're initialized, you can't use standard modules to define shared data that will be updated by clients on an ongoing basis. In a COM+ application, you must share read-write memory using another technique.

The Shared Property Manager

The COM+ Services Type Library includes a component known as the Shared Property Manager (SPM). (Its nickname is, of course, "the spam.") The SPM allows you to create and access shared data items in a COM+ application. Each data item is accessible to all objects running in the same process. The SPM also implements a locking scheme to synchronize access to data. This locking scheme can be critical to maintaining data consistency in the presence of concurrency.

The SPM provides a simple yet effective form of synchronization. Instead of having stand-alone properties, the SPM requires you to define each property within the scope of a *property group*. A property group provides a namespace for a set of properties. A property group is also a unit of synchronization. Going back to the example earlier in the chapter, what if you have data relating to a point and you want a writer object to change both the x coordinate and the y coordinate before a reader object can see either change? A property group provides a locking scheme that allows the writer object to finish its work before any reader object can see its changes.

Figure 7-8 shows how the SPM works from a high-level perspective. Different objects running in different activities each creates its own instance of a specific property group. However, the data for the group is laid out in memory only once in a processwide fashion. In addition to the property values, each property group has its own exclusive lock. Each shared property group instance implements an internal lock manager that relies on this exclusive lock to synchronize access to property data within the group.

The SPM is a name/value dictionary that lets you create and retrieve properties and property groups by name. Let's look at an example. Before you can create and retrieve properties and property groups, you must create an instance of the shared property group manager. Take a look at the following code:

```
Dim spam As SharedPropertyGroupManager
Set spam = New SharedPropertyGroupManager
Dim MyPoint As SharedPropertyGroup
Dim AlreadyExists As Boolean
' Create and/or bind to group MyPointData
Set MyPoint = spam.CreatePropertyGroup("MyPointData", _
                                        LockMethod, _
                                        Process, _
                                        AlreadyExists)
```

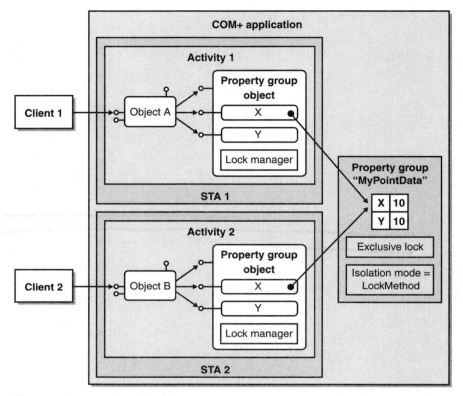

Figure 7-8 *The SPM provides synchronized access to shared data through properties in a property group. When you create a property group, you define its locking behavior by setting the isolation mode.*

The *CreatePropertyGroup* method takes four parameters. The first parameter lets you pass the name of the property group. If a property group of the same name already exists, the SPM binds you to it. If the property group doesn't exist, the SPM creates it and then binds you to it. The last parameter of *CreatePropertyGroup* is a Boolean output parameter that tells the caller whether the property group existed before the call.

The second and third parameters specify an *isolation mode* and a *release mode* for your property group. The isolation mode allows you to establish the locking behavior for the group, while the release mode tells the SPM how long you want the data for the group to remain in memory. Note that both of these parameters are passed *ByRef* and that the SPM ignores their input values if the property group already exists. Only the client that creates the group can set these values. If the property group already exists, the SPM returns the current isolation mode and release mode to the caller in these two parameters as output values.

When your object creates a property group instance and attempts to access some of its properties, it must first acquire the group's exclusive lock. Internally, the lock is associated with the activity in which your object is running. Once your object's activity has acquired the lock, objects in other activities will block when they attempt to access properties in the group. The next question is: How long does the activity hold to the lock? The answer depends on how you set up the group's locking behavior.

When you create a group, you establish the locking behavior by using an isolation mode of *LockMethod* or *LockSetGet*. You should use *LockMethod* if you need to maintain consistency across several of the properties in the group. When a group's isolation mode is set to *LockMethod*, each object acquires the exclusive lock and holds it for the duration of the current method call. The COM+ runtime supplies code in the interception layer to release the lock after your method returns. This scheme allows an object to read and write to several properties in a group without having to worry about the reads and writes of other objects.

You have a few good reasons to create a property group using an isolation level of *LockMethod*. You might want to read a property and then update its value without the risk of another client reading or updating its value between your two operations. Or you might have interdependencies among the properties in a group, as in the case of the data associated with a point. For example, you might want to change both the *x* position and the *y* position of a point without the risk of another client getting an inconsistent read. In such cases, each object requires a higher level of isolation when running a series of updates.

If you pass *LockSetGet*, the SPM acquires and releases the group's exclusive lock each time you access an individual property. Unlike with *LockMethod*, a lock is never held for the duration of a method. You should note that in some designs this can make your data vulnerable to inconsistency. However, when you don't need higher levels of isolation, holding locks for a shorter duration results in higher levels of concurrency.

You have to find the best balance between consistency and concurrency. Often it's desirable to place different properties in different groups. Some of your groups can use *LockMethod* while others use *LockSetGet*. This lets you add more granularity to your locking scheme to get the consistency you need without blocking users unnecessarily.

When you set the release mode for a group, you can pass a value of either *Process* or *Standard*. The value *Process* indicates that you want the property group to remain in memory for the lifetime of the process. The value *Standard* indicates that you want the property group to manage its lifetime using standard reference counting. When you pass *Standard*, the property group's data is released from memory as soon as the last client releases its property group object. In most cases, you'll create and release property group objects, but you'll want to keep the data associated with the group in memory. This means that you'll use *Process* much more often than *Standard*.

Of course, the SPM isn't really useful until you start creating and using shared properties. You can create a property using the *CreateProperty* method or the *CreatePropertyByPosition* method. Here's an example of creating two properties and setting their default values:

```
Dim spam As SharedPropertyGroupManager
Set spam = New SharedPropertyGroupManager
Dim MyPoint As SharedPropertyGroup
Dim AlreadyExists As Boolean
Set MyPoint = spam.CreatePropertyGroup("MyPointData", _
                                       LockMethod, _
                                       Process, _
                                       AlreadyExists)
' Create and/or bind to property X
Dim X_Position As SharedProperty
Set X_Position = MyPoint.CreateProperty("X", AlreadyExists)
If AlreadyExists = False Then X_Position.Value = 10
' Create and/or bind to property Y
Dim Y_Position As SharedProperty
Set Y_Position = MyPoint.CreateProperty("Y", AlreadyExists)
If AlreadyExists = False Then Y_Position.Value = 10
```

Like *CreatePropertyGroup*, *CreateProperty* simply binds you to a property if it already exists. You can retrieve an existing property by name or by position. If the property doesn't already exist, the SPM creates it and assigns the default value 0 (as a long integer) to its *Value* property. If you want a different default value, you should set it explicitly when the property is created.

The *Value* property of a shared property object is stored as a *Variant*. This situation gives you quite a bit of flexibility. You can store any Variant-compliant data type such as *Integer*, *Long*, *Double*, or *String* in a property. You can also store a Variant-compliant array. The following is an example of storing an array of strings in a shared property:

```
Dim data() As String
ReDim data(3)
data(0) = "Bob"
data(1) = "Carol"
data(2) = "Ted"
data(3) = "Alice"
MyProperty.Value = data
```

Once you're familiar with the SPM, you'll find that it's pretty easy to share data across a set of objects running in different activities. In a moment of weakness, you might even be tempted to assign a Visual Basic object reference to a shared property. However, you must resist this impulse. As you know, shared objects don't fit very well into the activity-based programming model. Because of their problems with thread affinity, shared Visual Basic objects don't fit in at all. There are also problems associated with context relativity. If you store an object reference in a property group, you can legally use the reference only from within the same context. The bottom line is that the SPM isn't for storing objects created with Visual Basic.

While storing object references in a property group is unacceptable, it's common to create a component for managing the data held in a specific group. It's just that your application will create objects from this component and release them even though the property group data remains in memory. The data in the property group defines a logical object in terms of primitive data types and arrays. You can simply create objects when they're needed and let them rehydrate themselves with the data in the property group. As long as each object lives entirely within the scope of a single activity, you can avoid problems relating to concurrency.

Limitations of the SPM

The SPM provides data that you can access quickly, but you should note that the data will be lost in the case of a system failure or an application crash. The reason that the SPM is fast is because nothing is written to disk. If the data you're sharing across a set of clients needs to be recoverable, you must use some persistent form of storage such as a database.

Data managed by the SPM is accessible only to objects running in a single process. If you need to share data across processes or machines, you must use something else. Once again, this might be a good reason to employ a database.

Keep in mind that read and write operations in the SPM are never transacted. While the SPM can provide isolation, it doesn't provide any rollback facilities. If you modify a shared property from inside a COM+ transaction, your changes are permanent, even when you roll back the transaction. And don't be fooled into thinking that your property group locks are held to the end of the current COM+ transaction. The locks in the SPM have nothing to do with COM+ transactions. The SPM releases its locks as soon as the current method finishes, which in most cases is before the end of the current transaction.

Also note that, unlike most database products, the SPM never uses read locks. It employs only exclusive locking. Once an object acquires the lock for a group, every other object is blocked. A database can provide an optimized form of concurrency by blocking only users who attempt to perform write operations. This additional level of locking granularity provides higher levels of concurrency because many readers can access the same data at the same time.

During the beta cycle for Windows 2000, COM+ included a service known as the In-Memory Database (IMDB). The IMDB, which was promoted as an improved version of the SPM, allowed operations on shared memory to be enlisted in transactions. It also provided more granularity with respect to locking. However, the IMDB had various problems, and customer feedback during the beta cycle ultimately led the COM+ team to pull the IMDB from the final release of Windows 2000.

While the IMDB was accessible through an OLE-DB provider and ADO, it didn't provide a database engine for running queries. Therefore, it wasn't very functional from the perspective of an experienced database developer. The real downfall of the IMDB was that it couldn't outperform a local Microsoft SQL Server database. In short, it was harder to use and not as functional, and it was no faster than maintaining shared data in a table in SQL Server.

I've taken the time to discuss the IMDB not so you'll know about things you can't use but to illustrate the benefits of using a local database to get around the limitations of the SPM. The SPM will always provide the fastest access to shared data, but if you need persistence, data that's shared across processes, read locks, or transacted operations, a local database can provide that extra support. As a COM+ developer, you should always think of the database as your friend. Don't be afraid to use it when you need it.

SHARING DATABASE CONNECTIONS

When you begin writing data access code for the middle tier, you'll notice a few things that are very different from writing data access code for a two-tier desktop application. You should know what database connection pooling is, how it works, and how it changes the way you should write data access code. This section will discuss the best way to design and write your ADO code when deploying middle-tier objects in the presence of OLE-DB connection pooling.

Why Do You Need Database Connection Pooling?

Establishing a database connection usually requires effort on the part of two computers. The client must pass the user's credentials to the database management system (DBMS), and the DBMS must verify the user's identity and return a handle back to the client. This requires network round-trips and processing cycles on both computers. The idea behind database connection pooling is simple: Because a connection is relatively expensive to open, an application can scale to accommodate more users if it can cache these connections and share them across multiple clients.

In a two-tier application, each client computer must establish its own connection to the DBMS, as shown in Figure 7-9. The fact that each client application runs in a separate process on a different machine makes it impossible to share connections. In this type of application, a database connection is often established when the user launches the client application and the connection is held open until the application terminates.

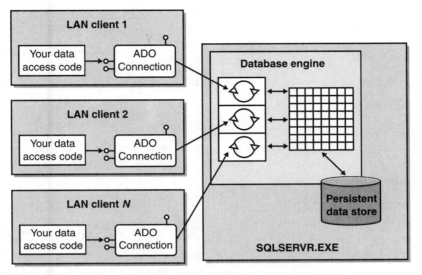

Figure 7-9 *In a two-tier application, each client must establish its own connection to the DBMS. Because each client application runs on a separate computer, there's no opportunity for sharing connections across users.*

In an attempt to conserve server-side resources, the designer of a two-tier application might decide to close a client's connection whenever the user allows 10 minutes to pass without any activity requiring access to the database. After the connection is closed, the user might issue a command to access the database. In such a case, the client application can transparently reestablish another connection. This approach allows the system as a whole to accommodate more users, but each user experiences a delay each time a new connection must be established with the DBMS.

The architecture for a three-tier application offers several advantages over that of a two-tier application. One significant benefit is the ability to share database connections. As clients submit requests from the presentation tier, objects running on behalf of many different users all use a common set of preopened connections. This sharing makes it possible to scale to levels that aren't possible in a two-tier application.

Figure 7-10 shows the high-level architecture of a three-tier application that uses database connection pooling. When you build this style of application, the use of connection pooling makes your code run faster and allows more users to get by on far fewer database connections. The best news of all is that you don't have to write the code to share and manage database connections across users. It's already built into OLE-DB and ODBC. As long as your OLE-DB providers and ODBC drivers support this feature, your ADO code can benefit from it automatically whenever it runs in a middle-tier environment such as COM+ or IIS.

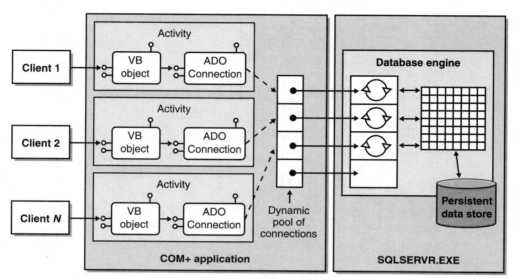

Figure 7-10 *In a three-tier application, database connections can be shared. Both ODBC and OLE-DB provide the basis for connection management and automatic connection pooling.*

How Does Connection Pooling Work?

Automatic connection pooling has been part of ODBC for a while, but it was not until the release of Microsoft Data Access Components (MDAC) 2 that connection pooling was added to OLE-DB as well. Connection pooling in OLE-DB is enabled by an OLE-DB service component that works with the OLE-DB provider that you use to talk to the DBMS. You simply open and close ADO connections and the connection pooling is conducted for you behind the scenes.

Let's look at an example. Suppose you're working with the native OLE-DB provider for SQL Server (SQLOLEDB). If all your data access code accesses a single database in one computer running SQL Server, OLE-DB can place and manage all your connections in a single pool. The first time an object in a COM+ server application creates a new ADO *Connection* object and invokes the *Open* method, OLE-DB must establish an actual connection to the DBMS. However, when you invoke the *Close* method, OLE-DB does not drop the connection to the DBMS. Instead, the connection is placed in a pool so that it can be used by other objects that need it.

When the code running on behalf of another user invokes the *Open* method on a second ADO *Connection* object, OLE-DB looks in the pool to see whether a preexisting connection is available. If it finds an established connection, your application doesn't have to contact the DBMS to establish a new connection. Instead, it can perform its work using the first connection. This speeds things up considerably.

Let's take a moment to consider the limitations of the connection-pooling scheme used by OLE-DB. A connection pool can be used only by objects in the same process. If all your objects run in a single instance of DLLHOST.EXE or INETINFO.EXE, they can all share the same pool.

You should also note that every connection in a pool must be associated with the same OLE-DB provider, server computer, database, user ID, and password. If your application is connecting to both SQL Server and ORACLE, OLE-DB maintains a separate pool for each DBMS. Likewise, you must use the same user ID and password to place all your connections in the same pool. If you want every object in a server application to use a single pool of connections, every component must use the same connect string.

When all the connections from the pool are in use and a client calls a method to open another connection, OLE-DB establishes a new connection with the DBMS. This allows the pool to grow dynamically. OLE-DB also places a timeout interval on each connection in the pool. OLE-DB automatically closes a connection that remains idle for more than 60 seconds. This allows the pool to shrink back to a more efficient size when a peak traffic time is followed by a time with lower activity.

You should also be aware that trappable ADO errors can occur when the DBMS reaches its maximum number of connections. You're on your own because neither OLE-DB nor ADO helps you handle the errors that are raised because of this problem. If SQL Server is configured to allow 50 connections and the connection-pooling scheme attempts to open the fifty-first connection, for example, your ADO code will experience an error in the call to *Open*. You must write contingency code to deal with this. One way to handle this error is to reattempt opening the connection another few times. The ultimate solution usually involves getting the database administrator to reconfigure the DBMS to allow for a larger number of connections.

There's another important limitation related to this database connection-pooling scheme. What happens if your COM+ application has a pool of 10 connections and the computer running the SQL Server database gets rebooted? Every connection in the pool is unusable. Should you shut down a COM+ server application when the database is restarted? This isn't an elegant solution, but many companies deal with the problem in this way.

Taking Advantage of Database Connection Pooling

So maybe writing data access code isn't as straightforward as you might have thought. A call to the *Close* method doesn't really mean close; it means *release* the connection back into the pool. Moreover, a call to *Open* doesn't really mean open—it means *acquire* a connection from the pool. As you've seen, a call to *Open* can result in growing the pool by one if all the existing connections are already in use.

Your objects should never be selfish with a database connection. The most important habit to get into is to acquire connections late and release them early. The sooner your objects release their connections, the greater chance that each object can acquire an existing connection in the pool. However, if your objects hold onto connections longer than necessary, your application might establish extra connections that it doesn't need. This will penalize you in terms of performance and resource usage.

You should design your components to acquire and release connections on a per-method basis. Here's a good starting point for a method that contains data access code:

```
Sub MyMethod()
    Dim conn As ADODB.Connection
    Set conn = New ADODB.Connection
    conn.Open sConnect ' (1) establish connection
    ' Your code goes here.  (2) conduct read/write operations
    conn.Close          ' (3) close connection
    Set conn = Nothing
End Sub
```

Declaring your ADO connection objects in the declaration section of your class modules typically doesn't help your design and can get you in trouble. In a COM+ application, your ADO Connection objects should always be closed at the end of each request. If you rely on *Class_Initialize* and *Class_Terminate* to open and close a class-level ADO *Connection* object, you'll likely hold onto connections longer than you need to. Look at the following class definition for the component *CCustomerManager*:

```
' Class CCustomerManager
Private conn As ADODB.Connection

Sub Class_Initialize()
    Set conn = New ADODB.Connection
    conn.Open sConnect
End Sub

Sub AddCustomer(ByVal Customer As String)
    ' Code to add new customer record using conn
End Sub

Sub Class_Terminate()
    conn.Close
    Set conn = Nothing
End Sub
```

CCustomerManager acquires a connection when it's created and releases the connection upon termination. The client code to use this component looks something like this:

```
Dim CustMgr As CCustomerManager
Set CustMgr = New CCustomerManager
CustMgr.AddCustomer "Bob"
Set CustMgr = Nothing
```

The problem with this approach is that connections are held open while you're waiting for the Visual Basic runtime to create and tear down objects. The connection is held longer than it needs to be. What's more, if the client forgets to set the *CCustomerManager* object equal to *Nothing*, it takes the Visual Basic garbage collector even longer to close the connection. Forgetting to set your objects equal to *Nothing* also exposes you to other problems in which objects aren't shut down properly. You're better off opening and closing your connections in methods that are explicitly called by the client.

Now imagine what would happen if you had a second component, *CProductManager*, that was similar to the *CCustomerManager* component and the client wrote code that looked like this:

```
Dim CustMgr As CCustomerManager
Set CustMgr = New CCustomerManager
CustMgr.AddCustomer "Bob"
Dim ProdMgr As CProductManager
Set ProdMgr = New CProductManager
ProdMgr.AddProduct "Dog"
```

This code has problems because it attempts to acquire a second connection before releasing the first connection within the scope of a single client request. This code requires two connections when it could get by with one.

During the design phase, you might occasionally encounter a situation in which it's acceptable to declare an ADO *Connection* object in the declaration section of a class module. This might be the case if you need to call multiple data access methods on one object in a single request. For example, the client might need to call the *AddCustomer* method multiple times and you don't want to keep releasing and reacquiring a connection from the pool in a single request. Look at the following class definition of the *CCustomerManager* class and note the addition of two new methods:

```
' Class CCustomerManager
Private conn As ADODB.Connection

Sub AcquireConnection()
    Set conn = New ADODB.Connection
    conn.Open sConnect
End Sub

Sub AddCustomer(ByVal Customer As String)
    ' Assume that AcquireConnection has been called.
    ' Code to add new customer record using conn
End Sub
```

(continued)

```
Sub ReleaseConnection()
    conn.Close
    Set conn = Nothing
End Sub
```

To use this new design, the client must explicitly call methods to acquire and release the connection. The client code is rewritten to look like this:

```
Dim CustMgr As CCustomerManager
Set CustMgr = New CCustomerManager
CustMgr.AcquireConnection
CustMgr.AddCustomer "John"
CustMgr.AddCustomer "Paul"
CustMgr.AddCustomer "George"
CustMgr.AddCustomer "Ringo"
CustMgr.ReleaseConnection
Set CustMgr = Nothing
```

As you can see, this design puts the responsibility on the client to do the right thing. Lots of programmers dream of a world in which objects can always take care of themselves. They feel that this is something that has been promised to them by object-oriented programming languages. They reason that an object should be able to transparently acquire and release its own resources. Unfortunately, this practice doesn't result in the most efficient code. The examples I've just shown you clearly demonstrate otherwise. You should open and close connections on a per-method basis or you should expect your designs to take on more complexity.

As you move into more complex designs, it's up to you to release database connections as quickly as possible once you acquire them from the pool. This usually requires more attention to detail and well thought-out collaboration between the objects in your application.

SHARING POOLABLE OBJECTS

So far, this chapter has discussed sharing threads, memory, and database connections across a set of clients. In addition to these types of resources, COM+ also provides a recycling mechanism for sharing a set of objects across a set of clients with a scheme known as *object pooling*. Object pooling can improve an application's scalability because it reduces the need to create and destroy objects throughout the lifetime of a process. I must state up front that Visual Basic isn't capable of producing components that create poolable objects. This limitation of Visual Basic is due to problems associated with thread affinity. However, you should still have a basic understanding of how object pooling works and why it's important.

Each pool represents a set of objects created from the same CLSID. Once client A has finished using an object, the COM+ runtime deactivates the object and places it back in the pool. When client B needs an object of the same CLSID, there's no reason to create another one. The COM+ runtime can simply take an object from the pool and activate it within the activity of client B. At a high level, object pooling is very similar to database connection pooling. Many different clients acquire and release a specific type of resource, and system-provided code matches up a small number of resources to a large number of clients.

Object pooling requires the use of *just-in-time activation*. When a client has finished using an object, the COM+ runtime must break the association between the client and the object. This is known as *deactivation*. When the client needs another object, the COM+ runtime must find another object and associate it with the client. This is known as *activation*. What's really neat about this scheme is that the client doesn't perceive that objects are being deactivated and reactivated. It simply acquires a connection to a logical object and invokes a series of method calls. The client has no idea that the physical object that executes the first method call might be different from one that executes the second method call.

Poolable objects are created from configured components with a *JustInTime-Activation* attribute setting of *True*. When COM+ creates a new context for an object that is configured for just-in-time activation, it adds a special Boolean flag known as the *done bit,* as shown in Figure 7-11. Every time a call returns from the object, the COM+ interception code examines the done bit. If the done bit is set to *True*, the COM+ runtime deactivates the object. Now, things get a little tricky because the client that created the object is holding onto a proxy that doesn't have an object on the other side. However, on the next method call the COM+ runtime performs a just-in-time activation to service the client's request.

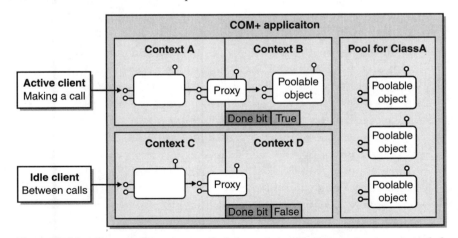

Figure 7-11 *Object pooling is controlled through just-in-time activation. A pooled object is typically activated and deactivated on each method call.*

As you can see, the done bit is a pretty important part of this scheme. In most cases, the done bit should be set to *True* to release a poolable object back to the pool as soon as possible. You can set the done bit to *True* in two ways. One way is to configure a method-level attribute named *AutoComplete*. When this attribute is turned on, the interception code sets the done bit to *True* before executing the method. You can also manipulate the done bit programmatically. The *IContextState* interface has a method named *SetDeactivateOnReturn* that allows you to set the done bit to either *True* or *False*. Note that the *ObjectContext* interface has a method named *SetComplete* that sets the done bit to *True* in addition to casting a vote to commit the current transaction.

Even though you can't create poolable objects using Visual Basic, you still need to understand how the done bit works if you plan to create transactional components. Transactional components are like poolable components in that they also require just-in-time activation. In Chapter 8, I'll revisit this topic and spend more time discussing the need to deactivate Visual Basic objects running in a transaction.

Why Is Object Pooling Important?

The primary motive behind object pooling is that some middle-tier objects are expensive to continually create and initialize. If a set of these "expensive" objects can be created once and recycled across a set of clients, the server computer can conserve the processing cycles associated with this ongoing object creation and initialization. Think of a pooled object in the same way that you think of any other shared middle-tier resource.

You shouldn't expect that any component will experience a significant performance boost when you add support for object pooling. While object pooling saves processing cycles associated with the continual creation and destruction of objects, it requires additional processing cycles for managing the pool. The system must insert an object into the pool after deactivation and must fish out another object for every just-in-time activation. For most lightweight components, the difference between using pooling and not using pooling is marginally small. However, certain types of components benefit dramatically from object pooling.

During the design phase you should ask yourself whether a component is a good candidate for object pooling. Specifically, you should ask whether the creation and initialization of this object type is both expensive and generic. If the answer is yes, object pooling can be beneficial. If the answer is no, object pooling probably won't be very valuable.

Let's look at an example of a component that can benefit from object pooling. Assume that you're designing a component that will establish a connection to a mainframe application. It will take each object about 5 seconds to establish the connection. That's the expensive part. However, once the object establishes the connection to the mainframe application, the object and its connection can be used across many different clients. That's the generic part. The object holds no client-specific state. It's equally useful to any client in its initialized state.

Figure 7-12 shows the Activation tab of the component's Properties dialog box (accessible through the Component Services administrative tool) where you can configure the object pooling settings for a component in a COM+ application. (These settings are always disabled for a Visual Basic component.) Notice that the Minimum Pool Size is set to 10. When you configure your component like this, the COM+ runtime automatically creates and initializes 10 objects when the application is launched. The initialization time for these objects is then amortized over the lifetime of the application.

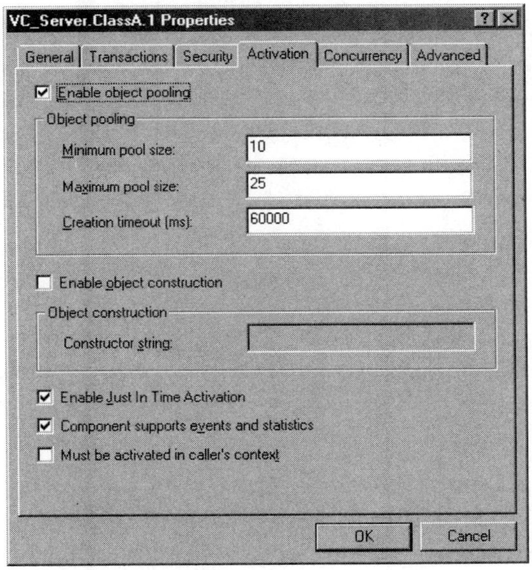

Figure 7-12 *You can configure a C++ component for object pooling by using the component's Properties dialog box.*

The primary advantage of object pooling is that each client doesn't have to wait 5 seconds while an object in the middle tier establishes a connection. The client simply acquires an object with an existing connection from the pool. In a scenario such as this, object pooling can significantly improve client response times as well as the application's overall throughput.

In addition to saving processing cycles associated with object creation and initialization, object pooling can also provide *resource throttling*. Throttling provides a way to limit the number of clients that use a set of objects and their associated resources. For instance, you might want to limit the maximum number of outstanding connections to the mainframe application at any one time. By configuring the component to be throttled, you can easily do so.

The Maximum Pool Size setting restricts how many users can use the component at any one time. If you specify a setting of 25, only 25 clients can use the component at a time. Once 25 clients have activated objects, any other clients will block until one of the other clients releases an object back to the pool. A blocked client will simply wait for the next available object.

As long as the done bit is set, an object is returned to the pool whenever a method returns to a client. Setting the done bit isn't required, but it's preferred in most situations. When the done bit is set, each client acquires, uses, and releases an object on a per-method-call basis. In our example, it means that only 25 clients can run method calls at the same time. If these objects don't set the done bit, the maximum size indicates how many clients can create connections to an object. As you can see, setting the done bit allows for throttling and provides higher levels of concurrency than you'd see were the done bit not set.

In addition to a maximum pool size, a component also has a configurable Creation Timeout setting. A client will block only for the duration of the creation timeout. If a client times out while attempting to activate an object from the pool, it experiences a runtime error. You must then deal with this by providing an error handler for the code that attempts to activate the object.

Let's summarize what object pooling is all about. It's about reusing objects for which initialization is both expensive and generic. I used an example of a component that must establish a connection to a mainframe application. There are many other situations in which you might encounter components that also meet this criterion. However, it's important to remember that a component can't really benefit from object pooling if it doesn't meet this criterion.

Object Pooling vs. Database Connection Pooling

Object pooling solves a few problems associated with the database connection-pooling scheme built into OLE-DB. With database connection pooling, you can't throttle the number of available connections. Object pooling is better because you tune each process to use the optimal number of connections. The COM+ runtime is your friend because it automatically blocks one client until another client releases one of the pooled objects.

Also note that poolable objects can detect when the connection they hold has gone bad. This means that a poolable object can establish a new connection when the existing connection has been dropped. This makes it possible to design poolable objects that are self-healing. You can hide certain problems that can't be hidden by using pooled database connections. When a SQL Server computer is rebooted and a pool of database connections has gone bad, the code that uses these connections requires an error-handler. Code that uses pooled objects can be shielded from such problems.

If these issues seem important, you might find it advantageous to add poolable components to your application. Poolable components can encapsulate the code that establishes and manages a set of connections to a database server or a mainframe application. You can also use them to establish sockets-based connections to other applications. However, a poolable component must meet several requirements. It must be created with C++, its *ThreadingModel* attribute must be set to *Neutral* or *Both*, and it can't exhibit thread affinity. There are a few other requirements as well.

Using C++ along with the Active Template Library (ATL) is the easiest and most straightforward way to create COM+ components that support pooling. The ATL Wizard does most of the work to set things up properly. However, adding support for a poolable component that's involved in a transaction dramatically increases the coding requirements. This is one area of COM+ development in which you unfortunately can't use Visual Basic.

SUMMARY

So, what have we learned? An application's ability to scale starts at the process level. And within each process there must be code dedicated to sharing resources as efficiently as possible. Some of this code is supplied by Microsoft, and some of it you must write.

Sharing data across a lot of users is hard. Concurrency and data consistency are antagonistic by nature. When you write code to get more of one, it usually means you get less of the other. The key to building the fastest possible application is to understand when locking must occur and to avoid locking when it's not necessary. I'll build on this theme in the next chapter, which covers transactions.

And speaking of COM+ transactions, you already have a pretty good head start learning how they work. Knowing about activities, just-in-time activation, and the done bit is critical to understanding the transactional programming model. These concepts are important if you intend to design and create transactional components.

Over the last few years, Visual Basic has advanced impressively in its ability to produce middle-tier components. If fact, many companies refuse to write their business logic and database access code in any other language. However, some areas of COM+ development still require C++. If you need a poolable component or some code that's written directly against OLE-DB, you must bring in the guy who's not afraid of pointers and semicolons. If he can give you what you need, pay him whatever he asks and definitely don't ask him to explain what he's done for you.

Chapter 8

Programming Transactions

At the end of the last chapter, I made a bold statement: The key to building the fastest possible application is in understanding when locking must occur and in avoiding locking when it's not necessary. However, some form of locking is inevitable in an application when many clients are contending for a finite pool of resources. One client must wait for another client to relinquish a thread, and one thread must wait for another thread to relinquish a processor. Each client needs exclusive access to various resources, and this need is detrimental to an application's concurrency and overall throughput.

When you're dealing with resources such as processors, threads, and database connections, you can respond to a growing user base by adding more hardware. Keeping the client-to-resource ratio at a reasonable level is an important part of reducing contention and maintaining acceptable response times. However, when you're dealing with the data that runs your business, the problem of contention doesn't have such a straightforward solution.

Let's say you're building an online commerce application that sells animals such as dogs, cats, and birds. You have a *Products* table that contains a row for each type of animal, and each row tracks the inventory level in the *Quantity* field. Now, here's the problem: There's only one place in the entire application where the inventory level for dogs is kept. The record that tracks the quantity of dogs represents a single point of contention across all clients. When multiple clients attempt to read and write to this value at the same time, consistency and concurrency issues arise. As the number of clients accessing the inventory level of dogs increases, it becomes harder and harder to prevent this contention from seriously compromising the performance of your application.

Just about every business application uses data in one form or another. Some applications are concerned only with querying and analyzing data, while others are primarily concerned with modifying data. Applications that modify data and have a large number of concurrent users are commonly referred to as *online transaction processing* (OLTP) systems. This chapter discusses the most significant issues involved with building this type of application.

You should understand several key OLTP concepts before you start writing transactions for a COM+ application. This chapter reviews the basics of transaction processing, including why a transaction must meet the "ACID rules" and what's meant by a transaction's isolation level. I'll also present two approaches to programming transactions. The first involves writing local transactions against a single database management system (DBMS) such as Microsoft SQL Server. The second involves writing distributed transactions using a more complex infrastructure supplied by COM+ and the Distributed Transaction Coordinator (DTC). Each technique is best suited for certain situations, so you must know the right questions to ask when you're deciding which approach to use.

It's really hard to create a highly optimized OLTP application using SQL statements that are portable across DBMSs from different vendors. If you're primarily concerned with application performance and scalability, you must often compromise on portability. As painful as it sounds, you must often write SQL statements and stored procedures that are particular to one specific DBMS. For this reason, I've chosen to use SQL Server and its native language, Transact-SQL, for the examples in this chapter.

I've chosen SQL Server for two reasons. First, it comes with my MSDN subscription, and second, it's the DBMS with which I have the most experience. I know that many of you use other DBMS products, such as Oracle and DB2. At a high level, the topics examined in this chapter are equally important no matter what DBMS you're using. However, when I give you a hint using Transact-SQL or talk about locking behavior and granularity, I'll leave it up to you to research your DBMS to see how those features are supported.

WHAT IS A TRANSACTION?

A typical command in an OLTP application conducts several read and write operations to perform a single unit of work. In essence, the command executes a transaction. A transaction can be defined as *a related set of operations that read and modify data on behalf of a single client*. As you'll see, the requirements are quite high in an OLTP application that runs many transactions per second.

In this chapter, I'll use a sample application that lets clients submit sales orders to purchase products from the Animal Market database. The database schema for this application is shown in Figure 8-1. To keep things simple, each order is submitted on behalf of a single customer for a specific quantity of one type of product. An example is an order in which Bob buys five dogs for $100 ($20 apiece) The application must perform some validation and make the following updates to properly record the purchase:

- Subtract the purchased quantity from the product's inventory level in the *Products* table

- Add the purchase price to the customer's account balance in the *Customers* table

- Add a new order record to the *Orders* table

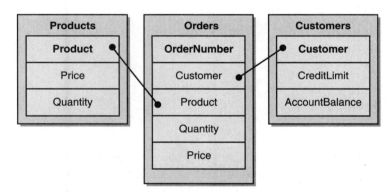

Figure 8-1 *The Animal Market application is based on this database schema.*

In a real-world application, you'd want to allow a customer to buy multiple products in a single order. However, I've avoided such a design because it would require a fourth table to track order details. My simpler database design will allow you to focus more on important OLTP concepts and less on relational database theory.

Here are the SQL statements you need to submit to the DBMS to record the purchase:

```
-- Decrement inventory.
UPDATE Products
SET Quantity = Quantity - 5
WHERE Product = 'Dog'
-- Charge customer.
UPDATE Customers
SET AccountBalance = AccountBalance + 100
```

(continued)

```
WHERE Customer = 'Bob'
-- Add new order record.
INSERT Orders(Customer, Product, Quantity, Price)
VALUES('Bob', 'Dog', 5, 100)
```

You might also want to perform some validation checks before writing a sales order. Here's an example of writing a batch of Transact-SQL statements that performs a validation before attempting an update. The batch raises an error if the requested quantity isn't in stock.

```
DECLARE @Quantity int

SELECT @Quantity = Quantity
FROM Products
WHERE Product = 'Dog'

-- Raise user-defined error 50001
-- if fewer than five dogs are in stock.
If (@Quantity<5)
BEGIN
    RAISERROR(50001,16,1)
    RETURN
END

UPDATE Products
SET Quantity = @Quantity - 5
WHERE Product = 'Dog'
```

This example leverages SQL Server's ability to raise custom error messages back to the client. A call to *RAISERROR* can use custom error messages that have been added to an application with the system-provided stored procedure *sp_addmessage*. You should know how to properly raise errors from SQL statements and how to catch them from a Microsoft Visual Basic component.

A real-world sales order will most likely have other validation checks in addition to the one shown above. However, I'll leave the rest to your imagination. At this point, I've shown enough SQL so that we can begin our discussion of writing transactions.

Transactional Systems

Writing an OLTP application without transaction support from your DBMS or from the underlying platform would be incredibly difficult because so many things can go wrong during a transaction. Users often submit requests that violate business rules. For example, what if an order request asks for a product that isn't in inventory? What if a customer doesn't have the available credit to make the purchase? System failures can occur as well. What if the transaction log has filled up, leaving the database in a read-only condition? What if the DBMS computer is unreachable due to a system crash or a network failure? All these scenarios prevent the user from successfully completing a transaction.

If you didn't get any assistance from your DBMS, you'd have to write lots of contingency code to deal with just about every possible failure scenario. If a transaction successfully completes the first update but can't complete the second, the first operation must be undone. For example, let's say you remove five dogs from inventory, only to discover that the customer doesn't have enough money to buy them. You have to submit a compensating UPDATE statement against the *products* table to replace the inventory you just removed. Or consider a more complex transaction, in which failure occurs on the tenth operation. You have to undo nine updates in order to return the database to its previous state.

Another problem with rolling back write operations in the manner that I've just described is that it doesn't even take concurrency into account. If a large number of clients were bombarding your application with many requests per second, you'd have to write all sorts of locking logic to deal with consistency and synchronization. For instance, look at the following SQL statement:

```
UPDATE Table1
SET Field1 = Field1 * 2
WHERE ID = 'ID28'
```

The statement seems simple enough: It doubles the value of *Field1*. But how can you undo this update? If you can guarantee that no other transaction has changed the value of *Field1*, you can undo it with the following statement:

```
UPDATE Table1
SET Field1 = Field1 * 0.5
WHERE ID = 'ID28'
```

However, if another transaction changes the value in between the submission of your initial SQL statement and your compensating undo statement, the data will be left in an inconsistent state. To guard against this, you would have to implement some kind of locking mechanism, preventing other transactions from changing this field value in between your two statements.

Fortunately, you don't have to write your application in this manner. OLTP application programmers can leverage transaction services provided by the underlying infrastructure. DBMSs such as SQL Server, Oracle, and DB2 provide extensive support for transaction processing. Other types of data sources, such as mainframe applications and message queues, often provide their own form of transaction support as well.

This built-in support makes writing a transaction much simpler. You start a transaction, conduct a series of read and write operations, and finish by committing or rolling back the transaction. The underlying system handles most of the difficult work of dealing with rollback and locking.

A Flashback Through the ACID Rules

If you've read anything about the theory behind transaction processing, you've no doubt heard of the ACID rules. A transaction must be *atomic, consistent, isolated,* and *durable.* When you write a transaction for an OLTP system, all participants should adhere to these rules. You've probably seen these rules countless times, but just to be redundant over and over again, let's review them once more.

- **Atomic**   A transaction must be an all-or-nothing proposition. Everything must be successfully updated or nothing should be updated.

- **Consistent**   Individual operations within a transaction can leave data in such a state that it violates the system's integrity constraints, but before a transaction is released, the system's data as a whole must be returned to a valid state.

- **Isolated**   The system must isolate, or hide, the uncommitted changes of each transaction from all other transactions (typically through locking).

- **Durable**   When a transaction is committed, the data sources involved must place all changes in stable storage, and these changes must be recoverable in the event of a system failure.

Take a moment to consider what the third ACID rule really means. The system must isolate a transaction's uncommitted changes from other transactions because uncommitted changes might be rolled back. Let's look at an example of a system that doesn't provide isolation. When transaction A makes a change, an interval of time passes before the change is committed. If transaction B can see and use the uncommitted changes of transaction A, problems can occur. What happens if transaction A is rolled back? Transaction B can be infected with data that never really existed. An uncommitted read is also known as a *dirty read.* As you can see, to run transactions concurrently, a system must isolate uncommitted changes to enforce data consistency.

As a programmer, you rely on a transactional system to provide the required levels of isolation through locking. A DBMS such as SQL Server incorporates a built-in transaction manager and a lock manager, as shown in Figure 8-2. The transaction manager is responsible for enforcing the ACID rules. It calls on its friend the lock manager to provide each transaction with its required level of isolation.

If transaction A modifies a record, all other transactions that attempt to read this record will block until transaction A is released. Once transaction A is committed, the lock manager allows transaction B to read the record in its new state. Once transaction A has been rolled back, transaction B can read the record in its initial state. In both cases, the lock manager prevents transaction B from seeing uncommitted changes. Transaction B must wait until transaction A has been released.

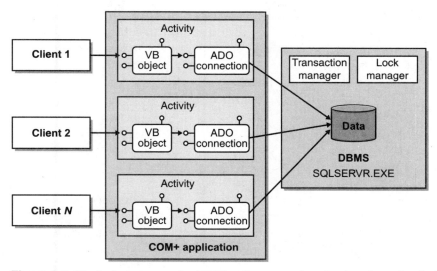

Figure 8-2 *The lock manager of a DBMS enforces synchronization through a locking policy.*

At this point, it's important to make a few observations. Data consistency requires isolation and isolation requires locking. Locking decreases concurrency because it results in blocking. Blocking reduces an application's overall responsiveness and throughput. From these facts, we can formulate two important rules for optimizing an OLTP application:

- Don't acquire unnecessary locks on data items.
- Try to minimize the time that any lock is held.

Locking and Granularity

Most lock managers use more than one level of granularity when they place locks on data. Coarse-grain locks (a table lock, for example) isolate larger amounts of data. Finer-grain locks (such as a record lock) isolate smaller amounts of data. If a transaction attempts to modify every record in a table, the lock manager can perform its work faster by acquiring and releasing a single table lock rather than acquiring and releasing many individual record locks. This is especially true for a table that has 100,000 rows.

However, a table lock has a definite downside—it seriously affects concurrency. Once transaction A acquires an exclusive table lock, transaction B must wait to access any record in the table. This is true even if the two transactions aren't interested in the same records. With record-level locks, a transaction locks only the data that it's actually using. Record-level locks are preferable when a transaction is modifying a single record in a large table. Finer-grain locks have much less impact on concurrency.

SQL Server adds one additional level of locking, known as a *page lock*. A page lock is somewhere between a record lock and a table lock in terms of granularity. SQL Server stores records in terms of pages. A standard page size helps SQL Server optimize disk I/O when moving data back and forth between memory and storage. It also provides a locking granularity that allows for faster performance than record-level locking but isn't as restrictive as table-level locking.

SQL Server 6 and earlier versions support only page-level and table-level locking. SQL Server 6.5 introduced a scheme in which you can use record-level locks at the last page in a table when you insert rows. However, this feature is off by default; you must explicitly enable it on a table-by-table basis. Version 7 is the first version of SQL Server to offer true record-level locking.

SQL Server 7 has a built-in optimizer that determines the level of locking for each read operation and write operation. If you're running an INSERT or an UPDATE that involves a single row, the optimizer typically uses record-level locking. If you have an update that involves many rows, however, the locking optimizer might escalate the level to page locks or possibly a table lock.

In most cases, you can rely on SQL Server's optimizer to choose the locking level for you. However, in some situations you might want to explicitly tell SQL Server to use row-level locking or a table lock. SQL Server includes a set of locking hints that influence locking granularity. You can place a hint in your SQL code like this:

```
UPDATE Products WITH (ROWLOCK)
SET Quantity = Quantity - 1
WHERE Name = 'Dog'
```

Write Locks vs. Read Locks

Most lock managers use two lock types: *write locks* and *read locks*. A lock manager uses write locks (also called *exclusive locks*) on data items to isolate the uncommitted changes of a transaction. The lock manager places read locks (also called *shared locks*) on data items when they're being read.

A write lock conflicts with other write locks and with read locks. A transaction that has a write lock blocks all other transactions from reading or writing to the data item in question. The data item remains locked until the transaction is committed or rolled back. This makes sense because the system must isolate uncommitted changes to ensure data consistency. However, this isolation has a price: The blocking reduces overall system concurrency and throughput.

Read locks don't conflict with other read locks. Many transactions can acquire read locks on the same data item concurrently. However, a transaction can't acquire a write lock on a data item that has outstanding read locks. This behavior ensures that a transaction doesn't overwrite a data item while another transaction is reading it. Table 8-1 summarizes how the lock manager handles lock requests when locks are already in place.

Table 8-1 **HOW THE LOCK MANAGER HANDLES LOCK REQUESTS**

	No Lock Held	*Read Lock Held*	*Write Lock Held*
Read Lock Requested	Lock acquired	Lock acquired	Request blocked
Write Lock Requested	Lock acquired	Request blocked	Request blocked

Isolation Levels

It's not all that difficult to determine how a lock manager uses write locks. When a transaction makes a change, the data item in question is exclusively locked from all other transactions. The system knows to hold this exclusive lock to the very end of the transaction. However, the lock manager's timing for acquiring and releasing read locks isn't as obvious. When a transaction reads a data item, how long should the system hold a read lock? Should the read lock be held for the entire transaction or just for the duration of the read operation?

You can adjust the amount of time a read lock is held by tuning the transaction's *isolation level*. While longer read locks help enforce data consistency and transaction isolation, they also degrade concurrency and throughput. In some situations, releasing read locks before the end of a transaction can provide an important optimization. Here are the four isolation levels supported by SQL Server:

- **Read Uncommitted** The transaction can read any data items whether or not they have outstanding write locks. Reading a data item with an outstanding write lock is known as a *dirty read*. Also, the transaction won't acquire (or release) read locks. This isolation level provides the fastest access but is vulnerable to inconsistent reads.

- **Read Committed** Transactions can read only data items that have been committed. A transaction running at this isolation level must wait until another transaction's write lock is released before accessing a data item. Read locks are held for the duration of read operations but are released before the end of the transaction. This is the default isolation level used by both SQL Server and ActiveX Data Objects (ADO) when you run a transaction without COM+.

- **Repeatable Read** This level is like Read Committed except that all read locks are held to the end of the transaction. Any data item that's read in any stage of a transaction can be read later with the same results; that is, all data read by the transaction remains in the same state until the transaction is committed or rolled back.

■ **Serializable** This level is like Repeatable Read with one extra qualification: A query that runs multiple times in a serializable transaction must always have the same results. Phantom data items can't be inserted by other transactions until the transaction is complete. For example, if a transaction running at this level runs a query to determine the number of records in a table, no other transaction can insert a row in the table until the transaction is completed. The lock manager typically enforces this isolation level through the use of a table lock or an index range lock. This is the default isolation level used by SQL Server when it is called by an object running in a COM+ transaction.

Every level except Serializable compromises isolation to improve concurrency and throughput. When you run transactions with an isolation level of Serializable, the transaction manager favors data consistency and isolation at the expense of concurrency and throughput. A transaction is said to be serializable if it isn't affected by other transactions. When every transaction is serializable, it has the same effect on an application as running the transactions one at a time. Running all your operations at the Serializable level is always best for data consistency—but worst for concurrency. Later in the chapter, you'll see there are ways to run different operations inside the same transaction at different levels of isolation.

PROGRAMMING LOCAL TRANSACTIONS

Writing a simple transaction against a single DBMS isn't very complicated. Let's say you're creating an application that keeps all of its data in one SQL Server database. One way to start and control a local SQL Server transaction is to use methods exposed by the ADO *Connection* object. Look at the following code:

```
Dim conn As Connection
Set conn = New Connection
conn.Open MyConnectString
conn.IsolationLevel = adXactSerializable
conn.BeginTrans
    ' SQL statements omitted for clarity.
    conn.Execute sqlDecrementInventory
    conn.Execute sqlChargeCustomer
    conn.Execute sqlAddOrder
conn.CommitTrans
```

While this might be the easiest approach, controlling a transaction through an ADO connection object results in inefficient locking because it takes at least three round trips to the DBMS to complete a transaction. You hold on to locks while calls are sent back and forth between your ADO code in the middle tier and the DBMS.

Whenever possible, you should run each transaction in a single round trip to the DBMS, especially if your ADO code and the DBMS run on separate computers.

There are two common ways to run a local transaction in a single round trip to the DBMS. You can submit a SQL batch that includes a set of statements, or you can invoke a stored procedure that holds the equivalent SQL logic. Both approaches require you to control the transaction programmatically by using Transact-SQL. Here's an example of a batch that runs a transaction:

```
-- Set isolation level to Serializable.
SET TRANSACTION ISOLATION LEVEL SERIALIZABLE
-- Run transaction to purchase five dogs for $100.
BEGIN TRANSACTION
    -- Decrement product quantity from inventory.
    UPDATE Products SET Quantity = Quantity - 5
    WHERE Product = 'Dog'
    -- Charge price to customer account.
    UPDATE Customers SET AccountBalance = AccountBalance + 100
    WHERE Customer = 'Bob'
    -- Add order record.
    INSERT Orders(Customer, Product, Quantity, Price)
    VALUES('Bob', 'Dog', 5, 100)
COMMIT TRANSACTION
```

This simple example doesn't include any code to validate data or deal with transaction rollback, but it illustrates how to execute a series of SQL statements in a single transaction. When you execute this batch using an ADO *Connection* or *Command* object, SQL Server uses its own internal transaction manager to enforce the ACID rules. You should observe that this batch also allows you to run and release a transaction in a single round trip.

SQL Server transactions use a default isolation level of Read Committed. The batch in the previous example adjusts the default isolation level to Serializable. All statements in this transaction run at this level. SQL Server 7 also allows you to add hints to adjust the isolation level on a statement-by-statement basis.

An alternative to including SQL batches in your data access code is to create stored procedures. Stored procedures can hold the same Transact-SQL logic, and they typically yield the best performance because of the way they're cached in memory in the DBMS. When you define a store procedure, you can include parameters defined for input, input/output, and output, as well as a return value. If you call a stored procedure that has output parameters or a return value, you should call it using an ADO command object.

Many people have suggested that stored procedures don't fit into multitier application design. They argue that the logic for validation and business rules should be maintained in a language such as Visual Basic instead of Transact-SQL. If you agree with this argument, you're more concerned with code maintainability than with application performance. Stored procedures will always run faster. If you decide to write most or all your logic in Visual Basic, you really need to pay attention to how many round trips you're making to the DBMS.

For example, if you try to maintain too much logic in Visual Basic, you might end up with a design in which you make one round trip to start a transaction, a second to get some data for validation, a third to execute an UPDATE statement, and a fourth to commit the transaction. In a larger, more complex transaction, this approach can lead to 20 to 30 round trips for each transaction. My point is that this approach simply doesn't scale. While calls are going back and forth between your data access code and the DBMS, locks are being held that degrade your application's throughput and scalability. Reducing round trips is a very important aspect of scalability.

CATCHING ERRORS FROM SQL SERVER'S NATIVE OLE DB PROVIDER

Database programmers often encounter a problem when they submit batches or execute stored procedures against SQL Server for the first time. If you're using the native OLE DB provider, it's easy to miss errors that are raised by a batch or a stored procedure. For example, if you write a batch with multiple SELECT, INSERT, UPDATE, and DELETE statements, the underlying data access layer returns a separate result for each statement. This happens even with a SQL statement such as an action query that doesn't return any rows. Each result carries an HRESULT, the *RowsAffected* value and possibly a recordset, and an error message associated with the execution of the statement. The fact that the native OLE-DB provider returns multiple results means you must process each one to make sure you handle errors raised by statements defined later in the batch. Here's a simple example of what your code should look like:

```
Dim rs As Recordset
Set rs = conn.Execute sqlMyBigBatch
Do Until rs Is Nothing
    Set rs = rs.NextRecordset ' Process all results.
Loop
```

PROGRAMMING DISTRIBUTED TRANSACTIONS

As you've seen, a single DBMS can enforce the ACID rules when it holds all the data involved in a transaction. For example, SQL Server supplies an internal transaction manager that provides commit and rollback behavior. The transaction manager also guarantees that committed data is recoverable in the event of a system failure.

But what happens if not all the data involved in a transaction resides on the same computer or in the same database format? OLTP applications that run such distributed transactions are far more challenging to implement. Imagine a situation in which the *Products* table is in a SQL Server database, the *Customers* table is in an Oracle database, and the *Orders* table is in DB2, as shown in Figure 8-3. To run a distributed transaction, you must use software that coordinates commit/abort behavior and recovery across several data sources at once.

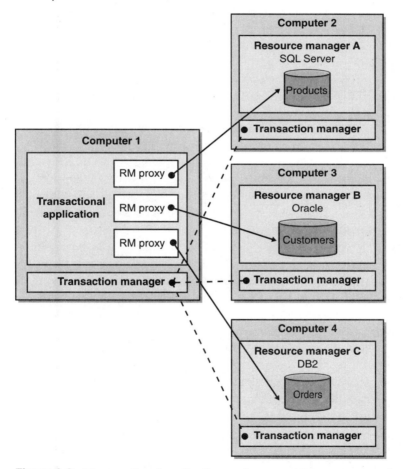

Figure 8-3 *A transactional application and transaction managers work together to monitor a distributed transaction and to execute the two-phase commit protocol across multiple resource managers.*

Quite a few software products use a similar high-level architecture to solve the problems associated with running distributed transactions. For example, CICS from IBM, Tuxedo from BEA Systems, and COM+ from Microsoft all use a high-level abstraction called a *transaction manager* (TM) and a special protocol called *two-phase commit.*

Much of the terminology related to distributed transactions was coined in the early days of CICS. The application that performs the read/write operations and ultimately controls the transaction is known as a *transactional application*. Each data source is known as a *resource manager* (RM). Each *node* (computer) in the system either runs a local session of a TM or communicates with a remote session of a TM. An application that's built on top of this infrastructure is often called a *transaction monitor*.

To see things in a clearer light, let's examine how these different applications and services interact. A transactional application calls a TM and makes a request to start a distributed transaction. The TM creates a transaction by generating a unique ID and initializing various data structures to manage the transaction's lifetime. This TM is in charge of running the two-phase commit protocol and is known as the *coordinating transaction manager* (CTM).

In addition to calling the TM to start a distributed transaction, a transactional application also enlists connections to one or more RMs. This enlistment process involves passing the distributed transaction's ID to an RM and telling the RM to subordinate control of the transaction to the CTM.

In some deployments, an enlisted RM communicates directly with the CTM. In other deployments, an RM enlists with a local TM, which is known as a *participating transaction manager* (PTM). During this type of enlistment, the CTM must also establish a connection with the PTM. Once each connection has been enlisted, the lines of communication are set up as shown earlier in Figure 8-3.

The transactional application and the CTM work together to enforce the ACID rules across the entire transaction. The transactional application issues commands to the CTM, and the CTM coordinates commit/abort behavior across the entire group of participants.

The CTM enforces the ACID rules in a distributed transaction by running the two-phase commit protocol. After the transactional application indicates that it wants to commit the transaction, the CTM runs phase 1 to prepare the transaction. In this phase, the CTM sends an "Are you prepared?" message to each participant. If everything goes according to plan, each participant responds with an "I'm prepared" message.

By responding with an "I'm prepared" message, an RM indicates that its changes are in a durable state and that it can either commit or roll back those changes on request. Once every participant has responded with an "I'm prepared" message, the CTM knows that the changes can be committed, and the CTM can complete phase 1.

Here's what happens at the end of phase 1 in a successful transaction. After receiving an "I'm prepared" message from each participant, the CTM writes to its log that the transaction has been committed and returns a successful response to the transactional application. At this point, the transactional application is free to start other work, and the locks acquired by the transaction are still being held.

In phase 2, the CTM sends a "Time to commit" message to each participant. When an RM receives such a message, it's free to release the locks and discard any residue required to roll back the transaction. After committing its changes, each RM sends an "I'm done" message to the CTM. Once the CTM receives this message from every participant, it assumes that all the work has been successfully completed and that it, too, can discard any residue required to roll back the transaction.

As a programmer building COM+ applications, you don't have to be overly concerned with the inner workings of the two-phase commit protocol, which is really just an implementation detail. When you commit a distributed transaction in COM+, you should assume that the system will enforce the ACID rules. Nothing in the COM+ programming model requires you to think about the two-phase commit protocol.

If you want to read more on the subject, pick up a copy of *Principles of Transaction Processing* by Bernstein and Newcomer (Morgan Kaufman Publishers, 1997), which explains the low-level details of the two-phase commit protocol that are important to system implementers and administrators (in addition to many other important topics). If you plan to make a living writing OLTP applications, this book is required reading.

The Distributed Transaction Coordinator

Microsoft's TM is the Distributed Transaction Coordinator. This product initially shipped with SQL Server 6.5, but products such as COM+ and Microsoft Message Queuing Services (MSMQ) now use it heavily as well. The DTC runs as a system service on Microsoft Windows 2000 and on Microsoft Windows NT. Figure 8-4 shows how the DTC can act as a coordinating TM and also as a participating TM.

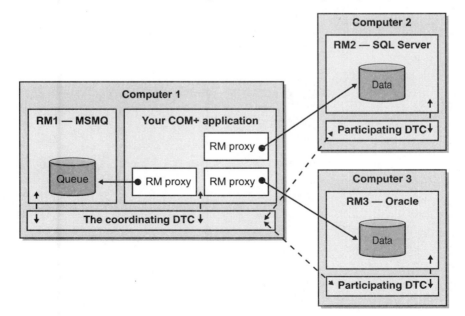

Figure 8-4 *The DTC is used by products such as COM+, MSMQ, and SQL Server.*

The DTC is based on a protocol called OLE Transactions, which defines a set of COM interfaces through which transactional applications and RMs communicate with the DTC. X/Open is another popular standard used by products such as Tuxedo, Encina, and TOP END. X/Open, like OLE Transactions, standardizes the way in which transactional applications and RMs communicate with TMs.

In the early days of MTS, SQL Server and Oracle were the only two RMs that provided interoperability with the DTC. Today, the list of RMs that work with the DTC is fairly long. Some RMs are written to use OLE Transactions. Other, X/Open-based RMs require bridging software to work correctly. For details about interoperability, you should consult the MTS SDK as well as the vendor of your resource manager. From this point on, I'll assume that you have one or more RMs that are interoperable with COM+ and the DTC.

Interacting directly with the DTC

You can execute distributed transactions using the DTC in two ways. The easy way is to use declarative transactions and let the COM+ runtime make all the complicated calls to the DTC for you. The second (and more manly) option is to create an application that communicates with the DTC directly. If you choose this second approach, you'll be writing your code in C++.

I'd like to digress for a second and describe the requirements of writing code directly against the DTC. You'll never actually do this as a Visual Basic programmer, but it's important to walk through the basic steps so that you can appreciate what the COM+ runtime does on your behalf when you run a declarative transaction.

The transactional application must first establish a connection with the DTC by calling *DtcGetTransactionManager* to obtain an *ITransactionDispenser* reference to the DTC proxy core object. The *ITransactionDispenser* interface contains a method named *BeginTransaction*. When you invoke this method, the DTC creates a new transaction object and returns a reference to your application. This transaction object exposes a *Commit* method and an *Abort* method through the *ITransaction* interface. When you create a transaction, you can specify both the default isolation level and a timeout interval.

Next, you must establish a connection to one or more RMs. For example, you can connect to a DBMS such as SQL Server or Oracle using an OLE DB provider. It's important to understand that the OLE DB provider acts as an RM proxy. After you've connected to a few RMs, you must explicitly enlist these connections by making calls to OLE DB. Once your connections are enlisted, you can execute SQL operations such as SELECT, INSERT, UPDATE, and DELETE. All your reading and writing activity is charged against your distributed transaction.

If the transactional application calls *Abort*, the coordinating DTC tells all the participants to roll back their changes and release their locks. If the transactional application successfully completes its work on all RMs, it calls *Commit* to tell the coordinating DTC to start executing the two-phase commit protocol. The coordinating DTC calls all the participants in parallel, and asks them if they're prepared to commit their work. The fact that it makes these calls in parallel means that the local DTC doesn't have to wait for the first participant to respond before sending the prepare request to the second participant. This approach improves performance significantly.

After the coordinating DTC receives an "I'm prepared" response from each enlisted participant, it logs the fact that the transaction was committed and returns a successful response to the transactional application. This is where phase 1 ends and phase 2 begins.

In phase 2, the coordinating DTC sends a "Time to commit" message to all participants in parallel. Each participant commits its changes, releases its locks, and sends an "I'm done" message to the coordinating DTC. Once the coordinating DTC receives all the "I'm done" messages, it can forget about the transaction because there's no longer any need to recover the transaction in case of a system failure.

As you can see, writing a distributed transaction in this manner requires a lot of attention to low-level details. You should also observe that this approach is similar to writing a local transaction in the sense that it's a procedural paradigm. You make explicit calls to begin, commit, and roll back the transaction. Fortunately, COM+ provides a declarative programming model that makes things much easier. However, you should keep in mind that behind the scenes with a COM+ transaction, things happen exactly as they've been described here. COM+ adds value by hiding the gory details of interacting with the DTC and enlisting RMs.

COM+ AND DECLARATIVE TRANSACTIONS

COM+ makes it much easier to run distributed transactions using the DTC by providing a programming model based on declarative transactions. You are responsible for creating objects in the scope of a COM+ transaction. When you do this, the COM+ runtime interacts with the DTC to create a distributed transaction. COM+ also enlists your RM connections behind the scenes.

After you create your objects in a transaction, you can use a handful of methods supplied by the *ObjectContext* interface or the *IContextState* interface to control the outcome of the transaction. As you'll see, you're responsible for releasing each transaction as soon as possible.

Let's start by examining how to create one or more objects in a COM+ transaction. Every configured component has a *Transaction* attribute. Figure 8-5 shows the Transactions tab of a component's Properties dialog box, which is available through the Component Services administrative tool. You can use this tab to view and modify the *Transaction* attribute for each component in a COM+ application. If you're using Visual Basic 5, you must first install your components and then adjust the *Transaction* attribute by hand.

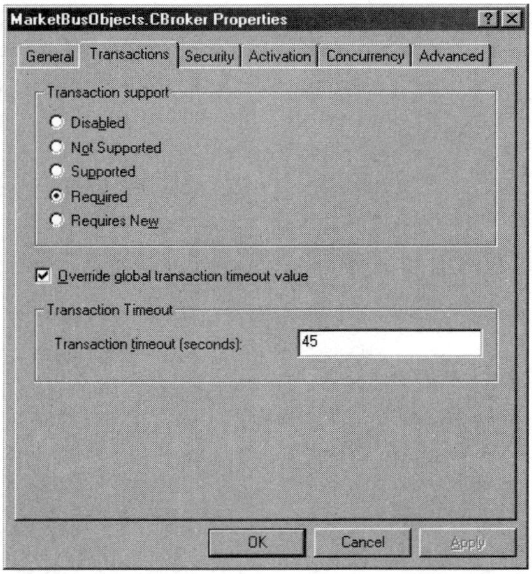

Figure 8-5 *When the COM+ runtime creates an object from a component, it looks at the component's* Transaction *attribute to determine whether the object should be created in a new transaction or an existing transaction.*

Visual Basic 6 added *MTSTransactionMode* to the property sheet of each public class module in an ActiveX DLL project. When you set this property, as shown in Figure 8-6, Visual Basic publishes the corresponding COM+ *Transaction* attribute in your server's type library. When you install your DLL in a COM+ application, the catalog manager automatically configures your components with the appropriate *Transaction* attribute.

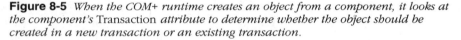

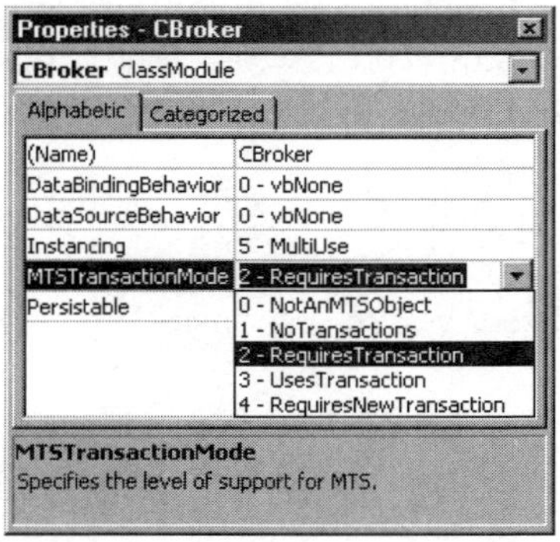

Figure 8-6 *When you install a DLL in a COM+ application, each component is configured with the* Transaction *attribute that corresponds to its* MTSTransactionMode *property.*

Notice the difference between the *MTSTransactionMode* property values for a Visual Basic class module and the *Transaction* attribute values in COM+. Don't let this variation bother you; it's just a slight difference in the wording between Visual Basic and COM+. Each of the four *MTSTransactionMode* property settings has a corresponding *Transaction* attribute setting, as shown in Table 8-2.

Table 8-2 *MTSTRANSACTIONMODE* PROPERTY SETTINGS AND EQUIVALENT COM+ *TRANSACTION* ATTRIBUTE SETTINGS

MTSTransactionMode Property *Setting*	COM+ Transaction *Attribute Setting*
RequiresTransaction	Required
RequiresNewTransaction	Requires New
UsesTransaction	Supported
NoTransactions	Not Supported
NotAnMTSObject (no debugging)	N/A
N/A	Disabled

Creating Objects in a COM+ Transaction

When the COM+ runtime creates a new object, it examines the component's *Transaction* attribute to see whether the new object should be created in a transaction. When the COM+ runtime creates an object that must run in a transaction, it also determines whether it should activate the object in a new transaction or in the transaction of its creator. In Chapter 7, I explained how COM+ matches objects to activities based on the *Synchronization* attribute. COM+ matches objects to transactions by using the *Transaction* attribute in the same manner.

Once an object is created in a transaction, it spends its entire lifetime there. When the transaction is committed or aborted, the COM+ runtime deactivates all the objects inside it by using the just-in-time activation scheme. This means that a Visual Basic object in a transaction must be destroyed when the transaction is released. As you'll see, this cleanup activity is essential to achieving the proper isolation semantics of a transaction. The objects and the state they've acquired must be destroyed at transaction boundaries to enforce the isolation requirement of the ACID rules.

A transactional object can be created by another object in the same COM+ application or by an external client. When the COM+ runtime receives an activation request to create a new object, it determines whether the object's creator is running in an existing COM+ transaction. It also inspects the *Transaction* attribute of the component. From these two pieces of information, it can determine how to proceed.

A component can have one of the following *Transaction* attribute settings:

- **Required**   The object is always created in a transaction. The object is placed in the transaction of its creator if one exists. If the creator isn't running in a transaction, the COM+ runtime creates a new transaction for the object.

- **Requires New**   The COM+ runtime creates a new transaction for the object.

- **Supported**   The object is placed in the transaction of its creator if one exists. If the creator isn't running in a transaction, the object is created without a transaction.

- **Not Supported**   The object is never created in a transaction.

An external client can initiate a transaction by activating an object from a configured component marked as Required or Requires New. The COM+ runtime determines that the new object must run in a transaction and that the creator isn't running in a transaction. The COM+ runtime therefore creates a new COM+ transaction and then creates the new object in it.

The first object created in a transaction, which is known as the transaction's *root object,* has an important role. It can create additional *secondary objects* in its transaction. If you're writing a method implementation for a COM+ object and you want to propagate another object in that transaction, you must create the object from components marked as Required or Supported.

You should note a subtle difference between Required and Requires New. A component marked as Required can be used to create either root objects or secondary objects. A component marked as Requires New can be used only to create root objects. As you learn more about the roles of the root object and secondary objects, you'll begin to appreciate the difference.

It's common to create COM+ transactions that contain multiple objects. However, let's first examine a transaction that contains only one object—the root object. Once you know exactly how the root object works, it'll be easier to understand what happens when you have several objects running in a transaction at once.

A tale of two transactions

When a client creates an object from a configured component marked as Required, the COM+ runtime creates a new COM+ transaction in which to place the new object. At some point the COM+ runtime also calls down to the DTC to create a new distributed transaction. You should think of the COM+ transaction as the *logical transaction* and the DTC-based transaction as the *physical transaction*. Note that the COM+ runtime doesn't create the physical transaction when it creates the logical transaction.

The COM+ runtime creates the logical transaction when it creates the root object, but it defers creating the physical transaction until the root object starts its work. Thus, a delay occurs between the creation of the logical transaction and creation of the physical transaction. The COM+ runtime delays creating the physical transaction as long as possible as an optimization to keep transaction times as short as possible.

In Chapter 7, I introduced the concept of just-in-time activation, which is extremely important to your understanding of declarative transactions. Here's a quick recap. The client never directly holds an object that supports just-in-time activation. Instead, the client holds onto a system-provided proxy that allows the COM+ runtime to play a special trick in the interception layer. The COM+ runtime activates an object at the beginning of each call and deactivates it before returning control to the client. The client can't tell what's going on, but each method call is serviced by a new and different object (assuming your transactional objects are not poolable).

A delay always occurs between the time the client creates an object and the time it issues the first method call. In MTS, the runtime defers starting the DTC-based transaction until the root object is activated at the first method call. COM+ adds a new optimization: The COM+ runtime doesn't start the DTC-based transaction until the root object makes its first "interesting" call. An interesting call is loosely defined as a call that requires the COM+ runtime to start the DTC-based transaction. An example of an interesting call is one that establishes a database connection that needs to be auto-enlisted or that queries for the *TransactionID*. In both cases, the COM+ runtime must call into the DTC and start a distributed transaction to complete its work.

When the COM+ runtime determines that it's time to start the distributed transaction, it issues a *BeginTransaction* call to the DTC. The COM+ runtime creates the physical transaction with an isolation level of Serializable and a default timeout interval of 60 seconds. This means that the transaction runs at the highest level of isolation and that you have one minute to complete your work.

This timeout interval is adjustable at the machine level as well as the component level. It's important to keep timeout intervals short because they help in the detection and resolution of deadlocks. (I'll talk about issues related to deadlocks later in the chapter.)

When the COM+ runtime calls down to create the physical transaction, the DTC creates a transaction object and passes the COM+ runtime an *ITransaction* reference. The COM+ runtime holds onto this reference for the lifetime of the logical COM+ transaction. The *ITransaction* interface lets the COM+ runtime call *Commit* or *Abort*. As you can see, the COM+ runtime has the ability to control the outcome of the transaction.

As a Visual Basic programmer, you shouldn't obtain an *ITransaction* reference to the transaction object and call *Commit* or *Abort* yourself. You're probably wondering, "So how do I control the transaction?" You have to know when the COM+ runtime calls *Commit* and *Abort* and determine how you can influence its decision.

Everything about declarative transactions is based on one major assumption: *The COM+ runtime decides whether to commit or abort the transaction when the root object is deactivated.* Before it makes this decision, you can do quite a lot to change the state of the transaction. You can invoke system-supplied methods that allow each object to vote on whether the transaction should succeed.

Three Important Flags: Happy, Done, and Doomed

Figure 8-7 shows a diagram of a client, a transaction, a root object, and the root object's context. It also shows some important internal flags that COM+ maintains. These flags are simply system-defined variables that have a value of True or False. For this reason, they're called *bits*. You should learn how to modify these bits and understand how they influence the COM+ runtime's decision to commit or abort a transaction.

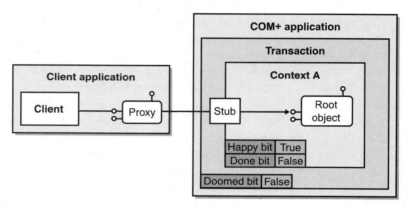

Figure 8-7 *The happy bit holds the object's vote on whether the transaction should be committed. The COM+ runtime knows when to deactivate the object by inspecting the done bit.*

The COM+ runtime lets each transactional object vote on whether the transaction should be committed or rolled back. The object's vote is stored in a context-specific area known as the *happy bit.* (Programmers without a sense of humor can call it the *consistency bit.*) This Boolean flag simply tells the COM+ runtime whether the object is willing to commit whatever work it's done. The default value for the happy bit is True.

The other important context-specific flag of an object in a transaction is the *done bit,* which allows an object to tell the COM+ runtime that it has completed its work. If the root object sets its done bit to True, it triggers its own deactivation. The motivation for doing this is to release the transaction as soon as possible. The default value of the done bit is False.

There's one other important flag, called the *doomed bit*. This is a single flag that is shared by every object and context in the transaction. This flag is initially set to False when a COM+ transaction is created. This flag is important because the COM+ runtime uses it when deciding whether to commit or abort the transaction.

When does the COM+ runtime inspect the doomed bit? And how can you change the value of the doomed bit? To answer these questions, you must understand the important role that a root object plays in every COM+ transaction. The COM+ runtime inspects the doomed bit when the root object is deactivated. If the root object is deactivated during an active transaction, the COM+ runtime inspects the doomed bit and releases the transaction by calling *Commit* or *Abort*. If the doomed bit is set to False, the COM+ runtime calls *Commit*. If the doomed bit is set to True, the COM+ runtime calls *Abort*.

The deactivation of the root object should always cause the end of the transaction's life cycle. When the root is deactivated, the transaction is released. As long as the root object remains activated, the transaction can remain alive and can hold all of its locks.

Now let's look at the two flags maintained in the context of every transactional object. The first one is the happy bit, which has an initial value of True. When an object running in a COM+ transaction is deactivated, the COM+ runtime examines its happy bit. If the happy bit is set to False, the COM+ runtime sets the transaction's doomed bit to True. Once the transaction's doomed bit is set to True, it can't be reversed. This has a powerful implication. If the root object or any secondary object in a transaction is deactivated in an unhappy state, the transaction is doomed to failure.

Let's look at a few scenarios to see how all this works. First, imagine that a client creates an object from a component marked as Required and invokes a method call that opens a connection to the DBMS and inserts a record. This results in the creation of a COM+ transaction and triggers the COM+ runtime to call down to the DTC to create the physical transaction as well. At this point, what happens if the client simply releases its reference to the root object? When the root object is deactivated, the COM+ runtime inspects its happy bit. The happy bit still has its initial value of True. Therefore, the COM+ runtime doesn't change the doomed bit. The doomed bit remains False, and the COM+ runtime calls *Commit* on the transaction. You can run a simple example and confirm these results by examining the Transaction Statistics in the Component Services administrative tool.

So that's pretty easy. You create an object in a transaction, call a method that does some work, and then release the object. It takes only three steps to successfully begin and commit a transaction with the DTC. This example shows how and when the COM+ runtime interacts with the DTC. We didn't write any code to explicitly begin or commit the transaction because the COM+ logical transaction does all of that for you.

Now let's write some code to force the COM+ runtime to roll back a transaction. All you do is set the root object's happy bit to False. One way to do this is by calling *DisableCommit* in a method with the following code:

```
GetObjectContext.DisableCommit
```

When the client invokes a method on the root object with this code, the COM+ runtime changes the value of the happy bit to False. Now, when the client releases its connection, the root object is deactivated. During the object's deactivation, the COM+ runtime sees that the happy bit is False and changes the value of the transaction's doomed bit to True. When the root object is deactivated, the COM+ runtime calls *Abort* on the transaction.

DisableCommit is complemented by another method named *EnableCommit*, which simply returns the happy bit to True. You can call each of these methods repeatedly. The happy bit is just a Boolean value, so whichever method is called last before the object is deactivated determines how the COM+ runtime handles the transaction. When you call one of these methods, you're simply voting on whether the transaction should succeed. You can call *EnableCommit* and *DisableCommit* as many times as you like within a given method. Only the last call before the object's deactivation matters.

The *SetComplete* and *SetAbort* Methods

In addition to *DisableCommit* and *EnableCommit*, the *ObjectContext* interface contains two other important methods for controlling a transaction: *SetComplete* and *SetAbort*. Like the other two methods, these cast a vote by modifying the happy bit. *SetComplete* sets the happy bit to True, and *SetAbort* sets it to False. However, *SetComplete* and *SetAbort* are different from the other two methods because they set the done bit to True. As you'll recall from Chapter 7, the done bit has a dramatic effect on an object's life cycle. *DisableCommit* and *EnableCommit* modify the done bit as well, but they set the done bit to False, which usually has no effect because it's the default value.

After the root object finishes executing a method call, it passes control back to the interception layer. This gives the COM+ runtime an opportunity to inspect the done bit before returning control to the client. If the done bit is set to True, the COM+ runtime deactivates the object. This is extremely important because it speeds up the release of the transaction. The root object can thus proactively release a transaction by calling either *SetComplete* or *SetAbort* and then returning control back to the client.

If an object that's the root of a transaction calls *SetAbort*, it has the effect of dooming the transaction. The COM+ runtime deactivates the object in an unhappy state, sets the doomed bit to true and aborts the transaction. If an object that's the root of a transaction calls *SetComplete* instead, the COM+ runtime deactivates the object and attempts to commit the transaction immediately. The COM+ runtime still inspects all the happy bits to decide whether to commit or abort the transaction in the same way that it does when you call *EnableCommit* and *DisableCommit*. *SetComplete* and *SetAbort* simply force the COM+ runtime to end the transaction much faster, which means that those expensive locks that your transaction was holding are released earlier. You don't have to wait for the client to release the root object.

You need to use *SetComplete* and *SetAbort* at the appropriate times. If you cast your vote by calling the *DisableCommit* or *EnableCommit* method in the root object, the transaction and all of its locks are held until the client releases the root object. Calling the *SetComplete* or *SetAbort* method is a much better approach because the root object forces the COM+ runtime to release the transaction. As you know, the most important thing you can do to improve concurrency and throughput in an OLTP environment is to reduce the amount of time that any transaction holds its locks.

You've seen that the COM+ runtime deactivates the root object and releases the transaction when you call *SetComplete* or *SetAbort*. This leads to another important question: How does the deactivation of the root object affect the client? When a client invokes a method that includes a call to *SetComplete* or *SetAbort*, the object is deactivated and destroyed. If the client had to deal with the fact that the object has died, you'd have a messy problem. Fortunately, the just-in-time activation scheme can hide the object's demise from the client.

If the client continues to call methods that call *SetComplete* or *SetAbort*, the COM+ runtime creates and releases a new root object and a new transaction each time. COM+ provides just-in-time activation followed by as-soon-as-possible deactivation. All of this creating and releasing occurs within the window of time that starts with a method call's preprocessing and ends with its post-processing. A COM+ transaction and the objects in it should be flashes in the pan. In the world of OLTP, shorter transactions result in better concurrency and throughput.

The *IContextState* Interface

So far, I've described four methods of the *ObjectContext* interface that allow you to control a transaction. COM+ introduces a new interface named *IContextState* that has similar functionality. Here are the four methods of this interface:

- ■ **_SetMyTransactionVote_** Sets the happy bit to True or False.
- ■ **_GetMyTransactionVote_** Reads the state of the happy bit.
- ■ **_SetDeactivateOnReturn_** Sets the done bit to True or False.
- ■ **_GetDeactivateOnReturn_** Reads the state of the done bit.

You should see that these methods allow you to change the happy and done bits just as the methods in the *ObjectContext* interface do. For example, you can replace a call to *SetComplete* with a call to *SetMyTransactionVote* and *SetDeactivateOnReturn*. As long as you know how to set the happy bit and done bit to True, it doesn't really matter how you do it.

So what's the difference between using the *ObjectContext* interface and the *IContextState* interface to control a transaction? First, *IContextState* let's you control the happy and done bits individually. Second, *IContextState* allows you to read the current state of those bits, unlike the *ObjectContext* interface. The third difference is that the COM+ runtime raises errors when you call an *IContextState* method on an object that isn't configured properly. Calls to *GetMyTransactionVote* and *SetMyTransactionVote* fail if the object isn't running in a transaction. Calls to *SetDeactivateOnReturn* and *GetDeactivateOnReturn* fail if the object doesn't support just-in-time activation.

So how do you choose between the *ObjectContext* interface and the *IContextState* interface when you write a transactional component? The truth is that it doesn't really matter much. Programmers who've been using MTS might prefer calling *SetComplete* and *SetAbort* because they're familiar with that approach. Other programmers might prefer *IContextState* because they want to read the state of the happy bit and the done bit. C++ programmers who are creating poolable objects that aren't involved in transactions should use *IContextState* because they'll want to manipulate the done bit without touching the happy bit.

As long as you know how the COM+ runtime behaves and you know how to manipulate the happy bit and the done bit, you can use either interface. In the rest of this chapter, I'll use the methods in the *ObjectContext* interface. You should simply note that you can use the methods of *IContextState* interchangeably.

The *AutoComplete* Attribute

One of the most important things to remember when you create the component for a root object is to release every transaction as soon as possible. The most common way to do this is by setting the done bit to True with a call to *SetComplete* or *SetAbort*. These calls are required because the default value of the done bit is False.

Each method of a configured component has an *AutoComplete* attribute that you can use to change the default value of the done bit to True. You can configure this attribute from the method's Properties dialog box in the Component Services administrative tool by selecting the Automatically Deactivate This Object When This Method Returns check box. This attribute sets the default behavior of a root object so that it deactivates automatically even if you don't include a call to *SetComplete* or *SetAbort*. This attribute also automatically sets the happy bit to False when the method raises an error back to its caller.

This feature is especially valuable for prewritten components that don't include calls to *SetComplete* or *SetAbort*. Perhaps you'll want to use such a component as the root of a transaction without having to modify any code. You can configure each method for *AutoComplete* to ensure that each method will start and release a transaction.

If you're writing a transactional component, the use of the *AutoComplete* attribute is optional. It offers convenience, but you'll have more control if you manipulate the happy bit and the done bit yourself. Moreover, it's important to remember that although the *AutoComplete* attribute changes the default value of the done bit to True, it doesn't guarantee that the done bit will remain True. You have to watch out because calls to *EnableCommit*, *DisableCommit*, and *SetDeactivateOnReturn* can set the done bit back to False and keep a transaction alive longer than you want.

The *ObjectControl* interface

The COM+ runtime manages the life cycle of every object that's created from a configured component. The life cycle of an object that supports just-in-time activation includes four stages: creation, activation, deactivation, and destruction. When you're programming COM+ transactions, you should be aware of when the transitions between these stages occur so that you can take appropriate action.

A Visual Basic class module provides an *Initialize* procedure. The code you write in *Initialize* is guaranteed to run when the Visual Basic object is created. However, *Initialize* always runs before the object has been activated. If you wait until after the object has been activated, the contextual information supplied by the COM+ runtime is richer and more reliable.

The *Terminate* procedure in a Visual Basic class is executed prior to the object's destruction yet after the object has been deactivated. *Terminate* is similar to *Initialize* in that it's fired when the object isn't in an active state. Neither *Initialize* nor *Terminate* gives you the control you need to manage your object's life cycle inside a COM+ transaction. Fortunately, the COM+ runtime can help by notifying your object just after activation and once again just before deactivation.

Here's how it works. The COM+ Services type library includes a definition for an interface named *ObjectControl*. When the COM+ runtime creates an object with support for just-in-time activation, it calls *QueryInterface* to determine whether the object supports this interface. If the object implements *ObjectControl*, the COM+ runtime calls methods in this interface to notify the object at important transition stages during its life cycle. This means that you should implement *ObjectControl* in every object that you think needs to receive these notifications. The *ObjectControl* interface contains the following three methods.

■   **Activate**   This method is called by the COM+ runtime after activation and just before the first method call is executed.

■   **Deactivate**   This method is called by the COM+ runtime just before the object is deactivated.

■   **CanBePooled**   For components that support object pooling, this method allows an object to tell the COM+ runtime whether it should be destroyed or placed in the pool. It's called by the COM+ runtime after deactivation. When you implement the *ObjectControl* interface in a Visual Basic component, an implementation of this method is required and meaningless.

So that your object receives these notifications, you should implement the *ObjectControl* interface in the MultiUse class modules in your ActiveX DLLs. Here's an example of a Visual Basic class module that implements this interface:

```
Implements ObjectControl

Private Sub ObjectControl_Activate()
    ' Your code for initialization after activation
End Sub

Private Sub ObjectControl_Deactivate()
    ' Your code for cleanup before deactivation
End Sub

Private Function ObjectControl_CanBePooled() As Boolean
    ' Object pooling not supported for Visual Basic components
    ObjectControl_CanBePooled = False
End Function
```

The COM+ runtime calls *Activate* just before the execution of the first method call. However, the *Activate* method executes while the object is in a fully active state. If your component is going to be configured for just-in-time activation, it's usually best to put your object initialization code inside *Activate* instead of *Initialize*. Likewise, you should place your cleanup code in the *Deactivate* method instead of *Terminate*.

Remember there are only two types of components that need just-in-time activation. Poolable components rely on just-in-time activation in order to release objects back to the pool in a more efficient manner. Components that run in COM+ transactions rely on just-in-time activation to keep transaction times short.

If you're creating a component that isn't poolable and that doesn't support transactions, you don't really need just-in-time activation. It's a small optimization to disable just-in-time activation for components that don't need it. Remember that the *ObjectControl* interface is just for objects that support just-in-time activation. If you have disabled just-in-time activation, you should use Visual Basic's *Initialize* and *Terminate* procedures for initialization and cleanup code.

Multiobject Transactions

As you know, the root object can create secondary objects in the same transaction by calling *CreateObject* on components that are marked as Required or Supported. (I'm sure you're well aware of this by now, but let me reemphasize that calling *New* on a class compiled into the same DLL causes serious problems in COM+.) Figure 8-8 shows a root object and two secondary objects in a COM+ transaction. Each object has its own context and its own happy bit and done bit.

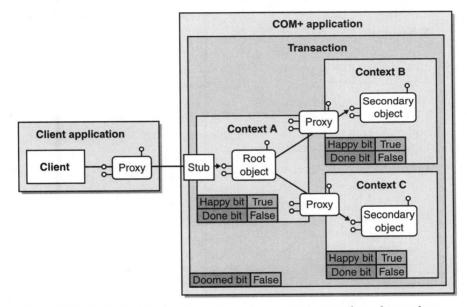

Figure 8-8 *Multiobject transactions always have a root. Secondary objects play a different role than the root object.*

A COM+ transaction is a democratic community in which each object gets to vote on whether the transaction should succeed. A secondary object follows the same rules as the root object. When a secondary object is deactivated, the COM+ runtime inspects its happy bit. If the happy bit is set to False, the COM+ runtime sets the transaction's doomed bit to True, which dooms the transaction to failure. There's nothing that any other object can do to set the doomed bit back to False. This means that any object in a transaction can prevent the transaction from committing.

It's common to have a design in which the root object creates secondary objects and uses them to complete the work for the transaction. If you plan to create multiobject transactions, you must understand how all the objects work together so that you can coordinate communication among them. More specifically, you should understand the responsibilities of secondary objects as well as the root object. Secondary objects play a much different role than the root object.

Let's look at the case in which the root object makes several successful method calls on a secondary object. As long as the secondary object doesn't set its done bit to True, it remains alive until it's released by the root object. The root object can make several successful calls on the secondary object and then call *SetComplete* to commit the transaction. When the root calls *SetComplete*, both objects are deactivated. The secondary object is deactivated first, followed by the root object. As long as neither object sets its happy bit to False by calling *SetAbort* or *DisableCommit*, the transaction is committed.

If a secondary object doesn't explicitly vote in the transaction outcome, it gives the COM+ runtime passive consent to commit the transaction because its happy bit is set to True by default. Also note that a secondary object doesn't need to set its done bit to True. This means that calling *SetComplete* or *SetAbort* in a secondary object is optional. This is quite different from a root object where calls to *SetComplete* or *SetAbort* are critical to releasing the transaction.

What happens if a secondary object wants to roll back a transaction? If a secondary object calls *DisableCommit*, it sets its happy bit to False. Now, the root object has a delicate situation on its hands. If the secondary object is deactivated in an unhappy state, it will doom the transaction. At this point, the root object has two choices. First, it can attempt to call another method on the secondary object and try to persuade it to change its happy bit to True. If this isn't possible, the second choice is for the root object to admit defeat. In this case, it should call *SetAbort* and raise an error back to the client.

One really important point is that the root should always be aware when a secondary object is unhappy. If the root object calls *SetComplete* in a transaction in which one or more secondary objects is unhappy, the COM+ runtime sees the conflict. The root object is trying to commit a transaction that must be rolled back. The COM+ runtime deals with this situation by deactivating all the objects and raising an *mtsErrCtxAborted* error back to the client.

Instead of calling *DisableCommit*, a secondary object can force a rollback by calling *SetAbort*. This has an interesting effect because the secondary object gets deactivated and dooms the transaction before control is returned to the root object. Now the root object is running in a doomed transaction. If the root object tries to activate another object in a doomed transaction, it experiences an *mtsErrCtxAborting* error. If the root object simply returns control to its caller without calling *SetAbort*, it's left activated in a crippled state. Future method calls on the root object will probably result in *mtsErrCtxAborted* and *mtsErrCtxAborting* errors being raised by the COM+ runtime.

These problems should lead you to one conclusion: When a secondary object wants to roll back a transaction by calling *DisableCommit* or *SetAbort*, the root object should also call *SetAbort* and halt any attempt to complete additional work. There's one small hitch: The root object can't examine the doomed bit. It can't ask the COM+ runtime whether a secondary object is unhappy. Therefore, your secondary objects should proactively communicate with the root object when they call *DisableCommit* or *SetAbort*. You can use the return value or output parameters in the methods of your secondary objects to indicate whether they're unhappy, or you can raise errors from the secondary objects back to the root object.

For example, if a secondary object decides to roll back the entire transaction in *Method1*, it can use the following sequence of calls:

```
GetObjectContext.DisableCommit
Dim ErrorCode As Long, Description As String
ErrorCode = myErrorEnum1 ' Something like (vbObjectError + 512)
Description = "The requested quantity is not available."
Err.Raise ErrorCode, , Description
```

If you follow this convention, a method implementation in the root object can assume that every secondary objects raises an error after setting its happy bit to False. This means that an error handler in the root object should call *SetAbort* and raise its own error to forward the secondary object's error description back to the client. If the root object can call methods on the secondary objects without experiencing an error, it can assume that everything is fine and call *SetComplete*.

Here's a typical method in the root object. Notice that all paths of execution result in a call to *SetComplete* or *SetAbort*.

```
Sub RootMethod1()
    On Error GoTo MyHandler
    Dim Secondary1 As CSecondary
    Set Secondary1 = CreateObject("MyDll.CSecondary")
    Secondary1.Method1
    Secondary1.Method2
    ' Commit transaction if all calls complete successfully.
    GetObjectContext.SetComplete
Exit Sub
MyHandler:
    ' Roll back transaction and get out ASAP on error.
    GetObjectContext.SetAbort
    ' Forward error information back to base client.
    Err.Raise Err.Number, , Err.Description
End Sub
```

Of course, this code shows only one of many possible approaches. If you take a different approach, you must carefully coordinate the communication between the secondary objects and the root object to follow these rules: Always call *SetComplete* or *SetAbort* in the root object, and never call *SetComplete* in the root object when a secondary object is unhappy.

You should keep in mind a few other important issues. First, you should be aware of a bug in the initial release of COM+ and Windows 2000 that prevents secondary objects from passing error descriptions to the root object after calling *SetAbort*. (See the sidebar below titled "Watch Out for the *SetAbort* Bug." This means that you might prefer using *DisableCommit* over *SetAbort*. The second thing to keep in mind is that a call to *DisableCommit* in a secondary object doesn't necessarily doom the transaction.

WATCH OUT FOR THE *SETABORT* BUG

Unfortunately, a bug in the initial release of COM+ can occur when a secondary object calls *SetAbort* and raises an error back to the root object. This bug is in the lightweight proxy that COM+ builds to connect the root object to a secondary object in the same STA. The bug is specific to Visual Basic components.

The bug overwrites any custom error description you're trying to propagate from the secondary object back to the root and replaces it with the dreaded description *method '~' of object '~' failed*. The workaround for this bug is to avoid calling *SetAbort* or *SetDeactivateOnReturn(True)* in secondary objects that raise errors. To roll back a transaction, a secondary object should call *DisableCommit* or *SetMyTransactionVote(txAbort)* instead. As long as the secondary object doesn't set its done bit, it can raise an error with a reliable description back to the root and still vote to roll back the transaction.

This bug raises two concerns. First, a lot of code written for MTS has secondary objects that call *SetAbort*. This bug doesn't exist in MTS, so many developers are in the habit of calling *SetAbort* and raising an error when a problem is encountered. This means that you might have to touch up MTS code when you port it to COM+.

The second problem is that a component must be written to be either a root object or a secondary object. The root object should always call *SetComplete* or *SetAbort*. But this is a catch-22 because secondary objects should never call *SetAbort*. The bug prevents you from writing a component that can be used interchangeably as the root object or a secondary object.

A fix for this bug will appear in the first service pack for COM+. Once this bug has been removed from COM+, you'll be able to port your MTS code more easily and write a component that can be used as either the root object or a secondary object.

If a secondary object calls *DisableCommit* and returns control to the root, it has indicated that it can't commit its work in its present state. However, *DisableCommit* doesn't deactivate the secondary object upon return to the root object. This is different from a call to *SetAbort*, in which the COM+ runtime deactivates the secondary object before the root object regains control. A call to *SetAbort* dooms the transaction to failure. When a secondary object calls *DisableCommit*, it says, "I am currently unhappy, but perhaps the root object can invoke another method and make me change my mind."

As you might imagine, using *DisableCommit* in this manner requires you to design a more elaborate communication protocol among the objects in a transaction. When a secondary object calls *DisableCommit*, the root object can try to persuade the object to change its mind by executing additional methods. However, the root object must ultimately call *SetComplete* or *SetAbort*. Therefore, the root object must find a way to make the secondary object happy or determine that the transaction can't be saved.

You should definitely avoid calling *DisableCommit* from the root object. You don't want to pass control back to the client when a transaction is pending. Never allow the client to control when the locks are released. This usually results in locks being left on data items for longer than necessary. This conflicts with your newfound "get in and get out" mindset. OK, enough said.

Database Connections and Auto-Enlistment

Now that we've covered the basics of how to commit and roll back a COM+ transaction, let's discuss how your database connections get enlisted. When you connect to an RM, the connection must be enlisted with the DTC, as you can see in Figure 8-9. This involves setting up a line of communication between the RM and one or more sessions of the DTC. As you saw earlier in this chapter, these lines of communication are used to execute the two-phase commit protocol.

Enlisting a connection in a COM+ application is actually quite easy. You simply have to follow two rules. First, you must establish the connection from an object running in a transaction. Second, you must be sure that you're using an RM that works with the DTC and that you're using an RM proxy that supports auto-enlistment. For example, SQL Server is an RM that works with the DTC, and the native OLE-DB provider for SQL Server is an RM proxy that supports auto-enlistment.

When you establish a typical connection from an object in a transaction using ADO, the RM proxy detects the need for auto-enlistment and makes all the required calls for enlistment behind the scenes. You open a database connection in the usual manner, and your write and read operations are automatically part of a distributed transaction. It couldn't be easier.

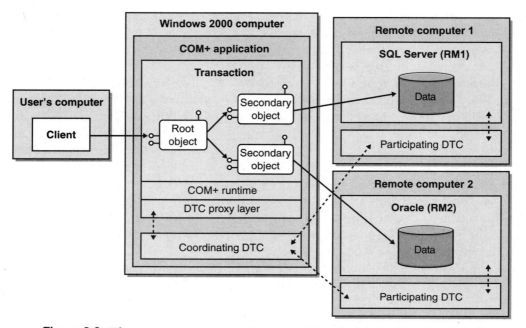

Figure 8-9 *When you create a connection to an RM such as SQL Server or Oracle from an object in a COM+ transaction, the COM+ runtime and the RM proxy automatically enlist the connection with the DTC.*

Let's look at an example. If you're working with SQL Server 7 and connecting through ADO with the native OLE-DB provider, you can connect using this code:

```
Dim conn As ADODB.Connection
Set conn = New ADODB.Connection
conn.Open MyConnectiString
```

As you can see, this is the same code that you'd write to establish any ADO connection. The COM+ runtime works with the native OLE-DB provider to auto-enlist any ADO connection made from inside a COM+ transaction. The RM proxy interacts with the DBMS to set up a communication channel with the coordinating DTC, as shown in Figure 8-9. You simply make your connections and begin accessing data. All of your changes are charged against a single distributed transaction that's controlled by the COM+ runtime.

In Chapter 7, I covered the basics of database connection pooling. In addition to standard database connection pooling, COM+ also allows for the pooling of enlisted connections. As you've seen, when a connection is established, it requires a round trip to the DBMS. Likewise, when connections are enlisted in a distributed transaction, they require even more round trips to the DBMS. The pooling of enlisted connections is a further optimization to reduce round trips.

When you close an enlisted connection from an object running in a transaction, COM+ returns it to a special pool. Most of the time, this pool won't contain more than one physical connection. If another object in the same transaction requests a connection using the same connect string, COM+ simply reuses the same enlisted connection, which means that several objects in a transaction can use the same enlisted connection. This scheme prevents redundant round trips to the same DBMS for enlistment to the same transaction. The COM+ runtime takes care of cleaning up the enlisted connection when the transaction is released.

COM+ Transactions and Stored Procedures with Transactions

When programmers want to call stored procedures from an object in a COM+ transaction, they often wonder what will happen if the stored procedure contains calls to control a local transaction, such as BEGIN TRAN, COMMIT TRAN, or ROLLBACK TRAN. How will these calls affect the behavior of the code when they're already running in a distributed transaction? The answer is simpler than you might suspect. Calls to BEGIN TRAN and COMMIT TRAN are ignored, while calls to ROLLBACK TRAN are honored.

A call to BEGIN TRAN is ignored because the transaction is already started. Furthermore, neither the DTC nor SQL Server supports the concept of nested transactions. A call to BEGIN TRAN must be ignored because it's impossible to start what's already been started.

It's also important to see that the stored procedure can't commit a distributed transaction if it didn't start the transaction. The stored procedure is just like a secondary object. It can vote to roll back the transaction, but it can't be the one that ultimately commits it. This means that calls to COMMIT TRAN are ignored as well.

If a stored procedure calls ROLLBACK TRAN, it dooms the transaction. In this sense, a stored procedure that calls ROLLBACK TRAN is just like a secondary object that calls *SetAbort* or *DisableCommit*. A root object will experience problems if it calls *SetComplete* after a stored procedure has rolled back the transaction. Therefore, it's important for a stored procedure to raise an error indicating its intention to roll back a transaction. If your stored procedure raises errors in this fashion, you can handle transaction rollback in a graceful manner inside the root object.

The Short, Happy Life of a Transactional Object

I've been building on a theme throughout this chapter: *To reach higher levels of concurrency and throughput, you must release your locks as quickly as possible.* When you're using transactional objects, the locks you acquire are held until you deactivate the root object. You should deactivate the root object as soon as possible by calling a method such as *SetComplete* or *SetAbort*. However, this aspect of the programming model can seem strange at first. COM+ must destroy all the objects associated with the transaction as part of the cleanup process. The root object and any secondary objects live for only the duration of a single method call.

This programming model is much different from that of classic object-oriented programming (OOP) and of COM, and it requires a new way of thinking. The OOP and COM paradigms fail to address scenarios in which state is discarded at the completion of each method call. Object-oriented clients assume that they can obtain a reference to a long-lived object. If a client modifies some state within an object, object-oriented programmers assume that the object will hold these changes across multiple method calls. But this isn't the case with transactional objects in COM+. Each object must die as part of the transaction's cleanup, and its state must go along with it.

This transparent destruction of transactional objects is often called *stateless programming*. In the short history of MTS and COM+, there's been a good deal of confusion about why statelessness is an essential aspect of programming transactions. Many people have suggested that stateless programming is about reclaiming memory on the computer running the COM+ application. They argue that destroying objects and reclaiming memory results in higher levels of scalability because of more efficient resource usage. Their argument is both confusing and inaccurate.

As a Visual Basic programmer, your only reason for setting the done bit to True is to ensure the semantics of a transaction. The idea is that a transactional object can see a data item in a consistent state only while the RM is holding a lock. If a COM+ object holds a copy of this data item after the lock has been released, another transaction can modify the original data item inside the RM. The original data item and the copy can thus get out of sync and violate the ACID rules of a transaction. The point of destroying objects at transactional boundaries is that any copy of a data item must be thrown away when the RM releases its locks. This is why COM+ requires that all transactional objects be destroyed when a transaction is released.

If you have an object that isn't involved in a transaction, holding state across method calls doesn't cause any problem. If you set a component's transaction support property to Not Supported and you don't call *SetComplete* or *SetAbort*, you can create stateful objects.

One strange aspect of programming declarative transactions is that an object dies before its transaction is released. This means that an object never truly knows the outcome of the transaction in which it was running. Even the root object is destroyed before the COM+ runtime starts running the two-phase commit protocol. This can bring up a few interesting issues when you're designing a transactional application.

Let's say you have a transaction with a root object and a secondary object. When the root is activated, it creates the secondary object and calls a method to perform some work. Assume that both objects are happy. When the root object calls *SetComplete* and returns, the COM+ runtime deactivates both objects and starts running the two-phase commit protocol.

What happens if the COM+ runtime experiences a failure in phase 1? It can't raise an error to the root object because the root object has already been destroyed. The only thing it can do in this case is to raise an *mtsErrCtxAborted* error back to the client. However, if your client is a forms-based Visual Basic application or an ASP page, it's not very elegant to send it an error code that's defined in the COM+ Services Type Library. It can often be helpful to add another nontransactional component to your design to deal with this error. This new component plays the role of a *transaction observer.*

Figure 8-10 shows two different clients running transactions. Client 1 is connected directly to the root object, while client 2 is indirectly connected to the root object through a nontransactional object. One of the biggest benefits of the latter design is that the client can be shielded from *mtsErrCtxAborted* errors that can occur during phase 1 of the two-phase commit protocol. The client invokes a method on the nontransactional object; the nontransactional object then invokes a method on the root object to run a transaction. The nontransactional object can observe the outcome of the transaction and can ultimately determine whether the transaction was committed or rolled back.

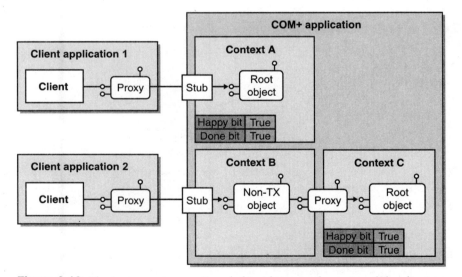

Figure 8-10 *Placing a nontransactional object between the root and the client can offer many benefits.*

A nontransactional object can also maintain client-specific state across multiple method calls. This can be advantageous in certain designs because a stateful object can reduce the need to pass parameters and reinitialize objects.

I'm not suggesting that you can always use stateful objects. In many situations (especially with Web-based applications), your objects live for the duration of a single client request, whether or not they're transactional. However, in a few places in distributed application design, stateful objects offer the best approach. When you encounter a situation in which it makes sense to keep a stateful object alive across a series of calls, be sure that the object isn't transactional and don't set the done bit to True—and remember, there's no good reason to call *SetComplete* from a Visual Basic object that's not running in a transaction.

TRANSACTIONAL DESIGN ISSUES

I'd like to cover just a few more issues in this chapter. I've explained how to program local transaction as well as how to program distributed transactions with COM+ and the DTC. Now let's compare these two approaches so that you can make an informed decision when choosing between them. I also want to talk about a few different strategies for partitioning your business logic and your data access code. As you'll see, each approach offers trade-offs with respect to application performance and code maintainability. I'll finish by discussing how to avoid deadlocks and how to tune a transaction.

COM+ Transactions vs. Local Transactions

The creators of MTS and COM+ put a great deal of work into the infrastructure for running distributed transactions. Consequently, Microsoft's documentation usually pushes COM+ transactions much more than local transactions. However, both approaches are viable. Many DBMSs and mainframe applications have built-in TMs that are capable of enforcing the ACID rules on their own, without the DTC. You should understand all the relevant issues so that you can make the best choice for any given project.

Running a local transaction in a single round trip always offers better performance than a COM+ transaction because a COM+ transaction requires extra calls between the COM+ application, the DTC, and the RM to enlist connections and run the two-phase commit protocol. However, it's hard to say how much better the performance will be because it depends on your hardware and your network configuration. The difference could be significant or it could be marginal. The only way to really know is to run benchmarks.

If your data is spread out across multiple computers or differing database formats or both, you have no choice but to use COM+ transactions and the DTC rather than local transactions. But even if you currently don't have to deal with multiple DBMSs, you might decide to use COM+ transactions to minimize the impact of integrating other DBMSs into your application in the future.

Another reason to choose COM+ transactions over local transactions is that COM+ transactions simplify your application designs and reduce coding requirements. In the case of a component that will be used as a secondary object, you don't even have to add any code. You can simply configure the component to support transactions, and all of its read/write activity will be charged against the distributed transaction started by the root object. If you're creating a component to play the role of the root object, you usually need to add some code—you'll probably add calls to *SetComplete* or *SetAbort*—but this is easier than working in a procedural paradigm in which the programmer is responsible for explicitly starting, committing, and rolling back transactions.

So it comes down to a choice between performance and scalability on one hand and flexibility and ease-of-use on the other. Do you want maximum speed? If so, make sure all your data is in one DBMS and use local transactions. Do you need to run distributed transactions? If so, use COM+ transactions. Do you like the way that declarative transactions simplify your life? If so, use COM+ transactions.

If you decide to go with COM+ transactions, you can always compensate for the extra round trips by obtaining faster hardware. You can also do a number of things to optimize the way COM+ and the DTC run distributed transactions. The Windows DNA Performance Kit, which is part of the Microsoft Platform SDK, is an excellent resource for tuning COM+ transactions. (It's not in the default installation, so you have to specify it during a custom installation.) The Windows DNA Performance Kit offers guidelines for application design and hardware tuning that significantly improve performance. It also backs up these recommendations with plenty of benchmarks.

Here are just a few of the guidelines you'll find in the Windows DNA Performance Kit:

- Place the DTC transaction log in a storage location that offers fast access. The default location for the log isn't as fast as it could be.

- Don't create transactions across process boundaries.

- If all of your data is in a single DBMS, such as SQL Server, you can improve performance by reconfiguring the Windows 2000 server that runs your COM+ application to use the DTC on the computer running SQL Server.

Don't mix COM+ transactions with local transactions

You should probably avoid running a COM+ transaction with a local transaction in a single request. For instance, what if a root object creates a nontransactional object and then both objects make a connection to the same DBMS? If the nontransactional object starts a local transaction, you can easily get into trouble. The problem is that the DBMS sees two different transactions and assumes that the distributed transaction belongs to one client and the local transaction belongs to another.

Why is it a problem if a single request from a client results in two different transactions? The biggest problem is that the locks of each transaction will block the other. If the root object runs a SELECT statement resulting in a table lock, the local transaction could block an attempt to access the locked table. Unfortunately, the table lock is held until all the objects are deactivated. As you can see, this is a recipe for deadlock. You should never respond to a client request by running a distributed transaction and a local transaction on the same database at the same time.

Partitioning Business Logic and Data Access Code

Early in the design phase, you must decide how important it is to separate business logic from data access code. In larger projects, it's best to maintain all your business logic in one set of classes and all your data access code in another. In smaller applications, a formalized separation might be overkill.

The transactional programming model of COM+ doesn't force you to take one approach or the other. For example, you can design a transaction with business logic in one component and data access code in another. A business logic component can serve as the root object by modeling a high-level workflow composer. This business component can run COM+ transactions using customized data access components that are configured to run in their creator's transaction. This formalized separation of business logic and data access code results in higher levels of maintainability because your business logic isn't intermingled with your ADO calls. It is also easier to port your applications across different DBMSs.

In a smaller application, you might decide that a formalized separation of business logic and data access code isn't important. Since you've already split the presentation tier code from your nonvisual logic, you might not feel the need to further partition your nonvisual logic. You can thus keep your design simple and get your code into production more quickly. If you can make the assumption that you'll only use one specific DBMS for the lifetime of the project, you don't have to deal with the issue of porting across different DBMSs.

Whatever you decide with regard to separating business logic from data access code, you should never lose sight of performance and the need to minimize round trips to the DBMS. Suppose you're writing a method to remove a requested quantity of a certain product from inventory. It's intuitive to write code to accomplish this task in two discrete database operations. First, you run a SELECT statement to open an ADO recordset on the *Products* table. This allows a Visual Basic object in the middle tier to determine whether the quantity currently in inventory is enough to satisfy an order request. If the requested quantity is greater than the inventory quantity, the object should roll back the transaction and raise an error back to the caller. If a requested quantity is less than or equal to the inventory quantity, the component can complete its mission by running an UPDATE statement against the *Products* table.

The upside to this approach is that it allows you to maintain your validation logic inside a Visual Basic component. The downside is that it takes two round trips to the DBMS to complete an operation that could be completed in one. There's obviously a trade-off between performance and maintainability. If you want the best performance, you should submit a SQL batch or execute a stored procedure.

If you decide to write logic in SQL, you must decide between using SQL batches and using stored procedures. Many Visual Basic programmers prefer stored procedures because they're a little faster and because the Visual Basic IDE makes it pretty awkward to maintain and edit SQL batches in Visual Basic source code. If you use stored procedures, you only need to write the ADO code to call stored procedures.

If writing validation logic in Visual Basic is more important, you can compromise by making one round trip to the DBMS to fetch all the data you need for validation and running your validation checks in the middle tier using Visual Basic. If you find any validation errors, you can roll back the transaction and raise an error back to the caller. If no validation errors occur, you can make a second round trip to the DBMS to complete your writing and commit the transaction. The trade-off with this approach is that you'll probably hold locks in between these two round trips.

Avoid mapping Visual Basic classes to tables

Programmers in search of object-oriented purity often forget the requirements of an OLTP system. The most important thing in a scalable design is a "get in and get out" mindset. The class-per-table approach usually doesn't cut it because it sacrifices performance and shorter lock times in favor of a higher level of maintainability.

For example, if you have individual classes for the *Products* table, the *Customers* table, and the *Orders* table, each class probably establishes its own connection and submits its SQL statements independently of the others. This means at least three round trips to the database. If each class makes several round trips on its own, this approach starts to get really expensive.

You can reduce the number of round trips by creating a model that uses a single Visual Basic class for each database connection. Such a class is often referred to as a *session component*. The purpose of a session component is to conduct all your operations in as few round trips as possible. Generally, the session component exposes a method for each transaction or command that can be run on the DBMS.

The advantage of designing in terms of sessions is that it offers the best performance and scalability. Unfortunately, there are a few disadvantages as well. You have to write more logic and validations in SQL and less in Visual Basic. This makes it harder to port your applications from one DBMS to another. You're also required to raise errors from SQL code and catch them in Visual Basic code. In addition, you might have to abandon your UML code generator unless it has a check box to turn on the Stop Thinking Like An Object-Oriented Guy From The 1980s And Start Thinking Like An Efficient OLTP Design Tool option.

Dealing with Deadlocks

Creating an OLTP application typically requires balancing two competing goals. On one hand, you want the highest possible levels of concurrency. On the other hand, you must have isolation to guarantee the consistency of your data. This means that the system must place locks on data items to block certain transactions while other transactions perform their work.

Locking is critical. Without it, you'd have no way to ensure data consistency. Most of the time, when a transaction is blocked, it simply waits its turn and then gets to do its work. However, sometimes locks acquired by transactions don't have the desired effect. In some situations, the locks held by two or more transactions conflict in such a way that the situation can't be resolved by waiting. This is known as a *deadlock*.

For example, suppose transaction A has acquired a write lock on data item X and is attempting to acquire a write lock on data item Y to complete its work. If transaction B has acquired a write lock on data item Y and is waiting on the write lock held on data item X, the two transactions have hit a stalemate. Without intervention, both transactions will wait indefinitely for the other to release its locks.

A single DBMS such as SQL Server can quickly detect a deadlock situation. SQL Server resolves a deadlock by terminating one of the transactions and sending an error message to the victim. When the locks of the victim are released, the other transaction can complete its work.

In a distributed transaction, some deadlock situations can't be detected by any single resource manager. This is why COM+ transactions have a default timeout of 60 seconds. If a transaction can't be completed within a minute, the DTC assumes that a deadlock has occurred and aborts the transaction. In either case, your code must be ready to deal with deadlock errors when they occur.

You should think twice before you reconfigure a component's transaction timeout interval to something higher than the default of 60 seconds. In most systems, transactions are short-lived—usually less than a second. If you reconfigure a component to have a 20-minute timeout interval and it experiences a deadlock, you can unintentionally create a set of meaningless locks that will sit there and block other transactions for 19 minutes and 59 seconds. The important point is that you should never casually change the timeout interval for a transactional component to a large number.

Coding to avoid deadlocks

To prevent deadlocks, you can employ a few standard techniques. A *cyclic deadlock* can occur when two programmers have written separate transactions for the same set of data. For example, one programmer might write a transaction that modifies the *Products* table and then the *Customers* table. If another programmer writes a second transaction that accesses those tables in reverse order, the chance of a deadlock is greater. You can reduce the chances of cyclic deadlocks by maintaining a consistent flow of data access across all the transactions that use the same set of data.

Deadlocks resulting from *lock conversion* are also common and require your attention. Let's say that you're writing a transaction that removes a specific quantity of a product from inventory. Your transaction starts by running a SELECT statement against the *Products* table to find out whether the requested quantity is in stock. If the inventory quantity is equal to or greater than the requested quantity, you then run an UPDATE statement to remove the quantity from inventory. We'll assume that the SELECT statement and the UPDATE statement are both run against the same record in the *Products* table.

In a high-volume OTLP application, there's a good chance that two separate transactions will both run the SELECT statement and acquire read locks before either can acquire the write lock required for the UPDATE statement. This results in a deadlock. Each transaction waits for the other to remove its read lock so that it can acquire a write lock. The problem is that the transaction first acquires a read lock on a data item and then tries to convert the lock to a write lock. If two transactions acquire the read lock at the same time, neither party can convert the lock to a write lock.

Many programmers assume that they are safe from deadlocks when a transaction is running at the Serializable level of isolation, but the Serializable level of isolation doesn't provide any protection from the problems of lock conversion. SQL Server supports another type of lock called an *update lock,* which can be used to solve this problem. You can use an update lock whenever you need to escalate a read lock to a write lock in the course of a transaction.

An update lock conflicts with write locks and with other update locks. A transaction will block while trying to acquire an update lock if another transaction has already acquired a write lock or an update lock. But unlike a write lock, an update lock doesn't conflict with read locks. If a transaction holds a read lock on a data item, another transaction can acquire an update lock. Likewise, if one transaction holds an update lock, other transactions can acquire read locks. An update lock prevents lock conversion problems without impacting concurrency as much as a write lock.

You can explicitly ask for an update lock by using the UPDLOCK hint in a Transact-SQL SELECT statement. Here's an example of using an update hint in a SELECT statement with ADO:

```
Dim sSQL As String
sSQL = "SELECT Quantity" & _
       " FROM Products WITH (UPDLOCK)" & _
       " WHERE Product = 'Dog'"
Dim rs As ADODB.Recordset
Set rs = New ADODB.Recordset
```

(continued)

```
rs.CursorLocation = adUseClient
rs.CursorType = adOpenForwardOnly
rs.LockType = adLockReadOnly
' Assume conn is an open connection.
rs.Open sSQL, conn
Dim Quantity As Long
Quantity = rs.Fields("Quantity")
' The update lock is now in place.
' Execute UPDATE statement if appropriate.
```

SQL Server also uses update locks if you use pessimistic locking with server-side cursors. The following code doesn't use the (UPDLOCK) hint, but it has the same effect:

```
Dim sSQL As String
sSQL = "SELECT Quantity" & _
       " FROM Products " & _
       " WHERE Product = 'Dog'"
Dim rs As ADODB.Recordset
Set rs = New ADODB.Recordset
rs.CursorLocation = adUseServer
rs.CursorType = adOpenDynamic
rs.LockType = adLockPessimistic
' Assume conn is an open connection.
rs.Open sSQL, conn
Dim Quantity As Long
Quantity = rs.Fields("Quantity")
' The update lock is now in place.
' Execute UPDATE statement if appropriate.
```

Both of these examples illustrate techniques that can be used to eliminate deadlocks caused by lock conversion. If your DBMS doesn't support update locks, it supports another lock type to prevent deadlocks from lock conversion. You can always obtain a write lock on a record using an UPDATE statement that sets a field equal to itself. This forces the lock manager to place a write lock on the record in question. This is a brute force approach, but it's commonly used.

While you can write your applications to eliminate some types of deadlocks, other types are unavoidable in a large OLTP system. Some deadlocks will be caught by the DBMS; others will be caught when a COM+ transaction reaches its timeout value. You must plan to trap deadlock errors when they occur and handle them as gracefully as possible. Sometimes you can handle a deadlock by resubmitting the transaction from an error handler. This can hide the deadlock from the user of the application. At other times, you might be forced to return an error to the caller along with instruction to "try again later."

A Final Word on Tuning

We've covered a great deal of territory in this chapter. As a final exercise, I'd like to put all this OLTP theory to work by sketching the workflow of a typical transaction. I'll use the example of submitting a sales order for the Animal Market application. When you start designing the workflow of a transaction, think about which operations cause the greatest amount of contention. Those operations should be run last.

For example, you should always run operations at lower isolation levels first. When you need to lock rows or tables that block other users, you should do that at the very end of the transaction. This practice is essential for minimizing lock times. And as you know, shorter lock times increase throughput and keep response times as low as possible. Here's one possible workflow design for the our sales order example:

■ Run a SELECT statement against the *Customers* table at Read Uncommitted to verify the customer's existence. Roll back the transaction and raise an error if the customer's name isn't in the database.

■ Run a SELECT statement against the *Products* table at Read Uncommitted to verify the product's existence and retrieve its price. Assume that product prices don't change during business hours. Roll back the transaction and raise an error if the product isn't in the database.

■ Insert a new record in the *Orders* table. Of the three tables being updated, this one has the least contention.

■ Update the *Customers* table. This table has the second-lowest amount of contention. Run a SELECT query with an update lock to read the customer's credit limit and account balance. Roll back the transaction and raise an error if the customer doesn't have enough available credit to make the purchase. If the customer has enough available credit, update the customer record to charge the sales price to the account balance.

■ Update the inventory in the *Products* table. This table has the greatest amount of contention. Run a SELECT query with an update lock to read the inventory level of the product. Roll back the transaction and raise an error if the product doesn't have enough units in stock. If there is enough inventory, update the product record to decrement inventory.

■ If no errors have occurred, commit the transaction.

SUMMARY

This chapter has covered techniques for programming local transactions as well as COM+ transactions. You should always choose the approach that makes the most sense for the project at hand. Either way, transactional programming is all about keeping application throughput high and response times low as the number of users increases. You do this by avoiding unnecessary locks and minimizing the length of time that locks are held.

Declarative transactions are at the core of the COM+ programming model. They're fairly easy to use and they solve the incredibly difficult problem of running distributed transactions against multiple resource managers. The COM+ runtime handles all the interactions with the DTC and makes sure that connections are properly enlisted. All you have to do is learn how to control the outcome of a transaction by setting the happy bit and the done bit.

By now, you're probably tired of hearing me go on and on about minimizing round trips, but avoiding unnecessary round trips between a COM+ application and your RMs is one of the keys to achieving optimal performance. You have to adopt an OLTP mindset to write a scalable application. Remember that using session components combined with stored procedures usually results in the best performance.

It should also be clear to you that optimizing an OLTP application requires a solid understanding of a database API such as ADO and an in-depth knowledge of the RMs you'll be using. You should also take the time to learn how each RM deals with transactions, locking, and concurrency so that you can write your Visual Basic components and SQL code to make the most of your hardware and software.

Chapter 9

Creating Components for IIS and ASP

As a developer, you can't ignore the phenomenon of the Web. Businesses are increasingly abandoning the two-tier style of development in favor of browser-based applications for the corporate intranet, and an increasing number of companies are building Web sites targeted at their outside sales force, suppliers, or stockholders. Online consumer sales at companies such as Amazon.com have reached mind-boggling levels. It seems as if every other day another bunch of 22-year-olds turn into multimillionaires when their "dot-com" company has its IPO.

The success of the Web is based on open and ubiquitous standards such as HTTP and HTML, which allow an application to reach a much larger audience than is possible by any other means. When you build a Web-based application, anyone with a browser, an IP address, and an Internet connection is a potential user. Some sites leverage advanced features such as Dynamic HTML (DHTML) and client-side scripting. Other sites use more generic techniques to support down-level browsers and thereby reach a wider audience.

Over the next few years, Extensible Markup Language (XML) is poised to take applications based on HTTP to the next level. HTTP has been an excellent protocol for transmitting formatted content, and now it's quickly becoming the medium for transmitting XML-based data from business to business.

This chapter describes how to build Web-based applications for Microsoft Windows 2000 Server. We'll examine the architecture of both Microsoft Internet Information Services (IIS) and Active Server Pages (ASP) because they provide the building blocks for communicating with HTTP on the Windows platform.

Because I want to focus on the more advanced aspects of developing Web applications, I'll assume that you've had some exposure to HTML and writing server-side scripts in ASP pages. I'll also assume that you have a basic familiarity with built-in ASP objects such as *Request, Response, Session, Application,* and *Server.* Finally, I'll assume that you know how to use HTML forms to capture input data associated with an ASP request. If you aren't familiar with the fundamentals of ASP, I suggest that you find some appropriate resources to supplement this book.

HTTP vs. DCOM

Many companies that have distributed applications use HTTP as the protocol for all client-to-server communication. I'd like to take some time at the beginning of this chapter to examine the key issues that make HTTP preferable to DCOM in certain situations This should help you understand when a distributed application must rely on a Web server such as IIS.

The first reason for using HTTP is the most obvious: It facilitates cross-platform development. HTTP is ubiquitous—implementations are available on all platforms. HTML processors are also available everywhere as well. You can thus reach many more potential users. Applications that rely on DCOM, on the other hand, can reach only users with a 32-bit version of Windows. When you add the fact that user interfaces built using HTML can run on many different browsers and operating systems, HTTP becomes a very attractive way to build cross-platform applications.

HTTP isn't just for serving up HTML-based user interfaces. Many applications use HTTP as an RPC-like protocol, sending arbitrary information to the Web server in POST requests and interpreting the response messages as appropriate. The most common format for sending this information is XML. XML is a text-based data format that allows applications developed by different organizations to exchange information in a platform-neutral way. Fortunately for Visual Basic programmers, Microsoft's XML parser is built into Windows 2000 and provides excellent support for reading, writing, transmitting, and receiving XML.

Another disadvantage of using DCOM throughout an application is that DCOM requires a significant amount of client-side configuration. Client computers must be configured with information about AppIDs, CLSIDs, ProgIDs, and IIDs. Client computers also require the registration of type libraries. This client-side configuration can be expensive to set up and maintain.

Here's an example of how client-side configuration requirements can be problematic. Let's say you've created a Visual Basic component and installed it in a COM+ server application. You built the component using a *MultiUse* class with public methods. As you know, you can generate an application proxy to install the type library on the client machine. But what happens if you want to add a few new methods to the second version of the class in an upgraded version of the DLL? If you add new methods and recompile the component under binary compatibility, all client computers will need the updated version of the type library. You therefore have to regenerate and reinstall a new application proxy. This client-side configuration requirement catches many developers and administrators off guard.

The point I'm trying to make is that the problems associated with DCOM and client-side configuration have a tangible administrative cost. You can avoid this cost by using HTTP and a standard Web browser because they lessen or eliminate the need for client-side configuration. Once again, using HTTP without a Web browser or HTML is another viable option.

Another problem with DCOM is that it is impractical for connecting computers that aren't running in a private Windows 2000 or Windows NT–based network. It can be difficult or impossible to authenticate and authorize users from across the Internet. DCOM is also notoriously difficult to configure across a firewall. Most firewall software is designed to allow HTTP requests to pass freely across ports 80 and 443. However, most firewall software makes it far more difficult to configure the ports required by RPC and DCOM.

DCOM also suffers from being a very connection-oriented protocol. For example, client computers using DCOM typically require at least six round trips to the server to run a command. The first three to four round trips are required to create the object. More round trips are required to establish a secure connection to the server process. The last round trip is used to invoke the desired method. Also, tearing down the connection requires at least two round trips, one to execute *Release* (from *IUnknown*) and one to tear down the TCP connection. HTTP is far more efficient. A client that relies on HTTP can execute its first method in roughly two round trips—one to establish the initial TCP connection and one to carry the actual request and response.

In Chapter 6, I described how DCOM uses a pinging mechanism to implement distributed garbage collection. This client-to-server pinging is necessary to properly release objects when client applications crash. While this pinging mechanism is important, it's also expensive and limits the number of DCOM clients that can effectively connect to a single server computer simultaneously.

DCOM also poses problems when you want to share a set of server computers across a set of clients. The connection-oriented nature of DCOM pins a client to a specific server, so you can't perform load balancing on a request-by-request basis. Moreover, the apartment-threaded nature of a Visual Basic component pins a client to a specific thread on a specific server. This means that an application based on Visual Basic and DCOM can't take full advantage of the thread-pooling scheme available to a COM+ server application.

An application based on HTTP is much easier to load balance and is far more scalable. Later in the chapter, I'll describe several HTTP load-balancing techniques that are the most common and effective ways of scaling an application. As you'll see, Visual Basic objects should always be created and released in the scope of a single HTTP request. HTTP-based load balancing is the most common way to scale an application to handle thousands of users.

Load-balancing schemes available with HTTP don't merely increase the number of potential users. They can also significantly improve an application's availability because each request for a specific user can be directed to a different server. If one Web server computer crashes or is off line for maintenance, clients can continue to use the application without interruption. This isn't possible when a client is connected through DCOM to a specific object running on a specific server computer.

Despite these arguments for preferring HTTP to DCOM, you must realize that Web-based development presents its fair share of challenges. Emerging standards make it challenging to build and maintain Web applications. It's also tricky to manage sessions of client-specific state when you use a connectionless protocol such as HTTP. Finally, it's difficult to create an effective callback notification system for client applications that are running in a browser on the other end of the Internet. But then again, I know you love a challenge.

THE IIS/ASP ARCHITECTURE

IIS is more than a simple Web server. It's a sophisticated server based on many popular protocols and Internet standards. In addition to HTTP, IIS handles protocols such as File Transfer Protocol (FTP), Network News Transfer Protocol (NNTP), and Simple Mail Transfer Protocol (SMTP). In this chapter, we'll focus on how IIS handles HTTP traffic. In particular, we'll examine how IIS plays the role of Web server for the Windows platform. The information in this chapter is based on IIS 5, which ships with Windows 2000 Server and Windows 2000 Professional.

The initial release of IIS was simply a service that served up static HTML pages. Recent versions of IIS are far more sophisticated. In addition to serving up static Web pages, IIS can run extensive server-side processing in response to HTTP requests.

You can take a few different approaches to server-side processing with IIS. Like many UNIX-based Web servers, IIS can run applications that are based on Common Gateway Interface (CGI). This CGI support makes it relatively easy to port existing Web applications to the Windows platform. However, CGI isn't the best approach when you build an application for IIS. Web development based on the native API for IIS is more flexible and offers much better performance. The native API for IIS is known as the Internet Server API (ISAPI).

Software written directly against ISAPI comes in two flavors: ISAPI extensions and ISAPI filters. ISAPI extensions are invoked in response to HTTP requests for a specific filename extension. ISAPI filters are invoked in response to all HTTP traffic for a specific IIS computer, site, or application.

Writing software directly against ISAPI provides the best performance and greatest flexibility, but it has several daunting requirements. ISAPI software must be compiled into DLLs that expose call-level functions as well-known entry points. Visual Basic doesn't support this, so most ISAPI development is done using C or C++. ISAPI programming also forces you to deal with low-level plumbing details such as implementing a thread-pooling manager and writing custom synchronization code. Most companies avoid creating ISAPI-based software because they don't have the expertise and they're not willing to invest the time and money to get it.

ASP is a popular alternative to ISAPI-based development. ASP doesn't eliminate the need for ISAPI, however. ASP is a runtime layer built on top of ISAPI that hides the low-level grunge of direct ISAPI programming. ASP is itself an ISAPI extension that allows you to write server-side logic using simple scripting languages. The ASP framework provides the convenience of a built-in thread-pooling scheme and eliminates the need to write custom synchronization code.

Since this book focuses on writing software with Visual Basic, I'll leave the topic of writing ISAPI filters and ISAPI extensions for another book. Here, I'll concentrate on what you can do using ASP pages and Visual Basic components.

The ASP Framework

Let's take a moment to review the fundamental concepts of ASP. The ASP framework is built around three important assumptions. First, since Web applications tend to generate pages from static data as well as dynamic data, an ASP page is usually a combination of HTML text (static data) and server-side script (code for generating dynamic data). Second, since developers want to build sites using component-based software, an ASP page can load and run objects from standard COM components. Third, since Web developers need help with state management because HTTP is largely a connectionless protocol, the ASP framework provides a scheme for managing client-specific state as well as application-wide state across HTTP requests.

As you know, an ASP page is a text file that contains HTML and server-side scripts. Server-side scripts can be written in a number of scripting languages, including VBScript and JScript (Microsoft's JavaScript implementation). The ASP runtime handles a request for an .ASP file by running a filter that looks for special tags that enclose instructions to be parsed and executed on the server. The ASP runtime executes these server-side scripts and returns an HTML stream back to the client. This HTML stream can include a combination of static HTML from the page and HTML that is generated dynamically as a result of server-side processing. An ASP developer can write server-side scripts to run business logic, access databases, and interact with COM objects.

In addition to providing an easy way to run scripts and Visual Basic objects on the Web server, the ASP runtime also provides support for state management. The ASP designers recognized the difficulty of managing application-wide variables and client-specific state when you develop applications based on a connectionless protocol such as HTTP. The ASP framework exposes a name/value dictionary called the *Application* object for sharing in-memory data across all the clients of a specific application. The ASP framework solves the more difficult problem of managing client-specific state through another name/value dictionary called the *Session* object.

The session-management facilities of the ASP framework are made possible by the passing of HTTP cookies between the IIS Web server process and the client's browser. The generation and management of these cookies as well as the caching of client-specific state is transparent to the ASP developer. Anyone who's programmed against the ASP *Session* object can tell you how easy it is. The ASP runtime does almost all the work behind the scenes.

ASP application variables and ASP session variables are accessible to ASP developers as well as to Visual Basic developers who are creating components for IIS. These ASP state management features make it much easier for you to build session-based applications in which clients build up server-side state over a series of ASP requests. However, you must understand how the use of ASP session-management can limit an application's scalability. Over the course of this chapter, I'll tell you several reasons why ASP session variables are inappropriate for large-scale applications.

IIS Applications

The main Web server process for IIS runs as a Windows service and is launched from an executable named INETINFO.EXE. All incoming HTTP requests are initially sent to this Web server process. If IIS sees that a request is for a static Web page (such as a file with an .HTM extension), it simply returns the page to the client. However, if IIS determines that the request should be routed to an IIS extension such as the ASP runtime, it calls upon a system-provided helper object known as the Web Application Manager (WAM).

If you look at the COM+ Applications folder of a Windows 2000 server (with IIS installed), you'll see a library application named IIS In-Process Applications. This application contains a free-threaded component named IISWAM.W3SVC that's installed along with IIS. This component is a WAM that routes incoming requests for ISAPI extensions to the proper DLL. For example, when a WAM receives a request with an .ASP extension, it redirects the request to ASP.DLL.

IIS uses an abstraction known as an *IIS application* to map URLs to physical directories. For this reason, an IIS application is also known as a *virtual directory*. The installation of IIS automatically creates a default Web site that serves as the root application. The path to the site's home directory is typically something like C:\InetPub \wwwroot. You can configure additional IIS applications by creating virtual directories using the IIS administrative tool called the Internet Services Manager. For instance, you can map a URL such as *http://LocalHost/MyApplication* to a physical directory of your choice. Once you create a virtual directory, you can simply add your HTML and ASP pages to the appropriate directory and everything from that point down in the directory hierarchy is part of the IIS Application (until you reach another IIS Application).

As you can see, it's pretty simple to get an IIS application up and running. If you're not familiar with setting up and managing IIS applications, you should read through the documentation that ships with IIS 5. The documentation for IIS is itself a virtual directory that's accessible through the path *http://LocalHost/iishelp*. It offers step-by-step instructions for creating and managing IIS applications.

IIS tracks configuration information for IIS-specific entities such as computers, sites, and applications in a special database called the IIS metabase. The IIS metabase is similar in concept to the COM+ registration database (RegDB) and the Windows Registry, but it is a separate data store used exclusively by IIS.

The IIS metabase is a hierarchical database file that holds key/value pairs. Some metabase keys are configurable through the Internet Services Manager. Other important metabase keys are accessible only programmatically through IIS Admin Objects, which are accessible through Active Directory Services Interfaces (ADSI).

Later in this chapter, I'll show a brief example that uses IIS Admin Objects with ADSI. You'll find a complete overview of writing administrative scripts and programs in the IIS documentation or the Platform SDK by searching on "Administering IIS Programmatically." These resources offer more information on accessing the metabase keys with Windows Script Host (WSH) files or with Visual Basic.

Processing an ASP Request

Figure 9-1 shows the flow of a typical ASP request. The request is initially handled by a WAM object, which routes it to the ASP runtime. The ASP runtime responds by creating an internal page object. The page object runs a filter on the requested ASP page to parse out any server-side processing instructions. Note that the programmatic interfaces exposed by WAM objects and by internal page objects are undocumented. You never have to interact with them directly. However, once you see how these system objects interact with one another, you'll have a much better understanding of how an ASP request is processed.

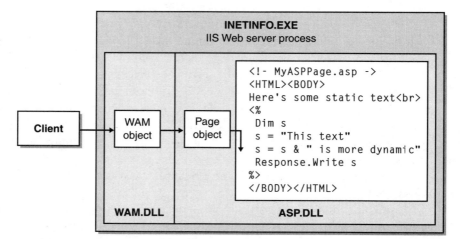

Figure 9-1 *WAM objects route requests for .ASP files to the ASP runtime, which responds by creating an internal page object to filter out and run server-side scripts.*

The WAM is a free-threaded object. When it calls into an ISAPI extension such as ASP.DLL, it uses a multithreaded apartment (MTA) thread that's been dispatched from a thread pool maintained by the IIS runtime. One of the trickier aspects of creating an ISAPI extension is dealing with concurrency and synchronization issues caused by this MTA thread pool. The ASP runtime makes things easier by switching each ASP request over to a single-threaded apartment (STA) thread before running the code in an ASP page. The ASP runtime manages a separate pool of STA worker threads. (Behind the scenes, ASP is actually using COM+ thread pooling to accomplish this.) The ASP designers created this thread-pooling scheme to provide an optimized balance between concurrency and resource usage while eliminating the need for programmer-assisted synchronization.

Figure 9-2 shows how the ASP runtime switches each request from an MTA thread to an STA thread. A dispatching mechanism in the ASP runtime places each request in a central request queue. STA threads in an ASP-managed pool monitor this queue and service requests on a first-in, first-out basis. Note that the size of this thread pool is dynamic. The ASP runtime spawns additional threads during high-traffic times and releases threads when things quiet down.

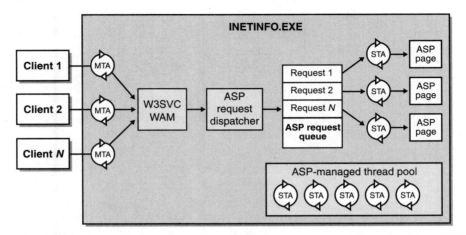

Figure 9-2 *ASP requests are placed in a central request queue, where they're serviced on a first-in, first-out basis by a pool of STA worker threads.*

Switching over to an STA thread effectively eliminates concurrency issues, but it also has a noticeable effect on performance. An ISAPI extension DLL that processes each request on a single MTA thread provides faster response times. You can easily see the difference in performance by benchmarking ISAPI extension DLLs against ASP requests. However, most companies are willing to give up a degree of performance in return for an environment in which it's far easier to write software. They assume that additional hardware can compensate for the overhead of the ASP threading scheme.

Note that IIS 5 provides an optimization that wasn't offered in earlier IIS versions. When the ASP request dispatcher encounters an ASP page that doesn't include any server-side processing tags, it simply processes the page on the MTA thread without sending it to the request queue. This improves performance noticeably. In earlier versions of IIS, you had to use pages with an .HTM or .HTML extension in order to avoid the overhead of a thread switch. Now all pages can have an .ASP extension regardless of whether they have server-side processing tags. The thread switch is incurred only when needed.

IIS provides a way to configure the maximum size of the STA thread pool and the maximum size of the request queue. The thread pool size is controlled by the *AspProcessorThreadMax* key in the IIS metabase. The default setting for this key is 25 per processor per process. On a quad-processor machine, that means that each process that hosts ASP can have up to 100 worker threads. For most production ASP applications, this default setting shouldn't be adjusted. I recommend that you avoid adjusting this key unless you've thought through all issues related to tuning a thread pool. It's easy to inadvertently degrade the responsiveness and throughput of your site by setting this value too high.

The primary reason to increase the value of *AspProcessorThreadMax* is to optimize an application in which ASP pages make long-running calls to COM objects running in other processes and on other machines. In most other scenarios, increasing the value of *AspProcessorThreadMax* hurts performance because of the additional overhead of switching more threads in and out of the Web server's processors. Note that you can't adjust this setting using the Internet Services Manager. You must change it programmatically using an administrative script or a Visual Basic application.

In some situations, the ASP request queue size can also require tuning. If the Web server gets more requests per second than it can handle, the request queue will grow larger and larger. When the queue grows too large, the response times for servicing incoming requests will decrease dramatically. IIS sets a maximum capacity for the queue so that the request backlog doesn't grow too large.

By default, the ASP runtime allows the queue to grow to 3000 requests. Once the queue has reached capacity, additional incoming ASP requests are rejected with a "Server Too Busy" error. This behavior is reasonable because it allows IIS to reject any request that it can't handle in a timely manner.

Adjusting the queue size allows you to change the point at which the Web server starts rejecting incoming requests. You must strike a balance between high availability and shorter response times. The whole point is to configure the queue size to handle short-term peaks but limit the queue's backlog during extreme workloads. If your Web server gets overloaded, it's better to send error messages back to your clients than to make them wait an unacceptably long time.

You can adjust the *AspRequestQueueMax* key as well as the *AspProcessorThread-Max* key programmatically using IIS Admin Objects and ADSI. For example, in a Standard EXE project you can reference the Active DS Type Library and write the following code:

```
Dim MyWebServer As ActiveDs.IADs
Set MyWebServer = GetObject("IIS://LocalHost/W3SVC")
MyWebServer.Put "AspProcessorThreadMax", 30
MyWebServer.Put "AspRequestQueueMax", 1500
MyWebServer.SetInfo
```

Let's review by summarizing how the ASP thread pool works for a default installation of IIS on a machine with a single processor. The pool has 25 STA worker threads available per process. (If you want more threads, you should acquire a dual- or quad-processor Web server machine.) When a request arrives, it's placed in the request queue. The ASP runtime dispatches an idle STA thread from the pool, if one is available. (Note that this scheme allows any thread in the pool to process the request.)

If all the STA worker threads are busy processing other requests, incoming requests are queued up and processed on a first-in, first-out basis. As long as the queue doesn't reach its default capacity of 3000 requests, all requests are processed.

Now that you understand the threading scheme built into the ASP runtime, let's talk about how to make the most of it as a Visual Basic programmer.

Creating Visual Basic Objects from ASP Pages

Let's begin this section by examining the relationship between a Visual Basic object and the ASP runtime environment. Since you'll be creating and configuring Visual Basic DLLs to run on the Web server, you should understand how object activation and lifecycle management work when you create COM objects from an ASP page. Fortunately, ASP makes it relatively easy to create Web-based applications that leverage Visual Basic components running on the Web server.

The following ASP page uses a server-side script written in VBScript to create a Visual Basic object and interact with it:

```
<%@ LANGUAGE="VBSCRIPT"%>
<HTML><BODY>
<H2>Customer List</H2>
<%
    Dim sProgID, CustomerManager
    sProgID = "MyWebDll.CCustomerManager"
    Set CustomerManager = Server.CreateObject(sProgID)
    Response.Write CustomerManager.GetCustomerListHTML()
%>
</BODY></HTML>
```

You can see how easy it is to create and use a Visual Basic object from an ASP page. Note that the ASP page filter recognizes the inline tags <% and %> as the beginning and the end of a server-side script. Alternatively, you can write server-side scripts in an ASP page using the *SCRIPT* tag with the *RunAt=Server* attribute.

I must emphasize that running Visual Basic components from server-side scripts doesn't prevent you from building cross-platform solutions. You can run as much COM code as you'd like on the Web server without creating any client-side dependencies on Microsoft Internet Explorer or the Windows platform. As long as you write platform-independent HTML, the client computers can run a wide range of browser and operating systems. It's up to you to know which HTML tags and client-side scripting techniques create browser-specific dependencies.

Replacing ASP scripts with Visual Basic components

You can reap quite a few benefits by moving business logic and data access code out of ASP pages and into Visual Basic DLLs. ASP pages are great for programming in the small, but managing an application that contains thousands of lines of code can be difficult. Here are a few things to keep in mind when you're deciding whether to place your logic in an ASP page or a Visual Basic component:

- You get higher levels of encapsulation and code reuse by using a programming language that is class-based and object-oriented, such as Visual Basic.

- The Visual Basic IDE offers compile-time type checking and the most effective use of IntelliSense. This results in greater productivity and fewer hours spent debugging (especially if you're programming against a COM-based library such as ADO).

- Visual Basic code is compiled; ASP scripts aren't. This means that logic in a Visual Basic DLL can run faster than a server-side ASP script. However, you can't always assume that moving logic from an ASP page into a Visual Basic component will speed things up. Creating and tearing down Visual Basic objects requires its own share of processing cycles. Moving code out of an ASP page and into a Visual Basic component can actually degrade performance for a request with minimal logic. But as the amount of code for a request increases, the compiled format of Visual Basic code will outperform the equivalent logic in an ASP page.

- Visual Basic code uses direct vTable binding when you program against COM libraries such as ADO. ASP scripts use *IDispatch* and late binding on every method call when they interact with a COM object. For example, if a request requires 20 or more calls against ADO objects, the performance penalty for late binding can be significant.

- COM-based DLLs created with Visual Basic can take full advantage of the integration between IIS and the COM+ runtime environment.

- You can access the Win32 API directly from an ActiveX DLL but not from a script in an ASP page. (Of course, your Visual Basic code can potentially crash the Web server process if you call a Win32 API function incorrectly.)

You should also keep in mind the issues relating to scripting clients that we discussed in Chapter 4. You have to deal with a few oddities when you write ASP code with a scripting language such as VBScript. First, variables in a server-side script can't be explicitly typed. They are implicitly cast as Variants. This can take some getting used to if you're a Visual Basic programmer.

Second, VBScript can retrieve method output parameters only when they're declared as Variants. If you try to call a method on a Visual Basic object that has an output parameter declared as a *String* or *Double*, the VBScript code will fail and generate a "Type mismatch" error. You should therefore design your Visual Basic methods so that output parameters (*ByRef*) are Variants if you intend to call them from ASP scripts.

You can propagate errors from a Visual Basic object back to an ASP page, but error handling isn't as graceful in VBScript as it is in Visual Basic. Error handling is typically conducted by using an *On Error Resume Next* statement and checking the error number after each call. This is cumbersome, but it works. Here's an example of handling an error with VBScript in an ASP page:

```
<%
    On Error Resume Next
    Dim sProgID, CustomerManager
    sProgID = "MyWebDll.CCustomerManager"
    Set CustomerManager = Server.CreateObject(sProgID)
    Response.Write CustomerManager.GetCustomerListHTML()
    ' Test to see if call experienced a runtime error.
    If Err.Number <> 0 Then
        Response.Write "<b>There has been a system error</b><br>"
        Response.Write Err.Description
    End If
%>
```

Lifecycle requirements for apartment-threaded objects

As you know, you can use Visual Basic to create apartment-threaded components that run in the STA model. If you want to create a component that supports a more sophisticated threading model, you must use a different language, such as C++. The good news for Visual Basic programmers is that this doesn't impose much of a limitation in an IIS application because the ASP thread pool is based on STA threads. An ASP page and the Visual Basic objects it creates often run on the same thread. As a result, you can avoid the overhead of COM's proxy/stub layer.

When you create an ActiveX DLL for an IIS application, be sure to leave your project's threading model set to the default setting of Apartment Threaded. Don't change it to Single Threaded, which forces your objects to run in the main STA of the IIS Web server process and causes your objects to load on a different STA thread than the ASP page that created them. This setting degrades performance because it creates an unnecessary proxy/stub layer. Moreover, single-threaded DLLs are undesirable because they can result in strange blocking problems.

It's important to remember that Visual Basic objects exhibit thread affinity. This means that a Visual Basic object can be accessed only by the thread that created it. This isn't a problem when you create and release an object within the scope of a single HTTP request. But if you attempt to hold onto a Visual Basic object across multiple requests by assigning it to an ASP *Session* variable, you end up pinning the client to a specific worker thread in the ASP thread pool.

To illustrate why this situation is undesirable, let's look at an example that highlights the issues that the ASP designers had to think through when creating their framework. Imagine a request from a client that creates an object and assigns it to an ASP *Session* variable. The object is created on one of the STA threads from the ASP thread pool—let's say thread 17. What if the next request from the same client is processed by thread 8? A problem occurs because thread 8 can't access an apartment-threaded object created on thread 17. The request would have to switch from thread 8 to thread 17 in order to access the object.

The ASP designers had to choose between two evils. They decided that pinning clients to threads was preferable to having a situation in which a single request requires access to multiple threads from an ASP-managed pool. They added code to the ASP runtime to determine when an apartment-threaded object is assigned to an ASP *Session* variable. Once a client session is assigned an apartment-threaded object, the ASP runtime routes every request through the same STA worker thread for the duration of the session. This is unfortunate because the ASP thread-pooling scheme works best when it can use the first available thread in the pool.

The ASP thread-pooling model dispatches any thread in the pool to service an incoming ASP request. However, when you assign a Visual Basic object to an ASP *Session* variable, ASP must locate (and possibly block on) the one thread that created the object. While the ASP runtime can serialize all future requests over the same thread, this situation doesn't allow an application to reach its potential in terms of performance and concurrency. One client can block on another's request even when several STA worker threads are sitting idle in the pool.

The important point to take away from all this is that Visual Basic objects should be used only at page scope. You should never attempt to hold onto a Visual Basic object (or any other apartment-threaded object) with an ASP *Session* variable because your application won't scale properly. Of course, you might be able to get away with doing this if your site doesn't get much traffic. But you should at least realize the implications of what you're doing.

You've seen the problems associated with apartment-threaded objects and ASP *Session* variables. Assigning a Visual Basic object to an ASP *Application* variable creates an even more severe problem. If you assign an apartment-threaded object to an ASP *Application* variable, the requests from many different clients must be routed through a single thread. (There's actually a special STA thread created for this purpose, so there's always a thread switch and a single point of contention.) This results in severe and unacceptable blocking behavior. If you release your Visual Basic objects at the end of every request, you can avoid this undesirable result.

Partitioning a Web Application into Separate Processes

IIS gives you the option of running your ASP pages in the Web server process (INETINFO.EXE) or in an isolated process. The default Web site and other IIS applications have a configurable Application Protection setting for controlling whether they run in INETINFO.EXE or in a separate, isolated process. Figure 9-3 shows how to adjust the Application Protection setting for an IIS application using the Internet Services Manager.

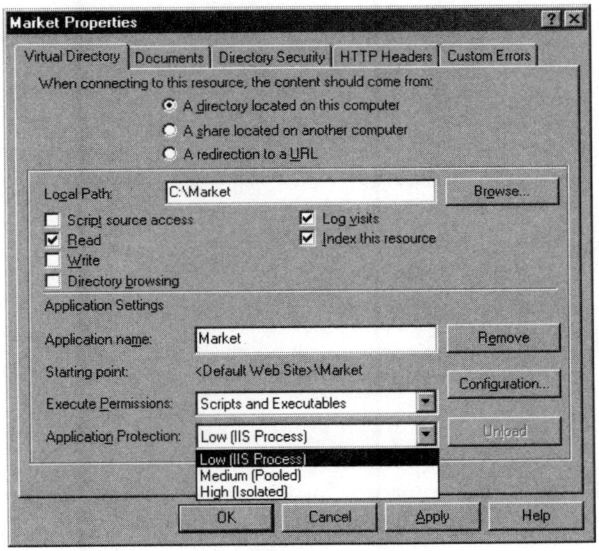

Figure 9-3 *You can configure an IIS application to run in INETINFO.EXE or in an isolated process.*

To achieve the highest levels of performance, you should run your ASP pages and Visual Basic objects in INETINFO.EXE, as shown in Figure 9-4. You can run your ASP pages in INETINFO.EXE by adjusting the Application Protection setting of the home directory or an IIS application to a value of Low (IIS Process). Note that this isn't the default setting for either the home directory or an IIS application in IIS 5.

If you want to run Visual Basic objects in INETINFO.EXE along with your ASP pages, you can add your components to a COM+ library application. You can achieve the same effect by registering your DLLs with REGSVR32.EXE and running them as nonconfigured components. Objects created from nonconfigured components are slightly faster than objects created from configured components because they don't require system-provided proxies with interception code. However, you should remember that nonconfigured components can't carry declarative attributes or interact with the COM+ runtime.

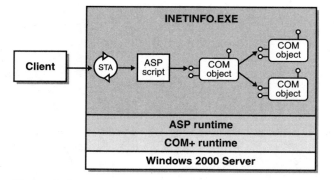

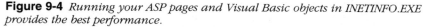

Figure 9-4 *Running your ASP pages and Visual Basic objects in INETINFO.EXE provides the best performance.*

Although running all your code in INETINFO.EXE provides the best performance, other factors might lead you to run your Visual Basic objects and your ASP pages in a separate process. Perhaps you're more interested in higher levels of fault tolerance. Or perhaps you want to run your Visual Basic components on a separate computer to share a set of business objects across multiple Web servers or to create a more secure environment. When you split an application into multiple processes, you typically give up some degree of performance in order to get something else in return.

The two primary reasons why companies avoid running Visual Basic code in INETINFO.EXE have to do with fault tolerance and upgrading application code. Fault tolerance is an issue because the code in a Visual Basic DLL can potentially crash INETINFO.EXE. For example, if you write a call to a Win32 API function that doesn't handle pointers correctly, you can bring down an entire Web site. Any Visual Basic DLL that contains *Declare* statements and API calls must be thoroughly tested before being released into production.

You should note that many developers and administrators overestimate Visual Basic's ability to crash INETINFO.EXE. If an ActiveX DLL fails to catch a standard runtime error, the error is simply passed back to the ASP page that created the object. If the ASP page doesn't catch the error, the ASP runtime simply reports the error back to the browser. While unhandled errors don't make for an elegant application, most Visual Basic code can run safely in INETINFO.EXE without the risk of a crash.

The second reason to avoid running Visual Basic code in INETINFO.EXE has to do with upgrading application code. Once a Visual Basic DLL has been loaded into INETINFO.EXE, the Web server process must be shut down before the DLL can be rebuilt or replaced. Some companies find the requirement to shut down INETINFO.EXE unacceptable for a production server. Later in this chapter, we'll look at a few options that allow you to replace a Visual Basic DLL in production without shutting down the Web server process. During development, you'll also want to avoid loading your DLLs into INETINFO.EXE because doing so makes it painful to recompile and test your code.

You can run your Visual Basic code in a separate process in several ways. The first approach we'll look at is configuring your Visual Basic components in a COM+ server application, as shown in Figure 9-5. Your Visual Basic objects are created in an instance of the COM+ container application DLLHOST.EXE. Each call from an ASP page to an object is executed across process boundaries with the help of a proxy/stub pair.

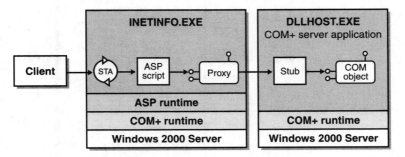

Figure 9-5 *When an ASP page creates an object from a component configured in a COM+ server application, the ASP page and the object are connected through a proxy/stub pair.*

During development, this approach makes it much easier to rebuild a DLL. After you test your DLL, you can simply shut down the COM+ server application and rebuild it. Moreover, you can switch back and forth between running objects in DLLHOST.EXE and in the Visual Basic debugger. If you set up your components for MTS/COM+-style debugging (as described in Chapter 6), you can single-step through code for a Visual Basic object that's been instantiated from an ASP page running in INETINFO.EXE. If you'll be debugging Visual Basic objects created from ASP pages, you should read the sidebar on the following page.

DEBUGGING VISUAL BASIC COMPONENTS CREATED FROM ASP PAGES

Visual Basic developers can encounter a problem when they first attempt to debug Visual Basic objects created from ASP pages under Windows 2000. When an ASP page attempts to create an object in the Visual Basic debugger, the ASP runtime reports the error message "The call to Server.CreateObject failed while checking permissions. Access is denied to this object." I'll cover security in greater depth in Chapter 11, but I want discuss this problem here so that you don't get hung up when you start debugging Visual Basic components targeted for an IIS application.

An IIS application has a default security setting that allows anonymous access. When an unauthenticated client submits an ASP request, the ASP page runs as an anonymous user under the IUSR_*MachineName* account. The process associated with the Visual Basic debugger (VB6.EXE) uses default access permissions that are configured on a machine-wide basis. The IUSR_*MachineName* account can't call into VB6.EXE until it has been added to the machine-wide default access permissions. You modify the security permissions using a utility called DCOMCNFG.EXE. If you run DCOMCNFG.EXE from the command line, you can change the machine-wide Default Access Permission setting on the Default Security tab. DCOMCNFG.EXE provides a standard Windows access control list (ACL) editor that lets you grant access permissions to IUSR_*MachineName* or any other user account. Keep in mind that this opens up a potential security hole that's probably far more acceptable for a development workstation than it is for a production server.

Another quick way to get around this security problem is to disable anonymous access for the default Web site using the Internet Service Manager and rely on Integrated Windows authentication during debugging. If you do this, ASP pages don't run as IUSER_*MachineName*. Instead, they run under the interactive user account—the same user account that the browser runs under. If you're doing all your debugging on a single machine, the Visual Basic debugger also runs under the interactive user account. Therefore, COM security checks allow ASP pages to create and interact with objects in VB6.EXE.

Note that the problem I've described in this sidebar is an issue only when you debug an ActiveX DLL in the Visual Basic IDE. The problem doesn't affect Visual Basic objects running in a COM+ application.

Another good reason to add your components to a COM+ server application is to run objects on a separate computer that serves as a dedicated application server. You might want to do this, for example, if you want to have a single application server that's used by many different Web servers. Or you might want to balance the processing load of the application across several computers or have your business objects run on a computer that's more secure than the Web server. Once you install your Visual Basic components in a COM+ server application on the application server computer, it's pretty easy to create an application proxy and install it on any Web server that needs to access it. ASP pages can then create objects from across the network.

As you know, out-of-process calls are expensive. Calls that cross computer boundaries are even more expensive. If ASP pages will be calling objects that live in other processes, you must design your components to minimize the number of round trips. This is an important aspect of distributed application design.

Isolated IIS Applications

You've learned one way to run your Visual Basic objects in a separate process outside of INETINFO.EXE. IIS also lets you run your ASP pages outside of INETINFO.EXE. If you set the Application Protection setting for an IIS application to Medium (Pooled) or High (Isolated), your ASP pages will run in an instance of the COM+ container application DLLHOST.EXE.

Figure 9-6 shows how things work when you set an IIS application's Application Protection setting to High (Isolated). IIS has to perform a little trickery to run ASP pages in an isolated process. When you change the setting of an IIS application to High (Isolated), IIS creates a new COM+ server application with a special WAM component. You can actually verify this by refreshing and examining the COM+ Applications folder in the Component Services administrative tool after you make the adjustment.

When IIS receives the first request for the isolated IIS application, the W3SVC WAM object in INETINFO.EXE creates an instance of this special WAM component, which forces the COM+ runtime to launch a new instance of DLLHOST.EXE. From that point on, all requests for this isolated IIS application are routed across these two WAM objects. The result is that all ASP pages associated with the isolated IIS application run in their own private process.

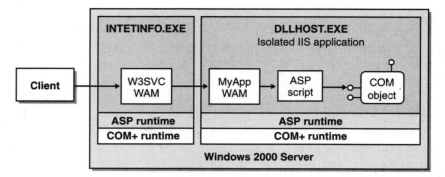

Figure 9-6 *When an IIS application has an Application Protection setting of High (Isolated), it runs in a private instance of DLLHOST.EXE.*

Keep in mind that there is a performance penalty for every request because it requires an out-of-process COM call from one WAM object to another. However, unlike the deployment scheme depicted in Figure 9-5, calls from ASP pages into a Visual Basic object don't have to go across process boundaries. As long as your components are in a library application or are registered as nonconfigured components, your objects are created in the same process and on the same thread as the ASP page that created them. Such a model gives acceptable performance even when an ASP page makes multiple calls into an object.

The final deployment scheme is simply a minor variation of the one you just saw. When an IIS application runs with Medium (Pooled) protection, it runs in a shared instance of DLLHOST.EXE along with any other IIS application that has the same setting. Note that Medium (Pooled) is the default Application Protection setting for the home directory as well as every new IIS application. Figure 9-7 shows how requests are routed to their proper destinations.

One motivation for running IIS applications in isolation has to do with security. INETINFO.EXE runs as a Windows service under the identity of the system. Isolated IIS applications, on the other hand, run under the identity of a more restricted user account. This means that isolating an IIS application can lower the risk of attacks on your Web site. I'll revisit this topic in Chapter 11 when I talk about IIS security.

You've now seen quite a few possible deployment scenarios. You can run all your ASP pages and Visual Basic objects in INETINFO.EXE. You can run your ASP pages in INETINFO.EXE and run your Visual Basic objects in a COM+ server application. You can run your ASP pages and objects outside of INETINFO.EXE. In fact, you can partition a Web application in just about any way that makes sense.

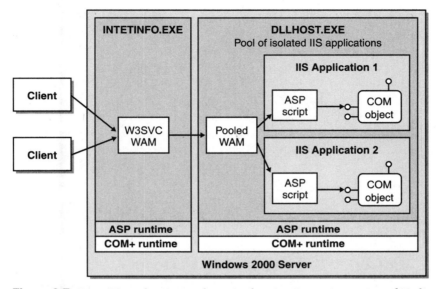

Figure 9-7 *Every IIS application with an Application Protection setting of Medium (Pooled) runs in a shared instance of DLLHOST.EXE.*

What's really neat about these deployment options is that they don't necessarily affect the way you write your ASP pages or your Visual Basic components. (The one exception is when you've created a Visual Basic component that has an in-process dependency for performance reasons.) When you finish writing your application, you can change from one deployment option to another without rewriting any code. You can simply change the Application Protection setting of an IIS application or the activation setting of a COM+ application.

For example, you can test and debug your code in the development environment by running your Visual Basic components in a COM+ server application. This makes it much easier to unload and recompile your DLLs. When it's time to put your code into production, you can configure your site to run your ASP pages and your Visual Basic objects in INETINFO.EXE to achieve the best possible performance.

SPLITTING CODE BETWEEN ASP PAGES AND COMPONENTS

Now that we've covered the basics of developing and deploying Visual Basic components for an IIS application, I'd like to discuss some of the important factors that affect the way you design an application for IIS. Deciding how to partition application code into ASP pages and Visual Basic components is critical.

If you're designing the high-level architecture for a new Web application, you can typically break down your application code into three logical tiers. You have data access code, business logic, and user interface code. In the initial design phase, it's important to decide how and where to package the code for each of these tiers.

For most of us, the decision where to put the data access code and the business logic should be easy. They should be written into components and distributed in COM-based DLLs. The components should then be configured in COM+ applications or run as nonconfigured components. Once the components holding your business logic and data access code are in place, the developers responsible for the user interface can create desktop and Web-based applications. The client applications that define the user interface use your business objects as an entry point into your company's IT infrastructure.

Creating a great Web application requires expertise in many different technologies. Many of these technologies center around the presentation tier. In this book, I won't cover how to build a sophisticated and interactive user interface (an undertaking that requires extensive knowledge of DHTML and JavaScript). Instead, I'll concentrate on the code that runs in IIS that sends the user interface portion back to the browser.

As you know, ASP pages are critical because they allow you to run server-side scripts that, in turn, allow you to activate and run COM objects in response to client requests. ASP pages are also used extensively to package the content, the layout details, and the user interface code behind Web pages. But exactly how much should you put into ASP pages? That's an easy question to answer: It depends.

Some Web developers like to define every aspect of the user interface using ASP pages. Others go to great pains to minimize what they need to put in their ASP pages. Many developers favor using a mixture of ASP pages and components for generating HTML dynamically. Whichever approach you take, some part of your application must be responsible for defining the user interface.

Any nontrivial Web application must do the following things: it must accept input that the user has entered in HTML forms, it must interpret user requests and run the appropriate commands, and it must generate HTML that contains page content and layout details and send it back to the browser.

Let's examine a few approaches to building the code for the presentation tier. Each approach offers its own set of trade-offs in terms of productivity, reusability, maintainability, extensibility, and performance. Whatever approach you choose, you have to write code against the built-in ASP objects (such as *Request* and *Response*) and you have to create and run business objects. You also have to generate HTML for page content and layout and send it back to the browser.

So how do you decide whether to put presentation tier code in ASP pages, compiled code, or a mixture of the two? You should ask yourself the following questions. How fast do you want to get your site up and running? Which is more important, development productivity or application performance? How important is code reuse? Are you willing to invest more time at the beginning of the project to improve the maintainability and extensibility of your site? Do you want to be able to change various aspects of your site without recompiling any code? Your answers to these questions will lead you to a decision.

Creating the User Interface with ASP Pages

Embedding your presentation tier code in ASP pages using a tool such as Microsoft Visual InterDev has its advantages and disadvantages. On the positive side, you can quickly create and modify the layout of Web pages. You can write server-side scripts that use ASP objects such as *Request, Response, Session,* and *Application.* You can create and run custom business objects. And finally, you can add the code and static HTML to define the pages that are sent back to the browser.

On the other hand, the Visual InterDev approach can be hard to manage if you're developing a large Web site, particularly if the site is constantly changing. Since all your presentation tier code is defined and deployed in text files, it's harder to find effective reuse techniques. You don't have an object-oriented mechanism by which you can encapsulate various parts of your logic from other parts. Instead, each page can become a smorgasbord of page content, layout details, code for dealing with user input, and calls to business objects.

The most common reuse technique for the Visual InterDev developer is to call Save As on an .ASP file and then customize the copy. This approach makes it pretty easy to change one page on the site. However, larger, site-wide changes can be more difficult. For example, supposed you need to slightly change the layout of a commonly used table report. If you have many .ASP files with redundant attribute settings for this report, you have to modify every page to accommodate this site-wide change. As you can see, this problem compromises your site's maintainability.

For smaller Web sites, this might not pose a huge problem. But with large sites, it's often necessary to change many .ASP files to add a new feature or modify the behavior of some client-side script. As you can see, this approach can compromise extensibility as well as maintainability.

Another disadvantage of larger ASP pages is that they can be slow. Because of the interpretive nature of script, larger ASP pages can't run as fast as compiled code. Moreover, every call that an ASP script makes to a COM object goes through *IDispatch* and uses late binding. This means that calls to business objects and calls to the built-in ASP objects are much slower than the same calls made from inside a compiled Visual Basic DLL. The performance degradation of late binding can be significant when a single ASP page makes hundreds or thousands of COM calls.

Creating the User Interface with Compiled Components

If you want to generate part or all of an application's user interface using Visual Basic components, you probably have to program against the ASP objects. It's important to note that you can do just about anything in an ActiveX DLL that you can do in an ASP page. You can thus write components that retrieve values from query strings and HTML form input controls using the *Request* object. You can use the *Response* object to write HTML and client-side script back to the browser. If you're familiar with the ASP object model, you know that there's a whole world of possibilities.

Let's look at what you have to do to program directly against the built-in ASP objects from Visual Basic components. First, you must reference both the COM+ Services Type Library and the Microsoft Active Server Pages Object Library in your ActiveX DLL project. Next, you retrieve ASP object references by name from the *Item* collection of the *ObjectContext* interface. The ASP objects that are available in the *Item* collection include *Request*, *Response*, *Session*, *Application*, and *Server*. It's that simple.

Look at the following method implementation:

```
Sub MyMethodCalledFromASP()
    Dim rsp As Response
    Set rsp = GetObjectContext.Item("Response")
    rsp.Write "Hello World!"
End Sub
```

This code works the way it does because of integration between the ASP runtime and the COM+ runtime. When a server-side script in an ASP page creates an object from a configured component, the ASP runtime passes the references for these five built-in ASP objects to the COM+ runtime. The COM+ runtime uses these references to populate the *Item* collection when it initializes the new object's context. This is just another example of how the COM+ runtime environment flows contextual information from the creator to a newly created object. After the object is initialized, the ASP objects are available for the duration of the ASP request.

Each configured component has an *IISIntrinsics* attribute that must be set to True in order for its objects to access the built-in ASP objects. Fortunately, the default value for this attribute is True. (The COM+ documentation incorrectly lists the default value as False.) You should also note that you can't configure the *IISIntrinsics* attribute using the Component Services administrative tool. You must adjust it programmatically. Of course, you don't have to change it in order to write the code just shown. However, you can perform an optimization by setting the value to False for configured components that don't program against the ASP objects.

At this point, I'd like to make two important observations about Visual Basic components that use built-in ASP objects. First, ActiveX DLLs that use the *ObjectContext* interface to retrieve ASP references must program against the COM+ Services Type Library and should therefore be deployed as configured components. Second, a Visual Basic object requires a call to the ASP runtime each time it accesses an ASP object. If a Visual Basic object and the ASP page that created it live in different processes, this out-of-process call will be expensive.

The key point is that a Visual Basic component that uses ASP objects must be deployed in a COM+ library application as opposed to a COM+ server application. Otherwise, your code's performance will be unacceptable. During development, when performance isn't critical, it's fine to test and debug a component that uses ASP objects in a COM+ server application or in the Visual Basic debugger. But once your code is in production, the component must be added to a COM+ library application so that its objects will run in the same process as the ASP page that creates them. As I stated earlier in this chapter, you can run ASP pages together with Visual Basic objects in three ways: in INETINFO.EXE, in an isolated IIS application, or in the pooled IIS application.

Creating a custom framework for generating a user interface

If your goal is to maintain as much logic as possible inside compiled components, you can adopt a favorite strategy of developers who wear their "COM Is Love" T-shirts day after day. They believe that all application logic should be packed into COM-style DLLs. For the purpose of this discussion, allow me to label such developers as *COM fanatics*. These COM fanatics believe that ASP pages are evil because they aren't distributed in a compiled binary form. COM fanatics make a concerted effort to minimize what goes into ASP pages on their sites. They've discovered a way to minimize an entire Web site to a single ASP page:

```
<%
    Dim ProgID, req
    ProgID = "WebFramework.ClientRequest"
    Set req = Server.CreateObject(ProgID)
    req.ProcessRequest
%>
```

Let's say that this ASP script relies on a custom component named *ClientRequest*, which is built into an ActiveX DLL project named *WebFramework*. The component exposes a single public method called *ProcessRequest*. This method serves as the sole entry point into a Web application based on the COM fanatic's custom framework. In this framework, the *ProcessRequest* method services each client request. Take a look at the following pseudocode:

```
Sub ProcessRequest()
    ' Determine what command the user wants.
    ' Instantiate and call business objects.
    ' Create HTML with content and layout.
    ' Send HTML back to browser.
End Sub
```

The COM fanatic must devise an application design that allows clients to run any of the various commands that the application offers. However, all the requests come through a single entry point. How does the *ProcessRequest* method determine which command to run?

One popular technique is to pass the client's command preference in a query string. This requires some extra work. You must append the proper query string to your URLs as you dynamically write them into your pages. For instance, you can write your URLs to take the following form:

```
MyPage.asp?Command=GetCustomerList
```

Listing 9-1 is a sample implementation of *ProcessRequest*. This code interprets the client's request by pulling the command value out of the query string. It also shows a simplistic way to structure code to generate and transmit HTML back in the response. This is one possible starting point for creating the COM fanatic's framework. Companies typically try an approach such as this when they begin putting together a custom Web-based framework. Their goal is to achieve higher levels of reuse, maintainability, and extensibility. However, putting together a custom framework that meets these goals requires a significant investment at the beginning of a project. You also have to tackle many other design issues along the way.

```
Sub ProcessRequest()
    Dim req As Request
    Set req = GetObjectContext("Request")
    Select Case req("Command")
        Case "", "GetStartPage"
            GetStartPage
        Case "GetCustomerList"
            GetCustomersList
```

Listing 9-1 *(continued)*

(continued)

```
        Case Else
             ' Handle unknown command.
    End Select
    Set req = Nothing
End Sub

Private Sub GetStartPage()
    ' Generate HTML for start page.
End Sub

Private Sub GetCustomerList()
    ' Create business object.
    ' Run query to retrieve customer data.
    ' Generate formatted HTML from customer data.
End Sub
```

Some companies spend lots of money trying to design and implement a custom framework before abandoning this approach and deciding that it's more cost-effective to go back to using ASP pages to define the user interface. If you decide to create such a framework, don't underestimate the up-front costs and the importance of a well-thought-out design.

Here are a few more things to think about. When you move to a component-based framework like this one, it's harder to use productivity-oriented page designers such as Microsoft FrontPage and Visual InterDev. If you do use a page designer, you usually can't use .ASP or .HTM files. You have to cut and paste snippets of HTML code into a database and then use these HTML snippets to parse together Web pages dynamically.

Another thing you should avoid is compiling any content or HTML layout details into your DLLs. For instance, if you define all your HTML layout tags in your DLL, you must recompile and redistribute your code whenever you want to change a minor cosmetic aspect of your site. Since you're trying to improve your site's maintainability with the framework, something's wrong if your framework creates new maintenance problems that you didn't have when the user interface was defined in ASP pages.

To achieve the highest levels of maintainability and extensibility, you should create a framework that uses a data-driven approach. You definitely want your application's view of business data (such as a customer list) to be data-driven, but you can take it much further. You should also strive for a data-driven approach when you define such things as page titles, page formatting, and navigation. This sort of data isn't exactly business data. It's metadata that the user interface portion of your application uses to do its job.

If you use a data-driven approach, you can create a framework that allows the site's Webmaster to add new pages by simply adding a new record to a database that holds your metadata. For example, you can create a database table named *Pages* that defines a set of fields such as *Title*, *Header*, and *Body*. The code in your framework can dynamically parse these elements into a Web page at runtime.

Likewise, you can easily make a site-wide change to such things as page formatting and the navigation toolbar if the metadata that defines them also lives in the database. If you get to a point where you can make site-wide formatting changes and add new pages without recompiling any code, you've done a good job.

As I've mentioned, if you take a data-driven approach, you should store HTML metadata and client-side script in a noncompiled medium. A database is usually the best choice. The framework can retrieve the metadata from the database at application startup or on an as-needed basis.

Let's say you decide to store all the HTML metadata in a DBMS such as Microsoft SQL Server or Oracle. When your ASP application starts, you can retrieve all your metadata from the database and load it into ASP *Application* variables. This will provide fast and easy access to metadata and let you quickly generate custom pages on the fly.

Using a Mix of ASP Pages and Components

The choice between ASP pages and Visual Basic components isn't an all-or-nothing proposition. Many companies find that the best balance is to use ASP pages to define the basic skeletons of their pages and to use components to generate the more tedious or processor-intensive aspects of the user interface.

Here are a few examples of what's possible. You can create a generic component that generates an HTML form with a set of input controls by inspecting the schema of a database table at runtime. You can create a custom Visual Basic component that creates formatted HTML tables by looping through an ADO recordset. If you're really progressive, you can write a component that leverages an XML parser to convert ADO recordsets into presentable HTML content.

As you can see, you have to consider quite a few issues when you decide how much user interface logic to put in ASP pages versus Visual Basic components. You also have to analyze the requirements of the project and assess the skills of your team members.

MANAGING STATE IN A WEB APPLICATION

Why does state management pose so many problems in a Web application? For the most part, it's because HTTP is largely a connectionless and stateless protocol. The lightweight nature of the HTTP protocol assumes that the Web server forgets all about the client the instant it's done processing a request. In contrast, DCOM and RPC provide a very connection-oriented protocol that makes it easy to maintain client-specific state on the server computer.

Many Web developers store HTTP cookies on the client computer to manage client-specific state across a series of requests. Your server-side software can generate a cookie to track each client session. You must write application logic to send cookies back and forth in requests and responses. In some applications, the developer must generate and transmit a cookie at the beginning of every session as well as look for cookies in each incoming request to identify a particular client.

As you know, the ASP framework provides state management features through two built-in ASP objects. The *Session* object is a name/value dictionary that provides a simple way to track client-specific state. The ASP framework provides the convenience of managing a cookie for each client session behind the scenes. The *Application* object is a name/value dictionary that allows you to store state that's available to any request running in the same IIS application.

I'll assume that you know how to read and write to ASP *Session* and *Application* variables from an ASP page. You should also know that it's possible to access ASP *Session* variables and ASP *Application* variables from a Visual Basic component. To refresh your memory, let me reiterate an important rule I covered earlier in this chapter: Never store a Visual Basic object in an ASP *Session* variable or an ASP *Application* variable.

Using all this knowledge, you often must decide how to maintain client-specific state across multiple requests. For instance, if you're designing a Web-based shopping cart application, you must build a session-based state machine that allows a client to select products and enter payment information across a series of requests.

The first question you must answer in the design phase is whether it's acceptable to store client-specific state on the Web server computer. You can't do this in some scenarios—such as when you're writing ASP pages and Visual Basic components for a Web farm environment. Storing client-specific state on a Web server only works if all the requests from a single client are routed across the same IIS computer, and many load balancing schemes used by Web farms do not impose such a restriction. Complicated environments such as Web farms typically require stateless techniques in which client-specific state is stored in a backend database or sent back and stored on the client using something like cookies or invisible HTML controls.

I'll defer the discussion of problems posed by a Web farm environment until later in this chapter. For now, we'll look at a simpler scenario. If you can make the assumption that you're writing ASP pages and Visual Basic components for a Web site based on a single IIS computer, you can use ASP *Session* variables to manage client-specific state.

When you use ASP *Session* variables to hold your state across requests, you should store simple values (primitive data types) instead of Visual Basic objects. When you store your state in ASP *Session* variables using data types such as Integer, Double, and String, IIS can process future requests using any available STA worker thread from the pool. When you use this approach, you can even use ASP *Session* variables to hold complicated data structures such as arrays and Variants.

Let's look at an example that uses a Visual Basic object to read and write state to and from an ASP *Session* variable. You can use the following code to write a simple string value to an ASP *Session* variable named *MyState*:

```
Dim sess As Session
Set sess = GetObjectContext("Session")
sess("MyState") = "Some data related to this client"
```

In a future request for the same client, you can retrieve the state from the same ASP *Session* variable as follows:

```
Dim sess As Session, s As String
Set sess = GetObjectContext("Session")
s = sess("MyState")
```

For a slightly more complicated example, let's say you need to store a set of line items for a client's shopping cart. You can accomplish this by storing a string array in an ASP *Session* variable, as shown here:

```
Dim sess As Session, LineItems() As String
Set sess = GetObjectContext("Session")
Redim LineItems(1 To 3)
LineItems(1) = "Product=Dog;Quantity=5"
LineItems(2) = "Product=Cat;Quantity=10"
LineItems(3) = "Product=Bird;Quantity=25"
sess("ShoppingCart") = LineItems
```

A future request can append additional line items to the array or run a transaction to purchase the items. Using ASP *Session* variables in this manner allows you to build stateful applications and sites that use a shopping cart metaphor (like Amazon.com).

The one key aspect of designing an application that uses ASP *Session* variables is that you must make an assumption about how your application will be deployed. Each client must be guaranteed that its requests will be serviced by the same IIS computer. In the next section, we'll look at some factors that might make it impossible for you to make this assumption.

Scaling a Web Application Through Load Balancing

A Web site is like an aspiring Hollywood actor. At the beginning of its career, its biggest problem is paranoia about forever living in obscurity. When it becomes famous, it has a new set of challenges. The volume of incoming requests increases dramatically and its fans have lofty expectations about the site's performance and are highly critical when these expectations are not met. Unfortunately, these challenges are sometimes more than a Web site can handle. Some Web sites respond to fame by going up in smoke, and they never recover. The Web sites that can handle the pressure more gracefully go on to become the places that thousands of users return to again and again.

Some Web sites (often the children of famous Web sites) are famous from the day they're launched. Others see their user base grow from hundreds to thousands to hundreds of thousands of users on their path to fame. To meet the demands and the expectations of their fans, these sites must scale accordingly.

I touched on the concept of scalability in earlier chapters, but it's important to look at it one more time. A simple definition of scalability is a system's ability to accommodate a growing number of clients and to give each client satisfactory levels of responsiveness. To reach this goal, a Web site must supply an adequate number of processing cycles per second to handle the volume of incoming requests. As you might expect, more clients require more processing cycles. So the question becomes, "Where do all these processing cycles come from?"

At first, you might be able to increase your site's scalability with a single-server solution. You can upgrade your Web server to a computer with a faster processor or multiple processors or both. This is what's known as *scaling up*. For example, you can buy a Web server with two or four really fast processors. The new computer will handle a larger client base than the previous computer. However, at some point a single server solution simply won't cut it. You can only scale up so far. Moreover, the computers at the high end of that market are prohibitively expensive. Once you hit a certain threshold, cost-effective scalability requires the use of multiple processors spread across multiple computers. You often hear people say that you need to *scale out* rather than scale up.

This is where load balancing comes into play. You have to distribute the workload of incoming HTTP requests across several not-so-expensive computers. We'll look at several approaches to meeting this challenge. For a Web-based application, it's better to address load balancing at the point where the HTTP request arrives at the site. This means you need a technique to distribute incoming HTTP requests across a set of IIS computers. A site that uses this approach is often called a *Web farm* or a *Web server array*.

Creating a web farm

Web designers have quite a few techniques for distributing HTTP requests across a set of servers. One simple approach is to design a Web site with a dedicated routing server that has custom code to redirect clients, as shown in Figure 9-8.

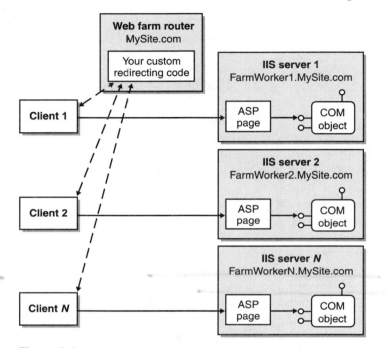

Figure 9-8 *You can build a session-based Web farm by using a routing server to distribute a set of clients across a set of IIS server computers.*

The routing server is given a well-known DNS name (such as *MySite.com*) and a dedicated IP address. Other servers in the farm have their own dedicated IP addresses and optionally DNS names. When a client's initial request reaches the routing server, the request is redirected to one of the other servers in the farm. You can redirect clients from the routing server using the *Session_OnStart* event in the global.asa file. The code in Listing 9-2 shows one possible implementation.

```
Sub Session_OnStart
    Const SERVER_COUNT = 3
    Dim sServer, sURL
    Randomize
    Select Case (Fix(Rnd * SERVER_COUNT) + 1)
        Case 1
            sServer = "FarmWorker1"
```

Listing 9-2   *(continued)*

(continued)

```
       Case 2
            sServer = "FarmWorker2"
       Case 3
            sServer = "FarmWorker3"
   End Select
   sURL = "http://" & sServer & ".MySite.com/MyApp/default.asp"
   Response.Redirect sURL
End Sub
```

This technique requires that the client's initial request to the routing server be for a page with an .ASP extension. The *Session_OnStart* event won't fire if the request is for a file with an .HTM or .HTML extension. The algorithm shown above redirects each new client to one of three servers in the farm. Once a client is redirected to an IIS computer in the farm, a session is created and the client sends all future requests to the same address. For this reason, you can think of this as a *session-based* load-balancing technique.

The algorithm I just showed you uses a random number for redirection, but you can design a more elaborate load-balancing mechanism. For instance, each server in the farm can send performance data back to the routing server. If each server periodically transmits a count of active sessions to the routing server, the load-balancing code can redirect each new client to the server with the fewest active clients.

Round-robin DNS is another common session-based load-balancing technique. With round-robin DNS, each logical DNS name (such as *MySite.com*) maps to several IP addresses. When a browser attempts to resolve the DNS name, the DNS server sends back one of the addresses from the list. The DNS server rotates the addresses in order to distribute a set of clients across a set of servers. Once a browser resolves a DNS name into an IP address, it caches the IP address for the duration of the client's session. Round-robin DNS is slightly faster than the redirection technique shown above but produces the same results. Different clients are given different IP address to balance the load across a set of servers.

To set up a Web farm with one of these session-based load-balancing techniques, you should use relative URLs in your ASP pages and Visual Basic code. For instance, you should use a URL such as */MyOtherPage.asp* instead of an absolute URL that contains a server's DNS name or IP address. This will ensure that each client continues to send requests to the same server once a session has started.

While both of these forms of session-based load balancing are fairly easy to set up, they have a few notable limitations. First, load balancing is performed only once for each client at the beginning of a session. The load-balancing scheme can get a little skewed. For instance, all the users who've been sent to FarmWorker1 might go to lunch while all the users who've been sent to FarmWorker2 continue to send requests. In this case, one server can get overloaded while another server sits idle.

A more significant problem has to do with a Web application's availability. Session-based load balancing exposes the IP addresses of the servers in the farm to the client. This is limiting because each IIS computer becomes a single point of failure.

What happens when one of the Web servers in the farm crashes or is taken off line for maintenance? The load-balancing algorithm must take this into account as soon as possible, but this can be problematic. If the routing server or the DNS server passes out an IP address for a server that's gone off line, clients receive a "Server not available" error. With some round-robin DNS systems, it can take you a long time to fix the problem once you've discovered that one of your servers has crashed. Things can get really bad if IP address mappings need to be propagated to other DNS servers throughout the Internet.

To make things worse, when a Web server goes off line, it affects every client for which it was holding session-specific state. In other words, when the Web server crashes, client sessions can crash along with it. As you can see, the load-balancing techniques you've seen so far can compromise the availability and fault tolerance of a Web application. Fortunately, you can use more sophisticated approaches to load balancing that sidestep these problems. The solution lies in exposing a single IP address to every client.

Designing a better Web farm

As you've seen, exposing multiple IP addresses for a single Web site can compromise availability and load distribution. It's better to expose a single IP address that maps to several physical servers. However, this solution requires low-level networking code to reroute incoming IP packets across a set of servers. Most companies opt for an off-the-shelf solution rather than rolling their own. We'll take a look at some of the more popular options in this section.

First, we'll look at how you can perform load balancing with a hardware-based product such as the LocalDirector switch from Cisco or the BigIP router from F5. Then we'll look at Network Load Balancing (NLB), a software-based solution included with Windows 2000 Advanced Server. You should note that many other vendors offer similar products. This market is quite competitive, so you should conduct your own research to determine who can offer you the best combination of price and performance.

Figure 9-9 shows the basic configuration of a site with a hardware-based solution. A router or switch listens for incoming requests on a single virtual IP address and can reroute them across a set of IIS server computers. Each computer in the farm has its own unique IP address. However, unlike the load-balancing techniques we discussed earlier, the IP addresses of the physical servers are never seen by clients. Load balancing is performed every time a request comes in across the "virtual" IP address. This approach is known as *request-based* load balancing.

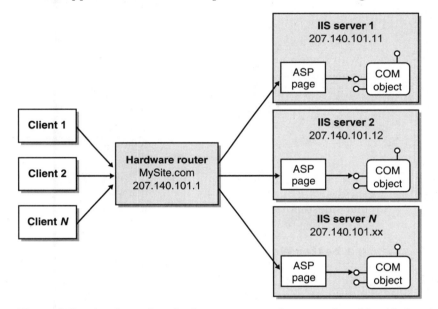

Figure 9-9 *A hardware-based solution can provide request-based load balancing. Client requests are made to a single virtual IP address and are rerouted across a set of physical IP addresses.*

NLB is a Windows service that represents a software-based solution for achieving request-based load balancing. NLB can be used by many types of applications that rely on IP traffic. In the rest of this chapter, we'll focus on using NLB to create a Web farm.

The NLB service is based on Convoy Cluster software purchased by Microsoft from Valence Research. Unlike LocalDirector or BigIP, NLB doesn't require a proprietary piece of hardware. It's installed as a Windows device driver on each machine in the farm, as shown in Figure 9-10. NLB can accommodate a Web farm of up to 32 servers.

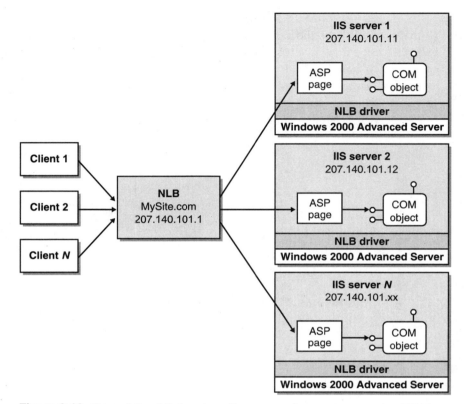

Figure 9-10 *Network Load Balancing allows a set of computers running Windows 2000 Advanced Server to monitor a single IP address.*

When you set up a Web farm using NLB, all the servers are in constant communication with each other. They exchange performance statistics and divide up the responsibilities of handling incoming requests. Every incoming request is seen by every server in the farm, and the NLB service has a proprietary algorithm to determine which server handles each request.

NLB has a few advantages over a hardware-based solution. It doesn't require a proprietary hardware device, and there isn't a singe point of failure. If you're going to use a hardware-based solution, you can usually buy a second failover device to improve availability and fault tolerance. Some companies find that a hardware-based solution with failover is too expensive for their needs. However, the argument for a hardware-based solution is that it has a one-time cost. With a software-based solution, you usually have to pay additional licensing fees every time you add another server to your Web farm. Once again, I'll leave it to you to do the research into which solution is best for your application.

LocalDirector, BigIP, and NLB differ significantly in their low-level plumbing details. But from a high-level perspective, they produce the same results. Each client makes a request using a virtual IP address, and the request is routed to one of many IIS server computers in the Web farm. Request-based load balancing has many advantages over session-based load balancing. Request-based load balancing is more granular because the load-balancing algorithm is run far more frequently. This results in a more even distribution of requests across servers.

The primary motivation for using request-based load balancing is to achieve higher levels of availability and fault tolerance. Both NLB and hardware-based solutions can detect when a server has gone off line and can quickly recover to avoid routing future requests to an unavailable IP address. Moreover, an administrator can safely take a server off line during operational hours. For example, the administrator can perform a *rolling upgrade,* which involves taking Web farm computers off line one by one. Rolling upgrades make it possible to do things such as shut down INETINFO.EXE in order to revise a set of Visual Basic DLLs. The idea behind a rolling upgrade is that the Web site as a whole never experiences an interruption in service.

Request-based load balancing also has disadvantages. One of the main disadvantages is that managing state in a Web farm becomes more complicated because you can't assume that a client's requests will be serviced by the same IIS computer. If you can't make this assumption, you shouldn't attempt to maintain state using ASP *Session* variables. You must design a more sophisticated approach to session management. There are also several important issues concerning the use of ASP *Application* variables in an environment that uses request-based load balancing.

Maintaining state in a Web farm

If users of your Web application will simply be browsing for information, you don't have as many concerns about maintaining state. However, if your Web application involves something like a shopping cart, you must carefully consider how to build up and store state for each client across requests.

You should start the design phase by asking yourself a simple question: Where can you maintain client-specific state in your application? You have three choices. First, you can store state on the client computer using cookies or store state in the HTML that you send to the browser. Second, you can store state in the middle tier in IIS. Third, you can store state in a back-end DBMS such as SQL Server.

When you design a Web application for a site based on a single IIS computer, storing state in IIS using ASP *Session* variables is usually the easiest and most straightforward approach. If you have a Web farm that uses session-based load balancing, you can also store client-specific state in IIS. However, if you have a Web farm that uses request-based load balancing, most techniques for storing data in IIS don't work correctly.

If you can't store state in IIS, you must resort to one or both of the other options. The main advantage of storing state on the client is that it can be done quickly. You don't need to make time-consuming trips to the back-end database. Some of the advantages of storing state in the back-end database are that the data is durable and you can store as much state as you need. Storing state on the client has size limitations and also raises security issues. Many companies don't want to store sensitive information on the client's computer. Moreover, some client-side security settings can prevent you from writing to the client's hard disk.

You should note that when you store state in a back-end database, you'll probably still be required to maintain a minimal amount of state on the client. For example, it's common to explicitly pass a customer ID or some other type of primary key between the client and IIS with every request so that you can map a user to one or more records in your database. Sometimes you can get away with using something that HTTP sends anyway, such as the client's IP address or user name. As you can see, it's possible to maintain a little client-side state but still keep the majority of your data in a database such as SQL Server, where it's safe and secure.

During the design phase, you should also consider the following questions when you're deciding whether to write your client-specific state to a back-end database. How will accessing the back-end database affect performance? Will the back-end database be a significant performance bottleneck? If so, you might consider eliminating or reducing trips to the back end. You should do some benchmarking and compare the response times of requests that involve database access against the times of requests that do not.

You can usually reduce the number of trips to the database but not avoid them completely. Here are a few more questions you should consider during the design phase. How costly will it be to you if client-specific state gets lost or corrupted? Do you want the same client-specific state to be available when a user moves to a different machine? Is your client-specific state so sensitive that you need to hide it from your users? Do you need to store so much client-specific state that it's not practical to store it all on the client?

You can usually find a suitable compromise in terms of how much to write to your database. For example, you might access the database on the client's initial request to validate a user name and password and to retrieve a set of preconfigured user preferences. Then, as the user starts adding items to a shopping cart, you can track those actions by storing state on the client computer. Finally, when the user purchases the items, your application can make a second trip to the database to record the transaction. In this scenario, the client's session might involve 20 to 30 requests, but only 2 will require a trip to the back-end database.

Passing state between IIS and the browser

Whether you're maintaining lots of client-specific state on the client or just a primary key, you need to know how to pass data back and forth between the browser and IIS. In this section, we'll look at three common techniques for doing this.

The easiest way to store state on the client is by using HTTP cookies. The ASP *Response* and *Request* objects make writing and retrieving a cookie value relatively simple. For instance, you can write a cookie into an HTTP response like this:

```
Dim rsp As Response
Set rsp = GetObjectContext.Item("Response")
rsp.Cookies("UserID") = "BrianR"
rsp.Cookies("UserName") = "Brian Randell"
rsp.Cookies("FavoriteFood") = "CheeseBurger"
rsp.Cookies("FavoriteQuantity") = "3"
```

If you write cookie values in an HTTP response, they'll flow back and forth with each request-response pair. Cookies are just as easy to read using the ASP *Request* object. The cookies in the example above live for the duration of the browser's session.

You can also store persistent cookie values on a user's hard drive. If you do this, these cookie values will live across sessions of the browser. This means that your site can remember all sorts of information and maintain user-specific preferences across visits. Users seem to appreciate sites that do this. To store a persistent cookie value to your user's hard drive, you simply add an expiration date as follows:

```
rsp.Cookies("UserID") = "BrianR"
rsp.Cookies("UserID").Expires = "July 1, 2001"
```

In a shopping cart application, you can use cookies to build up a complex data structure across successive hits. Here's an example of writing multiple values to a single cookie to store line items for a shopping cart:

```
rsp.Cookies("LineItemCount")= "3"
rsp.Cookies("LineItems")("Item1") = "Product=Dog;Quantity=5"
rsp.Cookies("LineItems")("Item2") = "Product=Cat;Quantity=10"
rsp.Cookies("LineItems")("Item3") = "Product=Bird;Quantity=25"
```

You should note a few important limitations of using HTTP cookies. First, they don't work across domains. Second, there's a limit on what you can store in a cookie. Most browsers support cookies of up to 4096 bytes. While you can write multiple cookies to one client, larger sets of data can become impractical to work with. Third, you can't assume that all clients support cookies. Some browser are simply too old to support them. Furthermore, some users disable cookies in their browsers after reading warnings from conspiracy theorists.

If you have to support clients that don't support cookies, you can't store data that will live on the client across sessions of the browser. You must also come up with a different technique to pass client-specific state back and forth. One popular technique involves using query strings to append named values to your URLs. For instance, instead of setting your HTML form's action to *\MyPage.asp*, you can append a query string to the URL like this: *\MyPage.asp?UserID=BrianR*.

Appending named values to URLs requires additional effort on your part. You must dynamically embed these name/value pairs to the end of every URL when you generate the HTML for your pages. Also, you're generally limited to about 2 KB when you manage state with query strings.

You should have one last client-side state management technique up your sleeve. This technique involves using a hidden field in an HTML form. If a user won't accept cookies and you want to store more state than you can append to a URL in a query string, this might be the solution you're looking for. Note that this technique requires the use of an HTML form and a Submit button. Here's an example of what your form might look like:

```
<FORM ACTION="MyPage.asp" METHOD="Post">
    <INPUT TYPE="Hidden" NAME="UserID" VALUE="BrianR">
    <INPUT TYPE="Submit" VALUE="Get Past Purchases">
</FORM>
```

A few more words on optimization

Products such as the NLB, LocalDirector, and BigIP allow you to turn off request-based load balancing and resort to session-based load balancing (also known as sticky sessions). For example, if you adjust the Affinity setting in NLB, you can tell the service to route each client to the same physical server once the first request goes through. This might be good news if you have a large, preexisting Web application that has dependencies on ASP *Session* variables.

The bad news is that resorting back to session-based load balancing compromises an application's performance and availability. You lose out on many of the benefits provided by request-based load balancing. It slows things down because the routing mechanism has to maintain client-to-server IP address mappings and perform a lookup for each request. It also makes your site vulnerable to problems with fault tolerance and distribution skew that we discussed earlier. What's more, additional problems arise when client requests are routed through a proxy server.

For example, it's possible for hundreds or thousands of clients to be associated with a single proxy server. This means that your load-balancing mechanism might see a large set of clients as a single IP address. You might have a situation in which 3000 users who share the same proxy server are beating the stuffing out of one of your Web servers while nine other servers in the farm are sitting around with nothing to do.

To make things even worse, America Online (AOL) has a proxy farm that's so big that it spans multiple class C addresses. However, a class C address is the coarsest level at which affinity works in NLB. This means that the requests of one AOL user are often routed across multiple NLB computers even when affinity has been turned on. In such a case, *Session* variables cause problems even when you're using sticky sessions.

My point is that if you can use request-based load balancing, you should resist going back to session-based load balancing, which is kind of like buying a Porsche and driving 30 miles an hour on the freeway. You should realize that all the "session-aware" features primarily support applications that have dependencies on middle-tier state. Your Web application will scale much better if you don't introduce these dependencies into your design.

Now, let's say you've been very disciplined throughout the design phase and you've created a Web application that has no dependencies on ASP session management. At this point, you can and should perform one more optimization: You should disable session management. As it turns out, IIS conducts a lot of session management work on your behalf unless you explicitly disable the session management feature. Leaving this feature enabled can unnecessarily waste precious resources such as processing cycles, memory, and network bandwidth.

So, what happens if you don't disable ASP session management? When a client requests an ASP page, the ASP framework checks to see whether the client is associated with an active session. If it's the client's first request, the ASP framework carries out a bunch of tasks to start tracking the client's session. ASP generates a unique SessionID and starts passing it back and forth in HTTP cookies. ASP also searches for the *Session_OnStart* event and executes it if it exists. If the ASP framework finds a valid SessionID in an incoming request and determines that the user is part of an active session, it must map the current request to any client-specific state that might have been stored in ASP *Session* variables in earlier requests.

The ASP framework also performs extra work to serialize all requests for any one session. This support eliminates concurrency problems relating to session state. However, this serialization of requests from any specific client is also costly and restrictive when it's not necessary. For example, let's say that your application defines two frames in the browser and each frame is based on an ASP page. One ASP page has to be completely processed before the ASP runtime begins processing the second one. If session management has been disabled, IIS can process both ASP pages at the same time on two different threads. This issue becomes especially important when the Web server computer has multiple processors.

As you can see, the ASP session management features are expensive. If you don't need them, you should turn them off by clearing the Enable Session State check box in the Internet Services Manager. You can turn off session management for an IIS application or for the entire site. You can also turn off session management by placing the following declaration at the top of all your ASP pages:

```
<%@ EnableSessionState=False %>
```

Caching Application-Wide State

The final topic I want to discuss in this chapter is how to manage application-wide state in a Web site. The ASP framework provides the *Application* object for sharing a single set of variables across a set of clients. Each ASP application variable is accessible to every request in a given IIS application.

Using ASP *Application* variables is similar to using the Shared Property Manager (SPM). It simply provides a way to cache data in memory within a process and share it across a set of clients. In fact, in many situations you can use ASP *Application* variables and the SPM interchangeably. Let me list the advantages of each approach.

If you'll be caching updateable data, the SPM can provide more granular locking because you can partition your cached data into several property groups. The locking scheme used by the ASP *Application* object allows for only a single coursegrained lock. Another potential benefit of the SPM is that it doesn't have a dependency on the ASP runtime. You can use the SPM to create a configured component that provides a caching scheme and then use the component in a COM+ application with both Web-based and DCOM-based clients.

Many ASP developers find that ASP *Application* variables are easier to use. These variables are also accessible directly from an ASP page, while the SPM is not. The ASP *Application* object also makes it easier to release memory that's no longer needed. The ASP *Application* object and the ASP *Session* object both provide a *Contents* property that exposes a *Remove* method and a *RemoveAll* method. The SPM doesn't provide similar functionality.

Whether you use the ASP *Application* object or the SPM to track application-wide data, you must decide during the initial design phase whether the code you write will run in a Web farm environment. When clients are routed across a set of IIS server computers, it's difficult to cache updateable data. You often have to make the assumption that cached data, once loaded from a database, will be used on a read-only basis.

Caching read-only data at the Web server is one of the best ways to improve response times and increase overall throughput. Caching techniques are valuable because they reduce the required number of round trips to the database. They can also conserve server-side processing cycles. For example, after retrieving the *products* table in an ADO recordset, you can format the data into an HTML table or into XML and cache it as a string value in an ASP *Application* variable. This technique reduces the need to convert data on a request-by-request basis.

If you're going to design a middle-tier caching scheme for read-only data, you should also make assumptions about how long your data will stay fresh. In some cases, you can load data into ASP *Application* variables once at application startup or whenever the data is first accessed. In other applications, you might decide to have data refreshed at periodic intervals.

Here's an example to illustrate what you can do to design a caching coherency scheme. Let's say that you want to cache an HTML table for the product list in an *Application* variable, and you assume that product data will change often enough that the HTML table should be refreshed every five minutes.

In your design, you create one ASP *Application* variable to hold the actual product list and another *Application* variable to track when the list was last refreshed from the database. Any ASP page or Visual Basic component can examine the time of the last refresh when retrieving the list. When the code running in a request determines that the interval between the current time and last-refreshed time is greater than the refresh interval, it can requery the database and regenerate the list for itself and any other request issued in the next five minutes. If you're a forward-thinking COM+ designer, you can also keep the refresh interval in a configured component's constructor string so that you can easily adjust it without recompiling any code.

SUMMARY

This chapter has covered some of the important issues relating to building large-scale applications with Visual Basic. Applications that use HTTP for client-to-server communication are far more scalable than applications that rely on DCOM and RPC. The Web and HTTP also open up a whole world of cross-platform development.

If you're designing and building Web sites with Windows 2000 Server, you must understand the architecture of IIS and ASP. These core technologies allow you to expose ASP pages and Visual Basic components to clients across the Internet as well as the corporate intranet, not to mention business-to-business extranets. As you've seen, many subtle aspects of the technology affect how you write your ASP pages and Visual Basic components. Unfortunately, many programming techniques and deployment schemes prevent an application from scaling to meet requirements for response times and overall throughput.

What I hope you take away from this chapter is that you must think long and hard about scalability early in the design phase. Many designers and developers who didn't design with scalability in mind now deeply regret the dependencies their applications have on ASP *Session* variables. Their applications will probably never make it in the big leagues.

It's often impossible to anticipate how busy and successful your site will become. If you know that your site will never get more than a few requests per minute, you don't have to worry about many of the details I covered in this chapter. But if you're not sure, you shouldn't take any chances. When you begin designing a Web application, start with the assumption that it might one day be the most popular site on the Internet.

Chapter 10

Introduction to Messaging and Asynchronous Communication

Messaging has traditionally been an integral part of distributed application programming, especially in larger, mission-critical systems. Messaging offers an extra dimension that you can't achieve using synchronous protocols such as RPC and HTTP. This chapter explains how messaging products such as IBM's MQSeries and Microsoft Message Queuing (MSMQ) enable companies to reap the benefits of messaging without having to hand-roll a sophisticated communication infrastructure.

This chapter explains why and when you should use messaging in a distributed application. It also explains how message queues can add responsiveness and reliability to an online transaction processing (OLTP) application that you can't get by other means. I'll also show you how to write applications that send and receive MSMQ messages using Visual Basic. While I can't show you every aspect of MSMQ programming in a single chapter, my goal is to get you started by showing you the most common techniques for creating applications that send and receive MSMQ messages.

The chapter also explains how MSMQ supports transactional messaging. You must send transacted messages to transactional queues in order to ensure exactly-once delivery. You'll learn two straightforward techniques for sending and receiving transactional messages with MSMQ and Visual Basic: You can leverage MSMQ's internal transactioning mechanism, or you can use a COM+ transaction, which leverages the Distributed Transaction Coordinator (DTC).

After I describe MSMQ, I'll introduce in this chapter the Queued Components service, which is part of COM+ and Windows 2000. The service is an ease-of-use framework that's layered on top of MSMQ. Queued Components provides the benefits of MSMQ without requiring you to deal with all the complexities of MSMQ programming. As you'll see, an understanding of MSMQ is helpful in learning how queued components work.

This chapter also describes the COM+ Events service, which helps you build applications that provide event notifications to other applications. Just as you should know the basics of MSMQ before you learn about queued components, you should understand how to design and configure queued components if you want to make the most of COM+ events.

While this chapter won't provide a complete reference to all these topics, it will explain their architecture and how they fit together, and it will help you decide among MSMQ, Queued Components, and standard COM method calls during the design phase. You'll learn the strengths and limitations of COM+ events, and you'll learn how to determine whether they're appropriate for your application. When you actually write applications that use MSMQ or Queued Components, however, you should consult the documentation in the Platform SDK and possibly other resources to supplement the material in this chapter.

WHY IS MESSAGING IMPORTANT?

The basic idea behind messaging is simple. A *message* is a request or other type of notification that's sent from one application to another. A *queue* is a named, ordered repository of messages that lives on a specific computer. Some applications issue requests by sending messages to the queue, while other applications remove messages from the queue and carry out the processing requested by the sender. Figure 10-1 shows how a queue is typically used in a distributed application.

A *sender application* creates and prepares a message by setting various properties in the message header and packing parameterized information into a payload, which is called the *message body*. It then writes the message to the queue. A *receiver application* removes the message from the queue as it reads it so the message is processed only once. The receiver application interprets the request, unpacks parameterized information from the body, and runs any commands requested by the message sender.

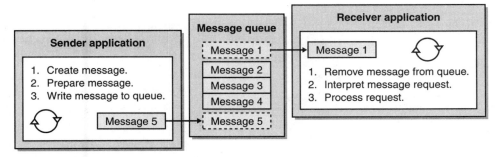

Figure 10-1 *A sender application creates and prepares a message and then writes it to the queue. A receiver application removes the message from the queue, interprets the message's request, and executes whatever processing the message requires.*

Message queues also support the concept of a *reader application,* which can examine a message in a queue without removing it. The act of reading a message is known as *peeking.* Peeking allows an application to be selective about the messages it removes from a queue.

Any application can assume more than one of these roles. It's common for an application to act as both a reader and a receiver on a single queue. The application can look at what's in the queue by peeking and receive only messages that meet certain criteria. It's also common for an application to receive messages from one queue while sending messages to a second queue. For example, it's common to create a workflow application in which various programs have both in-box queues and out-box queues. The out-box queue for one program is the in-box queue for another. After a program processes a request, it simply forwards the request to the next program in the workflow.

A messaging subsystem is a valuable building block in a distributed system because it allows applications to submit requests and send information to other applications in a connectionless, asynchronous manner.

Messaging vs. RPC and HTTP

In some ways, message passing is similar to a synchronous protocol such as RPC or HTTP; in other ways, it's very different. As you've seen throughout this book, COM uses RPC to issue interprocess requests between clients and objects. In Chapter 9, I explained how computers in a Web-based application communicate using HTTP. It's important to understand that RPC and HTTP are synchronous protocols. Their synchronous nature creates some noteworthy limitations, which I'd like to take some time to describe.

Let's start by looking at a couple of common problems with synchronous communication that you can solve by using messaging. The first problem with a synchronous protocol such as RPC or HTTP is that a client application's thread blocks during each request. The client application must wait while the server computer performs the requested task and returns a response. Also, if the server computer has a large backlog of requests from other clients, a client application might block on a response for an unacceptable period of time.

A messaging protocol, on the other hand, doesn't force client applications to wait. A client application can continue its work immediately after submitting an asynchronous request. You can return control back to the client faster, so you can improve response times. The trade-off is that you can't immediately inform the client of what happens because the message isn't processed until after the client regains control. The main assumption with messaging is that something must get done, but it doesn't have to be done right away. It's acceptable for the server to process the request in a few seconds, an hour, or a few days.

The second problem with a synchronous protocol is that it requires an established connection between two specific computers. In the case of a simple request sent from a client computer to a server computer, both the client application and the server application must be on line at the same time. For example, if the server is off line, a client application can't submit requests. Likewise, if no client applications are on line, the server application can't process any requests; it just sits around with nothing to do. In essence, neither side can get any work done unless the other side is up and running.

The requirements of connection-oriented communication are even higher in systems where requests are routed across two or more server computers. Figure 10-2 depicts a physical deployment scenario in which a client requests flows across three server computers.

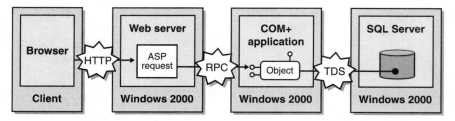

Figure 10-2 *Applications that rely exclusively on synchronous, connection-oriented protocols don't exhibit very high levels of fault tolerance. Every server computer must be on line in order for the system as a whole to be operational.*

The client sends a request to the Web server using HTTP. This request, in turn, fires an ASP page on the Web server, which uses DCOM and RPC to invoke a method on a business object running on an application server. The application server establishes an ADO connection to SQL Server using the native OLE-DB provider, which uses a proprietary, synchronous protocol called Tabular Data Streams (TDS). The important thing to note is that all three server computers must be on line and operational in order for the client to submit a request and receive a successful response. If any of the server computers goes off line, the application as a whole experiences downtime.

As you can see, distributed applications that rely exclusively on synchronous protocols can't provide the highest levels of fault tolerance and availability. An application server or a database management system (DBMS) might go off line due to a system crash or scheduled maintenance.

A messaging subsystem can offer higher levels of fault tolerance and availability because it acts as a buffer between the application that's issuing a request and the application that's processing the request. Client applications can continue to send request messages to a queue regardless of whether the receiver application is on line. When the server application comes back on line, it can resume processing request messages that have accumulated. A server can also continue its work after client applications have gone off line. As you can see, the queue acts as a buffering mechanism that allows either side to accomplish its work in the absence of the other.

The example in Figure 10-3 is similar to that in Figure 10-2, with one exception: Communication between the Web server and the application server is conducted using MSMQ messages instead of DCOM and RPC. The use of an asynchronous protocol means that clients can continue to make requests when either the application server or the database server has gone off line. The infrastructure of MSMQ simply stores request messages on the Web server until they can be successfully forwarded to the application server. The application server or the database server can go off line without causing any downtime for the overall application.

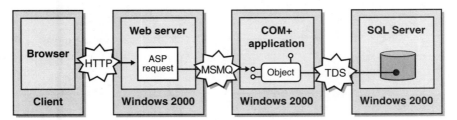

Figure 10-3 *Messaging offers higher levels of fault tolerance because clients can continue to successfully issue requests when one or more server computers is off line.*

A third problem with using a synchronous protocol is that requests are typically processed on a first come, first served basis. There's usually no way to prioritize calls with RPC or HTTP. A high-priority request must wait its turn if low-priority requests were submitted ahead of it. A messaging subsystem such as MSMQ can solve this problem by assigning priority levels to messages. Messages with a higher priority level are placed at the head of the queue, while lower-priority messages are placed at the end. The server can thus respond to the most important messages first.

The fourth (and arguably the most significant) problem with RPC and HTTP is that they're vulnerable to failures that lead to inconsistent results in OLTP applications. For example, let's look at what can go wrong when a client application invokes an RPC-based method call to run a COM+ transaction. Three types of failure can happen. First, the method call's RPC request message might fail between the client and the server. Second, the COM+ application might crash while the method call is executing a transaction. In both of these scenarios, the intended changes of the transaction are not committed. The third failure scenario is that the method call's RPC response message to the client might fail or be lost after the method call has successfully run and committed the transaction.

What happens if a client executes a method on a transactional object using DCOM and RPC from across the network and it doesn't receive a response. There's no real way of determining what happened. The client can't simply try to execute the same method because there's a chance the transaction will be run twice. From this example, you should observe that DCOM and RPC can't offer exactly-once delivery guarantees. HTTP is vulnerable to the same problems.

Transacted messaging provides a way to submit a transaction request with exactly-once delivery semantics. You can submit a transaction request with exactly-once semantics by breaking it down into three smaller transactions. In the first transaction, the client application sends a request message to a request queue on the server. In the second transaction, a listener application receives the request message, processes the request, and sends a response message to the client's response queue. In the final transaction, the client application receives the response message to find out what happened.

The important point here is that RPC is inferior to message passing because it doesn't allow the client to determine the exact status of a request. Later in this chapter, after I address the basics of MSMQ programming, I'll revisit this point and explain how to set up an application that allows you to run transactions with exactly-once semantics.

Now that you know how queues can improve your distributed applications, let's put this knowledge to work using MSMQ. As you program with MSMQ, you'll see that it requires more effort than writing COM-based method calls. When you use DCOM and RPC, you basically get all of your interprocess communication for free. When you use MSMQ, you have to invest more time in both application design and programming. However, when you consider the limitations of RPC, MSMQ is often well worth the time and energy you invest.

MSMQ

MSMQ 2 is built into Windows 2000; it doesn't run on earlier versions of Windows. MSMQ 1 runs on Windows NT, Windows 95, and Windows 98. It's not difficult to achieve interoperability between the two versions of MSMQ if you already have Windows NT and Windows 98 computers running in a Windows 2000 domain.

MSMQ 2 relies on Windows 2000 Active Directory to maintain a global catalog of configuration data. The MSMQ catalog spans a forest of Windows 2000 domains and tracks profiles of MSMQ-related entities such as computers, public queues, and security-related certificates. You can say that each MSMQ catalog defines an MSMQ enterprise.

The MSMQ Enterprise

To create an enterprise of MSMQ computers, you must first install MSMQ on a Windows 2000 computer that's been configured as a domain controller with Active Directory installed. A Windows 2000 domain controller is often called an Active Directory server. This first installation of MSMQ on an Active Directory server triggers the creation of MSMQ's enterprise catalog in Active Directory. A Windows 2000 forest can have multiple Active Directory servers with MSMQ installed. Each Active Directory server has a copy of the MSMQ catalog.

After you install MSMQ on an Active Directory server, it's pretty easy to install MSMQ on other computers in order to add them to the same MSMQ enterprise. You simply have to make sure that the other computers have been added to a domain in the same forest as the first Active Directory server before you install MSMQ.

The type of deployment I've just described is known as *MSMQ 2 enterprise mode.* You can also set up a group of computers in *MSMQ 2 workgroup mode,* which allows you to use MSMQ without needing a Windows 2000 domain controller or Active Directory. However, MSMQ 2 enterprise mode makes the MSMQ network far more capable. For this reason, this chapter will cover MSMQ only as it applies to computers that use Active Directory in a Windows 2000 domain.

You can configure MSMQ in a few different ways when you install it on a computer that's not an Active Directory server. You can set up an MSMQ computer as a routing server, an independent client, or a dependent client. A routing server can have its own queues. A routing server, as its name implies, can also act as a store-and-forward agent for messages targeted at a queue on another MSMQ computer. This is helpful when client applications can't send their messages directly to the target server. The routing server acts as an intermediate hop between the computer sending a message and the target computer, which holds the destination queue. Note that an

Active Directory server with MSMQ installed performs all the same tasks as a routing server. It simply holds a copy of the MSMQ catalog in addition to these other responsibilities.

You can also configure an MSMQ computer as an *independent client,* which doesn't perform store-and-forward duties but can create and manage its own local queues. This is a good installation choice for a remote computer such as a laptop because a client application can send messages to a network queue even when the laptop is disconnected. In such a situation, MSMQ creates a temporary local queue behind the scenes and caches messages as they're sent. Later, when the independent client computer reestablishes a connection to the network, the MSMQ infrastructure automatically forwards the messages to the destination queue.

A *dependent client* can't maintain queues locally. It can't function if it's disconnected from the network. It must be able to establish a connection to an Active Directory server or a routing server in order to send and receive messages. A desktop computer that's always connected to the LAN is typically the only type of machine that you'd run as a dependent client.

MSMQ embraces the concept of a *Windows 2000 site,* which is a set of computers on one or more subnets that all have high-speed access to one another. A site is usually a set of computers running on the same LAN. Each Windows 2000 site that contains MSMQ computers should have one or more Active Directory servers so that you can run queries against the MSMQ catalog without having to call across sites. Active Directory automatically maintains a copy of the MSMQ catalog on each domain controller and keeps this cached data up-to-date through replication.

You should understand that sending messages across sites is slower and less reliable than sending messages between two computers in the same site. MSMQ allows administrators to assign costs to each intersite link. MSMQ can then run an algorithm to determine the optimal routing for sending messages from one site to another. This administrative detail is an important aspect of tuning an MSMQ enterprise when computers are sending messages across sites that span large geographical distances.

The queue manager

The communication infrastructure of MSMQ relies heavily on a component known as the *queue manager.* The queue manager runs as a Windows service and is launched from MQSVC.EXE. MSMQ installs a queue manager on every computer that has store-and-forward responsibilities or that has its own local queues. The only type of MSMQ installation that doesn't get its own queue manager is a dependent client.

Each queue manager is assigned a unique GUID at installation time. MSMQ uses this GUID to track queues that are created and owned by a specific queue manager. It also uses this GUID to track messages that originate from the queue manager. It's important to realize that a computer never has more than one queue manager. This means that a queue manager's GUID also identifies the computer on which it's installed.

MSMQ tracks this GUID in Active Directory along with the information required to resolve the computer address when necessary.

In short, queue managers make possible all communication in MSMQ. A sender application must transmit a message to a queue manager. If the queue manager is the owner of the destination queue, it stores the message in the queue. If it doesn't own the destination queue, it forwards the message to another queue manager. If the computer with the destination queue can't be reached, the queue manager temporarily stores the message and forwards it later when communication can be established. Finally, receiver and reader applications communicate with the queue manager on the computer that holds the queue in order to receive or peek at messages.

I've already mentioned that MSMQ maintains a global catalog in Active Directory. Each queue manager also maintains additional data for local queues in a place called the local queue store (LQS). The LQS consists of a file for each local queue and configuration data that the queue manager uses to manage its local queues. Note that the LQS often duplicates information that's in Active Directory. The point of caching duplicate information is that the queue manager can use the LQS to eliminate network round trips and to handle messages at times when it can't connect to an Active Directory server.

MSMQ Programming

You can program with MSMQ in two ways. MSMQ exposes a C-level API as well as a COM-based component library. As a Visual Basic programmer, you're much better off using the component library when you program with MSMQ. Note that some MSMQ functionality is accessible only through the C-level API. Fortunately, you can meet most of the common requirements for message passing in a distributed application by using the component library. In the rare circumstance in which you need to use the C-level API, you can use Visual Basic *Declare* statements and call into the API directly. This chapter will examine the use of MSMQ's component library only. If you include a reference to MSMQ's type library (the Microsoft Message Queue 2.0 Object Library) in your Visual Basic project, you can use the MSMQ components.

MSMQ provides several components, each of which has quite a few properties and methods. I can't cover every aspect of programming with MSMQ's component library. I'll simply offer some programming examples that demonstrate the most common types of code required in a distributed application.

I'll assume that you have MSMQ installed on a Windows 2000 computer that's configured as an Active Directory server, a routing server, or an independent client. In addition to allowing you to write and test MSMQ programs, this type of MSMQ installation allows you to use the Computer Management administrative tool to carry out some basic MSMQ administrative tasks. This tool (shown in Figure 10-4) lets you manage and examine queues and messages. It's accessible via the Administrative Tools group, which is in the Programs group on the Windows Start menu.

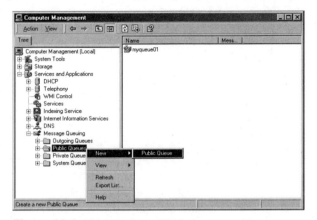

Figure 10-4 *The Windows 2000 Computer Management administrative tool lets you create and manage local queues.*

Creating a public queue

Let's begin our tour of MSMQ by creating a queue. You can create public queues and private queues. You can create a public queue in one of two ways—manually, using the Computer Management administrative tool, or programmatically.

Let's create a public queue manually. After you launch the Computer Management administrative tool, you simply right-click the Public Queues folder and choose Public Queue from the New menu. You must give the queue a name and specify whether you want the queue to be transactional. I'll describe transactional queues later in this chapter—for now, simply create a queue by giving it a name and leave the Transactional check box cleared. Click the OK button to create the queue.

After you create the queue, you can examine its attributes by right-clicking it and choosing Properties. You'll see a tabbed dialog box in which you can modify various properties of the queue. You'll notice that MSMQ automatically generates a GUID to serve as the ID for the queue. The GUID associated with a public queue is known as the *instance ID*.

To create a queue programmatically, you can use an *MSMQQueueInfo* object. First, you create the object and assign it a valid *PathName*, which should include the name of the computer and the name of the queue. For example, the following code uses an *MSMQQueueInfo* object to create a new queue:

```
Dim qi As MSMQQueueInfo
Set qi = New MSMQQueueInfo
qi.PathName = "MyComputer\MyQueue"
qi.Label = "My Queue"
qi.Create
```

Once you set the *PathName* property, you can create a queue by invoking the *Create* method. This example also sets the *Label* property of the new queue. A label is optional, but it can be helpful when you need to locate the queue later on.

The *Create* method has two optional parameters. The first parameter indicates whether the new queue is transactional. The second parameter, *IsWorldReadable*, indicates whether the queue will be readable to users other than the queue's owner. The default value for this parameter is *False*, which means that only the queue's owner can receive messages from the queue. If you pass *True* instead, the queue can be read by all users. Whatever value you pass, all users can send messages to the queue. You can also set queue security permissions by modifying the discretionary access control list (DACL) for the queue. You do this by opening the queue's Properties dialog box and navigating to the Security tab in the Computer Management administrative tool.

Note that you can abbreviate the *PathName* for a local queue so that you don't have to hardcode the name of the computer. You must do this if you want to write generic code that will run on many different computers. A single dot (as in .*MyQueue*) signifies that the queue path is defined on the local computer. You can use this abbreviated form when you create and open a local queue. For example, you can rewrite the previous code as follows:

```
Dim qi As MSMQQueueInfo
Set qi = New MSMQQueueInfo
qi.PathName = ".\MyQueue"
qi.Label = "Market Order Submission Queue"
qi.Create
```

You can also use an *MSMQQueueInfo* object to search for or open an existing queue. You run a query against Active Directory with an *MSMQQuery* object to determine whether a queue with a certain label exists. You run the query by invoking the *LookupQueue* method, which returns an *MSMQQueueInfos* object. The *MSMQQueueInfos* object is a collection of *MSMQQueueInfo* objects that match your lookup criteria. Here's an example of conducting a lookup by a queue's label:

```
Dim qry As MSMQQuery
Set qry = New MSMQQuery
Dim qis As MSMQQueueInfos
Set qis = qry.LookupQueue(Label:="Market Order Submission Queue")
Dim qi As MSMQQueueInfo
Set qi = qis.Next
If Not (qi Is Nothing) Then
    ' Open queue and send order message.
Else
    ' Degrade gracefully if queue cannot be located.
End If
```

In this example, a client runs a query against the MSMQ catalog in Active Directory to locate a queue with a well-known label. This dynamic lookup approach can provide flexibility because a client application doesn't have to know the name of the computer on which the queue resides. You can thus move queues around the network without having to rewrite applications.

Now let's open a queue and send a message. The next object you need to understand is an *MSMQQueue* object. The relationship between *MSMQQueueInfo* objects and *MSMQQueue* objects can be a little confusing. It's reasonable to conclude that an *MSMQQueue* object represents a physical queue because of its name. However, you're better off thinking of it as a queue handle. For example, you can open three different *MSMQQueue* objects on the same physical queue:

```
Dim qi As MSMQQueueInfo
Set qi = new MSMQQueueInfo
qi.PathName = ".\MyQueue"
Dim qSend As MSMQQueue
Set qSend = qi.Open(MQ_SEND_ACCESS, MQ_DENY_NONE)
Dim qPeek As MSMQQueue
Set qPeek = qi.Open(MQ_PEEK_ACCESS, MQ_DENY_NONE)
Dim qReceive As MSMQQueue
Set qReceive = qi.Open(MQ_RECEIVE_ACCESS, MQ_DENY_NONE)
```

You can see that an *MSMQQueueInfo* object represents a physical queue and that an *MSMQQueue* object actually represents an open handle to the queue. When you call *Open*, you must specify the type of access you want in the first parameter. When you open a queue with *MQ_RECEIVE_ACCESS*, you can peek at messages in addition to receiving them. However, if you want to send messages while also peeking at or receiving from the queue, you must open two *MSMQQueue* objects. Remember to invoke the *Close* method on an *MSMQQueue* object after you finish using it.

You can use the second parameter of *Open* to specify the share mode for the queue. The first possible setting for this parameter is *MQ_DENY_NONE*, which means that the queue can be opened by more than one application for receive access at the same time. You must use this setting when you open a queue using *MQ_PEEK_ACCESS* or *MQ_SEND_ACCESS*. However, when you open a queue with receive access, you can set the share mode to *MQ_DENY_RECEIVE_SHARE* to prevent other applications from receiving messages at the same time. When one application opens a queue with both *MQ_RECEIVE_ACCESS* and *MQ_DENY_RECEIVE_SHARE*, no other application can open the queue in receive mode. An application using this mode is the only one that can remove messages from the queue.

Creating a private queue

When you create a public queue, MSMQ assigns it an instance ID (a GUID) and publishes it in Active Directory. This allows other applications to open the queue by assigning the computer name and queue name to the *PathName* property. This also allows an application to locate the queue from across the network by running a query with an *MSMQQuery* object. However, the process of publishing a public queue takes up time and disk space and is sometimes unnecessary.

Imagine an application that consists of hundreds or thousands of independent clients that all require local response queues. In this situation, it makes sense to use private queues. Private queues must be created locally, and they're not published in Active Directory. They're published only in the LQS of the computer on which they reside.

As you'll see later in this chapter, you can send the return address for a private response queue in the header of a request message so that the receiver application can return a response message. You can thus establish bidirectional communication between a client application and the server. More important, using private queues means that you don't have to publish all those response queues in Active Directory, which saves both time and disk space.

You can create a private queue by adding *Private$* to the queue's *PathName*, as shown here:

```
Dim qResponseInfo As MSMQQueueInfo
Set qResponseInfo = New MSMQQueueInfo
qResponseInfo.PathName = ".\Private$\MyResponseQueue"
qResponseInfo.Create
```

MSMQ applications can send messages to private queues on other machines as long as they can find the queues. This isn't as easy as locating public queues because you can't open a private queue using a *PathName*—it isn't published in Active Directory. Later in this chapter, I'll show you a technique for passing the response queue's information to another application in a request message.

Locating a queue

Both public queues and private queues are assigned instance IDs by MSMQ at creation time. Each queue carries the same instance ID for its entire lifetime. When you open a queue using *PathName* or some other technique, a queue manager must ultimately resolve the instance ID before you can access the queue.

MSMQ generates an instance ID for a private queue using a different format from an instance ID for a public queue. As you know, MSMQ generates a unique GUID to serve as an instance ID for a public queue. A private queue's instance ID, on the other hand, is made up of the unique GUID of the local queue manager and a computer-specific queue ID. Here's an example of an instance ID for a private queue.

```
f38f2a17-218e-11d2-b555-c48e04000000\00000022
```

If you know the instance ID of a queue, you can open the queue using the *FormatName* property instead of the *PathName* property. Here's an example of two different *FormatName* properties, one for a public queue and one for a private queue:

```
PUBLIC=067ce2cb-26fc-11d2-b56b-f4552d000000
PRIVATE=f38f2a17-218e-11d2-b555-c48e04000000\00000022
```

Once you know how to generate the *FormatName* property, you can open a private queue on another computer using the following code:

```
Dim MyFormatName As String
MyFormatName = "PRIVATE=f38f2a17-218e-11d2-b555-c48e04000000\00000022"
Dim qi As MSMQQueueInfo
Set qi = new MSMQueueInfo
qi.FormatName = MyFormatName
Dim qSend As MSMQQueue
Set qSend = qi.Open(MQ_SEND_ACCESS, MQ_DENY_NONE)
```

In some cases, you can open a queue using either *FormatName* or *PathName*. But when you open a private queue, you can't use *PathName*. A private queue doesn't have an instance ID that's published in Active Directory. As you saw in the previous example, however, you can send a message to a private queue across the network by assigning the proper *FormatName* before invoking the *Open* method. Using *FormatName* rather than *PathName* is preferable when the target queue's information isn't published in Active Directory or when an Active Directory server isn't accessible.

Your final option for accessing a queue is using a *direct format name,* which specifies a protocol, a machine address, and a destination queue name. When you use this technique, you rely on the destination computer's LQS for queue name resolution. Here are a few examples of a direct format name:

```
DIRECT=TCP:209.27.34.23\MyQueue
DIRECT=TCP:209.27.34.23\private$\MyResponseQueue
DIRECT=OS:MyComputer\MyQueue
```

You typically use direct format names only as a last resort, when you can't use other techniques. For example, you must use direct format names to enable communication between two MSMQ computers that have been set up in workgroup mode. You must also use direct format names to enable communication across MSMQ enterprises. In other words, you must use direct format names to send messages between two computers that don't share the same Active Directory catalog.

The use of direct format names poses a major limitation. MSMQ isn't capable of temporarily storing a message on a routing server as the message passes from the sender to the recipient. The messages must be sent directly between the sender computer and the computer with the target queue. This means that the two machines must be able to establish a direct connection and that they can't benefit from the distributed store-and-forward mechanism that's built into the infrastructure of MSMQ.

Sending a message

Let's send our first message. MSMQ makes this task remarkably easy. You create a new *MSMQMessage* object and prepare it by setting a few properties. You then invoke the *MSMQMessage* object's *Send* method, and MSMQ routes your message to its destination queue. Here's a simple example of sending a message to a queue across the network:

```
Dim qi As MSMQQueueInfo
Set qi = New MSMQQueueInfo
qi.PathName = "MyServerComputer\MyQueue"
Dim q As MSMQQueue
Set q = qi.Open(MQ_SEND_ACCESS, MQ_DENY_NONE)
' Create a new message.
Dim msg As MSMQMessage
Set msg = New MSMQMessage
' Prepare the message.
msg.Label = "My superficial label"
msg.Body = "My parameterized request information"
msg.Priority = MQ_MAX_PRIORITY
' Send message to open queue.
msg.Send q
q.Close
```

As you can see, MSMQ's component library makes it easy to open a queue and send a message. The message in the example above has three properties set. *Label* is a string property of the message header that distinguishes or identifies a particular message. The two other message properties are the *Body* and *Priority*.

In MSMQ, a message body is stored as an array of bytes. The body is typically used to transmit parameterized data between the sender and the receiver. Our example shows that you can simply assign a Visual Basic string to a message body. The receiver can read this string from the message body just as easily. However, in many cases you'll use a message body that is more complex. For example, you might need to pass multiple parameters from the sender to the receiver. I'll revisit this topic in Chapter 12 in the section on data passing and describe your options for packing parameterized information into the body of an MSMQ message.

The last property used in the example specifies the message priority. A message has a priority value between 0 and 7; the higher the value, the higher the priority.

MSMQ stores messages with higher priority levels at the head of the queue. For example, a message with a priority level of 6 is placed in the queue behind all messages of priority 7 and behind messages of priority 6 that have already been written to the queue. The new message is placed ahead of any messages of priority 5 or lower. The MSMQ type library contains the constants *MQ_MAX_PRIORITY* (7) and *MQ_MIN_PRIORITY* (0). The default priority for a new message is *MQ_DEFAULT_ PRIORITY* (3).

Before I move on, I want to introduce a few other important message properties. When a message is sent to a queue, MSMQ assigns it an *ID* property. The *ID* property is a 20-byte array that uniquely identifies the message. MSMQ generates the ID by using two different values. The first 16 bytes of the ID are the GUID of the local queue manager. This means that the first part of the message ID is the same for all messages sent from the same computer. The last four bytes of the ID are a unique integer generated by the queue manager. In most cases, you don't need to worry about what's in the byte array. You should just assume that every ID is unique. However, if you need to compare two IDs to see whether they represent the same message, you can use VBA's *StrComp* function with the *vbBinaryCompare* flag.

Each message also has a *CorrelationID* property. Like the ID, this property is stored as a 20-byte array. Let's look at an example to see why this property is valuable. Let's say that a client application sends request messages to a server. The server processes the requests and sends a response message for each request. How does the client application know which request message is associated with which response message? The *CorrelationID* property takes care of this.

When the server processes a request, it can assign the ID of the incoming request message to the *CorrelationID* of the outgoing response message. When the client application receives a response message, it can compare the *CorrelationID* of the response message with the ID of each request message. This allows the sender to correlate messages. As you can see, the *CorrelationID* is useful when you create your own response messages. MSMQ also assigns the proper *CorrelationID* automatically when it prepares certain system-generated messages, such as acknowledgment messages.

Receiving and peeking at messages

To receive a message, you first open an *MSMQQueue* object with receive access and then invoke the *Receive* method to read and remove the first message in the queue:

```
Dim qi As MSMQQueueInfo
Set qi = New MSMQQueueInfo
qi.PathName = ".\MyQueue"
Dim q As MSMQQueue
Set q = qi.Open(MQ_RECEIVE_ACCESS, MQ_DENY_NONE)
Dim msg As MSMQMessage
```

```
' Attempt to receive first message in queue.
 Set msg = q.Receive(ReceiveTimeout:=1000)
If Not (msg Is Nothing) Then
     ' You have removed the first message from the queue.
     MsgBox msg.Body, vbInformation, msg.Label
Else
     ' You timed out waiting on an empty queue.
End If
q.close
```

There's an interesting difference between sending and receiving a message with MSMQ. You invoke the *Send* method on an *MSMQMessage* object, but you invoke the *Receive* method on an *MSMQQueue* object. (This doesn't cause any problems; it's just a small idiosyncrasy of the MSMQ programming model.) If a message is in the queue, a call to *Receive* removes it and returns a newly created *MSMQMessage* object. If there's no message in the queue, a call to *Receive* behaves differently depending on how the timeout interval is set.

By default, a call to *Receive* has no timeout value and will be blocked indefinitely if no message is in the queue. If you don't want the thread that calls *Receive* to be blocked indefinitely, you can specify a timeout interval. You can use the *ReceiveTimeout* parameter to specify the number of milliseconds that you want to wait on an empty queue.

If you call *Receive* on an empty queue and the timeout interval expires before a message arrives, the call to *Receive* returns with a null reference instead of an *MSMQMessage* object. The code in the previous example sets a timeout value of 1000 milliseconds. It also determines whether a message arrived before the timeout expired. If you don't want to wait at all, you can set the *ReceiveTimeout* value to 0. A *ReceiveTimeout* value of –1 indicates that you want to wait indefinitely. (This is the default if you don't pass a timeout value.)

You can call *Receive* repeatedly inside a *Do* loop to synchronously remove every message from a queue. The following example receives all the messages from a queue and fills a list box with message labels:

```
Dim qi As MSMQQueueInfo
Set qi = New MSMQQueueInfo
qi.PathName = ".\MyQueue"
Dim q As MSMQQueue
Set q = qi.Open(MQ_RECEIVE_ACCESS, MQ_DENY_RECEIVE_SHARE)
Dim msg As MSMQMessage
Set msg = q.Receive(ReceiveTimeout:=0)
Do Until msg Is Nothing
     lstReceive.AddItem msg.Label
     Set msg = q.Receive(ReceiveTimeout:=0)
Loop
q.Close
```

You can set the share mode to *MQ_DENY_RECEIVE_SHARE* so that your application won't have to contend with other applications while removing messages from the queue. Use a timeout value of 0 if you want to reach the end of the queue and move on to other business as soon as possible.

Sometimes you'll want to inspect the messages in a queue before removing them. You can use an *MSMQQueue* object's peek methods in conjunction with an implicit cursor to iterate through the messages in a queue. After opening a queue with receive access or peek access, you can call *Peek*, *PeekCurrent*, or *PeekNext*.

Peek is similar to *Receive* in that it reads the first message in the queue, but it doesn't remove the message. If you call *Peek* repeatedly, you keep getting the same message. Another problem with *Peek* is that it has no effect on the implicit cursor behind the *MSMQQueue* object. Therefore, you'll use *PeekCurrent* or *PeekNext* more often than *Peek*.

You can move the implicit cursor to the first message in a queue using a call to *PeekCurrent*. As with a call to *Receive*, you should use a timeout interval if you don't want to block on an empty queue. After an initial call to *PeekCurrent*, you can iterate through the rest of the messages in a queue by calling *PeekNext*:

```
Dim qi As MSMQQueueInfo
Set qi = New MSMQQueueInfo
qi.PathName = ".\MyQueue"
Dim q As MSMQQueue
Set q = qi.Open(MQ_PEEK_ACCESS, MQ_DENY_NONE)
Dim msg As MSMQMessage
Set msg = q.PeekCurrent(ReceiveTimeout:=0)
Do Until msg Is Nothing
    ' Add message labels to a list box.
    lstPeek.AddItem msg.Label
    Set msg = q.PeekNext(ReceiveTimeout:=0)
Loop
q.Close
```

The *ReceiveCurrent* method is often used in conjunction with *PeekCurrent* and *PeekNext*. For example, you can iterate through the messages in a queue by peeking at each one and comparing the properties of the current message against criteria of the messages you want to receive and process. For example, after calling *PeekCurrent* or *PeekNext*, you can compare the label of the current message with a specific label that you're looking for. If you come across a message with the label you're looking for, you can call *ReceiveCurrent* to remove it from the queue and process it.

Receiving messages using MSMQ events

The preceding example uses a technique for synchronously receiving messages, which gives you an easy way to read and remove all the messages that are currently in a queue. It also lets you process future messages as they arrive at the destination queue.

However, this approach also holds the calling thread hostage. If you have a single-threaded application, the application can't do anything else.

You can use MSMQ events as an alternative to this synchronous style of message processing. MSMQ events let your application respond to asynchronous notifications that are raised by MSMQ as messages arrive at a queue. You can therefore respond to a new message without having to dedicate a thread to block on a call to *Receive*.

Let's look at how MSMQ events work. The MSMQ eventing mechanism is based the *MSMQEvent* component. To use events, you must first create an *MSMQEvent* object and set up an event sink. Next, you must associate the *MSMQEvent* object with an *MSMQQueue* object that's been opened for receive access. You create the association by invoking the *EnableNotification* method on the *MSMQQueue* object and passing a reference to the *MSMQEvent* object. After you call *EnableNotification*, MSMQ notifies your application when a message has arrived by raising an *Arrived* event.

To create an event sink, you must use the Visual Basic *WithEvents* keyword and declare the source object's reference variable in the declaration section of a form module or a class module. The following code sets up an event sink for a new *MSMQEvent* object in a form module of a standard EXE project:

```
Private RequestQueue As MSMQQueue
Private WithEvents RequestEvent As MSMQEvent

Private Sub Form_Load()
    Dim qi As MSMQQueueInfo
    Set qi = New MSMQQueueInfo
    qi.PathName = ".\MyQueue"
    Set RequestQueue = qi.Open(MQ_RECEIVE_ACCESS, MQ_DENY_NONE)
    Set RequestEvent = New MSMQEvent
    RequestQueue.EnableNotification RequestEvent
End Sub
```

Once you set up the *MSMQEvent* object's event sink and call *EnableNotification*, you'll be notified with an *Arrived* event when MSMQ finds a message in the queue. Here's an implementation of the *Arrived* event handler, which processes messages as they arrive in the queue:

```
Sub RequestEvent_Arrived(ByVal Queue As Object, ByVal Cursor As Long)
    Dim RequestQueue As MSMQQueue
    Set RequestQueue = Queue  ' Cast to MSMQQueue to avoid late binding.
    Dim msg As MSMQMessage
    Set msg = RequestQueue.Receive(ReceiveTimeOut:=0)
    If Not (msg Is Nothing) Then
        ' Process message when it arrives.
    End If
    RequestQueue.EnableNotification RequestEvent
End Sub
```

Note that this example calls *EnableNotification* every time an *Arrived* event is raised. This is required because a call to *EnableNotification* sets up a notification only for the next message. If you want to receive notifications in an ongoing fashion, you must keep calling *EnableNotification* in the *Arrived* event. Also note that the code in the example receives every message that was stored in the queue when the *MSMQEvent* object was set up. In other words, MSMQ raises events for existing messages as well as future messages.

Creating listener applications using Visual Basic

I'm very fond of Visual Basic, but I must mention two limitations of this development tool when you use it to create server-side listener applications. First, in a mission-critical system it's best to deploy the listener application as a Windows service. This results in higher levels of availability. Second, if your listener application has to handle a high volume of incoming request messages, the best way to increase system through-put is to increase the number of worker threads that are receiving messages from the queue and processing requests. Typically, monitoring a queue with a thread pool of 5 to 20 threads results in the highest levels of throughput.

Some hardcore programmers have found ways to turn a Visual Basic application into a Windows service and to spawn additional COM-aware threads, but these are off-road techniques. They're not supported by Visual Basic and therefore result in code that can be pretty difficult to maintain.

Many companies use alternative approaches such as using C++ to create a custom listener application that exhibits maximum availability and throughput. Another approach is to leverage the multithreaded listener service that's built into the architecture of Queued Components. If you leverage the Queued Components service, you can get the multithreaded behavior while maintaining all your application code in Visual Basic. I'll explain how to do this later in the chapter.

You should also realize that you can sometimes get by with a server-side listener application that's a standard EXE project running on a single thread. You might not need to resort to C++ development or rely on Queued Components. This might be the case if you need to create a listener application that never receives more than a few messages per minute or a batch-processing application that runs once a day, at midnight, to process the messages that have accumulated in a request queue during the day. In such cases, a simple Visual Basic application can provide a much cheaper approach to creating a custom middle-tier listener application. As you'll see a little later, working in terms of raw MSMQ programming can also provide more options and flexibility than Queued Components.

Working with a response queue

When a client application sends a message to a request queue, it's often desirable to send a response message from the server-side listener application back to the sender. For example, a response message can contain a notification to inform the sender that the transaction ran successfully or that the transaction failed. A response message can also return a requested set of data back to the sender.

When you prepare a message in the sender application, you can add information to the message header that tells the listener application how to locate a response queue on the sender's computer. Each *MSMQMessage* object has a *ResponseQueueInfo* property. You must set up this property using an *MSMQQueueInfo* object. The receiving application can use *ResponseQueueInfo* to open the sender's response queue and send a receipt message. The code in Listing 10-1 shows how the listener application can receive a request message, open the sender's response queue, and send a response message.

```
Dim qi1 As MSMQQueueInfo, RequestQueue As MSMQQueue
Set qi1 = New MSMQQueueInfo
qi1.PathName = "MyComputer\MyQueue"
Set RequestQueue = qi1.Open(MQ_RECEIVE_ACCESS, MQ_DENY_RECEIVE_SHARE)
Dim msgRequest As MSMQMessage
Set msgRequest = RequestQueue.Receive(ReceiveTimeout:=0)
If Not (msgRequest Is Nothing) Then
    ' (1) Process message (implementation omitted for clarity).
    ' (2) Send notification back to client (implementation below).
    Dim qi2 As MSMQQueueInfo, ResponseQueue As MSMQQueue
    Set qi2 = msg.ResponseQueueInfo
    Set ResponseQueue = qi2.Open(MQ_SEND_ACCESS, MQ_DENY_NONE)
    Dim msgResponse As MSMQMessage
    Set msgResponse = New MSMQMessage
    msgResponse.Label = "Receipt for: " & msgRequest.Label
    msgResponse.Body = "Your sales transaction has been completed"
    msgResponse.CorrelationId = msgRequest.Id
    msgResponse.Send ResponseQueue
    ResponseQueue.Close
End If
RequestQueue.Close
```

Listing 10-1

When you create a listener application that returns response messages to the client application, you should typically assign the *ID* of an incoming request message to the *CorrelationId* of the outgoing response message. This technique is shown in Listing 10-1. When the client application receives a response message, it can compare the *CorrelationId* of the response message with the *ID* from each request message. This allows the sender to correlate messages.

You should also consider using private queues instead of public queues when you set up your response queues, especially in a distributed application with hundreds or thousands of clients. Unlike public queues, private queues are not published in Active Directory. Using public queues unnecessarily wastes processing cycles, network bandwidth, disk space, and administrative overhead.

Transactional Messaging

During the design phase, you should decide how you want MSMQ's queue managers to move your messages across the wire. You can choose a technique that's fast and less reliable or a technique that's slower but provides more guarantees. Performance and reliability are always at odds.

Each MSMQ message has a *Delivery* property. This property has two possible settings. The default setting is *MQMSG_DELIVERY_EXPRESS*, which means that the message is sent in a fast but unreliable fashion. Express messages are retained in memory only as they're moved across various routing servers toward their destination queue. If a computer crashes while holding express messages, the messages might be lost.

To ensure that a message isn't lost while being routed to its destination queue, you can set the *Delivery* property to *MQMSG_DELIVERY_RECOVERABLE*. The message is flushed to disk as it's passed from one computer to another. The disk I/O required with recoverable messages results in significant performance degradation, but the message won't be lost in the case of a system failure. When you send nontransactional messages, you must explicitly set the *Delivery* property if you want recoverable delivery. When you send transactional messages, the *Delivery* property is automatically set to *MQMSG_DELIVERY_RECOVERABLE*.

Even when you set the *Delivery* property to recoverable, you can still experience problems. A single message might be delivered to the destination queue more than once. In such a case, the listener application will process the same request multiple times, which can result in undesirable behavior. You can send messages in a more reliable fashion by using transactional queues.

When you send messages in a transaction, you get a few guarantees that you don't get with nontransactional messages. First, queue managers take extra precautions to ensure that messages aren't lost or duplicated. They also make sure that messages in a transaction are delivered in the order in which they were sent. Moreover, the sender can always determine when a message has failed en route to a destination queue.

Let's look at an example of in-order delivery. Let's say that you send message A and then you send message B to the same queue. Message A arrives before message B as long as they are part of the same transaction. This means that message A is placed closer to the head of the queue. However, other messages from other transactions might be interleaved with yours. MSMQ guarantees the ordering of messages only within a single transaction. Also note that due to these in-order guarantees, transacted messages can't be assigned different priorities. In MSMQ, every transacted message has a *Priority* value of 0.

MSMQ allows transacted messages to be sent only to transactional queues. You can't change the transactional attribute after a queue has been created. It is therefore important to indicate whether you want a queue to be transactional when you create it. You can use the first parameter of the *MSMQQueueInfo* component's *Create* method to indicate whether you want a transactional queue.

You can send and receive transactional messages with MSMQ in two ways. You can use MSMQ's internal transactioning mechanism, or you can use external transactions that are coordinated by the DTC using the two-phase commit protocol. Each technique offers distinct advantages.

MSMQ provides its own internal transactioning mechanism, which provides the best performance for transactional messaging. However, when you use internal transactions, MSMQ can't coordinate the transaction with any other type of resource manager, such as a SQL Server database. Internal transactions don't use the DTC. Instead, MSMQ uses a more efficient protocol that's tuned for transactional messaging. Consequently, internal transactions are much faster than externally coordinated transactions.

MSMQ supports the OLE Transactions protocol, which means that it's a valid resource manager that can participate in DTC-based transactions. You can use it along with other resource managers when you run declarative COM+ transactions. Your connection to a transactional queue can be enlisted with the DTC just like a connection to a SQL Server database. External transactions are also known as *coordinated transactions* because they're managed by the DTC.

While coordinated transactions are slower than internal transactions, you can incorporate message passing along with operations to other types of resource managers. For example, you can write a transaction that receives a request message, modifies a SQL Server database, and sends a response message. Because the three operations are part of a single transaction, the DTC enforces the ACID rules across all this writing activity. (See Chapter 8 for details about the ACID rules.)

MSMQ internal transactions

MSMQ provides a shortcut for sending a single transacted message: You pass the constant *MQ_SINGLE_MESSAGE* when you call *Send*. Here's what a call to *Send* looks like:

```
msg.Send q, MQ_SINGLE_MESSAGE
```

You'll want to send single messages in a transaction when you want exactly-once delivery. If you don't send a message in a transaction, the message is more likely to be lost or duplicated.

To send multiple messages in an internal transaction, you must create a new *MSMQTransactionDispenser* object. You can then invoke its *BeginTransaction* method to start a new transaction. A call to *BeginTransaction* returns an *MSMQTransaction* object. You can pass a reference to this *MSMQTransaction* object when you call a message-writing operation such as *Send*, *Receive*, or *ReceiveCurrent*. Here's an example that performs a receive operation on a transactional request queue while sending two messages to a transactional response queue:

```
Dim td As MSMQTransactionDispenser
Set td = New MSMQTransactionDispenser
Dim tx As MSMQTransaction
Set tx = td.BeginTransaction()
Set msg1 = RequestQueue.Receive(Transaction:=tx)
msg2.Send ResponseQueue, tx
msg3.Send ResponseQueue, tx
' Commit the transaction.
tx.Commit
```

Remember that messages sent to the same queue inside the same transaction have in-order delivery guarantees. In this example, you can assume that *msg2* will be placed in the queue ahead of *msg3*. However, there's no guarantee that messages from other transactions will not be interleaved between them.

The timing with which transacted messaged are added to and removed from transactional queues is tricky and it requires some attention on your part. Messages aren't sent to the response queue until the transaction has been committed. While the process isn't overly intuitive, it's important to see that a transacted message hasn't been delivered to the destination queue at the time the transaction commits. That's just the point at which the message begins its journey from the sender's computer.

When you receive a message in a transaction, it's removed from the queue immediately. Another application looking at this queue doesn't see the message even though the transaction hasn't been committed. However, if the transaction is aborted, the message is returned to the queue. This behavior is the same for transactional queues whether you're using internal transactions or external transactions.

You must follow a few rules when you program against transactional queues. If you violate one of these rules, MSMQ raises a runtime error.

- You can't send a message to a nontransactional queue from within a transaction.

- You can't send a message to a transactional queue if the message isn't part of a transaction.

- You can't receive and send messages to the same queue from within the same transaction.

- You can receive transactional messages only when the receiving application is running on the same computer as the transactional queue.

Another thing to keep in mind is that MSMQ transactions run at a lower isolation level than those in a DBMS such as SQL Server. As you'll recall from Chapter 8, SQL Server by default conducts the operations in a COM+ transaction with an isolation level of Serializable. MSMQ doesn't support the Serializable isolation level because of the way it manages locks during a transaction.

MSMQ provides an isolation level of Repeatable Read for a receiving application when other applications are sending messages to the same transactional queue. For example, the receiver might start a transaction and see the queue as empty. Later, within the same transaction, the receiver application might see phantom inserts made by other transactions. If MSMQ were to run transactions with an isolation level of Serializable, it would have to place an exclusive lock on the queue and block every send operation until the receiving transaction was complete. A locking scheme such as this would pose an unacceptable concurrency restraint in a queuing system.

When two transactions are run by two different receiving applications, however, the isolation level can be Read Uncommitted. For example, let's say that a single message is in a transactional queue. If transaction A receives the message from the queue, transaction B sees the queue as empty. If transaction A later aborts, the message is written back to the queue. The queue was really never empty, but transaction B saw it as empty because it read the queue in an uncommitted state.

MSMQ's inability to run serializable transactions isn't a flaw. Other messaging products, such as MQSeries, exhibit the same behavior. It's just an inherent problem with transactional queuing. Isolation is sacrificed to maintain higher levels of concurrency. As a result, you can't make as many assumptions as you can when you work with a DBMS that can run its operations with an isolation level of Serializable.

External transactions with MSMQ

The MSMQ type library contains a component for creating DTC-based transactions called the *MSMQCoordinatedTransactionDispenser*. This component's interface is identical to that of the *MSMQTransactionDispenser* component that you saw earlier in this chapter. Both components expose a single method, *BeginTransaction*, which returns an *MSMQTransaction* object. In fact, in most of your code you can use these two components interchangeably.

The difference between the two components is that the coordinated dispenser works with the DTC, while the internal dispenser doesn't. When you commit an external transaction, the DTC executes the two-phase protocol against MSMQ, which acts as a standard resource manager. The coordinated dispenser also lets you enlist a resource manager other than MSMQ into a transaction. However, Visual Basic offers no straightforward way to enlist another resource manager such as SQL Server using the *MSMQTransaction* object. You must explicitly enlist a database connection with a low-level call to ODBC or OLE-DB. You should probably avoid doing this in most production code written with Visual Basic. This means that most Visual Basic programmers should avoid using the coordinated dispenser directly.

Fortunately, you can get the same benefits of external transactions by sending and receiving messages from within a COM+ transaction. The COM+ runtime automatically enlists MSMQ as well as other resource managers such as SQL Server and Oracle into a declarative transaction. Here's an example that sends a message from a configured component that requires a transaction:

```
' Assume that this component requires a transaction.
Dim oc As ObjectContext
Set oc = GetObjectContext()
' (1) Write to a SQL Server database.
' (2) Send a message.
Dim qi As MSMQQueueInfo
Set qi = New MSMQQueueInfo
qi.PathName = "MyComputer\MyQueue"
Dim q As MSMQQueue
Set q = qi.Open(MQ_SEND_ACCESS, MQ_DENY_NONE)
Dim msg As MSMQMessage
Set msg = New MSMQMessage
msg.Body = "The database has been updated"
msg.Send q, MQ_MTS_TRANSACTION
q.Close
' (3) Commit the transaction.
oc.SetComplete ' or call SetAbort.
```

You can pass the constant *MQ_MTS_TRANSACTION* in a call to *Send*, *Receive*, or *ReceiveCurrent* to indicate that you want your writing operation to be part of the current COM+ transaction. You don't actually have to pass this parameter because this value is the default. Note that passing *MQ_MTS_TRANSACTION* results in a transacted operation if you make the call from within a COM+ transaction.

As in the case of an internal transaction, messages in a COM+ transaction aren't actually sent until the transaction has been committed. When you receive messages in a transaction, they're removed from the queue right away. If you call *SetAbort* to roll back a transaction, your messages are written back to the queue. Remember that there are no guarantees that the message will be placed back in the same position. The previous discussion of MSMQ isolation levels applies to external transactions as well as internal transactions.

Running a transaction with exactly-once semantics   Now that you've seen how to pass transacted messages, let's examine the problems associated with running a COM+ transaction without MSMQ. COM and RPC are vulnerable to communication failures that can lead to inconsistent results. This is often unacceptable in an OLTP application. In such cases, MSMQ can provide a solution.

Let's look at what can go wrong when a client invokes a COM-based method call to run a COM+ transaction. There are three possible causes of failure. First, the method call's request message might fail between the client and the server. Second, the COM+ application might crash while the method call is executing a transaction. In both of these scenarios, the intended changes of the transaction aren't committed. The third failure scenario is when the method call's response message to the client fails or is lost after the transaction has been successfully run and committed.

So here's the problem. What if a client submits a transaction by invoking a COM-based method call on a remote COM+ object but doesn't get a response? The client application has no way of knowing whether the transaction has been committed. If the client submits the same request a second time, the transaction might be committed a second time. As you can see, this creates a problem that COM and RPC can't solve.

Transactional message queues provide a way to submit a transaction request with exactly-once delivery semantics. You can run a transaction with exactly-once semantics by breaking it down into three distinct phases in which messages are sent and received from transactional queues. Figure 10-5 shows a high-level picture of how the queues are set up.

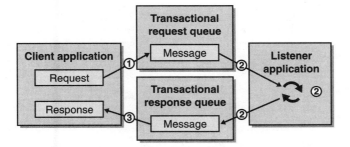

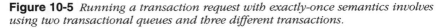

Figure 10-5 *Running a transaction request with exactly-once semantics involves using two transactional queues and three different transactions.*

First, the client submits a message to a request queue. Then the listener application accomplishes three steps in a single high-level transaction: It receives the client's message from the request queue, runs the transaction requested by the client, and sends a receipt message back to the sender's response queue. The server must successfully accomplish all three steps or the high-level transaction will be rolled back. If the transaction is rolled back, the client's message is returned to the request queue. This means that the listener application can receive the message from the request queue a second time.

Once the requested transaction has been successfully committed, a corresponding receipt message is placed in the response queue. The client application then receives a transactional message from the response queue indicating whether the transaction was completed successfully.

Transactional queues allow the sender to determine which state a request is in: waiting to be processed, being processed, or already processed. If the sender sees that the original message is still in the request queue, the request hasn't been processed. If the sender finds a corresponding message in the response queue, it knows that the request has been processed. If there's no message in either queue, the sender knows that the request is currently being processed. RPC isn't as good as transactional message passing because it doesn't give the client the same ability to determine the exact status of a request.

Dealing with poison messages and exception handling When you design applications with transactional messaging, you have to watch out for a common design problem. This problem occurs when a listener application aborts the transaction in which it receives the client's request message. For example, a listener application might be required to abort a transaction due to a business rule violation or because the database server is off line. However, if the request message is simply written back to the request queue, it causes a recursive loop: The listener application continues to receive the message, abort the transaction, and write the message back to the same request queue. This scenario is known as the *poison message problem*.

One common way to deal with poison messages is to run two separate transactions while processing the client's transaction request. The listener application creates an outer transaction to receive the request message, run a COM+ transaction to update the database, and send a response message back to the client. The COM+ transaction is run as a separate inner transaction. One easy way to accomplish this is to write a listener application that creates objects from a component whose transaction support property is set to *Requires New*.

Running two separate transactions can eliminate the poison message problem. If a business rule violation results in the rollback of the inner transaction, the listener application can determine that the client's transaction failed but still commit the outer transaction. This gives the listener application an opportunity to delete the original request message and send a response message with a failure notification back to the client.

Relatively speaking, it's not complicated to design a listener application that prevents poison messages that result from business rule violations, but you also have to deal with request messages that can't be processed due to other problems, such as system failure. When you design an application that will use transactional messaging, you should be careful not to underestimate the effort involved in dealing with poison messages and exception handling.

For example, what if a client submits a valid transaction request but the listener application can't process it right away? How do you write a listener application that can deal with a transacted request message when the database server is off line? You can't simply abort the transaction and write the request message back to the request queue. As you know, this creates a poison message scenario that puts the listener application into an infinite loop. Moreover, you can't simply commit the transaction and delete the request message without some type of contingency plan to prevent the client's request from disappearing into thin air. After all, the client submitted a valid transaction request and it's up to you to prevent it from falling on the floor.

One way to deal with this type of problem is to write an error message to a special exception-handling queue. For example, after receiving the transacted request message and determining that a system failure has occurred, you can send a copy of the message to an exception-handling queue that's regularly monitored by an administrator. This makes it possible for you to remove the original message from the request queue but still record the client's request. Once the database server is back on line, the administrator can run a utility program that you've written to process the request messages that have accumulated in your exception-handling queue.

I've presented just one simple approach to solving the exception-handling problems associated with transactional messaging. Many messaging applications have far more sophisticated designs. However, this example gives you an idea of the most important issues and how much time and effort is involved in creating a transactional listener application that does what it's supposed to do.

QUEUED COMPONENTS

The Queued Components (QC) service that's part of COM+ and Windows 2000 can provide many of the benefits of MSMQ programming, but in a much more transparent manner. QC integrates COM and MSMQ to provide the simplicity of COM-style method calls along with the benefits of messaging and MSMQ. As you've seen throughout this chapter, MSMQ programming requires more attention than COM does when it comes to issuing and responding to client requests.

When you use MSMQ, you have to think much more about the mechanics of communication. You have to prepare messages and explicitly send them to a specific queue across the network. On the receiving side, you must write a listener application to harvest these MSMQ messages and process their associated requests. Once you add in the extra complexity of establishing bidirectional communication (including response queues and Correlation IDs, for example), it's obvious that MSMQ programming is much more tedious than submitting requests using COM-based method calls.

One of COM's greatest strengths is its ability to abstract away the gory details of RPC and remote communication. As you saw in Chapter 3, the COM runtime and the universal marshaler work together to create a remote connection by transparently inserting a proxy/stub layer between a client and an object. This proxy/stub layer provides location transparency because it can seamlessly remote method calls between the client and the object.

In one sense, remote communication with MSMQ is similar to remote communication with COM. Someone sends messages from one computer and someone else listens for these messages on another computer. But COM is much simpler than MSMQ. COM's standard proxy/stub layer takes care of preparing, transmitting, and receiving RPC messages behind the scenes. With MSMQ, you have to do most of that work yourself.

A queued component is a COM component. But a queued component's methods can be remoted from one machine to another using MSMQ as an underlying transport, which means that queued components don't suffer from the same RPC-related limitations as standard COM components. As you'll recall, RPC imposes quite a few limitations because of its connection-oriented, synchronous nature.

Using a queued component is relatively simple. Here's how things work at a very high level. An application on the client computer creates a special QC proxy object and invokes one or more method calls. The COM+ runtime remotes these method calls by recording them in an MSMQ message and sending the message to a system-provided queue on the server computer. QC provides the required plumbing of a built-in listener service on the server computer. This listener service allows the COM+ runtime to monitor the queue and harvest messages as they arrive. After harvesting a message, COM+ creates an instance of the queued component and replays the messages that were recorded on the client computer.

You can see that QC provides the benefits of messaging while abstracting away the details of MSMQ programming. In the next section, we'll look into the finer details of using QC. You should note that QC doesn't provide as much flexibility as programming directly with MSMQ. If you understand the tradeoffs between using QC and using MSMQ, you can select the best approach for the project at hand.

The Architecture of Queued Components

Let's begin by revisiting the architecture of COM's standard proxy/stub layer, as shown in Figure 10-6. This architecture allows you to establish an RPC connection between a client and an object. As you'll recall from Chapter 3, when a client invokes a method, the proxy prepares and sends an RPC request message to the stub. After executing the method on the object, the stub prepares and sends an RPC response message back to the proxy. The details of preparing, sending, and receiving RPC messages are hidden behind the scenes by the proxy and the stub.

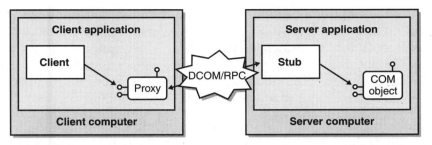

Figure 10-6 *COM's remoting architecture requires that a proxy/stub layer be introduced between the client and the object. The proxy and the stub rely on RPC to conduct synchronous, connection-oriented communication.*

Figure 10-7 shows the architecture of QC. When the client application properly instantiates an object from a queued component, it's not bound to the object that contains the method implementations but rather to a special proxy object called the *recorder*. In this sense, queued components have an architecture that's similar to COM's standard proxy/stub layer. A client can't tell the difference between a COM object, a standard COM proxy, and a QC recorder. However, the implementation details of the recorder are much different from that of a standard COM proxy.

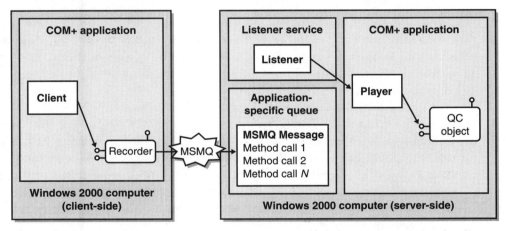

Figure 10-7 *A queued component can use MSMQ as its underlying transport. On the client side, method calls are automatically recorded and sent by the QC recorder component. On the server side, the QC listener service calls upon the QC player component to replay calls recorded in the MSMQ message.*

While a standard COM proxy knows how to communicate with the stub using RPC, the QC recorder object forwards method calls using MSMQ. The COM+ runtime creates recorder objects on the client computer from a configured component named *QC.Recorder*. The standard installation of COM+ adds this system-supplied component to a COM+ library application named COM+ Utilities.

Let me point out an important difference between a standard COM proxy and the QC recorder. COM's standard proxy/stub layer requires an established RPC connection. Each COM method call that's issued by the client is forwarded to the object in real time. For example, if a client executes two methods, the first call must return to the client before the second call can be executed. Queued components, on the other hand, are designed to work when the client computer can't establish a connection to the server computer.

When a client application creates an instance of the QC recorder and starts executing methods, the calls are not forwarded in real time. Instead, a recorder object buffers all the calls on the client computer by recording them in a single MSMQ message. The QC runtime doesn't try to send the message to the server computer until after the recorder object has been released. It's important to note that QC relies on the transactional messaging facilities of MSMQ. The fact that each message is sent inside the scope of an MSMQ transaction means that communication with QC has exactly-once delivery semantics.

I'll cover the details of configuring the server computer in a bit. Let's first look at the bigger picture. On the server computer, the queued component must be installed in a COM+ server application that's been configured as queued. When you configure a COM+ server application to be queued, COM+ automatically creates an application-specific public input queue for it. (COM+ also creates a few additional exception-handling queues.) Once a server application has been configured as queued, it can also be configured as a listener. When you configure a server application as a listener, COM+ sets up a service to monitor the queue and respond to incoming messages.

Let's assume that a queued component and its hosting COM+ server application have been properly configured and that the application is running. Now let's say a client application creates a recorder object and calls three methods. The recorder object responds by serializing the data required to replay these three methods in the body of an MSMQ message. When the client application releases the recorder object, the QC runtime attempts to send the message to the application's input queue on the server computer. If the client computer is disconnected from the network, the local queue manager stores the message and forwards it later, after it's been reconnected to the network. When the message is finally delivered to the application's input queue on the server computer, the QC listening service sees that it has arrived and begins to process it.

The QC listening mechanism involves a nonconfigured component named *QC.Listener*. While the listener monitors the queue, it delegates the responsibility of processing each MSMQ message to a player object. The listener creates a new player object for each incoming MSMQ message. Note that the listener creates player objects from a system-supplied configured component named *QC.ListenerHelper*. As it does with *QC.Recorder*, the standard installation of COM+ adds the *QC.ListenerHelper* component to the COM+ library application named COM+ Utilities.

A player object creates an instance of the queued component and executes each method recorded on the client computer. The MSMQ message carries with it all the information that the player needs to do its job. Once the player object has replayed all of its methods and released the instance of the queued component, its job is done. It is then released by the COM+ runtime.

Let's quickly review what it takes to remote a series of method calls using a queued component. Each series of method calls requires quite a few things. It requires the creation and destruction of a recorder object on the client computer, and it requires the COM+ runtime on the client computer to send one MSMQ message to the server computer. On the server computer, it requires the listener service to create and release a player object. Finally, during the player object's lifetime, the player object is responsible for reading information from the MSMQ message, creating an instance of the requested queued component, and replaying each method before releasing the object.

I'd like to point out a few key aspects of this architecture. First, player objects are thread-neutral. They run in the COM+ server application's MTA thread pool. If you're writing your code with Visual Basic, objects created from your queued components are loaded into threads in the STA thread pool. The bad news is that there's a thread switch between a player object and a Visual Basic object. The good news is that this architecture distributes all of your objects across all the threads in the STA thread pool. This means that QC provides multithreaded behavior. Your application can process several MSMQ messages concurrently, which leads to higher levels of throughput than what you can achieve with a single-threaded listener application.

Another point to keep in mind is that both the recorder component and the player component are configured to require a transaction. This has important implications for the server computer. The listener starts a new COM+ transaction when it creates a new player object. If you configure the transaction support attribute of a queued component as either Supported or Required, each instance of the queued component is created in the player's transaction. This is significant because aborting the player's transaction prevents QC from successfully processing a message received from the application's input queue. I'll revisit this topic a little later when I talk about exception handling.

Limitations of Queued Components

Now that I've covered the high-level architecture of QC, I can describe a few of its notable limitations. The first limitation is that QC relies on the MSMQ runtime. MSMQ must be installed on every client computer and server computer that uses QC.

The second important limitation is that QC's architecture relies on configured components on both the client computer and the server computer. The listening plumbing on the server also requires the COM+ container application DLLHOST.EXE. This means that QC can be used only by applications that run on a Windows 2000 computer. This unfortunate limitation prevents many companies from using QC for client-to-server communication. If your users are running earlier versions of Windows, QC might provide only a means for achieving asynchronous, disconnected communication from one server computer to another. For example, you might be able to use QC only for sending requests from a Web server to an application server.

The other noteworthy limitations involve several miscellaneous things you can do with MSMQ that are inaccessible through QC. Unlike MSMQ, QC doesn't allow you to query Active Directory for a queue using criteria such as a queue label. QC doesn't allow you to peek at messages. QC doesn't allow you to use Correlation IDs to correlate response messages. For one application, QC might provide all the functionality you need. For another application, you might decide to use MSMQ because it provides some needed feature that's not supported by QC.

Designing Queued Components

You can create a queued component in the same way that you create other configured components—by adding a multiuse class to an ActiveX DLL project. A queued component must implement at least one interface that's queueable. You should note that it's possible to create a user-defined interface that's queueable with either Visual Basic or IDL. Once you define a queueable interface, you can implement it in a multiuse class. However, in this chapter I'll keep things simple. I'll show you how to create a queued component by using a multiuse class with public methods. I've chosen not to work with a separate user-defined interface because I want to show the easiest way to create a queued component using Visual Basic.

A queueable interface has one important constraint: It can be used to communicate in only one direction. Therefore, the interface implemented by a queued component can contain methods with only input parameters. In other words, parameters can be sent only from the client computer to the server computer. Unlike COM method calls, which rely on RPC-based request/response pairs, a queued component can't return parameters from an object back to its client. Here are a few examples of methods that can be defined in a queueable interface:

```
Public Sub Method1()
    ' Implementation
End Sub

Public Sub Method2(ByVal i as Integer)
    ' Implementation
End Sub
```

```
Property Let Property1(ByVal s As String)
    ' Implementation
End Property
```

As you can see, every parameter must be marked using the *ByVal* attribute. An interface isn't queueable if it contains one or more methods that require an output parameter or a return value. For example, let's say you're trying to create a queued component using a multiuse class with public methods. The public methods that make up the default interface must all be queueable. Any of the following method signatures would render the class unusable as a queued component:

```
Sub Method3(ByRef i As Integer)
    ' Implementation
End Sub

' ByRef is the default calling convention.
Sub Method4(i As Integer)
    ' Implementation
End Sub

Function Method5() As Integer
    ' Implementation
End Function

Property Get Property1() As Integer
    ' Implementation
End Property
```

The key to designing queued components is to avoid method signatures that require passing data from the object back to the client. If you write the implementation for a multiuse class that follows these rules and compile it into a component in an ActiveX DLL, you can install it in a COM+ server application and configure it as a queued component.

Configuring a Queued Component

The first thing you do to set up the server computer is to create and properly configure a COM+ server application. Let's say you create a COM+ server application named MyApplication. You can manually configure this application to be queued and to be a listener by using the Component Services administrative tool, as shown in Figure 10-8. You can also automate the creation and configuration of a COM+ server application using scripts or using the COM+ Admin objects.

When you configure a COM+ server application as queued, COM+ automatically creates a public transactional queue with the same name. COM+ also creates several private queues to assist QC with exception handling.

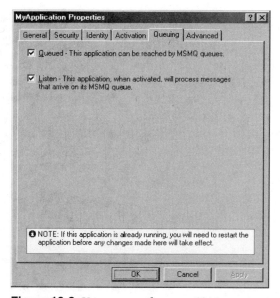

Figure 10-8 *You can configure a COM+ server application as queued and as a listener on the Queuing tab of the application's Properties dialog box in the Component Services administrative tool.*

You must do two more things to set up a queued application. First, you must configure the server application as a listener so that COM+ will monitor the application's queue for incoming messages. Second, you must start the application. The listening service works only when the application is running. You can start the server application manually using the Component Services administrative tool or you can start it programmatically using the COM+ Admin objects. Here's an example of Visual Basic code that starts a COM+ server application:

```
Dim cat As COMAdminCatalog
Set cat = New COMAdmin.COMAdminCatalog
cat.StartApplication "MyApplication"
```

You can also start a COM+ server application with a Microsoft Windows Script Host (WSH) batch file written in VBScript. Then you can configure the server computer to run this batch file on system startup by using the Windows Scheduler service. You can also schedule a queued application to run in the middle of the night if you'd like to process client requests in batch mode as opposed to real time.

In addition to configuring the application, you must also configure each queued component. First, you install the component in the queued server application. Then you configure the interface to be queued. Let's say that you want to use the default interface of a component named *MyQueuedComponent*. Once the component has been installed, you can locate the default interface (which is named _*MyQueuedComponent*) in the Interfaces folder of the Component Services administrative tool, as shown in Figure 10-9.

Figure 10-9 *Each configured component contains an Interface folder.*

Once you locate the interface, you can invoke its Properties dialog box. On the Queuing tab, you can configure the interface to be queued, as shown in Figure 10-10. If the Queued check box is disabled, it means COM+ has determined that the interface isn't queueable. This happens when a method in the interface has a *ByRef* parameter or a return value. Note that configuring an interface to be queued, like most other aspects of COM+ administration, can be done programmatically as well.

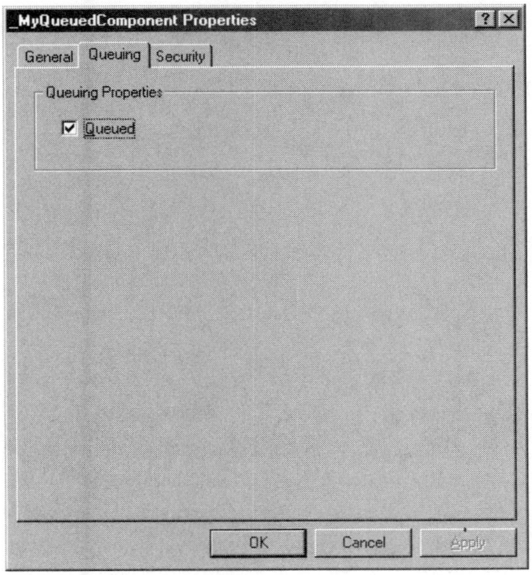

Figure 10-10 *An interface for a queued component must be configured as queued to enable asynchronous communication.*

Let me quickly summarize the configuration requirements for the server computer. First, you need to create a COM+ server application that's configured as queued and is configured to be a listener. Second, you must install the queued component in the application and make sure that one or more interfaces is configured as queued. The order of these two steps doesn't matter. Finally, you must start the server application. If you configure a server application to be a listener while it's running, you have to shut it down and restart it in order for the change to take effect.

Programming Queued Components from the Client

The most important aspect of client-side programming is creating the recorder object properly. If you want queued components to use MSMQ as an underlying transport, a client application must create a QC recorder instead of a standard COM proxy.

Let's say you've properly configured the queued component and its hosting COM+ server application, you've used the COM+ Export command to create an application proxy for this application, and you've installed the application proxy on the client computer. At this point, you're ready to use queued components from the client computer.

Note that the client-side configuration required for queued components is similar to that for other COM components. The client computer must have a registered copy of the type library as well as configuration information for ProgIDs, CLSIDs, and IIDs. It's also helpful to have a client-side AppID with a valid *RemoteServerName*. All of these details are handled for you if you install an application proxy on the client computer.

When you create a QC recorder object to act as a proxy for a queued component, you can't instantiate it using a standard technique such as calling the *New* operator or the *CreateObject* function. Look at the following code:

```
Dim obj1 As MyDll.MyQueuedComponent
Set obj1 = New MyDll.MyQueuedComponent
Dim obj2 As MyDll.MyQueuedComponent
Set obj2 = CreateObject("MyDll.MyQueuedComponent")
```

Both of these activation techniques result in standard COM activation. An instance of the queued component is created on the server computer, and the client is connected to it through COM's standard proxy/stub layer. Each method call is executed against the object in real time using RPC. In this scenario, you have a queued component but you're using it like a standard COM component.

To properly create the recorder object on the client computer, you must use a special activation technique. Look at the following code:

```
Dim rec As MyDll.MyQueuedComponent
Set rec = GetObject("Queue:/New:MyDll.MyQueuedComponent")
```

As you can see, you can properly create the recorder with a call to Visual Basic's *GetObject* function. However, in order for you to understand why this works, I need to explain the string argument that's passed to *GetObject* and explain the concept of a *moniker*.

Monikers have been part of COM for some time. A moniker is an object that finds or creates another object and binds it to a client. A moniker can be identified with a string such as the one passed to the *GetObject* function. I don't say much about monikers in this book because you can't implement them with Visual Basic. But you can use preexisting monikers from a client application written in Visual Basic using a call to *GetObject*.

The COM+ team added two new monikers to Windows 2000 to accommodate the needs of QC: the *Queue* moniker and the *New* moniker. When you call *GetObject* and pass a string that identifies the *Queue* moniker, a special moniker object is created behind the scenes, which creates a QC recorder object and binds it to the client. The *Queue* moniker relies on the *New* moniker to do its job. In the preceding example, I created a *Queue* moniker string in this format:

```
Queue:/New:MyD11.MyQueuedComponent
```

I passed the queued component's ProgID to the *New* moniker. You can also pass a CLSID with or without braces. This means there are three different formats that work the same way.

Note that the *Queue* moniker can accept parameters that make it possible to open the queue and send messages in a customized manner. You can see a list of all the available options in the Queued Components documentation in the Platform SDK. Here's an example of using a parameter to specify a server name that will override the declarative remote server name setting:

```
Queue:ComputerName=MyServer/New:MyD11.MyQueuedComponent
```

Now let's discuss the life cycle of the recorder object. While the recorder object remains active, method calls are simply recorded and buffered on the client computer. The QC runtime doesn't attempt to send the MSMQ message across the network until you release the recorder object. Look at the following code:

```
Dim rec As MyD11.MyQueuedComponent
Set rec = GetObject("Queue:/New:MyD11.MyQueuedComponent")
rec.Method1
rec.Method2 33
rec.Prop1 = "Some Value"
Set rec = Nothing
```

It's not until the last line, when the client releases the reference to the recorder object, that the QC runtime attempts to send the message. And, of course, if the client computer can't establish a connection with the server computer or another routing server in the enterprise, MSMQ caches the message locally until it can be forwarded to its proper destination.

The QC documentation also points out that you can create objects from a queued component using the *New* moniker, without the *Queue* moniker. Here's an example:

```
Dim obj As MyDll.MyQueuedComponent
Set obj = GetObject("New:MyDll.MyQueuedComponent")
```

Instantiating an object from a queued component in this manner has the same effect as the techniques I showed you earlier that use the *New* operator or the *CreateObject* function. The *New* moniker without the *Queue* moniker results in a call to *CoCreateInstance*. This means the client doesn't create a recorder object. Instead, it directly creates a remote instance of a queued component and is connected across a standard proxy/stub pair. This technique results in synchronous RPC-based communication. It also requires an established connection between the client computer and the server computer. If a direct connection can't be established between these two computers, the activation request fails.

It was a design goal of the COM+ team to create an infrastructure that made it easy to switch back and forth between synchronous and asynchronous calls. As you can see, once you've properly set up a queued component you can access it through connection-oriented, synchronous communication (COM) or through disconnected, asynchronous communication (QC). You can easily switch back and forth between these two radically different styles by simply changing the string the client application passes to *GetObject*.

Bidirectional communications

Establishing bidirectional communication with QC is possible, but it can also be tricky. The support that QC provides for returning response messages to a client isn't overly intuitive, especially when compared to how easy it is to use QC for sending messages in one direction. Let me provide an example to demonstrate what's required. The client application, in addition to creating a recorder object for the queued component on the server, must create a second recorder object using a local queued component. The client must send this recorder object as a parameter in an outgoing method. The queued component on the server can then use the recorder object that's been passed to return a series of method calls to the client computer.

It definitely adds complexity to an application when you want to use QC to send response messages back to client applications. You must create and configure a queued component and a queued COM+ server application on the client computer as well as the server computer. This approach works best when the client application is also another COM+ server application. However, it's not very elegant for a client application with a user interface.

What's hard about setting up a callback from a client application with a user interface? The problem is that the client application runs in one process while the callback objects are created and run in a separate instance of DLLHOST.EXE. It's tricky because you have to coordinate communication between these two processes.

Queued Components and Exception Handling

Let's step through how QC works when everything goes according to plan. The recorder object on the client computer sends an MSMQ message to the server computer. Remember that this message is sent to a transactional input queue. The listener service then creates a player object to receive the message. The QC player component is configured to require a transaction. Therefore, a player object runs in a COM+ transaction and can make a transacted receive. If the player object can successfully create an instance of the target queued component and successfully replay all the methods, it gives its consent to commit the transaction. When the player commits the transaction, QC assumes that the client's request has been processed, and the MSMQ message is deleted.

But what happens if things don't work out so smoothly? The infrastructure of QC provides support for exception handling and preventing poison messages. As I mentioned earlier, when you mark a COM+ application as queued, COM+ creates six additional private queues for exception handling in addition to the application's primary input queue. COM+ creates these extra queues to avoid the poison message problem.

Think about what would happen if the player object simply aborted the transaction when experiencing an error during the replay of a method. The MSMQ messages would be returned to the primary input queue and the QC infrastructure would try to reprocess the same message over and over again in an infinite loop. QC provides the additional queues to deal with exception handling in a more elegant fashion.

A few things can prevent a player object from successfully processing a client's request and deleting the associated MSMQ message. First, a player object aborts the transaction if it experiences a runtime error while replaying the methods from the MSMQ message. Second, any object created in the same transaction as the player object can also abort the transaction. For example, if your queued component is configured to require or support transactions, its objects are created in the same transaction as a player object. If your object calls *SetAbort*, the transaction aborts and the MSMQ message isn't deleted. Finally, the transaction times out if a player object can't complete its work within the computer-wide transaction timeout interval. By default, this interval is 60 seconds. A player object must replay every method, release your object, and commit the transaction before the timeout interval expires. If it doesn't do all this, the COM+ runtime automatically aborts the transaction.

When the player object's transaction is aborted, QC doesn't simply return the message to the same queue. If it did, it would experience the poison message problem. Instead, QC moves the message to the next queue in a chain of retry queues. In addition to an application's primary input queue, COM+ creates five retry queues and a final resting queue.

If you create a queued application named MyApplication, COM+ creates a public input queue with the name *myapplication*. It creates five retry queues with the names *myapplication_0*, *myapplication_1*, *myapplication_2*, *myapplication_3*, and *myapplication_4*. It creates a final resting queue named *myapplication_deadqueue* to store messages that can't be processed.

Here's how it works. If a player object can't successfully process a message from the primary input queue, QC moves the message to *myapplication_0*. After 1 minute, QC tries to process the message three more times. If these attempts fail, QC moves the message to *myapplication_1*, waits 2 minutes, and then attempts to process the message three more times. If the message continues to cause problems, QC moves it across all five retry queues and then into the final resting queue.

Each exception queue has a longer wait time than the queue before it. The wait times escalate from 1 minute to 2 minutes to 4 minutes to 8 minutes and finally to 16 minutes. After waiting 16 minutes with the message in *myapplication_4*, QC makes three final attempts and then moves the message to the final resting queue, where it becomes your responsibility to deal with it.

COM+ also supplies a utility named MessageMover, which you can use to automate the moving of messages between queues. MessageMover is a system-supplied component that's part of the COM+ runtime (COMSVCS.DLL). You can program against MessageMover in a Visual Basic application by including a reference to the COM+ Services Type Library.

Let's look at an example that shows how this utility component might be useful. Let's say you come in Monday morning to find that your application's database server has been off line for the last 48 hours. If clients submitted requests using queued components over the weekend, the final resting queue could be full of MSMQ messages that couldn't be processed. Using MessageMover, you can easily create an administrative application to move all these messages from the final resting queue back to the primary input queue. Once the database server is back on line, you should be able to move all the messages and QC will be able to successfully process them.

Programming with the MessageMover is easy. The following code can be added to a Visual Basic application to move all the messages from the final resting queue back into the primary input queue.

```
Dim MessageMover As MessageMover
Dim MessageCount As Long
Set MessageMover = New COMSVCSLib.MessageMover
```

```
MessageMover.SourcePath = ".\private$\myapplication_deadqueue"
MessageMover.DestPath = ".\myapplication"
MessageCount = MessageMover.MoveMessages
MsgBox MessageCount & " messages have been moved"
```

You can also create an exception class that can be called upon to automate the handling of a message that's been moved to the final resting queue. You create an exception class by creating a component that implements an interface named *IPlaybackControl* from the COM+ Services Type Library. This interface has two methods, *FinalServerRetry* and *FinalClientRetry*. You can write an exception class component to deal with failed messages on the client side as well as the server side. An exception class must also implement the queued interface that the client used to record methods in the original MSMQ message.

You can associate an exception class with a queued component by using the Advanced tab of the component's Properties dialog box in the Component Services administrative tool. In the Queuing Exception Class text box, enter the ProgID or the CLSID of the exception class.

When QC moves a message to the final resting queue, it looks to see whether the queued component has an exception class. If it does, QC creates an object and calls *QueryInterface* to establish an *IPlaybackControl* connection. Then QC calls *FinalServerRetry*. The way you implement this is fairly open-ended. For example, you can use the MessageMover utility to move the message to another queue. You can also send an e-mail to an administrator or log a Windows event.

After calling *FinalServerRetry* on the exception class object, QC calls *Query-Interface* once more to obtain another connection to the interface that defines the methods recorded in the message. QC can then replay the methods that were originally recorded into MSMQ by the client. This scheme gives the author of an exception class the opportunity to write contingency code to deal with the fact that the client's methods could not be replayed successfully. Once again, you can implement these methods in a number of ways. Note that if the call to *FinalServerRetry* and the calls to the individual methods succeed, QC assumes that you've taken care of things, and the MSMQ message is deleted. If you raise an error in the exception class, the message is moved to the final resting queue.

As you can see, QC supplies a pretty elaborate framework for dealing with poison messages and exceptions. In one respect, this is helpful because creating such a framework yourself isn't a trivial undertaking. In another respect, this framework doesn't provide as much flexibility as you might need in certain situations. If your application requires handling of poison messages in a different manner, you might want to avoid QC altogether and resort to raw MSMQ programming. The trade-off with this approach is that you have to create your own listener application and hand-roll your own exception-handling framework.

THE COM+ EVENTS SERVICE

COM+ Events is similar to QC in that it's a framework that's been added to COM+ and Windows 2000. This service helps you supply notifications to certain users and/or applications when interesting events occur. It's a new solution to a very old problem.

Many applications need to notify other applications when important things occur. Perhaps one application needs to inform another that a stock price has changed or that an inventory level has dropped below a certain point. COM+ Events makes it easier for applications to raise events and to respond to events.

In the COM+ Events model, applications that fire events are called *publishers*. Components and applications that receive and respond to events are called *subscribers*. The architecture of the COM+ Events service is said to be *loosely coupled* because publishers and subscribers don't require knowledge of one another. This is why the COM+ Events system also goes by the name Loosely Coupled Events (LCE). The act of decoupling is achieved through a layer of indirection between publishers and subscribers called an *event class*.

Here's how it works. An event class instance is an object who's implementation is provided by the system. However, an event class implements one or more interfaces that are defined by you. Each interface defines a group of methods that represent a set of events. When a publisher application instantiates an event class object, it can fire events. However, a publisher doesn't know or care about which subscribers are associated with an event class. A subscriber is associated with an event class through configuration data known as a *subscription*. An event class object uses subscription data kept in the COM+ catalog to locate and fire events on registered subscribers. Subscribers and subscriptions don't know or care which publishers are firing events on the event class. The key point here is that publishers and subscribers have no dependencies on one another.

This loosely-coupled architecture offers several benefits. First, you don't have to worry about subscribers when you design and write a publisher application. This means that there's less code to write and maintain. Also, once a publisher application is in production, you don't have to modify it if you want to add or remove subscribers. Furthermore, you don't have to modify subscribers or subscriptions when you want to add or remove the publishers that fire events on the event class.

The Architecture of COM+ Events

The high-level architecture of the COM+ Events model is depicted in Figure 10-11. The COM+ Events system deals with four main types of entities: publishers, event classes, subscribers, and subscriptions.

A publisher is an application that fires events. An event class object acts as a dispatching device for sending out event notifications. You define the interfaces for an event class, but COM+ actually implements the event class. The event class object locates each registered subscriber and forwards events as they're fired by a publisher. A subscriber is a class or an application that receives and responds to events. A subscription is a set of configuration data kept in the COM+ catalog that binds a subscriber to an interface in a specific event class. In other words, a subscription is a request to receive a specific set of events.

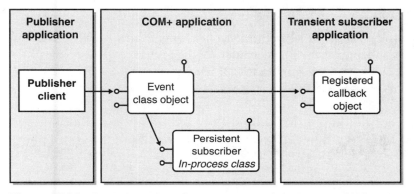

Figure 10-11 *The architecture of COM+ Events is based on a publisher, an event class, subscribers, and subscriptions.*

There are two types of subscriptions: persistent and transient. You can use a *persistent subscription* to configure a component to be a subscriber. When an event is delivered to a persistent subscription, the COM+ Event service creates a new object from a configured subscriber component and invokes the method associated with the event. The event service wakes up the subscriber component's application if it's not already running. Note that for a persistent subscription, an object is created and destroyed each time an event is fired.

If you register a callback object using a transient subscription, you can make a running application a subscriber. Once an application is running, it can register a callback object with a specific event class. This allows a transient subscriber to set up an event sink into which the event class can send notifications. In the case of a transient subscription, the event service doesn't have to create and destroy an object each time an event is fired. One big difference between the two types of subscriptions is that a transient subscription forces you to create a new subscription and register an active callback object programmatically. Unlike a transient subscriber, you can completely configure a subscription for a persistent subscriber by hand using the Component Services administrative tool.

You should note that an event system must exist on one specific computer. There is no integration with Active Directory to publish an event system as a network-wide resource. This means that the firing and dispatching of events always takes place on a specific computer. This raises fault tolerance issues because this computer represents a single point of failure for the entire event system.

Creating an event class

An event class is registered as a special type of configured component. An event class is a mapping of one or more event interfaces to a system-supplied implementation of a class. You define an event class interface as you would any other COM interface. You have the option of using Visual Basic or IDL. However, as you'll see, using Visual Basic is much easier.

To create an event class, you must create a definition for a coclass that implements the interface or interfaces that hold your events. This is a little strange because you don't supply an implementation for the coclass; COM+ supplies it for you. Here's a watered-down version of the IDL source code required to define an interface and coclass for an event class:

```
library MyTypeLibrary {
    [ uuid(IID_MyEventInterface) ]
    interface MyEventInterface : IUnknown {
        HRESULT OnThisHappened( BSTR Param1 );
        HRESULT OnThatHappened( BSTR Param1, double Param2 );
    }
    [ uuid(CLSID_MyEventClass) ]
    coclass MyEventClass {
        [default] interface _MyEventInterface;
    }
}
```

The difficulty with using IDL to define an event class is that you can't simply build a type library using MIDL.EXE and install it in a COM+ application. The type library must be embedded in a self-registering DLL. While you can do this using some C++ code and the Visual C++ development environment, you can't do it using the Visual Basic IDE.

The easy way to define an event class with Visual Basic is to simply create a multiuse class with public methods in an ActiveX DLL project. As you know, Visual Basic creates a definition for the default interface and the coclass in the DLL's type library. The resulting DLL is self-registering and meets all the requirements for installing the event class into a COM+ application.

Things will seem a little strange the first time you create an event class using Visual Basic because you define method signatures without any implementation. You might be tempted to set the instancing property of the class to *PublicNotCreatable* because you're defining a module of method signatures without implementation. You should resist this temptation, however, and leave the class's instancing setting at *MultiUse*. Here's a *MultiUse* class definition that can be used to define an event class:

```
' MultiUse class MyEventClass
Sub OnThisHappened(ByVal Param1 As String)
    ' No implementation
End Sub
```

```
Sub OnThatHappened(ByVal Param1 As String, ByVal Param2 As Double)
    ' No implementation
End Sub
```

If you decompile the DLL's type library using OLEVIEW.EXE, it will look something like this:

```
[ uuid(IID_Default_MyEventClass) ]
interface _MyEventClass : IDispatch {
    HRESULT OnThisHappened( BSTR Param1 );
    HRESULT OnThatHappened( BSTR Param1, double Param2 );
}
[ uuid(CLSID_MyEventClass)
coclass MyEventClass {
    [default] interface _MyEventClass;
}
```

This example keeps things simple by creating an event class that implements a single interface. This is the most straightforward approach. Keep in mind that you can define event classes that implement multiple interfaces. You can also exploit polymorphism by creating a design in which multiple event classes implement the same interface.

Installing and configuring an event class

Once you've compiled the multiuse class that defines your event class into an ActiveX DLL, you can install it in a COM+ application. When you install a component in a COM+ application using the Component Services administrative tool, you have a choice of installing a new component or a new event class. You should select the option to install a new event class. Note that the COM+ Admin objects also provide a special method for installing an event class.

When you install a new event class, COM+ never uses the implementation that's supplied by your DLL. That's why you don't need to include an implementation for any of its methods. Instead, COM+ creates a synthetic class implementation from a system-supplied component in ES.DLL. All that COM+ uses from your DLL's type library is the interface definition and the CLSID for the event class.

An event class is a configured component that has the same attributes as other standard configured components. However, it has a few additional attributes that are pertinent only to an event class. Figure 10-12 shows the Advanced tab of the Properties dialog box for an event class, on which you can configure LCE attributes that aren't available for configured components that aren't event classes.

In the Publisher ID field, you can enter a friendly name for an event class. Note that the Publisher ID is associated with an event class and not a publisher application. When you create a subscription for an event class, you have the option of identifying the event class using either its CLSID or its Publisher ID.

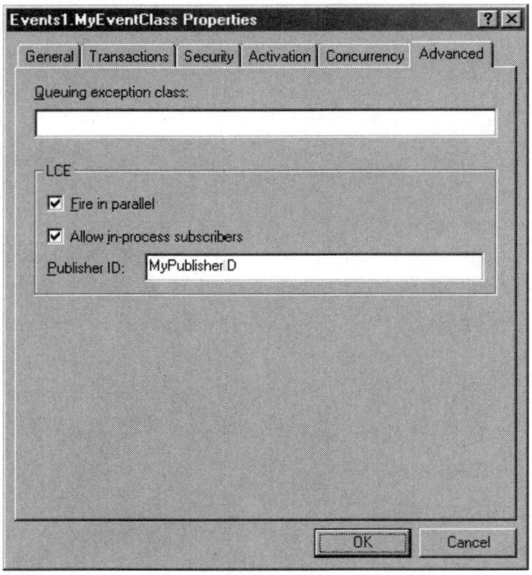

Figure 10-12 *The Advanced tab of an event class's Properties dialog box has a few extra settings for configuring loosely coupled events.*

If you clear the Allow In-Process Subscribers check box, you disallow subscribers from running in the same process as the event class. This option is selected by default. You might consider clearing it in some situations to achieve higher levels of security and fault tolerance.

The last option on the Advanced tab, Fire In Parallel, informs the COM+ event system whether to notify different subscribers on different threads. This option is cleared by default, which means that the event system uses a single thread to notify subscribers one by one, in a serialized fashion. If you select this option, the COM+ event system uses multiple threads to notify subscribers in parallel.

Configuring a persistent subscription

You can configure a component to be a subscriber by creating a persistent subscription. Like event classes, subscriptions are registered with the event system and their configuration data is stored in the COM+ catalog. A persistent subscription must be associated with either the CLSID or the Publisher ID of an event class. The subscription must also be configured with the IID that defines the set of events.

Let's say you want to create a persistent subscription for the event class I described earlier in the chapter. You can create a subscriber component using a *MultiUse* class in another ActiveX DLL project. However, it's important to remember that this subscriber component must implement the same interface as the event class.

When you create the ActiveX DLL project for the subscriber component, you should reference the type library from the DLL that holds the event class. This will allow you to implement the default interface used by your event class. Here's an example of a subscriber component that implements the same interface as the event class:

```
Implements MyEventClass

Private Sub MyEventClass_OnThisHappened(ByVal Param1 As String)
    ' Implementation for event response goes here.
End Sub

Sub MyEventClass_OnThatHappened(ByVal Param1 As String, Param2 As Double)
    ' Implementation for event response goes here.
End Sub
```

Once you compile this component into an ActiveX DLL, you can install it in a COM+ application and configure it as a persistent subscriber. You install a subscriber component in the same way that you install a standard component in a COM+ application. Don't install it as an event class.

One option is to install the subscriber component in the same COM+ application as the event class. However, if you want the subscriber to run in a separate process, you should install the subscriber component in another COM+ server application on the same computer.

Once you install the subscriber component, you can create a subscription for it by right-clicking the component's Subscriptions folder in the Component Services administrative tool and choosing the Subscription command from the New menu. This invokes the New Subscription Wizard. The wizard presents a list of the interfaces (IIDs) implemented by the subscriber component and asks you to select one to serve as the interface for the subscription. Next, the wizard presents a list of all the event classes on the local machine that implement the same interface. Your event class should be in this list if you've configured it properly. The last page of the wizard lets you assign a friendly name to the subscription and enable it. Note that the event system doesn't fire events to a subscription until it's been enabled.

Once you configure a component as a persistent subscriber, the COM+ event system creates an instance of it each time a publisher fires an event on the associated event class. Remember that the event system uses the subscriber component to create and destroy an object each time an event is fired. Also keep in mind that persistent subscriptions will survive a system shutdown, unlike transient subscriptions.

Creating a publisher

Once you create an event class and one or more persistent subscribers, creating a publisher application is pretty straightforward. Any application that can instantiate an event class object can fire events (subject to security restrictions). When you create a publisher application, you simply create an instance of the event class and call a method to fire an event. If you plan to run the publisher application on a different computer than the event class, you should use the COM+ Export feature to create an application proxy to install event class configuration information on the publisher application's computer. Here's a simple example of the code required in a publisher application to fire an event. As you can see, there's not much to it.

```
Sub FireEventFromPublisher()
    Dim MyEventClassObject As CMyEventClass
    Set MyEventClassObject = New CMyEventClass
    MyEventClassObject.OnThisHappened "this thing just happened"
    Set MyEventClassObject = Nothing
End Sub
```

The publisher application fires an event by invoking a method on the event class object, but ultimately the event is forwarded to subscribers by the event system itself. The event system is responsible for looking up subscription information from the COM+ catalog and forwarding the event to each subscriber. As you'll recall, you can configure an event class to fire events to subscribers one at a time or in parallel. In either case, the publisher application blocks until all the subscribers have processed their event notifications. In other words, the event system doesn't supply asynchronous behavior by itself. In the next section, I'll explain how to combine COM+ events with QC in order to fire events from a publisher application asynchronously.

Firing events asynchronously

By default, COM+ events are fired synchronously, in serialized fashion. A publisher application must wait while all subscribers handle the event and return control to the event system. Even if you've enabled the attribute for an event class to fire its events in parallel, the publisher still blocks until every subscriber has finished processing the event.

A scalable event notification architecture requires asynchronous communication. A distributed application is often inadequate if the publisher application is forced to wait while every subscriber processes its event notifications. Furthermore, some systems might require event notifications to be sent in an asynchronous and connectionless manner.

So far, everything I've said about the COM+ Events system is based on COM and RPC as opposed to MSMQ. Fortunately, COM+ Events has been integrated with QC in order to provide event notifications with the benefits of asynchronous, connectionless communication. Both event classes and persistent subscribers can be configured to use QC instead of synchronous COM calls. For companies with server computers that go off line or experience high traffic volumes, COM+ Events might impose too many limitations unless it's used with QC.

If you want to use the COM+ Events system with QC, all the limitations of queued components become the limitations of the COM+ Events model. Your event interfaces must abide by the same restrictions as any other queueable interface. This means that all events must be defined with only *ByVal* parameters and without return values. It also means that publisher applications and subscribers are restricted to Windows 2000 computers.

Transient subscriptions

In this chapter, I've gone through the basic steps of creating a persistent subscriber. While persistent subscribers are more common and far easier to use than transient subscribers, I want to briefly discuss how transient subscriptions work. As you'll recall, you can configure a persistent subscriber entirely by hand. It's harder to create a transient subscriber application because you must write code to create the transient subscription at runtime. This requires manipulating the COM+ catalog by writing code against the COM+ Admin objects.

A transient subscription is like a persistent subscription in the sense that it must be configured with a specific event class and a specific IID. The transient subscriber is like a persistent subscriber because it must supply a component that implements the same interface as the event class. However, the two types of subscribers are very different with respect to object lifetime and how they're created.

Once the running subscriber application creates a transient subscription using a specific event class and a specific interface, it must register a callback object that implements this interface. This callback object provides a sink that the event system can use to send event notifications. Unlike a persistent subscriber, the event system doesn't have to create and destroy an object each time it fires an event. The event system can fire many events on a long-lived callback object.

Transient subscriptions do have some drawbacks. Unfortunately, the COM+ Events system doesn't allow you to notify a transient subscriber asynchronously. Events can be dispatched only using COM, not MSMQ. For all practical purposes, this means that transient subscribers are restricted to running in the same LAN as the server computer with the event class. Synchronous callbacks also limit scalability.

Configuring security can also be a headache when you deploy transient subscribers because the client application or a custom server-side registration object must run under the identity of an account that has administrative access permissions to write to the COM+ catalog on the computer that holds the event class.

The last drawback to a transient subscription is that it's no longer useful after the transient subscriber application or the computer with the event class shuts down. If you don't explicitly remove a transient subscription from the COM+ catalog, it's removed automatically when the system restarts.

Additional COM+ Events features

I'd like to briefly mention a few more features of the COM+ Events model. First, it supports the filtering of events, so you can be more selective about which events are sent to a subscriber. A subscription has a *FilterCriteria* attribute that you can set to filter out events by specific criteria on a parameter-by-parameter basis. You can get even more control by creating a custom filter object and placing it between a publisher application and an event object. This gives you the ability to filter events on a per-subscriber basis. It also lets you determine which subscribers receive their event notifications first.

For more information about COM+ Events, see "The COM+ Event Service Eases the Pain of Publishing and Subscribing to Data" by David Platt in the September 1999 edition of *Microsoft Systems Journal (MSJ)*. You can find this article in the MSDN library. (Search on *Platt*.) David also provides details about QC in "Building a Store-and-Forward Mechanism with Windows 2000 Queued Components" in the June 1999 edition of *MSJ*. This article is also available in the MSDN library. In these articles, David unearths quite a few details that I haven't covered in this chapter. He also provides some valuable step-by-step instructions that can assist you when you're learning how to configure Visual Basic components that leverage these two COM+ services.

DECIDING AMONG MSMQ, QC, AND COM+ EVENTS

Now that I've covered the fundamentals of MSMQ, QC, and COM+ Events, I'd like to take a step back and describe a few important design issues. Let's say that you need to establish asynchronous, disconnected communication between two applications. As you've seen, QC eliminates the need for programming directly with MSMQ at the expense of some flexibility. If QC provides the functionality you're looking for, it can offer a savings in time and effort. However, you should keep in mind that many things are possible with MSMQ programming that aren't available with QC.

Communicating with computers running Windows NT, Windows 95, and Windows 98 is often a major concern. If this is a requirement, you must work with MSMQ directly. Many companies have determined that QC is best used for server-to-server communication. For example, QC makes it simple to send one-way asynchronous requests from a Web server to an application server. For an application that requires more sophisticated asynchronous communication, it's often better to spend the extra time and money to write your code using MSMQ.

You've seen that the COM+ Events service provides a value-added framework for dispatching event notifications. However, it's important that you understand its strengths and limitations. Many developers overestimate the capabilities of this service and then, after spending time working on prototypes and running stress tests, they decide that programming directly with MSMQ results in more adaptable and performance-oriented solutions.

Microsoft has aggressively pushed QC and COM+ Events as valuable new features and has had little to say about MSMQ. After all, MSMQ was already part of the platform and wasn't a hot new selling point.

Since I'm not a marketer, I've tried my best to convince you that MSMQ is one of the biggest selling points of the Windows 2000 platform. I'm not suggesting that QC and COM+ Events are never useful. I'm fond of QC because it gives Visual Basic developers a multithread listener service and a valuable exception-handling framework. But I urge you to use MSMQ when your design calls for it.

Let's conclude this chapter with an example that uses MSMQ and QC together. Let's say that you have to supply hundreds of client applications with event notifications when a stock price falls below a certain threshold. You start by designing a queued component to run on a Windows 2000 server computer. An application running on a different Windows 2000 computer might raise an event notification asynchronously using the queued component.

When the QC listening service processes the resulting message, it creates an instance of your queued component and lets you notify registered clients. If your queued component programs against MSMQ, you can send notifications to client applications running on Windows NT, Windows 95, and Windows 98. This type of solution promotes scalability because events are raised and dispatched asynchronously.

In a solution such as this, you must find a way to register clients who want to receive notifications. One approach is to create a private queue on each desktop and track the format name of each queue in a database or an XML file on the computer with the queued component that's going to be dispatching event notifications. When the queued component receives an event notification, it can iterate through all the format names and prepare and send a message to each client. Unfortunately, MSMQ doesn't currently support the broadcasting of messages, so you must prepare and send a separate message to each individual client-side queue.

SUMMARY

In this chapter, you've seen quite a few techniques for using Visual Basic to integrate messaging and asynchronous communication into a distributed application. What I hope you take away from this chapter is the *why* and *how* of moving data around the network using MSMQ messages.

Messaging can succeed in scenarios where RPC and HTTP fail. Asynchronous communication can significantly increase response times and system throughput. Messaging also improves availability because it provides reliable communication between computers that might become disconnected for any number of reasons.

Transactional programming takes messaging to another level. As you've seen, MSMQ can provide a level of reliability that you can't achieve using RPC or HTTP. Request messages can be submitted with exactly-once delivery semantics. However, you've also seen that transactional messaging involves a good deal of complexity. Someone has to deal with the poison message problem and exception handling.

Finally, you should be familiar with the strengths and weaknesses of each COM+ service so that when you need asynchronous or disconnected communication, you can make an informed decision about whether to use MSMQ or QC. In some applications, QC will meet your needs and can save you a good deal of time and money. Other applications will require MSMQ programming to implement specific functionality or to reach clients running on older versions of Windows. As you've seen, sometimes you can get creative and integrate these two services in a single solution.

Chapter 11

COM+ Security

It's impossible to overstate the importance of security in a distributed application. The data that runs your business is one of your company's most valuable assets. If you're providing access to this data through a COM+ application, it's critical that you know how to design and enforce security policies. An effective set of security policies must stop the bad guy from doing something you don't want him to do, but those security policies must also allow trusted users to use the application as it was intended without getting frustrating "Access denied" error messages.

Within a private network such as a corporate LAN, you can design a security policy to provide one degree of access to typical users and a higher degree of access to managers. For example, you might give managers read/write access permissions in places where other users don't have such permissions. When you deploy a distributed application on a public network such as the Internet, security becomes even more critical. If you don't secure the application properly, a competitor or some other malicious party can steal or destroy the data that is your company's lifeblood.

Enforcing security in a three-tier application is much different from securing a classic two-tier application. It requires a whole new way of thinking. You have to understand many of the core concepts of the Windows security model before you can make sense of the extra security-related features that COM+ provides.

COM+ inherits a few critical aspects of security from the underlying operating system, so I'll start the chapter with a quick Windows security primer to give you an understanding of authentication and authorization, how logon sessions relate to tokens, and how a process establishes its identity. Once you understand these core concepts, the added security features in COM+ will be easier to understand and use.

COM+ security is based on roles. As you'll see, the role-based model provides both declarative security and programmatic security. In one application, you might avoid any security-related programming and instead enforce security administratively using the Component Services administrative tool. In another application, one that requires conditional authorization checks or customized auditing policies, you might write security-related code to complement your declarative policies.

Security is especially important in today's world of interconnected computers. After covering how COM+ security works within a private network, I'll explain how COM+ integrates with IIS security. After all, many of you will be creating Web-based applications to reach users across the Internet. If you're exposing a COM+ application through ASP pages, you must understand how authentication works in IIS and how to configure access permissions to Visual Basic components. Once again, it's important to provide trusted users with the access permissions they require while preventing the bad guy from getting in and wreaking havoc.

I can't tell you everything you need to know about a topic as vast as Windows security in a single chapter, but I'll give you the background you need to design and deploy distributed applications that leverage the integrated security features of Windows 2000 and COM+. If you want to master Windows security, you must do further reading. One excellent resource that explains the inner workings of the Windows security model is Keith Brown's appropriately titled *Programming Windows Security* (Addison Wesley, 2000). Keith is one of the industry's leading experts in this arena; I highly recommend his book to complement this chapter.

SECURITY IN WINDOWS 2000

You can't get up to speed on COM+ security without understanding a few core concepts of the underlying Windows security model. If you're already familiar with this topic, feel free to skim this section. Otherwise, you should take the time to read this section carefully before moving to the section on COM+ security.

The first step in understanding security is learning how authentication works. You need to know what a security principal is and how it differs from an account. You should also understand the purpose of an authority and how it manages an accounts database. As you'll see, domain controllers are special computers that play a central role in allowing one principal to prove its identity to another.

I'll also describe how Windows enforces security at runtime using authorization checks. Windows uses logon sessions and tokens to cache authorization information about users. Windows also uses discretionary access control lists (DACLs) to map users and groups to permissions on specific resources. These pieces are the basic building blocks that allow you to configure an effective security policy.

This section will also focus on the additional complexities that are introduced when you perform authentication across the network. Fortunately, Windows provides authentication services transparently. A client application running on a desktop computer can safely communicate with a COM+ application on a server computer as long as a path of trust exists between them. As you'll see, the all-encompassing concept of trust permeates almost every aspect of security.

Principals and Authorities

Windows security is based on a central entity known as a *principal*. In Windows 2000, users and computers are recognized as security principals. (In Windows NT, computers aren't really recognized as first-class principals.) In this security model, one principal proves its identity to another principal through a process called *authentication*. Without authentication, it would be impossible to enforce a security policy. You'd have no way of knowing whom you were granting or denying access to.

Authentication is performed by an *authority*. An authority is a Windows service that verifies a principal's identity. For instance, when Bob (principal 1) enters his password in a logon screen and attempts to log on to the local computer (principal 2), an authority is called upon to determine whether it's really Bob. The authority keeps an encrypted copy of Bob's password and compares the password to what's been entered in the logon screen. If there's a match, Bob has proven his identity and the authority informs the local computer that it is indeed Bob who just logged on. In other words, the authority vouches for Bob's identity.

Each authority owns an accounts database of security-related configuration data. The authority maintains a separate account for each principal that it knows. When an account is created, the authority generates a unique identifier known as a *security ID (SID)*. A SID is similar to a GUID in the sense that it's a system-generated value that's unique in both time and space. However, the structure of a SID is different from that of a GUID. A SID always contains the ID of the authority that created it.

A principal account holds security-related data for a specific user or computer. For example, a user account can track group assignments and a password. The fact that the authority tracks user passwords enables users to prove their identity at runtime. A password is just one example of *principal credentials*—credentials that allow principals to prove their identities. In some scenarios, principals use more exotic forms of credentials to prove their identities, such as digital certificates and smart cards.

Local Accounts vs. Domain Accounts

Every computer running Windows 2000 or Windows NT runs an authority that owns an accounts database. Some computers run a *local security authority (LSA)*, which maintains local accounts. Other computers run a *domain authority,* which manages domain accounts. In both cases, the authority service is launched at machine startup time from LSASS.EXE.

In Windows 2000, principals can be identified using several different naming formats. Windows 2000 and Active Directory allow for the user principal name (UPN) format of *principal@authority*. For example, a domain account looks like Bob@MyDomain. In most cases, you can also identify a principal by using the older Windows NT Authority\Principle format, as in MyMachine\Bob or MyDomain\Bob. In fact, sometimes you have to use the older Authority\Principle format—such as when you assign an account name to serve as the identity for a COM+ application.

You can configure security within a relatively small group of computers without a domain authority. For example, one user can enable the local Guest account to allow other users to access local resources such as a shared directory without being authenticated. However, this approach doesn't provide much granularity. When you grant access to a resource, you must do it for everyone on the network. If you want to selectively grant access to specific users or a particular group, each user must be authenticated by an authority.

You can authenticate users in an environment without a domain authority through the use of duplicate local accounts. Each user must have an account on every computer in the network, and each account associated with a user must have the same user name and password. For example, if Bob is logged on to computer A and attempts to access a resource on computer B, the local security authority services on these two computers work together to try and authenticate him. If the authority on computer B determines that there is a local account with the same user name and password as the account that Bob logged on to on computer A, Bob is authenticated.

The problem with creating duplicate accounts is that they're hard to administer. For example, a network with 10 users and 10 computers would require 100 accounts. Imagine how difficult it would be for Bob to change his password. He would have to visit every computer on the network to do so. As you can see, managing security with duplicate accounts is feasible only in the smallest network scenarios. This approach simply can't scale because the administrative burden increases dramatically every time you add a new user or computer.

To create a security policy that can scale to accommodate a medium-sized or large population of users, you must set up your network to have one or more domain authorities. A domain authority manages a network-wide accounts database and performs authentication services for principals in the domain. Because a domain represents a set of users and computers, it is sometimes referred to as a *security boundary*.

A computer that runs a domain authority is called a *domain controller*. In Windows 2000, domain controllers maintain their accounts databases using Active Directory. Note that a domain can be configured with multiple domain controllers to improve performance, fault tolerance, and availability. When a domain has more than one domain controller, Active Directory uses replication to maintain a copy of the accounts database on each one.

The Windows security model is based on the concept of *trust*. Without trust, authentication would be meaningless. Users must trust their domain authority as well as the administrators of the domain authority. For example, Bob trusts the domain authority with his password, and he expects that the domain authority won't authenticate other users who are attempting to assume his identity.

Computers must also trust their domain authority. When you add a computer to a domain, the computer's local security authority implicitly trusts the domain authority. For example, when Bob attempts to access a resource on another computer in the domain, the local authority of that computer must trust the domain authority to verify Bob's identity. This is often called a *path of trust*.

Domain authorities can also trust one another. This makes possible authentication of users from one domain when they attempt to access resources on a computer in another domain. In Windows 2000, it's much easier to establish a path of trust between domains than in Windows NT. All Windows 2000 domains in the same forest have an implicit bidirectional trust set up between them. In Windows NT, trust relationships across domains must be configured manually in both directions. In Windows 2000, you must manually configure trust relationships to create a path of trust between domains that aren't part of the same forest.

User and Group Accounts

When it comes to securing a resource such as a COM+ application, it's more common to configure access permissions in terms of group accounts rather than user accounts. If you configure access permissions to resources in terms of user accounts, you must continually reconfigure these access permissions as individual users enter and leave the organization or change roles within the organization.

Working in terms of group accounts eases the administrative burden. A group typically represents a set of users who play a specific role or who make up an organizational unit. If you configure access permissions in terms of groups, you don't have to change them as often. It's also much easier to add and remove users accounts from these groups.

You can create group accounts within the scope of a local security authority or within the scope of a larger domain or forest. A *local group* (also called an alias) has an associated account in the local accounts database and is defined only on the local computer. A *domain group* is any group with a wider scope than a local group.

Windows 2000 recognizes three types of domain groups. The differences between these types have to do with whether a group is recognized across many domains in a forest or recognized only within a single domain. For the purposes of this chapter, I won't distinguish between the different types of domain groups.

It's important to understand the functionality of a local group. A local group exists only on a single computer. You use it to configure access permissions to resources on the local machine. You can add local users, domain users, and domain groups to a local group, but you can't nest local groups within one another.

In Windows 2000, you can nest domain groups. (Note that the domain authority must be running in native mode as opposed to mixed mode to do this). Nesting domain groups allows a company to map organizational groups to specific roles. For example, let's say that your company has one group for salespeople and another group for marketing folks and you need to grant users from both groups a fairly complex set of access permissions to some shared directories and files. While you can configure the same set of access permissions for both groups, it's usually easier to create a single role-specific group and assign the access permissions to that. Then you simply add the groups that contain users into the group that has the configured access permissions.

In a Windows NT domain, you can't nest domain group accounts. However, you can still nest domain groups within local groups. The scheme used by Windows NT doesn't provide as much flexibility as the scheme used by Windows 2000, but you can produce similar results in the two environments. The inability to nest domain groups in Windows NT means that local groups are more valuable in Windows NT than they are in Windows 2000. However, local groups still work the same way in Windows 2000 that they do in Windows NT.

Preconfigured Accounts

Windows 2000 includes a few preconfigured user and group accounts that are automatically assigned a set of commonly used privileges and access permissions. I'll briefly describe the accounts that are most pertinent to administering and securing a COM+ application.

Preconfigured accounts are created when the accounts database is created. For a local security authority, this happens when the operating system is installed. For a domain authority, this happens when a server is promoted to a domain controller, causing the creation of a new domain.

Each local security authority has a local Administrators group, which has an extensive set of privileges and access permissions by default. Many of these privileges and access permissions can't be reconfigured. Members of this group can create and configure COM+ applications by default. They can also install applications and services on the local machine and install and launch applications and services from across the network.

Every local security authority has an Administrator account, which is automatically added to the local Administrators group. It's important to see that the Administrator account is nothing special except for being a member of the local Administrators group. It doesn't have any explicitly assigned privileges or permissions. This account is important because it allows you to log on with administrative privileges and access permissions immediately after installing the operating system. After initially configuring a computer, many administrators delete or rename the Administrator account because it's an obvious choice for a break-in attempt.

Each domain authority has a Domain Admins group. The domain authority's Administrator account is automatically part of this group, and any user in this group can add other user and group accounts as well. The purpose of this account is to extend administrative privileges and access permissions to administrators who are responsible for managing the domain.

When you add a computer to a domain, the Domain Admins group is silently added to the local Administrators group. This means that a member of the Domain

Admins group is implicitly given administrator's privileges and access permissions on every computer in the domain.

Each domain authority has a Domain Users group, which includes all domain user accounts by default. Likewise, each local authority has a local Users group, which includes all local user accounts by default. When a computer is added to a domain, the Domain Users group is added to the local Users group as well. Note that the local Users group has the privilege to log on locally. This means that any user with a valid domain user account can log on to any computer in the domain (except a domain controller) by default.

Every local security authority and domain authority also has a Guest account. This account is disabled by default and its purpose is to provide access to principals that do not have an account that can be authenticated. For example, suppose you want to share a directory with users who are in a domain that doesn't have a trust relationship with your domain, or you want to share a directory with users who aren't in a domain at all. Since there's no path of trust between your computer and their authority, you'll need the Guest account.

When users try to access a resource on your computer, your local security authority attempts to authenticate them. If your local security authority can't find a matching user name in an accounts database, it looks to see if the Guest account is enabled. If it's disabled, unauthenticated users are denied access. If it's enabled, your local security authority maps unauthenticated users to the Guest account. By enabling the Guest account and configuring the appropriate access permissions, you can allow for anonymous access.

A problem can occur when you try to provide anonymous access using the Guest account. If a user account from an untrusted authority has the same user name as a user account in your local security authority or domain authority, the Windows security model checks to see whether the two accounts have the same password. If the passwords are identical, the user is authenticated under the identity of the trusted account. If the passwords don't match, the user isn't mapped to the Guest account; your local security authority simply denies access to the user. As you can see, the potential for conflicting account names makes using the Guest account a less-than-perfect solution for providing anonymous access. After all, lots of companies and organizations have a user account named Bob.

Each authority also recognizes two universal SIDs named Everyone and Authenticated Users. These SIDs are like group accounts in the sense that you can use them to configure access permissions. But they aren't really groups because they don't have accounts in any accounts database. The local security authority is hard-coded to associated these SIDs with the identity of a principal whenever it's appropriate.

The Everyone SID represents all users, including those who haven't been authenticated, which means that it includes users who've been mapped to the Guest account. The Authenticated Users SID includes all principals who've been authenticated by a trusted authority. Many administrators configure security permissions using the

Everyone SID even when the Authenticated Users SID would be a better choice. It's important that you understand the distinction between the two.

Logon Sessions and Tokens

Now that I've covered the basics of principals and authentication, let's focus on how a security policy is enforced at runtime. We'll begin with a look at logon sessions and tokens.

I'd like to start with a simple example. Let's say Bob logs on using a local account on his local computer. When he enters his password and tries to log on, the local security authority attempts to authenticate his identity. If authentication succeeds, the authority creates an *interactive logon session* and a *token* for Bob, as shown in Figure 11-1.

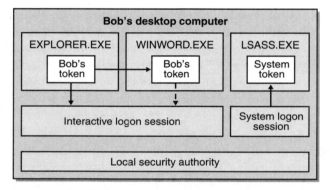

Figure 11-1. *Each process is created using a process token, which associates the process with an established logon session. The principal of this logon session serves as the identity for the process.*

The Windows security model makes a distinction between logon sessions and tokens. But you generally don't have to worry about differentiating between the two unless you're writing system-level security code in C++. As a Visual Basic programmer, you're better off thinking more in terms of tokens because that's what Windows uses to conduct security checks at runtime.

While Bob could have many different tokens on his local computer, he'll have only one logon session. You can think of a logon session as a collection of tokens associated with a specific identity. The local authority caches the SID for Bob's user account and the SIDs for all the local groups and domain groups of which Bob is a member in his tokens. The local security authority also caches any privileges he's been granted. As you can see, a token acts as Bob's badge because it contains the information that allows the system to conduct authorization checks whenever Bob attempts to access a resource.

One of the main advantages of using tokens in addition to logon sessions is that it allows one process to dynamically modify the authorization information associated with a principal without affecting other processes. For example, one process can add and enable a privilege for a token at runtime without affecting how other processes view the corresponding logon session. If processes were to use logon sessions directly instead of tokens, one process's modifications would be seen by others.

Here's a key point: Every process is created with a special token that gives the process its identity. This token is known as a *process token*. A process runs under the same identity as the principal associated with the process token's logon session.

Now let's go back to the example in Figure 11-1. When Bob successfully logs on to his local computer, the system starts up an instance of the Windows shell application (EXPLORER.EXE) and creates a process token from Bob's interactive logon session. If Bob launches another application from the shell, such as Microsoft Word (WINWORD.EXE), the system copies the process token from one process to another. However, both tokens point back to Bob's interactive logon session. Both of these processes run under Bob's identity.

The user associated with an interactive logon session takes on the identity of the Interactive User. (The identity of the Interactive User is crucial to our upcoming discussion of how to configure the identity of a COM+ application.) When no user is logged on to a computer, there is no interactive logon session and the Interactive User identity doesn't exist on the local computer.

What happens when Bob logs off his computer? His interactive logon session is shut down. When Windows shuts down his logon session, it also terminates every process that's running under the identity of one of his tokens. This example should shed some light on the relationship between logon sessions and tokens. Think of a logon session as a set of tokens. A logon session gives the operating system a way to manage a set of processes that are all running under the identity of the same principal.

In addition to interactive logon sessions, there are several other types of logon sessions, including system logon sessions, network logon sessions, service logon sessions, and batch logon sessions. You need a general understanding of when these types of logon sessions are created and how they're used.

When a computer is booted, the startup process creates a *system logon session,* a highly privileged logon session that essentially has no restrictions on what it can do. Many important Windows services run under the identity of the system. An example of such a service is the local security authority (LSASS.EXE), as shown in Figure 11-1. Once again, you must consider the concept of trust. Any code that runs under the identity of the system must be trusted. Note that the system logon session runs from the time the computer is booted until it's shut down.

You might assume that the system logon session is created using a local account in the accounts database, but this isn't the case. Windows 2000 is hardcoded to start and shut down the system logon session without requiring an account or an associated password. If Windows were to require a system account in the accounts database, this would simply open up another hole for the bad guy to steal the system's identity and circumvent your security policies.

The system logon session has no account, so it can't be recognized by other principals on the network. Note that privileged processes running as the system use the identity of the local computer account when they call out across the network. This enables other computers to authenticate requests from privileged services.

Let's look at an example to clarify this last point. When Bob logs on to his local computer using a domain account, his local security authority can't authenticate him without help from the domain authority. The local security authority on Bob's computer runs with a token created from the system logon session (as shown in Figure 11-2). However, when the local security authority calls out to the domain authority, it uses the identity of the local computer account. When the domain authority receives the request to authenticate Bob, it can determine that the request is coming from a computer that's a member of the domain.

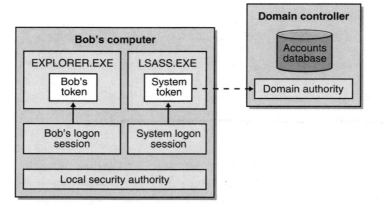

Figure 11-2. *When a process running under the identity of the system calls to another computer, the call is made using the identity of the local computer account.*

I'd like to point out two important things about a logon session. A logon session is always associated with one specific principal, and it's always limited to a single computer. So what happens if Bob attempts to access a resource across the network? The remote computer can't create a token to perform an authorization check using a logon session from another computer. The local security authority on the remote computer must create a *network logon session* and then create an associated token in order to determine whether Bob should have access to the requested resource.

Figure 11-3 shows that Bob has an interactive logon session on his local computer and a network logon session on another. It's important to understand that tokens created from Bob's interactive logon session and tokens created from his network logon session are usually quite different.

Tokens created from Bob's network logon session are similar to tokens created from his local logon session in that they contain the SID of his user account and the SID for each domain group to which he belongs. However, the set of privileges and

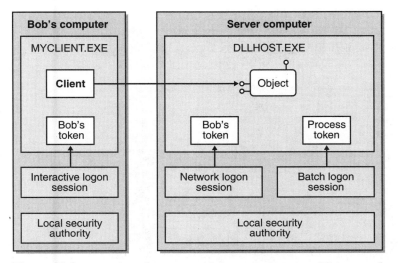

Figure 11-3. *A user can have network logon sessions in addition to a local interactive logon session.*

the SIDs of local groups are almost always different. For example, Bob might be a member of the local Administrators group on his own computer, but this doesn't mean that he's a member of the local Administrators group on the remote computer. In fact, it's likely that Bob is a member of the local Users group but not the local Administrators group on the remote computer.

The last two types of logon sessions I want to describe are *service logon sessions* and *batch logon sessions,* which are very similar. They're both used primarily for creating process tokens for local processes, and they allow you to run a process under an identity other than the system or the Interactive User.

When you configure a service on a Windows 2000 computer, you can run the service's process under the identity of the system or the identity of a user account. If you run the service under the system's identity, the service is given a process token that's associated with the system logon session. If you run the service using a user account, the operating system creates a service logon session and uses it to create the process token for the service's process.

Most processes don't require all the permissions and privileges that are extended to the system logon session. In fact, Windows doesn't even allow you to run an application under the system's identity. This configuration option is available only to Windows services. However, it's good practice to run even Windows services under a less privileged user account, if possible. Unnecessarily running a service under the identity of the system simply gives the bad guy one more opportunity to wreak havoc on your computer.

Unlike the process associated with a Windows service, the process for a COM+ application can't run under the identity of the system logon session. It must run under the identity of a specific user. You can configure the identity of a COM+ server application using the Identity tab of the application's Properties dialog box, as shown in Figure 11-4. You can configure a server application to run under the identity of the Interactive User or under the identity of a specific user account.

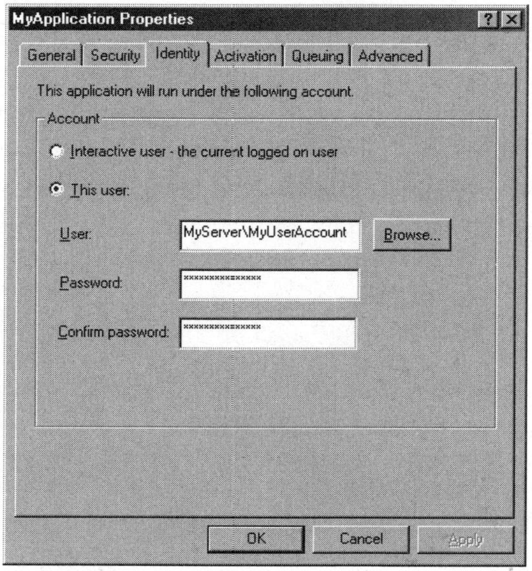

Figure 11-4. *On the Identity tab of a server application's Properties dialog box, you can specify which principal will serve as the application's identity.*

Running a COM+ server application as the Interactive User is a common thing to do during development, but it's not a good choice for a COM+ application running on a production server. Let's examine some of the problems with running an application under the identity of the Interactive User.

You typically want the process for a COM+ server application to run independently from the user who happens to be logged on to the server computer. The process for a COM+ server application that's configured with the identity of the Interactive User can run only during an interactive logon session. If no one's logged on to the server computer, client applications can't activate objects from across the network. You should also realize that the process for the COM+ server application is automatically shut down when the current user logs off. Moreover, the identity of the interactive logon session has different privileges and access permissions depending on which user is logged on.

Here's the bottom line: A COM+ server application can't run under the identity of either the system logon session or a service logon session, and you shouldn't run it under the identity of the Interactive User.

This brings us to the last type of logon session: the batch logon session. Batch logon sessions are similar to service logon sessions except that they're used for applications instead of services. When you configure a COM+ server application to run under the identity of a user account such as MyServer\MyUserAccount, the instance of DLLHOST.EXE associated with the server application is always launched with a process token created from a batch logon session. Note that when you configure the identity of a COM+ server application, you must use the Windows NT format for the account name. COM+ doesn't accept the newer UPN format (MyUserAccount@MyServer).

As you'll recall from Chapter 6, the COM+ Service Control Manager (SCM) launches the process for a COM+ server application when necessary. The SCM must also create the batch logon session in order to create the process token. However, to create the batch logon session, the SCM needs the password of the user account.

When you configure the identity of a COM+ server application to a specific user account, you must supply the user's password. The COM+ Catalog Manager writes the encrypted password to a secret place in the COM+ catalog, where the SCM can retrieve it when needed. Another important point is that the user account requires the Log On As Batch Job privilege in order to serve as the identity of a batch logon session. When you configure a COM+ server application to use a specific user account as its identity, COM+ automatically assigns the account this privilege.

The last thing I'd like to say about a COM+ application's identity setting has to do with testing and debugging components. In the development environment, it's common to run a COM+ server application under the identity of the Interactive User. One reason for doing this is that it's easier than creating and configuring a dedicated user account to serve as the application's identity. When you run your Visual Basic objects in DLLHOST.EXE, they run with your privileges and access permissions.

Another reason for running code under the identity of the Interactive User during development is that your objects can display message boxes to the user of the local computer. If a message box is invoked from an object running under the identity of a batch logon session, it's displayed on a virtual monitor that no user will ever see.

While it can be helpful to invoke a message box from an object in a COM+ application during development, doing so in a DLL that's put into production can have tragic results. Remember that compiling a production build for a DLL using the Unattended Execution option (as described in Chapter 4) is also a nice safety precaution.

Resources and DACLs

Now that I've covered the basics of logon sessions and tokens, I can explain how Windows conducts authorization checks at runtime. Many types of resources, such as directories and files on an NTFS partition, can be configured to allow access to certain users and groups while denying access to others. A securable resource has a set of security-related configuration data known as a *security descriptor*. The security descriptor holds the SID of the object's owner. The owner can configure who has access to the object. A security descriptor also can hold a security access control list (SACL) and a discretionary access control list (DACL).

A SACL is a list of configuration data used for auditing purposes. For example, you can set up auditing so that you'll know whenever a user modifies or deletes a particular file. I won't go into more detail about SACLs because COM+ doesn't use them. Later in the chapter, I'll describe how COM+ provides programmatic support for auditing.

A DACL is a list of access permissions that tells the system which tokens can access a resource and in what manner. Remember that a DACL is part of a security descriptor, so it's related to a specific resource such as a file or shared directory. Each entry in the DACL maps a SID for a user or group to a specific permission for that resource. For example, an entry in the DACL for a shared directory might indicate that Bob has read/write permissions. Another entry might indicate that the Marketing group has read permissions.

The Windows subsystem that uses DACLs to conduct authorization checks is known as the security reference monitor (SRM). When Windows calls upon the SRM to conduct an authorization check at runtime, the SRM compares the SIDs from a token to the SIDs in a DACL to determine whether a token (and its associated user) is authorized to access the resource. The SRM determines whether the principal has the access permissions to do what it's attempting to do.

I'd like to make two final points about authorization through the use of DACLs. First, if the security descriptor for a resource has a DACL, users must have explicit access permissions to access the resource. Second, if the security descriptor for a resource doesn't have its own DACL, it's given a NULL DACL and all users are implicitly granted all access permissions for the resource.

Network Authentication and Impersonation

Local authentication is fairly easy to conceptualize. But authentication over a network is far more complex. The authentication mechanism must facilitate passing sensitive information across the network in a manner that prevents the bad guy from reading and tampering with messages as they're sent from one computer to another.

Network authentication services are designed to prevent both *active attacks* and *passive attacks*. An example of an active attack is when the bad guy tries to hijack Bob's network logon session by executing method calls under the guise of Bob. The authentication service looks for evidence of such tampering and fails method calls when it finds that tampering has occurred. Network authentication services also prevent passive attacks, such as when the bad guy simply eavesdrops on messages in an effort to steal sensitive information. You can guard against eavesdropping by asking the authentication service to encrypt messages before they're sent across the wire so that the bad guy can't decipher their contents.

In order to use network authentication, two separate parties running on different computers must agree on a shared secret in the form of a cryptographic *session key*. This key is used to encrypt messages on the sending side and to decrypt them on the receiving side. When two parties use a session key to pass messages, they're said to be communicating across a *secure channel*.

In a Windows 2000 network, authentication and the creation of secure channels is performed by a loadable security module called a security support provider (SSP). To make SSPs plug-compatible with one another, Windows requires all SSPs to conform to a standard API called the Security Support Provider Interface (SSPI).

Figure 11-5 shows the layers that exist between a COM+ application and the SSP that's used to perform authentication services. This layered architecture is valuable because your applications are always shielded from the code that performs authentication services. Moreover, you don't need to write or buy an SSP. You can simply leverage one of the SSPs that ships with the operating system.

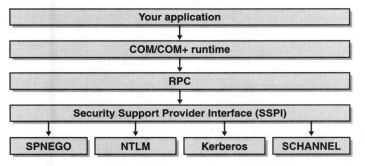

Figure 11-5. *SSPs are plug-in modules that perform authentication services.*

In most cases, you tell the SSP what level of authentication services you want by adjusting a declarative application attribute called the *authentication level*. The trade-off with different levels is that some authentication services are pretty expensive in terms of processing time. Setting the authentication level has a definite impact on performance.

NTLM and Kerberos are commonly used SSPs that provide authentication services for COM+ applications in a private network environment. NTLM is the default SSP for Window NT, and Kerberos is the preferred SSP for Windows 2000. Windows 2000 continues to support NTLM for backward compatibility with Windows NT. Secure Channel (SCHANNEL, which I'll describe later in the chapter) is an SSP most often used with HTTP.

The default SSP for Windows 2000 is called Simple Protected Negotiation (SPNEGO). SPNEGO isn't really an authentication service provider; it's a service that helps two computers negotiate the best SSP when they need to communicate in an authenticated fashion.

It's important to understand that the SSP must be supported by both computers in order for a secure channel to be established. Kerberos is usually used when two Windows 2000 computers establish a secure channel. NTLM is used when a Windows NT computer establishes a secure channel with a Windows 2000 computer or another Windows NT computer. The two computers involved can negotiate and agree on an SSP entirely behind the scenes.

NTLM and Kerberos have a few high-level similarities. For example, the authentication protocols for both SSPs can use a trusted domain controller to help establish a secure channel between two computers. Figure 11-6 shows an example of the parties involved when a secure channel is established between a client application and a COM+ server application. After the two computers negotiate which SSP to use, the SSP executes a handshake protocol to produce a secret session key that is shared by the two machines. This makes possible the establishment of a secure channel.

The low-level details of how NTLM and Kerberos work are fairly complex. NTLM uses a challenge-response protocol, and Kerberos uses an authentication scheme based on the distribution of tickets from services running on a Windows 2000 domain controller. While the details are interesting, I won't discuss them any further. (Keith Brown's book is an excellent resource for those of you who want to read more.) For Visual Basic programmers, the details of how NTLM and Kerberos establish a secure channel are just implementation details. They're hidden from you for your own good.

While knowing the implementation details of each SSP isn't all that important, you should observe that NTLM has a few notable limitations compared to Kerberos. First, NTLM doesn't support *mutual authentication*. While NTLM allows the server computer to be sure that it's receiving method calls from an authenticated client, it can't guarantee that the client's method calls will be executed only on the intended server computer. Kerberos supports mutual authentication so that the bad guy can't redirect Bob's method calls to an untrusted server by using some routing trickery.

The Kerberos ticket-passing scheme is more scalable than the NTLM challenge-response protocol. Kerberos has a more intelligent caching scheme, which results in fewer round trips to domain controllers. Consequently, Kerberos performs better in a larger network environment. Furthermore, Kerberos is significantly faster than NTLM when it comes to creating a secure channel between two computers that live in different, yet trusted, domains.

The final limitation of NTLM is that it doesn't support delegation. This means that NTLM limits the way a distributed application can make use of impersonation. However, later in the chapter I'll argue that you should avoid using delegation in COM+ applications anyway. If you agree with my argument, this last limitation of NTLM won't really be a limitation at all.

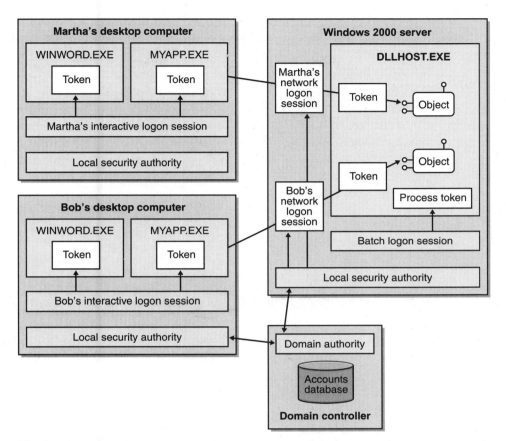

Figure 11-6. *Network authentication with NTLM or Kerberos requires the participation of a trusted domain controller in order to establish a secure channel between two computers.*

Setting the authentication level

Each COM+ server application has an *AuthenticationLevel* attribute that you can set to tell the SSP how actively you want it to perform authentication services. Any call that doesn't meet the requested level of authentication will fail. Higher levels of authentication provide more protection against tampering and snooping, but they also have a greater impact on performance. Table 11-1 lists the responsibilities of the SSP at each authentication level.

Table 11-1 **SSP AUTHENTICATION LEVELS**

Authentication Level	Configuration Value	Description	Protects Against
(None)	1	Method calls are never authenticated. This setting effectively turns off security.	N/A
Connect	2	Authentication occurs only once, when the connection is established.	Tampering
Call	3	Authenticity is guaranteed only for the first RPC packet of each method call. (This level is unsupported and is always promoted to Packet anyway.)	Tampering
Packet	4	Authenticity is guaranteed for each packet header in every method call.	Tampering
Packet Integrity	5	Same as Packet authentication level plus encrypted checksum of payload, which guarantees detection of tampering.	Tampering
Packet Privacy	6	Same as Packet Integrity authentication level plus payload encryption for privacy.	Tampering and snooping

You can adjust the authentication level for a COM+ server application on the Security tab of the application's Properties dialog box in the Component Services administrative tool, as shown in Figure 11-7. The authentication level is set on an application-wide basis when a COM+ server application is launched. Behind the scenes, the COM+ runtime sets the authentication level during application initialization by retrieving the configured value from the COM+ catalog.

The configured authentication level of a COM+ server application is only half the story, however. COM+ (or COM on a non–Windows 2000 computer) also examines the authentication level of the client application when it determines what level to use. You should understand that the process-specific authentication level on either side is a minimum authentication level—a low-water mark. When the client process and the server process have different low-water marks, COM uses the higher of the two.

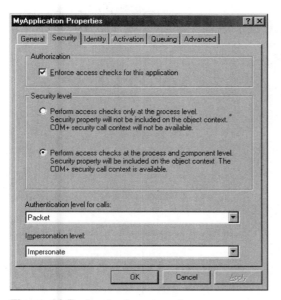

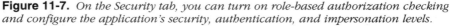

Figure 11-7. *On the Security tab, you can turn on role-based authorization checking and configure the application's security, authentication, and impersonation levels.*

When you configure the authentication level of the server application, you're guaranteed that authentication will run at that level or higher. However, if you want to turn off authentication or run it at a lower level, you must make sure that the client application doesn't request an authentication level that's higher than what you want.

When you install a Visual Basic client application that's based on a Standard EXE project, you can configure its authentication level in two ways: the easy and incorrect way or the hard and better way. The easy and incorrect way is to adjust the machine-wide default authentication level. You can easily do this using an administrative utility named DCOMCNFG.EXE. However, this opens a security hole on the client computer, particularly if you adjust the machine-wide authentication level to None.

The hard and better way to configure a client application's authentication level is to add a custom set of AppID keys to the Windows Registry. This technique works for client applications running on Windows 2000 or Windows NT. Figure 11-8 shows the keys and named values that you must add to the Registry. Note that you must map the name of the client application's executable image to a custom AppID and you must configure the AppID key with a named value that holds the configured authentication level.

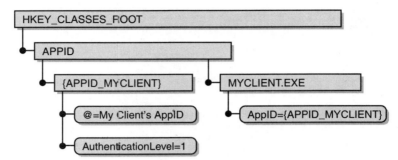

Figure 11-8. *These AppID settings are required when you configure the AuthenticationLevel setting for a client-side application based on a Standard EXE project. If there's no AppID, the application uses the machine-wide default AuthenticationLevel setting.*

You should note a few issues related to adding these entries to the Windows Registry of the client computer. First, the key that holds the GUID for the AppID must have an *AuthenticationLevel* named value of type DWORD (not String). Its value must also match one of the configuration values shown in Table 11-1. Second, after you add the AppID key to the Registry, you can adjust its authentication level using DCOMCNFG.EXE.

So far, I've only described how to set the authentication level declaratively. However, it can sometimes be beneficial or necessary to raise or lower the authentication level programmatically. In such situations, you must write the code in a low-level language such as C++ that can talk directly to COM's security API. The COM library exposes functions such as *CoInitializeSecurity* and interfaces that allow you to adjust the authentication level and other security settings on a process-wide basis. These functions also allow you to make more granular changes. For instance, you can change security-related settings for the channel associated with a proxy/stub pair. You can thus raise or lower the authentication level on a call-by-call basis.

Some companies have created a custom shim DLL using C++ to complement Visual Basic components and to gain extra programmatic control. However, if you want to maintain all your code in Visual Basic, you should assume that the authentication level is a static process-wide value.

I'd like to conclude with one more point about authentication levels. Remember that remote communication using COM should generally be restricted to a private network, in which messages associated with COM method calls are typically less vulnerable than on a public network such as the Internet. In a controlled environment, it's not always necessary to crank up the authentication level to one of the higher values (such as packet privacy). However, each company must decide for itself. If you can run authentication services at a lower level, you'll definitely experience better run-time performance.

Setting the impersonation level

In addition to an authentication level, a remote connection between a client and an object also has an *impersonation level*. The authentication level provides for privacy on the wire and allows the server computer to determine the identity of the caller; the impersonation level protects the client. Because authentication allows a client to effectively pass its security credentials across the network, the impersonation level determines how the server process can use the client's token. Higher levels of impersonation allow the server to do more with the client's security credentials. Table 11-2 lists the options for configuring the impersonation level.

Table 11-2 **IMPERSONATION LEVELS**

Impersonation Level	*Description*
Anonymous	The server can't see the client's credentials. This level is unsupported across the wire and is transparently promoted to Identify in Windows 2000 and Windows NT. This level is supported locally, but it causes all method calls to fail. You should always avoid this setting.
Identify	The server can see the security credentials and can use them only for identification and authorization.
Impersonate	The server can use the client's security credentials to access local resources.
Delegate	The server can use the client's security credentials to access local and remote resources. (Not available through NTLM.)

It's important to see that the impersonation level, unlike the authentication level, is determined entirely by the client. When you configure the impersonation level in a COM+ server application, the setting has an effect only when its objects act as clients that call methods on objects in other processes.

As with the authentication level, Visual Basic programmers can't easily change the impersonation level at runtime. If you're running a Visual Basic client application, the impersonation level used is the machine-wide default. Once again, you can change this default setting using DCOMCNFG.EXE.

Let me take a step back and explain the philosophy behind impersonation. Impersonation is a mechanism that allows a client application to delegate its security credentials to another process so that the other process can perform a task under the identity of the client. At the physical level, impersonation has some pretty heavy requirements. It requires the server application to discontinue running a client request under the identity of the process token and to switch to the identity of the client's token. While running under the identity of the client, the thread servicing the request can do only things that the client has been authorized to do. Moreover, if any operation in the request is audited by the system, the client's user name will show up in the Windows event log.

In some situations, impersonation works great—such as when you need access to a file server. If Bob accesses a shared directory across the network and tries to delete a file, he is assisted by a redirector service that runs under the identity of the system. But Bob's request isn't processed on a thread running under the identity of the system. Instead, before the redirector service attempts to delete the file, it uses impersonation to switch the thread to a token created from Bob's network logon session. The scheme works because Bob must have access rights in order to delete the file. It also means that Bob can be audited if he attempts such an undertaking.

A Web server is another type of service that relies on impersonation. For example, IIS runs as a service under the identity of the system. However, it wouldn't be very safe if IIS were to process every client request using the system's identity. IIS uses impersonation to switch worker threads to a less privileged identity. (Later in this chapter, I'll revisit this topic in greater detail.)

When it comes to building multitier applications using COM+, impersonation works much better in theory than in practice. The first reason to avoid impersonation is that it's somewhat difficult to set up and use, particularly if you want an object running in a COM+ server application to impersonate its client while making an off-host call.

For example, say that Bob runs a client application and wants to activate an object from a COM+ server application running across the network. Bob's interactive logon session on his local computer caches an encrypted copy of his password. When Bob activates an object, the server computer must authenticate him in order to create a network logon session. The local computer must supply the cached copy of Bob's password during the authentication process. You can say that the password in Bob's interactive logon session represents his network credentials.

In order for the server computer to call to a third computer and impersonate Bob, it must also cache an encrypted copy of Bob's password. This type of impersonation, which extends across two or more network hops, is known as delegation. To use delegation, you must use Kerberos because delegation isn't supported by NTLM. The client application must be configured with an impersonation level of Delegation. Moreover, both the client's user account and the user account that serves as the server application's identity must be configured with special property settings in Active Directory. The client's user account must have the Account Is Sensitive And Cannot Be Delegated property disabled. The server application's account must have the Trusted For Delegation property enabled.

Once you've jumped through the administrative hoops, you still have to request impersonation programmatically on a request-by-request basis in the method implementations of your components. There are several programmatic techniques for switching a thread from the process token to the client's token. However, these techniques are much more practical to use from C++ than from Visual Basic.

Now that I've listed a few technical reasons why you should avoid impersonation and delegation, let me give you some design reasons. When you use impersonation in a COM+ application, you're simply passing the buck to the administrator who's managing the data tier. Instead of enforcing a security policy, you're leaving everything up to the person who manages data-tier resources such as databases and shared directories. This security philosophy simply doesn't scale with a distributed application.

Impersonation forces the data tier administrator to explicitly grant and deny access permissions to user accounts or group accounts in an organization. When the administrator creates a new group, he or she might have to reconfigure access permissions in several database servers as well as a file server. A security policy becomes increasingly hard to manage as the number of data tier servers increases. Moreover, it's hard to discern the intentions of a user when you configure access permissions for a resource.

For example, if you grant a group read/write access permission on a file, you can't really enforce which parts of the file can be modified. You can't distinguish between a user who wants to make a minor change to a file and a user who wants to delete the entire contents of the file.

When you design a distributed application, you can substantially reduce the administrative burden by conducting all your authorization checks at the point at which client requests enter the middle tier. Most companies who've successfully deployed distributed applications on a large scale have found that this is the only sane approach.

It can also be far more effective to configure access permissions based on components and methods rather than on resources such as files and database tables. Both components and methods have associated semantics that make it easier to discern the user's intentions. For example, one method might make a minor change to a file and another method might delete its contents. You can decide which users should be allowed to execute each method. This makes for a far more effective security policy.

From a performance perspective, it's much better to immediately fail a method call in a COM+ application rather than forward the request downstream and have it be rejected by a file server or a database server. The earlier you can fail a call, the better. Moreover, in larger applications the processing cycles of the database server are often the most precious. If this is the case, you shouldn't waste processing cycles by conducting authorization checks on the database server when this work can be offloaded to the middle tier.

In another performance-related matter, impersonation and delegation reduce or eliminate the opportunity to conduct database connection pooling because every connection in a pool must have the same user and password. From the perspective of the DBMS, each connection in a pool has the same user identity.

To sum up, you should run authorization checks in the middle tier as close to the client as possible. This approach requires a significant mind shift for many companies, especially those that have worked extensively with two-tier applications. I recommend that you design a security policy based on the idea that the data tier trusts the user accounts that serve as the identities for middle-tier applications. These middle-tier user accounts are dedicated to running objects in COM+ applications. They're different from other user accounts in that they aren't associated with a human, so database administrators don't really know who's accessing their database.

Keep in mind that the database administrator needs to trust these middle-tier user accounts only enough to grant typical user permissions. For example, a middle-tier user account usually needs read/write permissions on tables and execute permissions on stored procedures. There's no need to grant administrative permissions to middle-tier accounts for activities such as creating and dropping tables.

Database administrators lose a degree of control that they had in the past, and they're no longer responsible for configuring access permissions for the company's user and group accounts. They can't perform user-by-user auditing using the various monitors provided by most commercial DBMSs. While some people (especially database administrators) see this loss of control as scary or threatening, it's a necessity when you deploy a large-scale, 3-tier application.

SECURITY IN COM+

Now that I've covered the essentials of Windows security, I can describe the security features that are specific to COM+. COM+ security comes in two forms: declarative and programmatic. As you'll see, both types are based on an important abstraction called a role.

Declarative security puts the responsibility of enforcing security policies on the shoulders of system administrators. When an application is deployed, an administrator decides who gets access to an application. As the security requirements for the application change over time, the administrator can address them without having to write or rewrite any security-related application code. This also lessens the need to recompile and redistribute DLLs. As with most other aspects of COM+ administration, you can configure COM+ security using the Component Services administrative tool or through the COM+ Admin object model.

In COM+, you can augment declarative authorization checks with programmatic security. In certain situations, programmatic authorization checks can provide greater control because you can add conditional logic. You should also note that while

Windows security provides many declarative auditing features, these aren't supported by COM+. If you want your application to audit the actions of its users, you must resort to programmatic security. However, the good news is that writing the code to perform customized auditing is quite easy.

Roles and Authorization

One of the central figures in the COM+ security model is the *role*. Let's look at why the COM+ team decided to base all authorization on roles. Earlier in the chapter, I described the practice of nesting groups within groups. A common motivation for nesting one group within another is to map several organizational units to a single security profile. For example, you might decide to nest the Sales group and the Marketing group in the DatabaseReader group. When you configure a set of access permissions for the DatabaseReader group, these permissions are also implicitly extended to the Sales group and the Marketing group.

Using multiple levels of grouping can simplify security administration in larger organizations because it reduces the number of accounts for which you must configure access permissions. It can also eliminate the need to reconfigure access permissions when users and groups are added or removed. The role-based model of COM+ security is based on these same principles. However, instead of nesting groups within groups, you nest groups within roles.

I must point out that COM+ roles are fundamentally different from groups. COM+ roles are defined within the scope of a COM+ application, whereas groups are defined in an accounts database and are thus associated with a specific authority. Roles are identified using strings, while groups are identified using SIDs. The COM+ security model decouples roles from SIDs to provide greater flexibility.

At design time, you define a set of roles. A role is a set of users in a COM+ application who share a common set of access permissions. Each role has a descriptive name and defines a security profile for a specific type of user. For example, you might design an application that includes three roles: Reader, Writer, and Manager. The authorization checks that you set up (either declaratively or programmatically) are always conducted in terms of roles. Roles are a comfortable abstraction for designers and programmers to work with, and they eliminate the need to be concerned about accounts (and their SIDs) during the development process.

At deployment time, an administrator maps a set of users and groups to the roles in your application, as shown in Figure 11-9. Note that a user or group can be added to multiple roles. Likewise, each role is likely to have many different users in its membership. The many-to-many relationship between users and roles creates a valuable degree of flexibility.

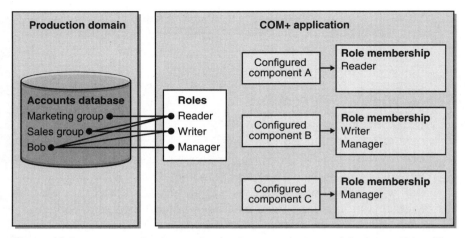

Figure 11-9. *You use roles during the development process to define security profiles and configure authorization checks. At deployment time, an administrator maps a set of users and groups to the roles defined in a COM+ application.*

One big benefit of the role-based model is that you can preconfigure access permissions for the entire application in the development environment. Access permissions are always specific to roles, and roles are defined within the scope of the COM+ application. Thus, role-based access permissions have no dependencies on SIDs. This is a key point. The use of roles in the COM+ security model eases deployment of a single COM+ application in multiple production environments.

When you distribute a COM+ application with a preconfigured security policy, you should include documentation that explains the semantics of each role. This information will be important to the administrators who map sets of users and groups to the roles you've defined.

If you're designing a secured application that you intend to deploy in many different production environments, you should also consider limiting the number of roles and minimizing the complexity of their semantics. Consider an application that defines 27 roles and contains four or five pages of documentation to describe each one. How many administrators will want to read through 100 pages of documentation when they put the application into production? Remember that your security policies can't be enforced as you intend unless an administrator can figure out how to properly map users and groups to your roles.

Configuring Declarative Security

Let's take a quick look at the steps you must take to set up declarative security checks for a COM+ server application. To configure and enforce role-based authorization checks, you must complete the following steps:

1. Enable authorization checking by selecting the Enforce Access Checks For This Application check box on the Security tab of the application's Properties dialog box.

2. On the Security tab, select either component-level security (the default) or process-level security.

3. On the Security tab, set the authentication level and impersonation level.

4. Create a set of roles in the server application.

5. Add a role to the membership of each component, interface, and method to which you want to grant access.

6. Map user and group accounts to the roles you've created. (An administrator usually does this at deployment time.)

When you create a new COM+ server application, declarative authorization checks are disabled by default. You enable them by selecting the Enforce Access Checks For This Application check box on the Security tab of the server package's Properties dialog box. This is the application-wide switch to turn on security. When security is turned off, just about anyone who can be authenticated to access your computer can create objects and execute methods.

COM+ applications also have a *Security Level* attribute that by default is configured for component-level checks as well as process-level checks. You can adjust this attribute to disable component-level checks in favor of process-level checks only. In most cases, you'll want to stick with the default setting. In just a bit, I'll describe what happens when you configure an application to use only process-level checks. For now, let's assume that you're going to stick with component-level security checks.

Designing roles is the hard part. Once you decide which roles to use, it's easy to add them to a COM+ application. In the Component Services administrative tool, you just right-click an application's Roles folder and choose New and then Role. Note that you can add roles and configure role-based authorization checks using the COM+ Admin Objects as well.

Once you add the appropriate roles to a COM+ application, you can configure a set of declarative authorization checks. This is where you configure which users get access permissions to various methods. You can add role-based authorization checks at the method level, the interface level, or the component level.

Every component has a *ComponentAccessChecksEnabled* attribute, which is on by default. This means that once security is enabled, callers are denied access unless they're in an authorized role associated with the method they're attempting to execute. If the caller isn't in one or more of the roles that are authorized to call the method, COM+ returns a standard "Access denied" error to the caller.

Figure 11-10 shows how the roles available to a method appear in its Properties dialog box. You must decide whether to configure access permissions at the component level, interface level, or method level. Each approach can be beneficial in certain situations, and you can mix and match all three. If you assign a role at the interface level, the role is implicitly associated with all its methods. If you assign a role at the component level, the role is implicitly associated with all its interfaces and all its methods. The design of your components will typically influence whether you use broad strokes (component-level checks) or fine-grained strokes (method-level checks). Note that method-level checks are a welcome addition in COM+. MTS doesn't support declarative checks at the method level, so developers must resort to programmatic checks more often.

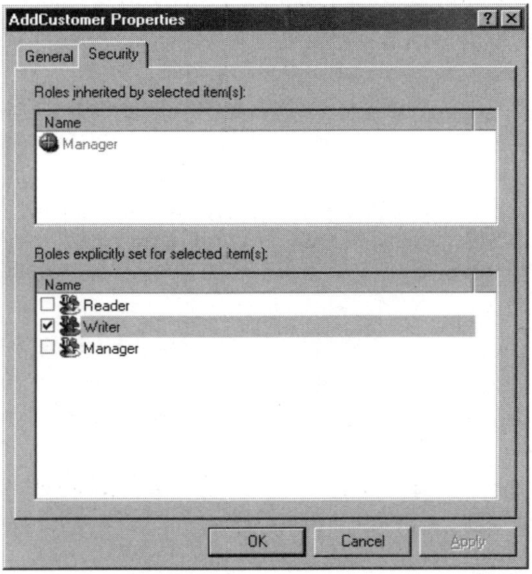

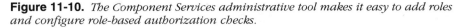

Figure 11-10. *The Component Services administrative tool makes it easy to add roles and configure role-based authorization checks.*

Enforcing Authorization at Runtime

When a COM+ server application with security enabled isn't running, a client faces two initial barriers to activating an object and calling a method. The client must have the appropriate launch permissions as well as the appropriate process-wide access permissions.

COM+ automatically configures these two access permissions behind the scenes. It constructs a DACL by taking the SIDs from the union of all roles defined in the application. Note that the SID for the system identity is added to this DACL as well. At runtime, the system compares the SIDs in the client's token to the SIDs in the DACL.

If the client's user account is explicitly or implicitly associated with at least one role, it has both launch permissions and access permissions. However, if the client doesn't map to at least one role, it can't launch the application or execute a method call.

When the COM+ runtime determines that the client is trying to do something for which it doesn't have authorization, it fails the call and returns the well-known HRESULT *E_ACCESSDENIED*. If the client is a Visual Basic application, the Visual Basic runtime catches the *E_ACCESSDENIED* HRESULT and raises a trappable "Access denied" error.

If you understand how the DACL influences runtime authorization checking, you can understand what happens in a COM+ application when security is disabled. COM+ prepares a NULL DACL for the application's launch permissions and process-wide access permissions. The NULL DACL indicates that all SIDs have implicit access permissions. In other words, anyone can launch the application and anyone can execute method calls into the application.

You should note that users who can't be authenticated by your server might have problems executing method calls even if you've disabled the application-wide security switch. If you want to allow unauthenticated users to execute methods, you must lower the application's authentication level to *None*. Note that running at an authentication level of *None* usually involves setting up a client-side AppID so that you can also adjust the client application's low-water mark to *None* (as described earlier in the chapter).

When an application has security enabled and you adjust the *Security Level* attribute to conduct only process-level checks, COM+ performs a single application-wide authorization check when a call enters the boundaries of the application. It does this using the DACL that I just described. Note that when an application is configured in such a manner, you have little granular control. If the client's token contains at least one SID that maps to any SID associated with any role in the application, the client has complete access to the entire application.

In most cases, you should leave the *Security Level* attribute at its default setting, which tells COM+ to run the authorization checks you've configured at the method, interface, and component levels. Once again, the COM+ runtime uses a simple algorithm to determine whether a call should succeed. It verifies that the caller is in at least one role associated with the method (or its interface or component). If the caller is in one or more of those roles, the call succeeds. If the caller isn't in an authorized role, the COM+ runtime fails the call by returning an "Access denied" error to the client.

Now let's look at a more complicated scenario. Let's say that component A and component B are both configured in a server application that has authorization checking enabled. A client application creates an object from component A, which in turn creates an object from component B, as shown in Figure 11-11. Let's say that the client application is running under the identity of a user account, which is in a role that's authorized to access component A. However, the user account isn't in a role that's authorized to access component B. What happens if the client attempts to execute a method on the component A object, which then attempts to execute a method on the component B object? The call will succeed because no intra-application security checks are implemented. You must understand the implications of this example when you design your security policies.

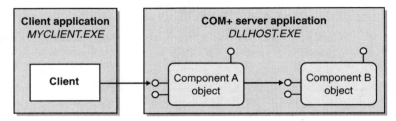

Figure 11-11. *COM+ runs authorization checks only when a call crosses an application boundary.*

Let's look at a minor variation on the example in Figure 11-11. If you install component A in a server application and you install component B in a library application, there will automatically be a security check between them. This, of course, assumes that both applications have security checks enabled. However, you should be careful not to get too carried away with configuring security on components that aren't used directly by clients. Components that aren't used by clients directly to create objects should be configured to deny all access. They should, however, be designed to trust other components in their application that call methods on behalf of authorized clients.

Calls between server processes can also be tricky. For example, what happens if a client application running as Bob makes a call to server application A, which then makes a call to server application B (as shown in Figure 11-12)? You might expect server application B to perform its security checks using Bob's security credentials, but this isn't the case. COM+ performs its security checks from hop to hop rather than from end to end. You must understand the difference between the *direct caller,* which is the party one hop up the call chain, and the *original caller,* which is the party at the top of the call chain. COM+ always performs its security checks using the credentials of the direct caller. Note that COM+ propagates Bob's identity downstream to server application B but that this contextual information should be used only for auditing purposes.

In this example, Bob is the original caller. The principal account serving as the identity for server application A is the direct caller. Server application B conducts its security checks using the direct caller. This security scheme requires server application B to trust that server application A has verified that Bob is authorized to do what he's attempting to do.

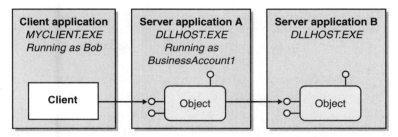

Figure 11-12. *COM+ runs role-based authorization checks when a call enters the boundaries of an application that has security enabled. However, security checks are always conducted using the token of the direct caller rather than the original caller.*

As you can see, you must be careful. When you give a role access permissions to a component, you typically give the members of the role implicit authorization to access any resources that the component uses. These resources often include other components, databases, Web servers, and file servers. Once again, the model encourages you to perform authorization checks as early as possible and to avoid relying on authorization checks that are conducted downstream from the initial point of authentication.

Programmatic Security

COM+ offers programmatic security to complement and extend what you can do using declarative security. You can write your own security checks using the *ObjectContext* interface or the *SecurityCallContext* interface. The two interfaces have some overlapping functionality, and in many cases either one will suffice.

Let's look at a quick example of how to obtain and use a *SecurityCallContext* reference in a method implementation. This example checks whether the method is executing in a secured application; if not, the call fails.

```
' Define standard HRESULT for access-denied errors.
Const E_ACCESSDENIED = &H80070005

Dim scc As SecurityCallContext
Set scc = GetSecurityCallContext
If scc.IsSecurityEnabled() Then
    ' Conduct secured operation.
Else
    ' Raise an access-denied error to caller.
    Err.Raise E_ACCESSDENIED, _
            "MyDll.MyClass.MyMethod", _
            "Access denied"
End If
```

IsSecurityEnabled tells you two things. First, it tells you whether the current call is running in a COM+ application that has security enabled. Second, it tells you whether the component has been configured to run authorization checks at the component, interface, and method levels. If you want your code to run only in a secured COM+ application, you can use the code in the previous example to raise an "Access denied" error back to the caller in the event that the application isn't secured. Note that the example uses a standard HRESULT when raising an error back to the client. This is the same HRESULT that COM+ uses when it fails a declarative authorization check.

You can also write code to test whether the caller belongs to a particular role. The *IsCallerInRole* method accepts a single string parameter for the role you want to test. The method returns *True* if the caller's user account or one of the user's group accounts maps to this role. You have to watch out because *IsCallerInRole* always returns *True* when it's called in an application in which security has been disabled. Some programmers make a habit of calling *IsCallerInRole* together with *IsSecurityEnabled*, as shown here:

```
Const E_ACCESSDENIED = &H80070005

Dim scc As SecurityCallContext
Set scc = GetSecurityCallContext
If scc.IsSecurityEnabled() And _
    scc.IsCallerInRole("Manager") Then
    ' Conduct a secured, manager-only operation.
Else
    Err.Raise E_ACCESSDENIED, _
            "MyDll.MyClass.MyMethod", _
            "Access denied"
End If
```

You have to choose whether it's necessary to call *IsSecurityEnabled* together with *IsCallerInRole*. The benefit of always calling these methods together is that you can prevent a user from conducting a sensitive operation in the case where a COM+ application hasn't been properly configured. The benefit of calling *IsCallerInRole* without *IsSecurityEnabled* is that it allows an administrator to turn off your programmatic authorization checks simply by turning off declarative authorization checks. The ability to turn off all authorization checks can be important when the administrator needs to perform diagnostic testing on an application.

As you can see, *IsCallerInRole* lets you conduct custom authorization checks on a method-by-method basis. This gives you more control than declarative security because your authorization checks can contain conditional logic. For example, you can write the *SubmitOrder* method so that only users in the role of Manager can submit a purchase order if the request exceeds $5,000, as shown in the following code:

```
Const E_ACCESSDENIED = &H80070005
Dim scc As SecurityCallContext
Set scc = GetSecurityCallContext
Dim Amount As Currency
```

```
' Determine the purchase amount.
Amount = GetAmount()
' Check for Manager role on any amount that exceeds $5,000.
If Amount > 5000 Then
    If Not scc.IsSecurityEnabled() Or _
        Not scc.IsCallerInRole("Manager") Then
        ' (caller <> manager) AND (amount > $5,000)
        GetObjectContext.SetAbort ' Abort transaction if one is running.
        Dim ErrDesc As String
        ErrDesc = "Manager required when amount exceeds $5,000"
        Err.Raise E_ACCESSDENIED, , ErrDesc
    End If
End If
' Now conduct secured operation.
```

Note that COM+ generates an *mtsErrCtxRoleNotFound* error if you call *IsCallerInRole* in a COM+ application that has security enabled and you pass a role name that doesn't exist.

Both COM+ and MTS support all the security-related functionality exposed by the *ObjectContext* interface. However, the *SecurityCallContext* interface is new to COM+. *IsSecurityEnabled* and *IsCallerInRole* are supported by both interfaces and work in the same way. However, the *SecurityCallContext* interface supplies the *IsUserInRole* method as well as several collections with information about upstream callers; these aren't available through the *ObjectContext* interface.

You can use the *IsUserInRole* method to conduct a customized authorization check on an upstream caller. For example, this code checks whether the original caller is in the role of Manager:

```
Dim oc As ObjectContext
Set oc = GetObjectContext()
Dim scc As SecurityCallContext
Set scc = GetSecurityCallContext()

Dim OriginalCaller As String
OriginalCaller = oc.Security.GetOriginalCallerName()
If scc.IsSecurityEnabled() And _
    scc.IsUserInRole(OriginalCaller, "Manager") Then
    ' Conduct manager-only operations.
Else
    Err.Raise E_ACCESSDENIED, _
            "MyDll.MyClass.MyMethod", _
            "Access denied"
End If
```

Although the *IsUserInRole* method might be tempting, you should use it sparingly. Unlike its cousin the *IsCallerInRole* method, *IsUserInRole* typically requires a round trip to a domain controller. From a design perspective, the use of *IsUserInRole* runs counter to the practice of conducting authorization checks as close to the user as possible. If you find yourself using this method too often, you should consider redesigning your application to conduct authorization checks further upstream.

Adding customized auditing code

In addition to allowing you to add conditional authorization checks, COM+ programmatic security also provides contextual information about the identity of upstream clients. You can retrieve identity information about both the object's creator and the object's caller. (A COM+ application must be configured for component-level access checks in order for the following examples to work.)

Even though the Security property exposed by the *ObjectContext* interface contains information about both the creator and the caller, they're typically one and the same. In fact, the contextual information associated with the creator is something that was created for MTS and is now considered deprecated in COM+. You should be concerned only with the name of the caller. The following code retrieves the original caller's user account name:

```
Dim oc As ObjectContext
Set oc = GetObjectContext()
Dim Caller As String
Caller = oc.Security.GetOriginalCallerName()
```

The main reason that COM+ provides the account and authority names of upstream callers is to provide contextual information for customized auditing. You can conduct an audit within a method implementation by writing the name of the original caller to the Windows event log or to a database.

In some situations, you might want to audit users when they successfully complete a transaction. In other situations, you might want to audit the times when authenticated users try to perform operations for which they aren't authorized. For example, if you determine through a programmatic authorization check that a user is attempting to do something sneaky, you can write the following code to log that fact in the Windows event log:

```
Dim Caller As String, LogMsg As String
Dim oc As ObjectContext
Set oc = GetObjectContext
Caller = oc.Security.GetOriginalCallerName()
LogMsg = Caller & " has attempted to look at everybody's salary."
App.LogEvent LogMsg, vbLogEventTypeError
```

This example uses the *Security* property of the *ObjectContext* interface. The property's *GetOriginalCallerName* method returns the caller's account name in the *Authority\Principal* format, as in MyDomain\KeithB. The *Security* object also exposes the *GetDirectCallerName*, *GetDirectCreatorName*, and *GetOriginalCreatorName* methods. As I mentioned earlier, *GetDirectCreatorName*, and *GetOriginalCreatorName* are considered deprecated under COM+ and should not be used. In most cases, it's the name of the original caller that you want to audit.

The technique I've just shown using the *ObjectContext* interface is the easiest way to get information about upstream callers. Using the *SecurityCallContext* interface is a little more complicated but can provide more detailed information, including the name of every upstream caller in the call chain.

A *SecurityCallContext* object provides an *Item* collection with several useful elements, as shown in Table 11-3. You can use this collection to determine the number of upstream callers as well as the application's minimum authentication level. It also lets you get at information about the original caller and the direct caller. When you want information about a particular caller, you must use the *SecurityIdentity* interface. This interface is defined in the COM+ Services type library.

Table 11-3   ELEMENTS OF THE *SECURITYCALLCONTEXT* OBJECT'S *ITEM* COLLECTION

Item	Type
NumCallers	Integer
MinAuthenticationLevel	Integer
Callers	*SecurityCallers* reference
DirectCaller	*SecurityIdentity* reference
OriginalCaller	*SecurityIdentity* reference

A *SecurityIdentity* object provides an *Item* collection with the elements shown in Table 11-4. You can use this object to determine the caller's account name and SID as well as the SSP, authentication level, and impersonation level used to make the call. Here's a simple example that retrieves the account name and authentication level of the original caller:

```
Dim scc As SecurityCallContext
Set scc = GetSecurityCallContext()
Dim Caller As SecurityIdentity
Set Caller = scc.Item("OriginalCaller")
Dim UserName As String, AuthLevel As Integer
UserName = Caller.Item("AccountName")
AuthLevel = Caller.Item("AuthenticationLevel")
```

Table 11-4   ELEMENTS OF THE *SECURITYIDENTITY* OBJECT'S *ITEM* COLLECTION

Item	Type
SID	*Binary array*
AccountName	String
AuthenticationService	Integer
AuthenticationLevel	Integer
ImpersonationLevel	Integer

COM+ also lets you examine each caller in the logical call chain, which is known as the *causality*. (See Chapter 6.) For example, what happens if a client application calls into one server application, which calls into a second, which calls into a third, which calls into a fourth, and so on? COM+ flows contextual information about each caller down the call chain. The server application that is furthest downstream can obtain contextual information about the caller's identity at each hop.

To get at this information, you must retrieve the *Callers* item from the *SecurityCallContext* interface. This item is an object reference of type *SecurityCallers*. A *SecurityCallers* object provides a collection with a *SecurityIdentity* reference for each caller. Here's an example that inspects each caller in the causality:

```
Dim scc As SecurityCallContext
Set scc = GetSecurityCallContext()
Dim Callers As SecurityCallers
Set Callers = scc.Item("Callers")
Dim Caller As SecurityIdentity
Dim Item As Integer
For Item = 0 To (Callers.Count - 1)
    Set Caller = Callers.Item(Item)
    ' Access identity of caller.
Next Item
```

Once again, I must reiterate that COM+ exposes all this contextual information about upstream callers for auditing purposes. If you need to call *IsUserInRole* to conduct an authorization check on a caller in the middle of the causality, you should probably rethink your security scheme and move your authorization checks to the point where the user is actually authenticated.

SECURITY IN IIS

I'd like to conclude this chapter with a discussion of IIS security and how it fits in with the other security-related topics I've talked about. Whether you're building Web-based applications that use ASP pages as a gateway to one or more COM+ applications, Web-based applications with HTML-based user interfaces, or Web-based applications that use HTTP but not HTML, your clients will go through IIS to get to your Visual Basic components. This should be sufficient motivation for you to learn how IIS security integrates with COM+ security.

Figure 11-13 shows life inside a typical Web application built with ASP pages and Visual Basic components. The first thing to notice is that INETINFO.EXE is the client's entry point into the middle tier. INETINFO.EXE is therefore the process that must authenticate the client. This means that you must rely on one of the authentication modes supported by IIS.

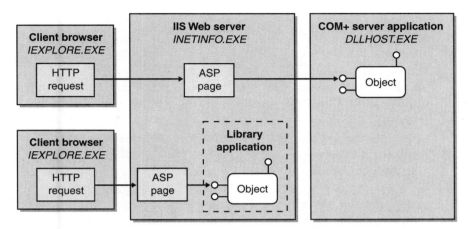

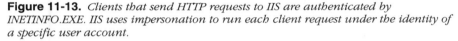

Figure 11-13. *Clients that send HTTP requests to IIS are authenticated by INETINFO.EXE. IIS uses impersonation to run each client request under the identity of a specific user account.*

The second thing to notice is that IIS must run each HTTP request under the identity of a specific security principal. INETINFO.EXE runs under the identity of the system, so if IIS were to process client requests using its process token, each request would run under the system's identity and would have virtually no restrictions. Obviously, this isn't a good solution. Instead, IIS uses impersonation so that client requests can run under the identity of more restricted user accounts.

I described the threading architecture of IIS and ASP in Chapter 9. As you'll recall, when a client requests a simple .HTM page, IIS processes the request on an MTA thread. However, when a client requests an .ASP page, IIS hands the request to ASP.DLL, which switches the request to an STA thread in order to run the page. Even though the threading architecture is complicated, impersonation works correctly in IIS even when the request is processed by an STA thread from the ASP thread pool. This means that client requests always run under the identity of a user account and never under the identity of the system.

Well, almost always. IIS does a reliable but not foolproof job of switching client requests to a user-specific token. There's a small risk of an attack in which a bad guy switches the thread that's processing his request back to the system token. As you can imagine, you really don't want the bad guy running his malicious code under the identity of the system. This essentially removes any restrictions on what he can do.

In Chapter 9, I also described how IIS uses WAM components to run IIS applications in isolation. One motivation for running an IIS application in isolation is to improve fault tolerance. A second motivation is to eliminate the risk of a bad guy performing the kind of attack I just described.

A WAM component for an isolated IIS Application is configured to run in a special COM+ server application. IIS automatically creates one of these COM+ server applications behind the scenes whenever it's necessary. When IIS creates one of these special COM+ server applications, it configures the application's identity using a special user account called IWAM_*Machine*, where *Machine* is the NETBIOS name of the local computer. This account is a local user account that's far more restricted than the system account. Even if the bad guy switches his request to the process token, he still can't run under the system's identity. As you can see, running an IIS application in isolation can be a valuable safety precaution. For this reason, many companies prefer to run their IIS applications outside of INETINFO.EXE by setting the Application Protection setting to Medium (Pooled) or High (Isolated).

By now, you know that IIS always runs client requests by impersonating various user accounts. But which user account does IIS use for a request? It depends on which authentication mode IIS is using. Before I dive into the topic of the modes that IIS uses to authenticate clients, I'd like to take a step back and talk about some important issues related to authentication using HTTP.

HTTP Security Standards

HTTP has become a widely accepted protocol because it allows you to reach clients running a variety of different operating systems and browsers, and it gives your application the potential to reach any user on the Internet. However, these benefits usually come with a few uncertainties.

When you use HTTP, you can't always assume that the client's identity can be authenticated with a user account in a Windows 2000 domain. In fact, you can't always assume that the client is running Windows. What's more, you might have to assume that the client computer and the Web server have to communicate through a firewall. What this boils down to is that an authentication mechanism such as Kerberos or NTLM won't suffice over the Internet.

Let me quickly review how Windows authentication works between a user and a remote server computer running within a private network. As you know, a path of trust must exist between the user's authority and the server computer. If the user and the server computer belong to the same domain or belong to domains with a trust relationship, the server computer can authenticate the user's calls using Kerberos or NTLM. Kerberos also provides the additional benefit of authenticating the identity of the server to the user.

Network authentication with Kerberos or NTLM requires a domain controller. The domain controller runs a protocol that helps the client and the server discover a common session key. This "shared secret" makes possible the establishment of a secure channel. Messages are encrypted using the session key on the sending side, and they're decrypted using the same session key on the receiving side. This process is often referred to as *symmetric-key encryption*.

Distributing a shared secret between any two computers on the Internet simply isn't feasible. It would essentially require every authority to have a bidirectional trust relationship with every other authority.

Fortunately, HTTP has matured to the point where a good deal of standardization has taken place in the areas of security and authentication. Secure Sockets Layer (SSL) has been adopted as the most common authentication protocol used with HTTP. SSL conducts authentication in a cross-platform fashion and it can be used to authenticate users from different organizations even if they don't belong to a common authority. SSL authentication is more accommodating than Kerberos or NTLM, but it's still based on the concept of trust.

In the SSL authentication scheme, one party doesn't have to divulge its secret to another. Encryption is based on two keys instead of one. One key is used to encrypt messages, and a second key is used to decrypt them. An entity can thus distribute a public key while keeping the other key private. This scheme is known as *asymmetric-key encryption*.

Here's how asymmetric-key encryption works at a very high level. Let's say that I give you my public key. I can encrypt a message with my private key and send it to you. You can then decrypt my message using my public key. If you trust the fact that I'm the only one with a private key capable of encrypting the message, you can be sure that I sent the message. Likewise, you can use my public key to encrypt your messages before you send them to me. Once again, if you trust that I'm the only one with the private key for decrypting the message, you can be sure that your messages won't be read by anyone else.

There are a few things to note about asymmetric-key encryption. The example I just gave of authentication doesn't involve mutual authentication. You know about me, but I know nothing about you. If I needed to authenticate you so that I could be sure it was really you on the other end, you'd have to give me a public key as well. However, it should be clear from the example that mutual authentication isn't required in order to establish a secure channel. As long as one party exchanges its public key with another, the two can communicate in a secure fashion.

You should also keep in mind that asymmetric-key encryption is computationally expensive compared to symmetric-key encryption—somewhere in the neighborhood of 1000 times more expensive. This means that using public/private key pairs has a significant runtime cost. One other point I should mention is that SSL authentication doesn't rely strictly on asymmetric-key encryption. SSL is also capable of passing a secret session key using asymmetric-key encryption in order to set up a faster channel based on symmetric-key encryption. As you can see, SSL attempts to speed things up when it can.

Certificates

As you've seen, public/private key pairs allow you to create a secure channel without the need for shared secrets or a domain controller. However, the distribution of public keys raises another security concern. For example, what if a bad guy passes you a public key and tricks you into thinking that it's my public key? If you're fooled into encrypting messages with his public key, you'll be sending messages that he can read. To prevent this security hole, the distribution of public keys usually involves certificates and a central authority that must be trusted by all public key recipients.

A certificate (also known as a *digital certificate*) is a document that attests to the association between a public key and an entity such as a human or a company. A certificate attests that the public key held by the certificate actually belongs to the entity named in the certificate. The common Internet standard for certificates is defined by the International Telecommunications Union (ITU) in ITU-T Recommendation X.509. An X.509 certificate consists of the following fields:

- Version
- Serial number
- Signature algorithm ID
- Issuer name
- Validity period
- Subject (user) name
- Subject public key information
- Issuer unique identifier
- Subject unique identifier
- Issuer signature

A certificate must be signed with the issuer's private key. Without this key, the certificate would have no value. The issuer's signature can be verified using the issuer's public key. If an entity trusts the issuer, the entity can also be confident that the public key contained in the certificate belongs to the subject named in the certificate.

Certificates are issued by a certificate authority (CA). A CA is a trusted service or entity that vouches for the identities of those to whom it issues certificates. More specifically, a CA vouches for the authenticity of the public key held in the certificate. However, in order for this entire scheme to work, a path of trust must exist. You have to trust a CA in order to trust the digital certificate it issues.

Many third-party companies, such as VeriSign, act as CAs. When you want to obtain a certificate from a third-party CA, you have to prove your identity. After all, if the CA is going to vouch for you, it wants to be sure that you're really you. When you send a certificate request to a CA, you must also send a public key for which you have a matching private key. The CA creates the certificate by packaging your name and your public key together with its signature and then sends the certificate to you.

You should note that a certificate is useless unless the certificate recipient has the public key of its issuer. So how do you obtain the CA's public key in a reliable and secure fashion? The public keys of CAs such as VeriSign are well known and are installed with browsers such as Netscape Navigator and Microsoft Internet Explorer. When two parties both have the public key of a CA, a path of trust exists between them.

CAs can certify subordinate CAs, which can then issue their own certificates. It is therefore possible to create a hierarchy of CAs with parent-child relationships. The top-level CA must be trusted without a certificate from any other CA, and its public key must be independently known. CA hierarchies make it possible to create paths of trust between nonaffiliated entities. Microsoft has a product named Microsoft Certificate Server (MCS) that allows a company to issues its own certificates.

SSL and HTTPS

Microsoft supports a suite of four related protocols for dealing with certificate-based security: Secure Sockets Layer (SSL) 2 and 3, Transport Layer Security (TLS) 1, and Private Communication Technology (PCT) 1.

Microsoft created PCT to compete with SSL 2. However, over the last few years SSL 3 has become the de facto authentication protocol to use with HTTP. PCT is now considered outmoded and should be avoided. TLS 1 is essentially a newer version of SSL 3, so I'll use the term SSL for either SSL or TLS.

SCHANNEL (Secure Channel) is Microsoft's implementation of all four protocols. SCHANNEL is an SSP that plugs into the Windows security architecture just as NTLM and Kerberos do. SCHANNEL allows applications such as IIS and Internet Explorer to use SSL when they conduct authentication based on asymmetric-key encryption.

SSL is used in two ways. The more common approach is to use SSL with a *server certificate*. This allows clients to authenticate the Web server. The server has no idea who the client is, but a server certificate is all that's needed to establish a secure channel. The Web server can exchange messages with an unauthenticated client without the risk of the bad guy deciphering what the messages mean.

The second approach is to use *client certificates* with a server certificate. The obvious benefit to using client certificates is that it allows the Web server to authenticate its clients. Each client can be mapped to a user account, which makes it possible to rely on standard authorization techniques such as restricting access through role-based security. However, this scheme can be hard to set up because each client needs its own certificate. Once again, MCS can help if you want to pursue the option of distributing client certificates.

Client certificates can be mapped to user accounts in a Windows 2000 domain. When mapping certificates to user accounts, you have two options. You can map each certificate to its own user account, or you can map many certificates to a common user account. For example, you can map every certificate for each user in the Sales department to a single user account. The documentation that ships with IIS and MCS is a good place to start when you want information on creating and distributing certificates to your clients.

Once you have a certificate on the Web server (and optionally a certificate on the client), you can use Secure HTTP (HTTPS). HTTPS is nothing more than HTTP over SSL. HTTPS differs from HTTP in that it always uses encrypted communication using a secret session key. Also, HTTPS uses port 443 by default, whereas HTTP uses port 80 by default. When the client first establishes a connection to IIS using HTTPS, public keys are exchanged in certificates using a negotiation protocol known as SSL authentication.

Once you have a server certificate, clients can communicate using either HTTP or HTTPS. However, you can also configure an entire IIS Web site or a virtual directory to require HTTPS. If you have heavy security requirements, you can use HTTPS for every request. However, keep in mind that HTTPS is slower than HTTP because it uses asymmetric-key encryption to set up a secret session key. If some parts of your site are less sensitive than others, you might consider using a mixture of HTTP and HTTPS.

IIS Authentication Modes

Now that we've covered the basics of how certificates and SSL work, let's look at the five IIS authentication modes. These are listed in Table 11-5 in the order in which IIS attempts to use them at runtime.

The first choice of IIS is the fastest mode, Anonymous Access, which avoids authentication altogether. In this mode, the Web server doesn't know or care about the identity of the client. However, IIS must still use impersonation so that the request doesn't run under the identity of the system account. By default, IIS uses an account named IUSR_*Machine*, which is created when IIS is installed. IUSR_*Machine* is only the default anonymous user account; you can assign a different user account to the anonymous user account using the Internet Services Manager.

Since IIS always tries to process a client request without authenticating the client, if you want IIS to authenticate client requests so that they run under the identity of the user's account, you must do something to prevent anonymous access.

Table 11-5 IIS AUTHENTICATION MODES

Authentication Mode	Description	What It Impersonates	On By Default?
Anonymous Access	Doesn't authenticate client	IUSR_*Machine*	Yes
Certificate-Based Authentication	Authenticates using SSL and client certificate	User accounts	Yes
Integrated Windows Authentication	Authenticates using Kerberos or NTLM	User accounts	Yes
Digest Authentication	Authenticates using password passed in encrypted form and a Windows 2000 domain controller	User accounts	No
Basic Authentication	Authenticates using password passed as clear text	User accounts	No

There are two common ways to prevent IIS from running a request using anonymous access. The first approach involves disabling anonymous access. Using the Internet Services Manager, you can disable anonymous access for an entire site, a virtual directory, or individual files. The second way to force IIS to authenticate clients is to reconfigure the permissions for .HTM and .ASP files so that the IUSR_*Machine* account doesn't have the proper access permissions to read them. You can configure permissions for individual .ASP files or for entire virtual directories as long as they're on an NTFS partition. If IIS fails when attempting to access a file using the IUSR_*Machine* account, it then attempts to authenticate the client using one of the other modes.

The second choice of IIS is Certificate-Based Authentication. This approach has by far the greatest administrative setup cost, but it's the preferred technique for authenticating clients and running their requests under the identity of established user accounts. Note that information about the client certificate is available programmatically. In fact, it's available through both the ASP object model and through interfaces in the COM+ Services Type Library.

Integrated Windows Authentication mode relies on Kerberos or NTLM. The client and the Web server negotiate which protocol to use, and a secure channel is set up in the manner described earlier. The limitation of this mode is that it requires Windows and Internet Explorer. It also uses ports that are restricted by most firewall software. While this approach doesn't scale well on the Internet, it works great when client computers and the Web server run within a private Windows network and trust a common authority.

Digest Authentication mode is new in IIS 5. It's disabled by default, so you have to turn it on in order to use it. When a user initially connects to the site, the user is prompted for a user name and password. Digest authentication is like NTLM in that it uses a challenge-response protocol and doesn't transmit the password over the Internet as clear text. However, it has a few significant problems that render it unusable in most situations. The most notable problem is that you must run the Web server on a domain controller. This opens you up to some pretty bad attacks. If the bad guy compromises your domain controller, he compromises everything in the domain. The other problem with digest authentication is that user accounts must be reconfigured in the accounts database to store their passwords as encrypted clear text.

Basic Authentication mode is also disabled by default. As with Digest Authentication mode, the user is prompted for a user name and password. The browser transmits the user name and password in the HTTP authentication header using a Base64/UUEncoded encoding scheme. This encoding scheme was not designed to protect messages, so you should assume that the password is actually being sent over the Internet as clear text. Therefore, you should use Basic Authentication mode only with HTTPS. If you don't use HTTPS, this mode results in some pretty bad exposure.

The strength of Basic Authentication mode is that it's a longtime HTTP standard and is supported by most browsers. It works through firewalls and proxy servers, and it doesn't require much effort to set up (especially compared to certificate-based authentication).

You should note one other interesting thing about using basic authentication with IIS and ASP. The password is available to ASP scripts and Visual Basic components using the *AUTH_PASSWORD* variable in the *ServerVariables* collection. You can't disable this option, so you have to put a fair amount of trust in the people who are writing scripts and components. For example, a sneaky developer could write user name and password pairs out to a log file and use this information to mount an attack.

So which of the five authentication modes should you choose for your application? It depends. Each has its strengths and weaknesses. Certificate-Based Authentication and Basic Authentication are the most popular modes for authenticating clients over the Internet.

You might get the impression that anonymous access is only for situations in which you don't care who the client is, but this isn't always the case. In some situations, you'll want to authenticate your clients but it won't make sense to maintain a Windows user account for each one. This is often the case when an application is designed to accommodate thousands or tens of thousands of users. If you want your application to scale to such heights, one option is to use a Microsoft product named Site Server, which has built-in support for tracking user profiles in a custom database. Another option is to hand-roll a custom security model.

For example, if you use anonymous access with HTTPS, you can create a secure channel. A client can safely transmit a user name and password across the Internet, and your application can supply a logon routine to perform custom authentication by running a lookup in an application-specific database to verify the user name and password. At this point, you'll probably need to generate some type of custom session key, which you send back and forth using HTTP cookies. A custom security framework such as this requires a substantial amount of code, but it provides greater flexibility and scalability.

Using IIS authentication with role-based security

Once you authenticate the client, you're only halfway home. To secure your application, you must also assign the proper access permissions to your .ASP files and your configured components. If your .ASP files (and other related files) are stored on an NTFS partition, you can configure them to grant or deny read access permissions or read/execute access permissions to users, groups, and aliases. It's relatively easy to configure access permissions on individual files and directories using Windows Explorer.

However, when you configure access permissions at the file and directory level, you can't take advantage of role-based security. As you'll recall, role-based security is valuable because it allows you to preconfigure authorization in a COM+ application and then deploy it in many production environments. Don't forget that the programmatic side of role-based security provides the benefits of conditional authorization checks and customized auditing.

There are three ways you can configure a COM+ application that will be used by ASP page clients: You can configure it as a library application, local server application, or remote server application. Let's look at the strengths and weaknesses of each of these deployment schemes.

If you use a library application, your objects load onto the same STA thread as the ASP page that creates them. However, COM+ inserts a lightweight interceptor proxy between the ASP page and the object. This allows COM+ to run its declarative authorization checks each time a call is made from the ASP page to the object. You should observe that these authorization checks are run using a logon session and a token created in conformance with one of the IIS authentication modes. One of the advantages of using a library application is that it provides the best performance.

If you use a local server application, your objects load into a private and local instance of DLLHOST.EXE. Once again, COM+ inserts an interception layer between the ASP page and the object in order to conduct role-based authorization checks. Running authorization checks in DLLHOST.EXE requires the creation of another token. However, both processes are on the same computer, so there's no need to create a second logon session.

Take another look at Figure 11-13. The uppermost request is passed from INETINFO.EXE to DLLHOST.EXE. It's important to see that impersonation allows the user's identity to propagate from one server process to another. For example, if IIS authenticates the client as Bob, the ASP page in INETINFO.EXE runs under Bob's identity. When the call is made to DLLHOST.EXE, authorization checks can be conducted using Bob's token as well. This works smoothly because of a new feature in Windows 2000 called *dynamic cloaking*. (This doesn't work as well in Windows NT and IIS 4.)

I've told you about using components from library applications and local server applications. Now I'll describe the third option and try to talk you out of using it. If you attempt to use a remote server application, you're likely to be in for heartache and frustration. Conducting role-based authorization checks on a computer that's one hop away from the Web server requires propagating a logon session across the network. This can be challenging or even impossible.

The problem is that most authentication modes used by IIS create a logon session without network credentials. In other words, the logon session doesn't include a password or some other proof of its identity. Without network credentials, the Web server can't propagate a logon session to another machine. In these cases, delegation doesn't work.

There are many ways to configure the authentication mode that IIS uses, and most of them don't result in a logon session with network credentials. However, with some effort you can make delegation work with basic authentication, certificate-based authentication, or Kerberos.

However, you should consider avoiding delegation because it goes against the practice of authenticating and authorizing as close to the client as possible. Delegation is expensive because it requires propagating the client's identity from the Web server downstream to another server. This degrades performance. Whenever possible, try to perform authentication and authorization on the Web server itself.

FURTHER READING

Security is a daunting topic. I hate to admit it, but this chapter is just the tip of the iceberg. There's so much more to learn in areas such as domain administration, certificate distribution, and cryptography. What's more, you should keep up on which IIS attacks are most common so that you can stay a few steps ahead of the bad guys. I have to apologize because I've left you with lots of homework.

If you want to master the administrative side of IIS and MCS, you should read the documentation that ships with these products. The Windows 2000 Resource Kit is also a valuable resource. It details how to get around in Active Directory and has good coverage of IIS.

If you really want to understand the guts of the Windows security model—especially if you're writing security-related code in C++—Keith Brown's *Programming*

Windows Security is required reading. Even if you don't like to read C++ code examples, the book is valuable because it clearly explains the core concepts of Windows security.

SUMMARY

The chapter started with a discussion of the core concepts of Windows security. Everything is based on principals. Authorities are services that allow one principal to authenticate another. Logon sessions and tokens are data structures created at runtime to cache authorization information about principals. Each process gets a process token that associates it with a principal and establishes its identity. A DACL is a configurable list of access permissions that makes it possible to run authorization checks against a principal's token at runtime.

Network authentication is performed by plug-in modules known as SSPs. Kerberos and NTLM are SSPs that are used to provide authentication services for computers communicating within a private network. The authentication level determines how actively the authentication service does its job. You should authenticate and authorize as close to the client as possible, which means that you should avoid COM+ application designs that involve impersonation or delegation.

The COM+ security model is based on roles. Roles decouple access permissions from SIDs, which makes it easier to deploy a single application in multiple production environments. You can preconfigure declarative role-based authorization checks, and you can also write code to conduct conditional authorization checks and audit user activity.

If you're creating a Web-based application, you must learn how IIS integrates with COM security. IIS uses impersonation to avoid running client requests under the identity of the system. The user account that IIS impersonates is determined by the IIS authentication mode. Using certificate-based authentication and basic authentication are two common ways to map Internet users to Windows user accounts. It's not uncommon to run requests under the anonymous Internet user account (which is IUSR_*Machine* by default).

Once a client is authenticated, the access permissions you've configured determine what the client can do. If you want to use role-based security, you should use configured components installed in a library application or local server application. You should try your best to avoid the use of remote server applications. Conducting authorization checks on an application server a hop away from the Web server is expensive because it requires impersonation and possibly delegation. You should always prefer conducting authorization checks on the Web server itself.

Chapter 12

Designing Scalable Applications

Throughout this book, you've seen a lot of detail about COM and COM+. Because this is the final chapter of the book, this is my last opportunity to put everything in perspective. Knowing the details is important, but it's equally important to see how all the little pieces fit together. How do you take all the things you've learned in this book and deploy an application that scales to fit your needs? In this chapter, I'll present a few physical deployment models and consider their implications for scalability.

Another theme of this chapter is how to select the best protocol for the job at hand. As a COM+ developer, your arsenal includes DCOM, HTTP, and MSMQ. Each protocol has its share of strengths and weaknesses. You must understand each one's capabilities if you want to avoid painting yourself into a corner.

I'll also describe techniques for passing data across the network. Passing data from and to the server is an essential aspect of any distributed application. I'll conclude the chapter with a few words on miscellaneous issues such as passing updatable recordsets and caching data in the middle tier.

SCALABILITY REVISITED

You can define scalability in a number of ways. In one sense, scalability is a measure of how many users your application can handle at the same time. In another sense, scalability can be an indicator of whether your application can meet the availability requirements of a mission-critical business application. You can also define scalability as your application's ability to accommodate users who are outside the sanctity of your company's LAN or don't have an associated user account in your company's Windows 2000 domain. A Web developer might define scalability as an application's ability to reach every last user on the Internet. You have to decide which aspects of scalability are valuable and which should be requirements for your application.

How many users do you need to accommodate today? How many users do you expect your application to serve in the future? On average, how often does each user submit a request to the server? By answering these questions, you should be able to calculate roughly how much traffic you need to handle. If you need to handle hundreds or thousands of requests per second, you should be prepared to design an application that can accommodate this level of traffic.

You must also consider where your users are located. Can your application scale to accommodate users who are outside a closely administered LAN? Perhaps your application will be used by employees who are telecommuting via ISDN, DSL, or cable modem. Maybe you need to accommodate an employee who is on the Internet via an MSN dial-up connection in a hotel room on the other side of the planet. Perhaps your application will need to accommodate users from any location on the Internet.

Can your application reach users running a variety of different browsers and operating systems? Is your application flexible and reliable enough to accommodate a scenario in which your company's system administrator can't possibly configure the computers of your users? Scaling to reach every user on the Internet definitely involves tradeoffs in terms of what technologies you can use on client-side computers.

The point I'm trying to make is that the ultimate scalable application would be able to run transactions and retrieve data for millions of Internet users concurrently, and each user would be able run any operating system and require no customized configuration. That's a pretty tall order. However, the requirements for scaling your applications typically won't be this high. You should know the associated costs of the various aspects of scalability, and you can avoid paying for things you don't really need. That's why it's critical to determine your exact requirements for scalability as early in the design phase as possible.

Before you design a distributed application, you must decide how clients will communicate with your servers. Which underlying protocol will allow clients to submit their requests to the server—DCOM, HTTP, or MSMQ? Your choice will have a profound effect on your application's scalability.

In this book, we've examined the inner workings of DCOM, HTTP, and MSMQ. As you know, these protocols are the building blocks of a distributed application. Each protocol has its advantages and drawbacks. Let's take a look at how each of these protocols fits into the big picture of large-scale application design.

The Original Vision of COM

In the 1990s, COM became an important technology for building component-based applications. It was adopted by many product groups within Microsoft, so many Windows developers had no choice but to follow suit. As a result, just about every Windows developer now uses COM in one form or another.

Many developers, myself included, thought that DCOM was on its way to becoming one of the industry's dominant application protocols for client-to-server communication. We shared a vision that large-scale applications could be built using a physical model like the one shown in Figure 12-1.

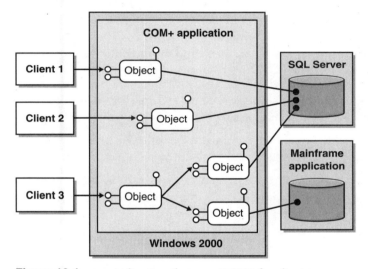

Figure 12-1. *An application that uses DCOM for client-to-server communication has trouble scaling beyond the LAN. DCOM also makes it hard or impossible to scale an application to accommodate thousands of users.*

COM offers location transparency by providing a transparent wire protocol (DCOM). As you know, this makes it relatively painless to establish a remote connection between a client computer and a server computer. In this sense, COM provides an inexpensive entry point into the world of distributed computing. This has led many people to conclude that DCOM is an obvious choice for building multitier applications.

As the 1990s came to a close, it became apparent that DCOM had too many limitations related to scaling a large application. For example, DCOM is far less able than HTTP to take advantage of load balancing products such as Microsoft's NLB and Cisco's LocalDirector. DCOM's connection-oriented nature makes it impossible to take advantage of request-based load balancing, thus limiting the number of concurrent users and preventing an application from achieving the highest possible levels of fault tolerance and availability.

The list of DCOM's shortcomings keeps growing. DCOM doesn't work well across firewalls, and its security model doesn't scale well on public networks such as the Internet. DCOM also requires a version of Windows on every client computer and a significant amount of custom configuration and administration on each client computer.

All these problems with DCOM boil down to one important fact: while DCOM works well for small to medium-size groups of users in a LAN environment, it becomes more problematic and unreliable as you add more clients or move them farther from the server.

At this point, I'm afraid I might be depressing you. After all, throughout this book I've endorsed COM as an essential technology and I've forced you to look at hundreds of pages of COM's low-level details. I'm not suddenly telling you not to use COM, but we need to take a step back and examine things on a higher level.

COM and COM+ provide four important things:

- The glue that allows you to assemble applications using components written in the language or languages of your choice.

- A value-added runtime environment that exposes system services through the use of context-based and attribute-based programming.

- The means with which to call between processes running on the same computer, such as when an ASP page executes a method on an object running in a COM+ server application.

- A wire protocol (DCOM) that allows you to communicate across computer boundaries.

You might decide that DCOM isn't usable in your application, but the first three aspects of COM and COM+ will still be valuable to you.

USING HTTP IN COM+ APPLICATIONS

As fate would have it, HTTP has emerged as the leading protocol for client-to-server communication. One key to this protocol's success has been that it's fairly simple to implement and is supported on every major platform. Its ubiquitous nature makes it valuable.

The phenomenon of the World Wide Web has had a profound effect on the way we build distributed applications. The industry as a whole has directed much of its recent attention to technologies related to Web servers and browsers. Companies are pouring millions of dollars into research and development to advance the capabilities of HTTP in many essential areas, such as load balancing and security.

Microsoft, like most other vendors, has recognized the strategic importance of HTTP. In fact, the architects of COM+ built their platform based on this assumption: An application must use HTTP for client-to-server communication to achieve the highest levels of scalability.

Figure 12-2 depicts a COM+ application with a scalable deployment architecture. Note that this application doesn't rely on DCOM. Instead, clients submit requests to IIS using HTTP. The Web farm plays a central role in this architecture because it allows a COM+ application to process hundreds of requests per second and to achieve higher levels of fault tolerance and availability.

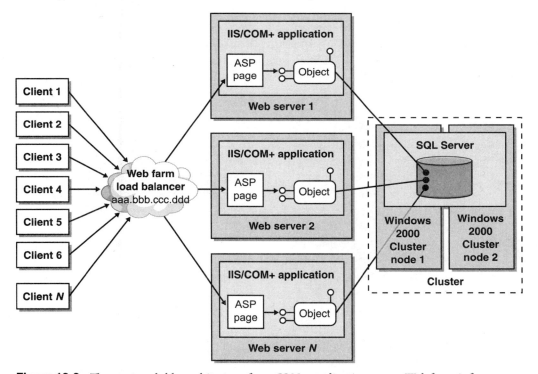

Figure 12-2. *The most scalable architecture for a COM+ application uses a Web farm infra-structure and request-based load balancing. This architecture forces you to use HTTP for client-to-server communication.*

This architecture provides the means to scale out. You can accommodate more clients by adding more mid-priced server computers to the Web farm. As I discussed in Chapter 9, a Web farm that uses request-based load balancing also provides higher levels of fault tolerance and availability. Chapter 9 also pointed out some important considerations when you design ASP pages and components for a Web farm environment that uses request-based load balancing. As you'll recall, many techniques involving ASP *Session* objects and other middle-tier caching techniques simply don't work. However, that's the price of admission when you want to create a large-scale application.

You can see from Figure 12-2 that the database server doesn't lend itself to scaling out in the same manner as the servers running IIS and COM+ applications. In most cases, the database server computer represents a single point of contention. This means that you must scale up the database server instead of scaling out. To accommodate a growing number of users, you must buy a more expensive multiprocessor computer that provides adequate processing cycles, memory, and hard disk space.

As you can see, Web servers can be scaled out but the database server can't. This should lead you to conclude that it's best to do as much of your processing on the Web server as possible. You should look for opportunities to offload work such as security-related authorization checks from the database server to Web servers in the farm.

The database server also represents a single point of failure. If the database server crashes, your application is dead in the water. You can address this vulnerability by using clustering technologies. Cluster Service in Windows 2000 is intended primarily to provide failover support for applications such as databases and messaging systems. Cluster Service allows several physical computers to assume the identity of a single computer. Each computer plays the role of a node, which can take over if another node fails. Cluster Service supports two-node failover clusters in Windows 2000 Advanced Server and four-node failover clusters in Windows 2000 Datacenter Server.

As I explained in Chapter 10, you can further address issues related to fault tolerance and availability through the use of messaging. Once an HTTP request arrives at the Web server, you can use either MSMQ or QC to capture the client's requests. This allows an application to remain operational when the database server is off line. Messaging can also help speed up response times when the database server has a large backlog of requests. You should also understand that MSMQ isn't limited to sending messages between different computers. You can always send MSMQ messages between two applications running on the same Web server computer. This approach is pretty straightforward and allows you to reap the benefits of asynchronous execution and exactly-once delivery.

Microsoft is expected to release a product named AppCenter Server in the second half of the year 2000. AppCenter Server is a suite of products designed for companies that are deploying and administering applications in a server farm environment. AppCenter Server will include new support for administering and monitoring NLB and Cluster Service and will include a third form of loading balancing through the Component Load Balancing (CLB) service.

CLB allows you to distribute a set of COM clients across a cluster of server computers. Each server computer in the cluster is typically configured with the same set of COM+ applications. CLB is based on a load-balancing algorithm that runs when a client activates a COM object. CLB is thus a session-based load balancing technique as opposed to a request-based load balancing technique.

In an application that uses CLB, all clients send activation requests to a central routing server. The routing server acts as an object broker by redirecting each activation request to one of the COM+ server computers in the cluster. The Component Services administrative tool already includes various configuration options for CLB because the COM+ team originally planned to ship CLB with the initial release of Windows 2000.

It's important to understand that CLB is based on DCOM and thus has the same limitations as DCOM. Therefore, CLB is most valuable when used in a LAN environment. In the grand scheme of things, the request-based load balancing provided by products such as NLB and Cisco's LocalDirector are far more valuable to a distributed application.

Separating HTTP from HTML

I'd like to review the requirements for scaling an application one more time in order to make a point. Here are some of the common requirements for a large-scale application:

- The application must be able to handle thousands or tens of thousands of users concurrently.

- The application must provide high levels of fault tolerance and availability.

- The client must be able to access the application through a firewall.

- The application must provide access to users across the Internet.

- The application must provide secured access to users who aren't closely affiliated with your company.

- Users can access the application without requiring a system administrator to configure their computers.

- The application must be accessible to users running on platforms other than Windows, such as Linux and Macintosh.

As you've seen, HTTP is vital to meeting all seven of these requirements. However, using HTML with HTTP isn't as critical. In fact, only the last requirement and, to a lesser extent, the requirement before that one actually force you to use HTML.

Ask yourself whether your application really requires the use of HTML. If you're creating an e-commerce site and you want to reach every last user on the Internet, the answer will be yes. If you're building a business application for your employees, suppliers, or customers, HTML will often be optional.

Nothing in the scalable deployment model shown in Figure 12-2 forces you to use HTML. If you can assume that your users will all run a 32-bit version of Windows, you have a few alternatives. For example, your application's presentation tier can be a traditional desktop application built using Visual Basic. You can thus leverage the Visual Basic forms designer (the tool you've grown to love so much over the last decade). The only new trick you have to learn is how to write the code in Visual Basic to submit an HTTP request to IIS. As you'll soon see, this isn't difficult.

You should also ask yourself whether you can build a better user interface using HTML or using Visual Basic. In my experience, HTML-based applications (even those built using DHTML and lots of client-side JavaScript) can't begin to match the elegance and ease-of-use of most Visual Basic applications. If you do elect to build your client applications with Visual Basic, will you really miss developing HTML-based interfaces for the browser? I know a lot of developers who most definitely won't.

Visual Basic makes it easy to create forms to capture and validate user input. Many developers have become accustomed to using grid and treeview controls and presenting the user with tabbed dialog boxes. These features are often beyond the capabilities of HTML and the browser. If you've been attempting to get around the limitations of HTML by downloading ActiveX controls to run in Microsoft Internet Explorer, you've already required your users to run a 32-bit version of Windows. You might as well take the next logical step and use Visual Basic to create the entire client application.

Think of the additional complications forced upon you by the browser. When it comes to managing client-side state, you must choose between cookies, query strings, and hidden forms. When you create a Visual Basic application to run on the user's desktop, managing state is much easier. What's more, it's easy to save an ADO recordset or an XML document to the user's hard disk. You don't have to worry about the security sandbox imposed by a Web browser.

I'm not saying that HTML and browser-based development are going away anytime soon. HTML is still one of the best ways to solve the problems of cross-platform development and eliminate client-side configuration issues. However, it's your job to realize when HTML is a requirement and when it's not.

I can't help but mention one other issue at this point, which is more political than technical. Let's say that you follow my advice and create a Web-based application using a desktop application built with Visual Basic. Someone in management or in your company's marketing department might accuse you of being behind the times. In a design meeting, someone might ask, "Why isn't the application Web-based?" You must convince the others that the application is Web-based. It's really all about HTTP and not so much about HTML and the browser. If you need to throw around a few buzzwords to prove your point, just tell them, "HTML was last year. This application is built from the ground up using XML." Maybe that'll get them off your back.

Executing Method Calls Using HTTP and XML

There are a few ways to submit an HTTP request from a client application created using Visual Basic. I'll present an example using Microsoft's XML parser because it provides one of the easiest and most flexible approaches. Version 2 of Microsoft's XML parser ships with Windows 2000, but Microsoft has been releasing new versions at fairly frequent intervals. You should use the most recent version, which you can download from *msdn.microsoft.com/xml/default.asp*.

Unfortunately, I can't teach you how to use XML in this book. But I will present a simple example to demonstrate what it takes to submit an XML-based HTTP request to IIS from a Visual Basic application. In this example, a client application submits an HTTP request to the Web server using a simple XML document to pass an input parameter. An ASP page retrieves this input parameter, executes the requested method, and returns output parameters to the client using another XML document.

The example is based on a configured component named *CCustomerManager*. Let's say that this configured component has been installed in a COM+ server application on a Web server computer. We'll execute one of the component's methods, *GetCustomer*, which has one input parameter and two output parameters. Here's what the method implementation looks like:

```
' Parameters are defined as Variants to accommodate ASP page.
Sub GetCustomer(ByVal Name, ByRef CreditLimit, ByRef AccountBalance)
    Dim conn As Connection, rs As Recordset
    Set conn = New Connection
    conn.Open sConnect
    Set rs = New Recordset
    rs.Open "SELECT CreditLimit, AccountBalance" & _
            " FROM Customers" & _
            " WHERE Customer='" & Name & "'", conn
    CreditLimit = rs("CreditLimit")
    AccountBalance = rs("AccountBalance")
    rs.Close
    Set rs = Nothing
    conn.Close
    Set conn = Nothing
End Sub
```

Since the *CCustomerManager* component has been installed in a COM+ server application, it's accessible to COM clients from across the network. However, we'd like to execute this method from a client application using HTTP as well. Let's start by adding an ASP page named GetCustomer.asp to the Web server with the following code:

```
<%@ Language=VBScript %>
<%
    Response.ContentType = "text/xml"
    set dom = Server.CreateObject("MSXML.DOMDocument")
```

(continued)

```
    set obj = Server.CreateObject("WebMarket.CCustomerManager")
    dom.load Request
    dim Name, CreditLimit, AccountBalance
    Name = dom.selectSingleNode("//Name").text
    obj.GetCustomer Name, CreditLimit, AccountBalance
%>

<Response>
    <CreditLimit><%=CreditLimit%></CreditLimit>
    <AccountBalance><%=AccountBalance%></AccountBalance>
</Response>
```

This ASP page includes a few interesting things. Obviously, the ASP page must create an instance of the *CCustomerManager* component in order to execute the *GetCustomer* method. However, before executing the method, the ASP page must retrieve the input parameter. This example assumes that the client has sent the input parameter in an XML document embedded in the body of the HTTP request.

The ASP page creates a *DOMDocument* object in order to deal with the incoming XML document. It populates this object by calling the *load* method and passing the ASP *Request* object. This technique works as long as the client has sent a well-formed XML document in the body of the request. (Note that this technique works with IIS 5 and Windows 2000 but not with IIS 4 and Windows NT Server.) Once the XML document has been loaded, the ASP page can extract the input parameter and execute the method. After executing *GetCustomer*, the ASP page prepares an XML response document to return to the client. Note that the ASP page explicitly sets the content type of the response to *"text/xml"* rather than the default, *"text/html"*.

In the final step, we submit an HTTP request to execute *GetCustomer* from a desktop application written with Visual Basic:

```
Const sURL = "http://localhost/MyApplication/"
' Create an XMLHTTPRequest object to issue the request.
Dim httpRequest As MSXML.XMLHTTPRequest
Set httpRequest = New MSXML.XMLHTTPRequest
' Prepare an XML document to pass the input parameter.
Dim Name As String, xmlRequest As String
Name = txtName.Text
xmlRequest = "<Request>" & _
                "<Name>" & Name & "</Name>" & _
            "</Request>"
' Open a connection to the Web server and send the request.
httpRequest.open "POST", sURL & "GetCustomer.asp", False
httpRequest.send xmlRequest
```

```
' Check for success/failure.
If httpRequest.status <> 200 Then
    ' Raise error when return status isn't 200.
    Err.Raise MyErrorCode, , "HTTP transport error: " & httpRequest.status & _
                        " - Description: " & httpRequest.statusText
End If
' Use a DOMDocument object to retrieve the method's output parameters.
Dim ResponseDoc As DOMDocument
Set ResponseDoc = httpRequest.responseXML
Dim CreditLimit As Currency, AccountBalance As Currency
CreditLimit = ResponseDoc.selectSingleNode("//CreditLimit").Text
AccountBalance = ResponseDoc.selectSingleNode("//AccountBalance").Text
```

Microsoft's XML parser provides an *XMLHTTPRequest* component that allows a client application to submit an HTTP request to the Web server. As you can see, the client application constructs a simple XML document that holds the method's input parameter. The client then invokes the *XMLHTTPRequest* object's *open* method followed by the *send* method to execute the code in the ASP page on the Web server.

Note that the third parameter of the *open* method indicates whether to submit the HTTP request asynchronously. Our example passes a value of *False* so that the call is conducted synchronously. The call to s*end* blocks until the Web server returns a response. After the call returns, the client application creates a *DOMDocument* object for extracting the output parameters from the response XML document.

I've presented this example to prove a point: a client application can use HTTP in the same way that it uses DCOM to communicate with a server computer. What's neat about this example is that you can create a client application that can go back and forth between using DCOM and using HTTP. In a LAN environment, DCOM might be preferable at times because it can provide faster response times with a heavyweight connection. But when you need the benefits of HTTP, that option is available as well.

You should observe that the technique of submitting requests via HTTP is available to non-Windows clients as well as to Windows clients. The only requirement is that the client knows how to use HTTP and XML. This opens up a world that DCOM can't tap into.

Also note that the technique of submitting XML-based HTTP requests programmatically is not limited to applications with a user interface. For example, imagine a scenario in which a COM+ application running on a public Web server is required to call a business object running on a different application server. The use of HTTP will be important if your company has placed a firewall between the public Web server and the application server for security reasons. The firewall makes it hard to make the call using DCOM. However, if the application server exposes the business object to clients using HTTP, the public Web server can execute methods on the business objects without any problems.

SOAP and Web Services

The example I just presented shows three important things about executing methods using HTTP:

- It allows you to expose COM+ applications using a highly scalable Web farm architecture.

- It allows you to integrate desktop applications built with Visual Basic.

- This approach is fairly grungy. It involves creating an ASP page for each method and explicitly preparing and parsing two XML documents in order to execute each method call. The code is fairly boilerplate in nature, but writing all those ASP pages and the required client-side code can get tedious.

Compared to DCOM, executing methods with HTTP in this fashion is particularly messy. DCOM hides the details of packing parameters into RPC messages and unpacking them on the other side. A client using DCOM simply invokes a method, and everything magically happens behind the scenes. So you might ask, "If they can make it so easy with DCOM and RPC, why can't they do the same for HTTP?"

Well, they can. In fact, many companies have been working hard to create a standard for executing method calls across HTTP. You've probably heard developers talking about Simple Object Access Protocol (SOAP). SOAP is a new specification whose goal is to standardize how clients execute methods across HTTP. It does this by defining a standard set of HTTP headers and an XML payload for transmitting method parameters and return values.

One of the most promising aspects of SOAP is that it provides a means of bridging heterogeneous systems. Keep in mind that SOAP is based entirely on HTTP and XML. Nothing about it ties you to the Windows platform on either the client side or the server side. This clearly isn't the case with DCOM.

For example, a Visual Basic client application can issue a SOAP request to a server computer running a UNIX operating system and an Apache Web server. The method's implementation can be written in Perl. Conversely, a non-Windows client application can submit a SOAP request to a server computer running IIS and Windows 2000 Server. The only requirement that SOAP imposes is that both the client and server must understand HTTP and XML.

One of the driving philosophies behind SOAP is to "invent no new technology." Most platforms already have functional Web servers and can communicate with HTTP. More and more platforms are picking up support for XML as well. SOAP tries to leverage the ubiquitous nature of HTTP and XML. It doesn't address issues such as load balancing and security because the underlying transport already takes care of them. SOAP simply extends HTTP by defining how clients prepare requests and how the server responds to them. At its most basic level, SOAP is like an interface in COM. It allows the client application and the Web server to agree on how to communicate.

SOAP is still in its early stages. The SOAP specification won't have much value until there are client-side and server-side implementations. You can obtain the SOAP specification and write these implementations yourself. (At the time of this writing the latest specification is available at *http://msdn.microsoft.com/xml/general/ soapspec-V1.asp.*) If you write a SOAP-based application by hand, your code will look a bit like the example I presented earlier. However, you'll have to add a considerable amount of code to deal with things such as propagating application-specific errors and properly packaging complex data structures.

However, the real potential behind SOAP is that it allows software companies such as Microsoft to add support to their development tools and to the underlying platform. This will benefit developers because, over time, Microsoft and other vendors will make executing a method call over HTTP as easy as using DCOM is today.

Microsoft has become very fond of the term *Web service,* which simply describes an application that exposes its functionality through SOAP-based HTTP requests. Creating such Web services that rely on client-side and server-side implementations of SOAP isn't a trivial task. Microsoft, like many other companies, must address complex issues such as parameter marshaling and error propagation so that SOAP works as smoothly as DCOM does today.

Microsoft is currently working on a suite of development tools and utilities for developers who want to integrate SOAP into their applications. These tools and utilities will be packaged in the Web Services SDK. (The name of this SDK might change before you read this.) I haven't been able to obtain a beta copy, so I can't give you any details about how this SDK will support SOAP. I also have no information about when the Web Services SDK will be available. By the time you read this, however, you'll probably be able to download the SDK from MSDN.

I can say with confidence that SOAP will be a big part of Microsoft's development strategy for the foreseeable future. The Web Services SDK is likely to go through several releases, each one extending the capabilities of the one before it. You can also expect future versions of COM+ and Visual Basic to have built-in support for SOAP. A day might come when you can simply adjust a declarative component attribute setting or change a property value at runtime to switch back and forth between using DCOM and HTTP.

APPLICATION DESIGN ISSUES

In this section, I'd like to talk about some important general design issues relating to multitier application development. I'll start by describing techniques for passing data using DCOM, MSMQ, and HTTP and then cover techniques for passing disconnected recordsets and caching data in the middle tier.

When it comes to passing data across the network, it should be obvious that round trips are your enemy. No matter what protocol you use, calls across the network are expensive and should be made only when necessary. It's almost always better to send lots of data in a single round trip than to use multiple round trips to accomplish the same thing.

It's also important that you appreciate the different data-passing mechanisms of DCOM, MSMQ, and HTTP. The parameters of COM method calls are often strongly typed. As you saw in Chapter 3, strongly typed parameters allow the universal marshaler to optimize the way it moves data across the network. When you pass data using MSMQ or HTTP, your data is much more loosely typed. The underlying MSMQ transport sees the body of an MSMQ message as a single, typeless payload. Likewise, the underlying HTTP transport sees the body of an HTTP request as a single, typeless payload. This makes passing data with MSMQ and HTTP fundamentally different from passing data with DCOM.

If you're accustomed to COM and strongly typed interfaces, communicating across application boundaries using MSMQ and HTTP will require a new perspective. You can't communicate the semantics of your data using method signatures; you must use other techniques. This restriction makes such things as documentation and self-describing data structures all the more important. When you pass data with a loosely typed transport, ADO recordsets and XML schemas can be valuable because they have metadata that describes the payload that's being moved between applications. Keep in mind that a transport that works with loosely typed data doesn't require you to install and configure application-specific type libraries.

Passing Data Using COM

One of the best things about COM is that it hides the details of interprocess communication. The code you write for an in-process object automatically works for an out-of-process object. You don't have to change anything in your Visual Basic class module. The client-side code that you write doesn't care whether the object is close by or far away.

As you know, COM is much easier to use than HTTP or MSMQ when it comes to passing data across process and computer boundaries. As you saw in Chapter 10, QC tries to make MSMQ as simple as COM, but MSMQ still has certain limitations and inflexibilities that make COM method calls more versatile.

Throughout this book, I've argued that DCOM is unusable in many situations. But there are still times when you can (and should) rely on COM's proxy/stub architecture—for example, when you need to make a synchronous call between two processes on the same machine. COM is not only easier to use than MSMQ and HTTP, in quite a few cases it also yields better performance.

You might encounter a situation in which you want server computers to communicate with one another using DCOM in a high-speed LAN environment. For example, in an application that uses request-based load balancing, you can use a COM+ server application running on a dedicated server computer to share session state across a farm of Web server computers.

As you can see, sometimes it's beneficial to pass data using COM. When you design a component that will be accessed from another process, you should be sure that it exposes methods that are designed to move data as efficiently as possible. Let's look at some practical considerations for designing methods that will be executed across a proxy/stub layer.

COM makes it trivial to move data based on primitive VBA types such as Integer, Double, and String. You simply create method signatures using these types to define your parameters and return values. It's also relatively easy to pass more complex data types such as arrays, UDTs, and Variants. You can also get tricky by passing arrays of UDTs or arrays nested within other arrays. The universal marshaler is your friend. It's happy to handle the details of packaging the data and shipping it to the other side.

When you're designing the interfaces for your component, you should be cautious about passing object references. Neither Visual Basic nor the universal marshaler supports moving an object across COM's proxy/stub architecture by value. This means that you can pass a Visual Basic object only by reference, not by value.

When you declare an object parameter using *ByVal*, the reference is marshaled from the client process to the process of the method being called. When you declare an object parameter using *ByRef*, the reference is marshaled in both directions. However, the COM object (and all the precious data in it) never leaves the process in which it was created.

When you pass a Visual Basic object reference across process or computer boundaries, the object doesn't actually move. The only thing that passes to the other side is a COM-savvy pointer that lets the recipient establish a connection back to the object being referenced. When the recipient wants to access a property or a method through the object reference, it must travel back across another proxy/stub pair to where the object lives. This type of marshaling is called *standard marshaling*. You should see that passing object references with standard marshaling is a bad thing when it results in excessive network round trips.

COM provides pass-by-value semantics for a special category of objects. In order to pass an object by value, the object must implement a standard COM interface named *IMarshal*. Such an object is said to provide *custom marshaling*. The benefit of using this type of object is that you can pass its data as payload across process and computer boundaries in simple COM method calls.

Objects that provide custom marshaling have a couple of notable requirements. They must be written in C++, not Visual Basic, and they must be installed and run as nonconfigured components.

Passing ADO recordsets using COM

To most Visual Basic programmers, the ADO *Recordset* object is the most common example of a component that implements custom marshaling. You can pass ADO recordsets across process and computer boundaries in COM method calls using either parameters or method return values. When you pass an ADO recordset by value, you must use a client-side static cursor. You must also disconnect the recordset by setting its *ActiveConnection* property to *Nothing*.

Here's an example. The *GetCustomerTable* method of the *CCustomerManager* component uses its return value to pass a disconnected recordset back to the caller:

```
Function GetCustomerTable() As Recordset
    Dim conn As Connection, rs As Recordset
    Set conn = New Connection
    conn.Open sConnect
    Set rs = New Recordset
    rs.CursorLocation = adUseClient
    rs.CursorType = adOpenStatic
    rs.LockType = adLockReadOnly
    Set rs.ActiveConnection = conn
    rs.Open "SELECT Customer, CreditLimit, AccountBalance" & _
            " FROM Customers"
    Set rs.ActiveConnection = Nothing
    conn.Close
    Set conn = Nothing
    Set GetCustomerTable = rs
End Function
```

After you expose this method in the *CCustomerManager* component, writing the client-side code to marshal the recordset from one process to another is simple:

```
Dim CustomerManager As CCustomerManager
Set CustomerManager = New CCustomerManager
Dim rs As Recordset
Set rs = CustomerManager.GetCustomerTable()
' Recordset object in now available in client process.
```

Passing an ADO recordset in this manner is an effective way to move small, medium, or large sets of data across process and computer boundaries. Once a recordset has been marshaled into the recipient's process, the data is close at hand and can be accessed quickly. Moreover, an ADO recordset carries additional metadata that describes its contents (such as the names and data types of its columns). I'll revisit this topic and describe a few more high-level design issues about passing ADO recordsets around the network later in the chapter.

Passing Data Using MSMQ and QC

As you saw in Chapter 10, MSMQ and QC let you reap the benefits of asynchronous or disconnected communication. It's a nice way to send requests and notifications between applications. Note that, like DCOM, MSMQ has trouble going through firewalls and can be tricky to configure for Internet clients. However, it can still be used in some situations for client-to-server communication. Moreover, both MSMQ and QC are very valuable for server-to-server communication.

The application that sends the message packs the message body. It's often desirable to transmit a set of request-specific parameters, so during the design phase you should consider how to pack data into the body of an MSMQ message. On the receiving side, you must be able to unpack these parameters before you process the request. In Chapter 10, I talked about sending and receiving messages, but my examples passed only a simple VBA string in the message body. Now let's look at some techniques for passing messages that hold more complex data structures.

The body of an MSMQ message is a Variant that's stored and transmitted as a Byte array. You can read and write the usual VBA data types (such as Boolean, Byte, Integer, Long, Single, Double, Currency, Date, and String) by using the message body. MSMQ tracks the type you use in the message header. This makes it quite easy to store a single value in a message body. But it doesn't solve the problem of packing several pieces of data at once. To pack several pieces of data into a message, you must understand how to use the Byte array behind the message body.

Using an array behind the message body can be tricky because you can use only an array of Bytes. If you assign another type of array to the message body, MSMQ automatically converts it to a Byte array. Unfortunately, once your data has been converted to a Byte array, there's no easy way to convert it back to the original array type on the receiving side. This means that a simple technique such as sending your parameters in a String array won't work.

QC also has an unfortunate limitation when it comes to passing arrays. Visual Basic doesn't allow you to define array parameters using *ByVal*; you must use *ByRef*. However, using *ByRef* in a method signature prevents the entire interface from being queueable. This means that the methods of a queued component can't use parameters or return values to move arrays.

Despite QC's limitations with arrays, a queued component generally makes it much easier to pass data than direct MSMQ programming does. You simply define *ByVal* parameters in your method signatures, and the QC runtime packs all the data into an MSMQ message for you. Also remember that a client application can call the same method multiple times on a recorder object. This can produce the same results as passing an array across the network.

The technique of pairing names and values in strings is popular with MSMQ programmers. This approach allows you to pack parameterized information into the message body using a single string value. But in this scenario the sending party is responsible for constructing the string and the receiving party is responsible for extracting the name/value pairs by parsing the string on the other side.

A string that contains name/value pairs is an example of loosely typed data. Both the sender and the receiver have to agree on the format of the string ahead of time. If you decide to go down this road, the use of XML schemas and an XML parser on each side can make the loosely typed nature of the MSMQ body far more manageable.

Packing a message body using a *PropertyBag* object

PropertyBag objects are useful because they can automate most of the tedious work of packing your parameterized information into a message body and unpacking it later. A *PropertyBag* object allows you to work in terms of name/value pairs. You read named properties from and write named properties to the *PropertyBag* object, and the object takes care of serializing your data in an internal Byte array.

Each *PropertyBag* object has a *Contents* property, which represents its internal Byte array. You can write named values into this Byte array using the *WriteProperty* method. Once you write all your parameters into a *PropertyBag* object, you can use the *Contents* property to serialize the Byte array into the message body, as shown here:

```
Dim msg As MSMQMessage
Set msg = New MSMQMessage
Dim PropBag As PropertyBag
Set PropBag  = New PropertyBag
PropBag.WriteProperty "Customer", "Bob"
PropBag.WriteProperty "Product", "MohairSuit"
PropBag.WriteProperty "Quantity", 4
msg.Body = PropBag.Contents
msg.Send q
```

The *PropertyBag* object writes your named values into a stream of bytes using its own proprietary algorithm. Once you pack up a Byte array in the sender application, you need a second *PropertyBag* object on the receiving side to unpack it. You can unpack the message by loading the Byte array into a new *PropertyBag* object and calling the *ReadProperty* method:

```
Dim msg As MSMQMessage
Set msg = q.Receive()
Dim PropBag As PropertyBag
Set PropBag = New PropertyBag
PropBag.Contents = msg.Body
Dim Customer As String, Product As String, Quantity As Long
Customer = PropBag.ReadProperty("Customer")
Product = PropBag.ReadProperty("Product")
Quantity = PropBag.ReadProperty("Quantity")
```

As you can see, the *PropertyBag* object makes your life much easier because it packs and unpacks your parameters for you. You can use this technique in other places as well. For example, you can define a Byte array parameter for a standard COM method and pass name value pairs between a client and a COM object. You can also use *PropertyBag* objects to store persistent name/value pairs in ASP *Application* variables and ASP *Session* variables.

Using persistable objects

Another technique for passing parameterized information using MSMQ or QC uses persistable objects. These are objects whose data can be stored and transmitted in the body of an MSMQ message. However, MSMQ can store objects in a message body only if they implement one of two standard COM interfaces: *IPersistStream* or *IPersistStorage*.

The interface definitions for *IPersistStream* and *IPersistStorage* contain parameters that are incompatible with Visual Basic. You can't implement these interfaces in a straightforward manner using the *Implements* keyword. Fortunately, Visual Basic 6 has added support for persistable classes. When you create a persistable class, Visual Basic automatically implements *IPersistStream* behind the scenes. When you work with persistable classes, you can read objects from and write objects directly to the message body. You can also create queued components that pass persistable objects as parameters. In the case of MSMQ or QC, the data associated with a persistable object is written into the body of an MSMQ message and a clone object is created on the other side when the receiving application retrieves the message.

Every public class in an ActiveX DLL or ActiveX EXE project has a *Persistable* property. You must set this property to *Persistable* at design time to make a persistent class. When you make a class persistent, the Visual Basic IDE lets you add a *ReadProperties* method and a *WriteProperties* method to the class module. You can add the skeletons for these two methods using the wizard bar (which consists of two combo boxes at the top of the class module window in the Visual Basic IDE). You can also add the *InitProperties* method, although it isn't required when you use MSMQ or QC.

You can use the *ReadProperties* and *WriteProperties* methods to read properties from and write properties to an internal *PropertyBag* object. Visual Basic creates this object for you behind the scenes and uses it to implement *IPersistStream*. Remember that your object must implement *IPersistStream* in order for MSMQ to write the object's data to a message body. When MSMQ calls the methods in the *IPersistStream* interface, Visual Basic simply forwards these calls to your implementations of *ReadProperties* and *WriteProperties*.

Using persistable classes with MSMQ is a lot easier than it sounds. For example, you can create a new persistable class and add the properties you want to pack into the message body. Next, you provide implementations of *ReadProperties* and

WriteProperties. Here's an example of a persistable Visual Basic class module that models a sales order request:

```
' COrderRequest: a persistable class
Public Customer As String
Public Product As String
Public Quantity As Long

Private Sub Class_ReacProperties(PropBag As PropertyBag)
    Customer = PropBag.ReadProperty("Customer", "")
    Product = PropBag.ReadProperty("Product", "")
    Quantity = PropBag.ReadProperty("Quantity", "")
End Sub

Private Sub Class_WriteProperties(PropBag As PropertyBag)
    PropBag.WriteProperty "Customer", Customer
    PropBag.WriteProperty "Product", Product
    PropBag.WriteProperty "Quantity", Quantity
End Sub
```

As you can see, there isn't much to creating a persistable class. Once you have a persistable class like the one shown above, you can use it to pack a message body like this:

```
Dim msg As MSMQMessage
Set msg = New MSMQMessage
' Create and prepare order request object.
Dim Order As COrderRequest
Set Order = New COrderRequest
Order.Customer = txtCustomer.Text
Order.Product = txtProduct.Text
Order.Quantity = txtQuantity.Text
' Assign the object to the message body.
msg.Body = Order ' WriteProperties is called.
msg.Send q
```

When you assign an object to the message body, MSMQ performs a *Query-Interface* on the object to see whether it supports *IPersistStream* or *IPersistStorage*. Since your object supports *IPersistStream*, MSMQ knows that it can call a method on this interface named *Save*. When MSMQ calls *Save*, Visual Basic forwards the call to your implementation of *WriteProperties*. This gives you an opportunity to write your named property values into the *PropertyBag* object, and they're automatically copied into the message body as an array of Bytes.

In the receiver application, you can easily rehydrate a persistent object from a message body by creating a new reference and assigning the message body to it:

```
Dim msg As MSMQMessage
Set msg = q.Receive(ReceiveTimeOut:=0)
Dim Order As COrderRequest
```

```
Set Order = msg.Body ' ReadProperties is called.
Dim Customer As String, Product As String, Quantity As Long
Customer = Order.Customer
Product = Order.Product
Quantity = Order.Quantity
```

When you assign a message body to a reference using the *Set* keyword, MSMQ creates a new instance of the object and calls the *Load* method of *IPersistStream*. Visual Basic forwards this call to your implementation of *ReadProperties*. Once again, you use the *PropertyBag* object passed as a parameter to extract your data.

QC makes passing persistable objects even easier because you aren't required to explicitly receive the message. If you pass a persistable object to a method of a queued component, the QC runtime automatically creates the cloned object before your method begins to execute.

One thing to keep in mind when you use this technique is that you must install and configure the DLL that holds the persistable class on both the sender's computer and the receiver's computer. This is required because the MSMQ runtime must re-create a local copy of the object on both computers in order for this scheme to work. Note that this configuration issue can make the use of persistable classes less desirable than some of the other techniques presented in this chapter.

Passing ADO recordsets using MSMQ

It turns out that you can also pass an ADO recordset in the body of an MSMQ message. An ADO recordset component, like a persistable class, implements *IPersistStream*, so you can simply assign an ADO recordset to a message body and MSMQ and ADO will work together to pack all the data associated with the recordset into the message body. You can also define a method in a queued component using a recordset parameter as long as you mark the parameter with the *ByVal* keyword.

As in the case of passing recordsets in a COM method call, this technique works only if you're using an ADO recordset with a client-side static cursor. This technique is powerful and also extremely easy to use. Look at the following code:

```
Dim conn As Connection
Set conn = New Connection
conn.Open sConnect
Dim rs As Recordset
Set rs = New Recordset
rs.CursorLocation = adUseClient
rs.CursorType = adOpenStatic
rs.LockType = adLockReadOnly
rs.Open "SELECT Customer, CreditLimit, AccountBalance" & _
        " FROM Customers", conn
' Pack recordset into a new message.
Dim msg As MSMQMessage
Set msg = New MSMQMessage
```

(continued)

```
msg.Body = rs
' Send message to queue.
msg.Send ResponseQueue
ResponseQueue.Close
rs.Close
Set rs = Nothing
conn.Close
Set conn = Nothing
```

On the receiving side, you can harvest the recordset from the message body just as easily. Here's an example of a client application that rehydrates a recordset and binds it to a data-aware grid control:

```
Dim msg As MSMQMessage
Set msg = q.Receive()
Dim rs As Recordset
Set rs = msg.Body
' Bind recordset to grid.
Set grdDisplay.DataSource = rs
```

Think of the design possibilities that open up when you use this approach. For example, say you're designing an application for a remote sales force. When users are connected to the network, you can download the most recent customer list to local queues on their laptop computers. Later, when users are disconnected, they can continue to add new sales orders and update customer information. Behind the scenes, you can track all of these inserts and updates in local ADO recordsets. When a user reconnects to the network, these recordsets can be transparently forwarded to a listener application that adds the new orders and posts customer updates to the database.

Passing Data Using HTTP

Using Visual Basic and Microsoft's XML parser, you can easily write code to transmit an XML document in an HTTP request. You saw a few examples of this earlier in the chapter. After all, an XML document is just a string. The challenging part is deciding what to put in it. Designing the XML schemas on which an XML document is based is a critical undertaking.

Over the next few years, XML will become more popular as a means of passing data across application, organization, and vendor boundaries, and it will create more opportunities for companies to exchange information with one another electronically. Placing an electronic order with a supplier is an obvious example, but ways to apply XML can go far beyond that. XML allows you to integrate COM+ applications with heterogeneous applications built using Corba and Enterprise JavaBeans.

XML is too important for you to ignore. If you haven't already learned about this technology, you should definitely get started and get comfortable using Microsoft's XML parser. The more you know about XML, the better. Also keep in mind that while it's highly fashionable to transmit XML documents using HTTP, you can just as easily pass them around using COM and MSMQ.

Passing ADO/XML recordsets using HTTP

You should look for opportunities to take advantage of the powerful integration of Microsoft's XML parser and ADO 2.5, which allows you to easily pass ADO recordsets from the Web server back to a client application in an HTTP response. As you'll see, you can also post an updated recordset from a client application back to the Web server in an HTTP request.

Let's look at an example. Here's an implementation of the *GetCustomerTable* method of the *CCustomerManager* component:

```
Function GetCustomerTable() As Recordset
    Dim conn As Connection, rs As Recordset
    Set conn = New Connection
    conn.Open sConnect
    Set rs = New Recordset
    rs.CursorLocation = adUseClient
    rs.CursorType = adOpenStatic
    rs.LockType = adLockBatchOptimistic
    Set rs.ActiveConnection = conn
    rs.Open "SELECT Customer, CreditLimit, AccountBalance" & _
            " FROM Customers"
    Set rs.ActiveConnection = Nothing
    conn.Close
    Set conn = Nothing
    Set GetCustomerTable = rs
End Function
```

This implementation of the *GetCustomerTable* method is similar to one shown earlier. The only difference is that this implementation assigns the recordset's *LockType* property a value of *adLockBatchOptimistic*, which allows you to update the disconnected recordset in the client application.

Now let's look at an ASP page that allows a Visual Basic client application to call the *GetCustomerTable* method and retrieve the recordset using HTTP:

```
<%@ Language=VBScript %>
<%
    Response.ContentType = "text/xml"
    set obj = Server.CreateObject("WEBMARKET.CCustomerManager")
    set rs = obj.GetCustomerTable()
    rs.Save Response, 1
%>
```

The ASP page calls the *CCustomerManager* object to retrieve the recordset object. It then serializes the recordset into the body of the HTTP response by calling the *Save* method and passing the ASP *Response* object as the first parameter.

Let me provide a little background for what's going on behind the scenes. As its first parameter, the *Save* method of an ADO recordset can accept any object that implements the *IStream* interface. Things work nicely with IIS 5 because the ASP *Response* object implements *IStream*. In other words, the ASP *Response* object gives the ADO recordset object a place in which to write a serialized stream of data. When the ASP page calls *Save*, the ADO runtime serializes the recordset's data and writes it into the HTTP response.

Note that the ASP page passes a value of 1 as the second parameter to the *Save* method. This value tells the ADO runtime to serialize the recordset using ADO's XML format. In a Visual Basic application that references the ADO type library, it's better to pass the constant *adPersistXML* instead of the hard-coded value 1.

Now look at the code in the client application that retrieves the recordset from the Web server:

```
Const sURL = "http://localhost/MyApplication/"
Dim rs As Recordset
Set rs = New Recordset
rs.Open sURL & "GetCustomerTable.asp"
' Now access the recordset programmatically
' or bind the recordset to a data-aware grid.
```

It's amazing how little code is required when you're using ADO 2.5. The *Open* method of an ADO recordset object accepts the URL of any ASP page that can send back a recordset serialized as an XML document. You don't even have to write any code that uses the XML parser.

After the client retrieves the recordset, the sky's the limit. You can bind the recordset to a grid, and you can perform sort, filter, and find operations. If the recordset was created with a *LockType* setting of *adLockBatchOptimistic*, you can update the recordset in the client application and send it back to the Web server to post the user's changes to the database.

Let's look at an example that sends an updated recordset back to the Web server. The code is slightly more complicated than the last example because you have to use a *DOMDocument* object.

```
Const sURL = "http://localhost/MyApplication/"
Dim rs As Recordset
' Use the recordset object from a grid control.
Set rs = grdCustomers.DataSource
Dim RequestDoc As MSXML.DOMDocument
Set RequestDoc = New MSXML.DOMDocument
rs.Save RequestDoc, adPersistXML
Dim httpRequest As MSXML.XMLHTTPRequest
Set httpRequest = New MSXML.XMLHTTPRequest
httpRequest.Open "POST", sURL & "PostCustomerTable.asp", False
```

```
httpRequest.send RequestDoc
' Check for success/failure.
If httpRequest.Status <> 200 Then
    ' Raise error when return status isn't 200.
    Err.Raise MyErrorCode, , "HTTP transport error: " & httpRequest.Status & _
                            " - Description: " & httpRequest.statusText
End If
```

The tricky part of sending the recordset back to the Web server is serializing it into an XML document. The technique used in this example relies on a call to the recordset's *Save* method. The client application passes a *DOMDocument* object as the first parameter. The *DOMDocument* object, like the ASP *Response* object, implements the *IStream* interface. This means that the ADO runtime can write serialized XML data to the *DOMDocument* object. The *DOMDocument* object can then be passed as a parameter to the *Send* method of the *XMLHTTPRequest* object. That's all that's required to send an XML document holding the data for the updated recordset back to the Web server.

Now let's look at the code in the ASP page that handles this incoming request on the Web server:

```
<%@ Language=VBScript %>
<%
    dim rs
    set rs = Server.CreateObject("ADODB.Recordset")
    rs.Open Request
    set obj = Server.CreateObject("WEBMARKET.CCustomerManager")
    obj.PostCustomerTable rs
%>
```

The ASP page creates a new recordset object and loads it with the XML data from the ASP *Request* object. This works because the ASP *Request* object in IIS 5 also implements *IStream*. The ASP page then creates an instance of *CCustomerManager* and calls the *PostCustomerTable* method, passing the recordset. The final link in the chain is the implementation of the *PostCustomerTable* method of the *CCustomerManager* component:

```
Sub PostCustomerTable(ByVal rs As Recordset)
    Dim conn As Connection
    Set conn = New Connection
    conn.Open sConnect
    Set rs.ActiveConnection = conn
    rs.UpdateBatch
    Set rs.ActiveConnection = Nothing
    conn.Close
    Set conn = Nothing
End Sub
```

The implementation of *PostCustomerTable* establishes a connection to the database and then associates the incoming recordset with this connection. After the recordset has been associated with an active connection, this method implementation executes the *UpdateBatch* method. The ADO runtime then works with your OLE-DB provider to create and submit the required INSERT, UPDATE, and DELETE statements. As you can see, updatable recordsets can save you lots of programming effort because all the required SQL statements are generated and submitted behind the scenes.

Read-Only Recordsets vs. Updatable Recordsets

The practice of passing ADO recordsets around the network has always been somewhat controversial. Some purists feel that passing a disconnected recordset to a client application violates the spirit of the three-tier model. They believe that data access code and database schema information should be hidden away in the middle tier. But others argue that the practical benefits outweigh the theoretical disadvantages.

Passing ADO recordsets to a client application is beneficial for several reasons. Once you download a recordset to a user's desktop computer, you can leverage ADO's client-side cursor engine to perform sort, filter, and find operations to your heart's content. You can bind recordset objects to data-aware controls. I know you're never supposed to admit to other Visual Basic programmers that you use bound controls, but you'll have to agree that they're pretty handy at times.

Passing recordsets to the client yields a few key benefits in terms of scalability. First, the client doesn't have to submit a request to the Web server (which must call to the database server) to perform sort, filter, or find operations. The ADO client-side cursor engine performs these operations locally, making the client application very responsive. Second, client applications submit few requests to server computers, which means that network traffic is reduced. Third, you can offload work to desktop computers, thus saving valuable processing cycles on the database server computer.

It's important to understand the distinction between read-only recordsets and updatable recordsets. Working with read-only recordsets is usually far less complicated. The use of updatable recordsets requires attention to concurrency and optimistic locking. It also requires extra contingency code to deal with runtime errors caused by update conflicts.

When you call *UpdateBatch* to post an updated recordset back to the database, you'd better be prepared to act when things don't go as expected. Many programmers avoid updatable recordsets because they believe that they create more problems than they solve. Other programmers find that updatable recordsets are useful, but only in certain situations. You need to determine when they're useful and when they're not.

If you use updatable recordsets, you should understand how ADO uses optimistic locking to deal with update conflicts. When a client application modifies rows in a disconnected recordset, the changes are cached in memory. However, ADO maintains a copy of the original row values as well as the new row values. Both values are transmitted when the recordset is sent back to the Web server. When the middle-tier component finally calls the *UpdateBatch* method to write the changes back to the database, ADO does some extra work to detect whether any updates have been made by other users since the recordset was copied from the database.

ADO detects update conflicts by adding WHERE clauses to its INSERT, UPDATE, and DELETE statements. This allows ADO to determine whether it's updating each row in its original form. ADO inspects the rows affected value on a statement-by-statement basis to ensure that each update has been made successfully. If ADO sees that an UPDATE statement has affected no rows, it determines that another user has modified the record. This update conflict causes ADO to raise a runtime error in the call to *UpdateBatch*.

The hard part about using updatable recordsets is handling partial failures. What if a client posts an updated recordset with 20 changes but 3 of these changes can't be written due to conflicts? Should you roll back the other 17 updates? This can be a difficult question to answer because a lot depends on the application. The bottom line is that the ADO optimistic concurrency mechanism is generic, but your contingency code must be customized to fit your needs. In some cases, you'll be required to implement a fairly complex conflict resolution scheme. This could involve sending a recordset of records that couldn't be written due to conflicts back to the client.

When you consider whether to use updatable recordsets, you must look at the data in question and determine the probability of conflict. Sometimes updatable recordsets have little or no chance of conflict—for example, if you're passing a customer recordset that represents all accounts from a specific salesperson's territory. If no other salesperson needs to update the same set of records, you can assume that conflicts are unlikely. However, if you need to pass the same customer recordset to many different users, the chances of conflict are much higher and updatable recordsets will be much tougher to use.

Let's say that your application requires a more sophisticated locking and concurrency scheme. Perhaps you want an application design where a user can retrieve a customer record for editing and lock out other users for a specific period of time. If you assume that the average user should get five minutes of "think time" to work with the record once it's been retrieved, you need to somehow lock the record to prevent others from updating it.

The first thing to note is that the optimistic locking scheme that ADO provides for client-side cursors won't give you what you want. Disconnected recordsets never leave locks on the database. Their only contribution to avoiding conflicts is that they check to determine when update conflicts have occurred. However, in our example we need a lock on the database to prevent others from updating the record.

Using a server-side cursor and pessimistic locking isn't a good solution either. Pessimistic locks should be held only for short periods—typically, the time it takes to run a transaction. One problem with a server-side pessimistic lock is that it requires you to keep a recordset object alive with an established connection. That doesn't work well in the middle tier. The second problem has to do with fault tolerance. If the client application crashes or the user falls asleep at the wheel after obtaining a pessimistic lock, the lock might be held for a long, long time.

The solution to this problem is to write a custom locking scheme. When you want users to be able to obtain a logical lock on a record, it's usually a good idea to use a timeout interval to give users a certain window of time in which to make and submit changes.

A custom locking scheme usually requires you to add extra fields to your database tables. Each table that will support the scheme needs extra columns for information about the lock owner and when the lock was acquired. Then you must add code to assign an owner and update the time that the lock was acquired.

When a user attempts to retrieve and edit a record, your code must determine whether the record is currently locked by another user. Your code must examine the last lock time and see if an existing lock has exceeded the timeout interval. If another user owns a lock, you can raise an error back to the user. However, if no lock is currently being held, you can update the lock owner and lock time information in the record before returning the record to a user for the preconfigured editing period.

As you can see, the automatic locking provided by ADO and OLE-DB can't accommodate sophisticated concurrency policies. You often need a custom scheme like the one I've just presented, which involves extra work in the design and implementation phases.

Caching Data in the Middle Tier

There are two primary reasons to cache data on the Web server—to improve response times (because it eliminates round trips to the database server) and to conserve processing cycles on the database server.

I'm going to jump right in and show you how to convert an ADO recordset to a string in the middle tier. This technique allows you to cache an ADO/XML recordset in an ASP *Application* variable or in a shared property using the SPM. ADO 2.5 has introduced the *Stream* object, which makes things pretty easy. Look at the following code:

```
Dim conn As Connection
Set conn = New Connection
```

```
conn.Open sConnect
Dim rs As Recordset
Set rs = New Recordset
rs.CursorLocation = adUseClient
rs.CursorType = adOpenStatic
rs.LockType = adLockReadOnly
Set rs.ActiveConnection = conn
rs.Open "SELECT Customer, CreditLimit, AccountBalance" & _
        " FROM Customers"
Set rs.ActiveConnection = Nothing
conn.Close
Set conn = Nothing
' Write recordset data into string variable using XML format.
Dim strm As Stream, MyXML As String
Set strm = New Stream
rs.Save strm, adPersistXML
MyXML = strm.ReadText
rs.Close
Set rs = Nothing
' Now cache MyXML in an ASP Application variable.
```

As I mentioned, the *Stream* object is new to ADO 2.5. In earlier versions of ADO, you could store persistent recordsets in disk files, but not in memory, because you didn't have any way to write the data associated with a recordset to a variable. The *Stream* object in ADO 2.5 makes this task trivial.

Once you write the XML data to an ASP *Application* variable or a shared property in the SPM, you can reuse it in future requests. You can use this data to load an ADO recordset object or a *DOMDocument* object. You can also manipulate the XML data on the Web server, pass it back to the client in an HTTP response, or both.

Note that you should avoid placing ADO Recordset objects and ADO Stream objects in either ASP *Application* variables or shared properties in the SPM. They have threading characteristics that make this practice very undesirable. You're always safe to store XML text in these middle-tier variables because this data is just a string. One other option that you have is to load read-only XML data into a *DOMFreeThreaded-Document* object. This object has sophisticated threading capabilities, which makes it acceptable to store the object in an ASP *Application* variable or a shared property in the SPM. This technique can conserve processing cycles because you don't need to reload XML data into a *DOMDocument* object on a per-request basis.

In some applications, it's also valuable to perform Extensible Stylesheet Language (XSL) transforms on the Web server—especially if you're supporting down-level browsers that can't make any sense of XML. These clients require formatted HTML tables. You can cache the XML data that represents the input to the XSL transform. You can also cache the resulting HTML table that's generated by the XSL transform. If many clients want the same view of a table, you don't have to keep reprocessing the same task. You can do the work once and leverage the results across many requests. The tradeoff is that you might require lots of memory on the Web server. However, memory is often much easier and cheaper to obtain than processing cycles.

When you cache data in the middle tier, you have to make some assumptions about how often the data will need to be refreshed. Some data changes so often that it can't be cached for any reasonable period of time. Other data remains static for days or months at a time. Still other types of data, possibly from a data warehouse, are historic and can be considered read-only. Once you make assumptions about the nature of your data, you must then decide how often it needs to be refreshed. Static data lends itself much more easily to caching techniques.

In Chapter 9, I described some of the issues involved with refreshing cached data at regular intervals. While some aspects of refreshing data aren't complicated, designing a caching coherency scheme for a Web farm environment can be very complicated, especially for applications that must maintain session state for users who are constantly redirected across a set of different servers in a Web farm. In many cases, the easiest approach is to simply write session state out to a database.

SUMMARY

I'd like you to take away a few important points from this chapter. First, scalability comes in many forms. While most applications require several forms of scalability, a given application usually does not require all of them. It's up to you to define your application requirements early on so you know what's important and what's not.

I also described in this chapter the critical roles HTTP and the Web farm architecture play in scaling a COM+ application. This means that most applications should base all client-to-server communication on HTTP rather than DCOM. Remember that it's also possible to use HTTP without HTML. HTML is important only when you need to provide cross-platform and down-level browser support. Visual Basic desktop applications that use HTTP will become increasingly common. They can be integrated into a scalable architecture, and they can provide a user interface that's far more sophisticated than those based on Web browsers.

While I haven't taught you much about XML in this book, I encourage you to spend the time to become proficient with it. You should also download Microsoft's XML parser and become familiar with its documentation. If you're just starting out, get a good book that teaches XML from the ground up. *XML in Action* by William J. Pardi (Microsoft Press, 1999) is a good entry-level book.

If you really want to master XML, I encourage you to read *Essential XML: Beyond Markup* by Don Box, Aaron Skonnard, and John Lam (Addison Wesley, 2000). OK, so I'm a little biased because one of the authors wrote the foreword to this book. However, *Essential XML* is a groundbreaking book that explains the heart and soul of XML. It goes way beyond the syntax of XML parsers and explains why XML is critical to our industry at this moment in time.

So, this is where the second edition of this book comes to an end. That means I should leave you with a summary of what you've learned. At the end of the day, COM and COM+ are simply technologies that help you build distributed applications. COM is the glue that allows you to assemble applications using components written in a variety of languages. COM+ is a runtime environment that offers valuable services such as thread pooling, declarative transactions, and role-based authorization checks.

COM+ and Windows 2000 also constitute a platform that provides many valuable services. IIS and ASP are essential services because they provide a basis for exposing functionality through HTTP and scaling an application through a Web farm architecture. MSMQ and QC are important because they add the extra dimension of asynchronous and disconnected communication. Taken together, these pieces provide the infrastructure that allows you to build large-scale applications that meet the needs of today's businesses. Now it's time to go out and apply what you've learned.

Index

Page numbers in italics refer to figures or tables.

Index

Index

Queue moniker, 355–56
queues, 318, *319*. *See also* messaging; MSMQ
  (Microsoft Message Queuing); Queued
  Components (QC)

R

Raise method, 113, 118–21
RAISERROR statement, 230
Read Committed level, 235
reader applications, 319
read locks, 234, *235*
read-only recordsets, 444–46
Read Uncommitted level, 235, 341
receiver applications, 318, *319*
receiving messages, 332–34
  using MSMQ events, 334–36
recorder objects, 21, 347–48, *347*, 354–57
record-level locks, 233
recordsets, ADO
  caching, in middle tier, 446–48
  custom marshaling and, 85
  passing, using COM, 434
  passing, using HTTP, 441–44
  passing, using MSMQ, 439–40
  passing read-only, vs. updatable, 444–46
references
  circular, 71–72
  class-based, 29, 31, 42–43
  object (*see* object references)
RegDB registration database, 18, 155–57, *156*,
  165
RegisterTypeLib function, 150
Registry
  authentication levels, 389–90, *390*
  CLSIDs and, 65–66, *65*
  configured components and, 156, 163–64
  GUIDs and, 61
  interface forwarding and, 134, *135*
  nonconfigured components, 157, 287
  remote activation and, 165–66, *166*
  server registration, 66, 93–94
  threading and, 197–98, *198*
  type library registration, 150
  universal marshaler interfaces and, 82–83,
    82, 83
REGSVR32.EXE utility, 66, 93, 157, 287
REGTLIB.EXE utility, 150
Release method, 70–72, 168
release mode, 210
remote activation, 164–66, *166*

remote communication. *See* out-of-process
  COM
Remote Procedure Call. *See* RPC (Remote
  Procedure Call)
remote servers, 91
Repeatable Read level, 235, 341
request-based load balancing, 307–9, 312–13
Request objects, 428, 443
resource manager (RM), 240, 259–60, *260*
resource sharing, 189–225
  database connections (*see* database
    connection pooling)
  memory (*see* memory sharing)
  objects (*see* object pooling)
  scalability, processes, and, 189–90
  security and, 383–84
  threads (*see* thread pooling)
  two-tier applications and, 4
  Web-based applications and, 9
resource throttling, 223–24
Response objects, 441–42
response queues, 336–37
Retained in Memory setting, 95
return values, 114, 148–49. *See also* parameters
reusability
  binary, 13, 50
  black-box, 36–37, 38
  COM and, 12–13, 27
  object-oriented programming and, 29
  white-box, 35–36
roles
  COM+ security and, 395–96, *396*
  IIS authentication and, 415–16
  MTS and, 15
ROLLBACK TRAN, 261
rolling upgrades, 309
root objects, 246, 255–58
round-robin DNS load balancing, 305
routing servers, 304–5, *304*, 323–24
RPC (Remote Procedure Call)
  COM and, 7, 79–81, *80*, 346, *347*
  DCOM and, 14
  messaging vs. HTTP and, 319–22, *320, 321*
RPCSS.DLL file, 64
runtime
  COM+, 159–60
  enforcing authorization at, 398–401, *400,
    401*
  errors, 115
  type inspection, 28, 44–45, 47

Subliminal Systems

Dedicated to making your company more
successful with multi-tier application development
using Windows 2000 and Windows NT technologies

- Consulting Services (architecture reviews & development team mentoring)
- Conference Talks
- Hands-on Training Through DevelopMentor

MICROSOFT LICENSE AGREEMENT

Book Companion CD

IMPORTANT—READ CAREFULLY: This Microsoft End-User License Agreement ("EULA") is a legal agreement between you (either an individual or an entity) and Microsoft Corporation for the Microsoft product identified above, which includes computer software and may include associated media, printed materials, and "online" or electronic documentation ("SOFTWARE PRODUCT"). Any component included within the SOFTWARE PRODUCT that is accompanied by a separate End-User License Agreement shall be governed by such agreement and not the terms set forth below. By installing, copying, or otherwise using the SOFTWARE PRODUCT, you agree to be bound by the terms of this EULA. If you do not agree to the terms of this EULA, you are not authorized to install, copy, or otherwise use the SOFTWARE PRODUCT; you may, however, return the SOFTWARE PRODUCT, along with all printed materials and other items that form a part of the Microsoft product that includes the SOFTWARE PRODUCT, to the place you obtained them for a full refund.

SOFTWARE PRODUCT LICENSE

The SOFTWARE PRODUCT is protected by United States copyright laws and international copyright treaties, as well as other intellectual property laws and treaties. The SOFTWARE PRODUCT is licensed, not sold.

1. **GRANT OF LICENSE.** This EULA grants you the following rights:

    a. **Software Product.** You may install and use one copy of the SOFTWARE PRODUCT on a single computer. The primary user of the computer on which the SOFTWARE PRODUCT is installed may make a second copy for his or her exclusive use on a portable computer.

    b. **Storage/Network Use.** You may also store or install a copy of the SOFTWARE PRODUCT on a storage device, such as a network server, used only to install or run the SOFTWARE PRODUCT on your other computers over an internal network; however, you must acquire and dedicate a license for each separate computer on which the SOFTWARE PRODUCT is installed or run from the storage device. A license for the SOFTWARE PRODUCT may not be shared or used concurrently on different computers.

    c. **License Pak.** If you have acquired this EULA in a Microsoft License Pak, you may make the number of additional copies of the computer software portion of the SOFTWARE PRODUCT authorized on the printed copy of this EULA, and you may use each copy in the manner specified above. You are also entitled to make a corresponding number of secondary copies for portable computer use as specified above.

    d. **Sample Code.** Solely with respect to portions, if any, of the SOFTWARE PRODUCT that are identified within the SOFTWARE PRODUCT as sample code (the "SAMPLE CODE"):

       i. **Use and Modification.** Microsoft grants you the right to use and modify the source code version of the SAMPLE CODE, *provided* you comply with subsection (d)(iii) below. You may not distribute the SAMPLE CODE, or any modified version of the SAMPLE CODE, in source code form.

       ii. **Redistributable Files.** Provided you comply with subsection (d)(iii) below, Microsoft grants you a nonexclusive, royalty-free right to reproduce and distribute the object code version of the SAMPLE CODE and of any modified SAMPLE CODE, other than SAMPLE CODE, or any modified version thereof, designated as not redistributable in the Readme file that forms a part of the SOFTWARE PRODUCT (the "Non-Redistributable Sample Code"). All SAMPLE CODE other than the Non-Redistributable Sample Code is collectively referred to as the "REDISTRIBUTABLES."

       iii. **Redistribution Requirements.** If you redistribute the REDISTRIBUTABLES, you agree to: (i) distribute the REDISTRIBUTABLES in object code form only in conjunction with and as a part of your software application product; (ii) not use Microsoft's name, logo, or trademarks to market your software application product; (iii) include a valid copyright notice on your software application product; (iv) indemnify, hold harmless, and defend Microsoft from and against any claims or lawsuits, including attorney's fees, that arise or result from the use or distribution of your software application product; and (v) not permit further distribution of the REDISTRIBUTABLES by your end user. Contact Microsoft for the applicable royalties due and other licensing terms for all other uses and/or distribution of the REDISTRIBUTABLES.

2. **DESCRIPTION OF OTHER RIGHTS AND LIMITATIONS.**

    - **Limitations on Reverse Engineering, Decompilation, and Disassembly.** You may not reverse engineer, decompile, or disassemble the SOFTWARE PRODUCT, except and only to the extent that such activity is expressly permitted by applicable law notwithstanding this limitation.

    - **Separation of Components.** The SOFTWARE PRODUCT is licensed as a single product. Its component parts may not be separated for use on more than one computer.

    - **Rental.** You may not rent, lease, or lend the SOFTWARE PRODUCT.

    - **Support Services.** Microsoft may, but is not obligated to, provide you with support services related to the SOFTWARE PRODUCT ("Support Services"). Use of Support Services is governed by the Microsoft policies and programs described in the user manual, in "online" documentation, and/or in other Microsoft-provided materials. Any supplemental software code provided to you as part of the Support Services shall be considered part of the SOFTWARE PRODUCT and subject to the terms and conditions of this EULA. With respect to technical information you provide to Microsoft as part of the Support Services, Microsoft may use such information for its business purposes, including for product support and development. Microsoft will not utilize such technical information in a form that personally identifies you.

- **Software Transfer.** You may permanently transfer all of your rights under this EULA, provided you retain no copies, you transfer all of the SOFTWARE PRODUCT (including all component parts, the media and printed materials, any upgrades, this EULA, and, if applicable, the Certificate of Authenticity), **and** the recipient agrees to the terms of this EULA.

- **Termination.** Without prejudice to any other rights, Microsoft may terminate this EULA if you fail to comply with the terms and conditions of this EULA. In such event, you must destroy all copies of the SOFTWARE PRODUCT and all of its component parts.

3. **COPYRIGHT.** All title and copyrights in and to the SOFTWARE PRODUCT (including but not limited to any images, photographs, animations, video, audio, music, text, SAMPLE CODE, REDISTRIBUTABLES, and "applets" incorporated into the SOFTWARE PRODUCT) and any copies of the SOFTWARE PRODUCT are owned by Microsoft or its suppliers. The SOFTWARE PRODUCT is protected by copyright laws and international treaty provisions. Therefore, you must treat the SOFTWARE PRODUCT like any other copyrighted material **except** that you may install the SOFTWARE PRODUCT on a single computer provided you keep the original solely for backup or archival purposes. You may not copy the printed materials accompanying the SOFTWARE PRODUCT.

4. **U.S. GOVERNMENT RESTRICTED RIGHTS.** The SOFTWARE PRODUCT and documentation are provided with RESTRICTED RIGHTS. Use, duplication, or disclosure by the Government is subject to restrictions as set forth in subparagraph (c)(1)(ii) of the Rights in Technical Data and Computer Software clause at DFARS 252.227-7013 or subparagraphs (c)(1) and (2) of the Commercial Computer Software—Restricted Rights at 48 CFR 52.227-19, as applicable. Manufacturer is Microsoft Corporation/One Microsoft Way/Redmond, WA 98052-6399.

5. **EXPORT RESTRICTIONS.** You agree that you will not export or re-export the SOFTWARE PRODUCT, any part thereof, or any process or service that is the direct product of the SOFTWARE PRODUCT (the foregoing collectively referred to as the "Restricted Components"), to any country, person, entity, or end user subject to U.S. export restrictions. You specifically agree not to export or re-export any of the Restricted Components (i) to any country to which the U.S. has embargoed or restricted the export of goods or services, which currently include, but are not necessarily limited to, Cuba, Iran, Iraq, Libya, North Korea, Sudan, and Syria, or to any national of any such country, wherever located, who intends to transmit or transport the Restricted Components back to such country; (ii) to any end user who you know or have reason to know will utilize the Restricted Components in the design, development, or production of nuclear, chemical, or biological weapons; or (iii) to any end user who has been prohibited from participating in U.S. export transactions by any federal agency of the U.S. government. You warrant and represent that neither the BXA nor any other U.S. federal agency has suspended, revoked, or denied your export privileges.

DISCLAIMER OF WARRANTY

NO WARRANTIES OR CONDITIONS. MICROSOFT EXPRESSLY DISCLAIMS ANY WARRANTY OR CONDITION FOR THE SOFTWARE PRODUCT. THE SOFTWARE PRODUCT AND ANY RELATED DOCUMENTATION ARE PROVIDED "AS IS" WITHOUT WARRANTY OR CONDITION OF ANY KIND, EITHER EXPRESS OR IMPLIED, INCLUDING, WITHOUT LIMITATION, THE IMPLIED WARRANTIES OF MERCHANTABILITY, FITNESS FOR A PARTICULAR PURPOSE, OR NONINFRINGEMENT. THE ENTIRE RISK ARISING OUT OF USE OR PERFORMANCE OF THE SOFTWARE PRODUCT REMAINS WITH YOU.

LIMITATION OF LIABILITY. TO THE MAXIMUM EXTENT PERMITTED BY APPLICABLE LAW, IN NO EVENT SHALL MICROSOFT OR ITS SUPPLIERS BE LIABLE FOR ANY SPECIAL, INCIDENTAL, INDIRECT, OR CONSEQUENTIAL DAMAGES WHATSOEVER (INCLUDING, WITHOUT LIMITATION, DAMAGES FOR LOSS OF BUSINESS PROFITS, BUSINESS INTERRUPTION, LOSS OF BUSINESS INFORMATION, OR ANY OTHER PECUNIARY LOSS) ARISING OUT OF THE USE OF OR INABILITY TO USE THE SOFTWARE PRODUCT OR THE PROVISION OF OR FAILURE TO PROVIDE SUPPORT SERVICES, EVEN IF MICROSOFT HAS BEEN ADVISED OF THE POSSIBILITY OF SUCH DAMAGES. IN ANY CASE, MICROSOFT'S ENTIRE LIABILITY UNDER ANY PROVISION OF THIS EULA SHALL BE LIMITED TO THE GREATER OF THE AMOUNT ACTUALLY PAID BY YOU FOR THE SOFTWARE PRODUCT OR US$5.00; PROVIDED, HOWEVER, IF YOU HAVE ENTERED INTO A MICROSOFT SUPPORT SERVICES AGREEMENT, MICROSOFT'S ENTIRE LIABILITY REGARDING SUPPORT SERVICES SHALL BE GOVERNED BY THE TERMS OF THAT AGREEMENT. BECAUSE SOME STATES AND JURISDICTIONS DO NOT ALLOW THE EXCLUSION OR LIMITATION OF LIABILITY, THE ABOVE LIMITATION MAY NOT APPLY TO YOU.

MISCELLANEOUS

This EULA is governed by the laws of the State of Washington USA, except and only to the extent that applicable law mandates governing law of a different jurisdiction.

Should you have any questions concerning this EULA, or if you desire to contact Microsoft for any reason, please contact the Microsoft subsidiary serving your country, or write: Microsoft Sales Information Center/One Microsoft Way/Redmond, WA 98052-6399.

OWNER REGISTRATION CARD

Register Today!

0-7356-1010-X

Return the bottom portion of this card to register today.

Programming Distributed Applications with COM+ and Microsoft® Visual Basic® 6.0, Second Edition

FIRST NAME

MIDDLE INITIAL

LAST NAME

INSTITUTION OR COMPANY NAME

ADDRESS

CITY

STATE

ZIP

( )

E-MAIL ADDRESS

PHONE NUMBER

U.S. and Canada addresses only. Fill in information above and mail postage-free.
Please mail only the bottom half of this page.

**For information about Microsoft Press®
products, visit our Web site at
mspress.microsoft.com**